George Grub

An ecclesiastical history of Scotland

From the introduction of Christianity to the present time

George Grub

An ecclesiastical history of Scotland
From the introduction of Christianity to the present time

ISBN/EAN: 9783743341746

Manufactured in Europe, USA, Canada, Australia, Japa

Cover: Foto ©ninafisch / pixelio.de

Manufactured and distributed by brebook publishing software (www.brebook.com)

George Grub

An ecclesiastical history of Scotland

AN

ECCLESIASTICAL HISTORY OF SCOTLAND

FROM THE INTRODUCTION OF CHRISTIANITY TO
THE PRESENT TIME.

BY GEORGE GRUB, A.M.

IN FOUR VOLUMES.

VOL. II.

EDINBURGH:
EDMONSTON AND DOUGLAS.
1861.

CONTENTS.

CHAPTER XXVIII.

From the death of Archbishop Foreman in 1521, to the death of Archbishop James Beaton in 1539.

Government of James V.—James Beaton, Archbishop of St. Andrews—Attempted Reform of the Cistercian Order—Foundation of St. Mary's College—John Mair, Provost of St. Salvator's College — Alexander Mylne, Abbot of Cambuskenneth—Succession of Bishops—John Bellenden, Archdeacon of Murray—Gavin Dunbar, Bishop of Aberdeen—Introduction of Lutheran Doctrines into Scotland—Patrick Hamilton, Abbot of Ferne—His opinions—His death—Death of Henry Forrest and others—School of Reforming Divines within the Church—John Winram, Sub-Prior of St. Andrews—Gavin Logie, Principal of St. Leonard's College—Robert Richardson, Canon-Regular of Cambuskenneth—Friar Alexander Seaton—Friar William Airth, ... 1

CHAPTER XXIX.

From the death of Archbishop James Beaton in 1539, to the death of Cardinal Beaton in 1546.

Death of James V.—Accession of Mary—Regency of the Earl of Arran—Cardinal David Beaton, Archbishop of St. Andrews—Succession of Bishops—Gavin Dunbar, Archbishop of Glasgow—Persecution of the Protestants—Condemnation of Sir John Borthwick—The Protestants favoured by the Regent—The Scriptures allowed to be read in the vulgar tongue—Persecution renewed—War with England—The Border Abbeys destroyed by the English—George Wishart—His residence in England—His return to Scotland—His trial—His death—Death of Cardinal Beaton—His character, . . . 15

CHAPTER XXX.

From the death of Cardinal Beaton in 1546, to the end of the Earl of Arran's Regency in 1554.

Regency of the Earl of Arran—John Hamilton, Archbishop of St. Andrews—James Beaton, Archbishop of Glasgow—Succession of Bishops—John Knox—His residence in the Castle of St. Andrews—His call to be a Protestant Minister—His Controversies with the Clergy—Council at Edinburgh in 1549—Members of the Council—Canons enacted—Persecution of the Protestants—Death of Adam Wallace—Council at Edinburgh in 1552—Publication of a Catechism—Alleged dispute about the Paternoster, ... 29

CHAPTER XXXI.

From the end of the Earl of Arran's Regency in 1554, to the Council of Edinburgh in 1559.

Regency of Mary of Lorraine—Succession of Bishops—David Panter, Bishop of Ross—Robert Reid, Bishop of Orkney—Return of John Knox—The effects of his preaching—His letter to the Regent—His departure from Scotland—His condemnation and appeal—Bond subscribed by the Protestant leaders—Resolutions agreed to by them—Trial and death of Walter Mylne—Provincial Councils in 1558—Toleration conceded to the Protestants—Advice given to the Bishop of Aberdeen by his Chapter—Council at Edinburgh in 1559—Articles of Reformation laid before the Council—Remonstrances presented to the Council—Canons enacted—Conclusion of the Council, ... 39

CHAPTER XXXII.

From the Council of Edinburgh in 1559, to the Parliament of August, 1560.

Quintin Kennedy, Abbot of Crossraguel—Publication of his Compendious Tractive—Summary of its Argument—Reply by John Davidson, Principal of the College of Glasgow—Correspondence between Quintin Kennedy and John Willock—The Regent's Proclamation against the Protestants—Arrival of Knox in Scotland—His Sermon at Perth—Destruction of the

Monasteries there—Spoliation of the Cathedral of St. Andrews
—Destruction of the Abbey of Scone—Civil War—Queen
Elizabeth assists the Protestants—Destruction of the Monasteries at Aberdeen—Death of Mary of Lorraine—Treaty of
Edinburgh—Protestant Ministers appointed to the chief towns
—John Row, Minister at Perth—Alleged imposture at the
Nunnery of St. Catharine of Sienna—Improbability of the
Story—Appointment of Superintendents—Parliament at
Edinburgh—Confession of Faith presented by the Protestants
—Feeble opposition to it—Its ratification—The authority of
the Pope taken away—The Mass proscribed—Conclusion of
the Parliament, ... 60

CHAPTER XXXIII.

From the Parliament of August 1560, to the return of Queen Mary to Scotland, in August, 1561.

The Confession of Faith—The compilers of the Confession—The
Book of Discipline—The Book of Common Order—The
Superintendents—First General Assembly—Proposed alteration in the Law of Marriage—Convention of the Estates—
Aberdeen Clergy summoned before the Estates—Act for
demolishing Abbey churches and cloisters—Commissioners
sent by the Estates, and by the Roman Catholic nobles, to
Queen Mary—Return of Mary to Scotland, ... 89

CHAPTER XXXIV.

From the return of Queen Mary to Scotland, in August 1561, to the Reasoning between the Abbot of Crossraguel and John Knox, in September, 1562.

Difficulties of Queen Mary—Her prudent government—Her interview with Knox—Efforts of the Protestant Ministers to
obtain a competent maintenance—John Craig, minister at
Edinburgh—Controversial discussions between the clergy and
the ministers—Ninian Winzet, Schoolmaster at Linlithgow—
His Tractate addressed to the Queen—His eighty-three questions delivered to Knox—He is obliged to leave Scotland—
Reasoning between Quintin Kennedy and John Knox, . . 106

CHAPTER XXXV.

From the Reasoning between the Abbot of Crossraguel and John Knox, in September, 1562, to Queen Mary's Marriage with Darnley in July, 1565.

Rebellion of the Earl of Huntly—Second Interview of Mary with Knox—Meeting of the General Assembly—Excommunication of Paul Methven—Prosecution of the Primate and other ecclesiastics—Knox's Sermon on the Queen's Marriage—Riot at Holyrood—Knox summoned before the Council—Discussion between Lethington and Knox—Marriage of Mary with Darnley, ... 128

CHAPTER XXXVI.

From Queen Mary's Marriage with Darnley in July, 1565, to her Abdication in July, 1567.

Rebellion of the Earl of Murray—Knox's sermon at St. Giles'—Attempts of the Queen to restore the Roman Church—John Sinclair, Bishop of Brechin—John Leslie, Bishop of Ross—Murder of Riccio—Question as to Knox's participation in the crime—Proposal to send a Nuncio to Scotland—Baptism of Prince James—Murder of Darnley—Meeting of Parliament—The Queen's Marriage with Bothwell—Her Imprisonment—Her Abdication, ... 143

CHAPTER XXXVII.

From Queen Mary's Abdication in July, 1567, to the death of Archbishop Hamilton, in April, 1571.

Coronation of James VI.—Regency of the Earl of Murray—Escape of Queen Mary from Lochleven—Her defeat at Langside—Her flight to England—Deprivation of the Principal and regents of King's College, Aberdeen—Negotiations between Murray and Elizabeth—Murder of the Earl of Murray—Regency of the Earl of Lennox—Death of John Hamilton, Archbishop of St. Andrews, ... 160

CHAPTER XXXVIII.

From the death of Archbishop Hamilton in April, 1571, to the death of John Knox in November, 1572.

Regency of the Earl of Mar—Letter of Erskine of Dun to the Regent—Erskine's opinions as to Ecclesiastical Polity and the Episcopal office—His remonstrances against the usurpations of the State—Ecclesiastical Convention at Leith—Sermon preached at the Convention, by David Ferguson—Ecclesiastical Polity agreed to by the Commissioners of the Convention and of the Privy Council—John Douglas appointed Archbishop of St. Andrews—General Assembly at St. Andrews—General Assembly at Perth—Residence of John Knox at St. Andrews— His return to Edinburgh—His illness—His parting interviews with his friends—His death and character, ... 170

CHAPTER XXXIX.

From the death of John Knox in November, 1572, to the resignation of the Regency by the Earl of Morton in March, 1578.

Regency of the Earl of Morton—Proceedings of the General Assembly—Protestant ministers appointed to the vacant bishoprics—Objections made to the office of Bishop—Andrew Melville, Principal of the College of Glasgow—Limitations of the powers of the Bishops—Patrick Adamson, Archbishop of St. Andrews—Resignation of the Regency by the Earl of Morton—Ecclesiastical condition of Scotland—Intellectual and moral results of the Reformation, ... 189

CHAPTER XL.

From the resignation of the Regency by the Earl of Morton in March, 1578, to the Raid of Ruthven in August, 1582.

Influence of the Duke of Lennox—His designs in favour of the Roman Church—Roman Catholic Missionaries in Scotland— Sermon of Walter Balcanquhal—Meetings of the General Assembly—General Assembly at Dundee—Condemnation of the titular Episcopacy—Subscription of the King's Confession —Second Book of Discipline—Differences between the First and Second Book of Discipline—The Tulchan Bishops—Distinction between them and the titular bishops — Conflict between the Church and the State—List of grievances drawn up by the General Assembly—Andrew Melville at Perth— Raid of Ruthven, ... 207

CHAPTER XLI.

From the Raid of Ruthven in August, 1582, to the death of Queen Mary in February, 1587.

Meetings of the General Assembly—Execution of the Earl of Gowrie—Robert Brown, the English sectary, in Scotland—

Flight of Andrew Melville and other ministers—Archbishop Adamson's intercourse with the English bishops—His opposition to the Presbyterian discipline—Ecclesiastical supremacy of the King ratified by Parliament—Royal declaration regarding the supremacy—The Earl of Arran driven from power—Return of the ministers from exile—Archbishop Adamson excommunicated by the Synod of Fife—His appeal to the King and Parliament—Declaration by the General Assembly—Proceedings of the English Government against Queen Mary—Her trial and condemnation—Remonstrances of King James—Death of Mary, ... 229

CHAPTER XLII.

From the death of Queen Mary in February, 1587, to the establishment of Presbyterianism in June, 1592.

Indignation of the Scots on the death of Mary—The Spanish Armada—Insurrection of the Roman Catholic nobles—Marriage of King James with Anne of Denmark—Death of John Erskine of Dun—Letter from Elizabeth to James—General Assembly of August, 1590—Sermon of James Melville—Speech attributed to King James—Relations between the English and Scottish Churches—Rise of Puritanism—Bancroft's Sermon at Paul's Cross—Irritation of the Scottish Presbyterians—Illness of Archbishop Adamson—His retractation—His death—General Assembly of May, 1592—Parliamentary ratification of the Presbyterian Church, ... 245

CHAPTER XLIII.

From the establishment of Presbyterianism in June, 1592, to the accession of King James to the Crown of England in March, 1603.

Renewed insurrection of the Roman Catholic nobles—They are excommunicated by the Provincial Assembly of Fife—Suppression of the insurrection—Death of John Leslie, Bishop of Ross—Sermon of David Black—Tumult of the seventeenth of December at Edinburgh—Robert Bruce, minister at Edinburgh—Account of his conversion—Ecclesiastical convention at Perth—General Assembly at Dundee—Publication of the Basilicon Doron—General Assembly at Montrose—The Gowrie Conspiracy—Vacant bishoprics filled up—Accession of James to the crown of England—Death of Archbishop Beaton, . 262

CHAPTER XLIV.

From the accession of King James to the Crown of England in March, 1603, to the consecration of the three Scottish Bishops in October, 1610.

Coronation of King James—Conference at Hampton Court—Convocation of 1604—John Spottiswood, Archbishop of Glasgow—General Assembly at Aberdeen—Imprisonment of John Forbes and other ministers—Treatise by James Melville—Trial of the ministers—Parliament at Perth—Scottish ministers summoned to London—Imprisonment of Andrew Melville—General Assemblies at Linlithgow—Court of High Commission erected—General Assembly at Glasgow—Episcopal Government restored—Consecration of three Scottish Bishops at London, ... 280

CHAPTER XLV.

From the consecration of the three Scottish Bishops in October, 1610, to the Perth Assembly of August, 1618.

Consecration of the other Bishops—Directions issued by the King—Acts of the Glasgow Assembly ratified by Parliament—William Cowper, Bishop of Galloway—Execution of John Ogilvie—Death of Archbishop Gladstones—John Spottiswood appointed Archbishop of St. Andrews—Absolution of the Marquis of Huntly—Creation of Doctors of Divinity—General Assembly at Aberdeen—New Confession of Faith—King James visits Scotland—Imprisonment of David Calderwood—New erection of Cathedral Chapters—General Assembly at St. Andrews—Patrick Forbes, Bishop of Aberdeen—His letter to Archbishop Spottiswood—General Assembly at Perth—Sermon of Archbishop Spottiswood—Five Articles agreed to by the Assembly, ... 298

CHAPTER XLIV.

From the Perth Assembly of August, 1618, to the death of King James VI. in March, 1625.

Synod of Dort—Death of Bishop Cowper—Scottish Ordinal of 1620—The Perth Articles ratified in Parliament—Dissatisfaction in consequence of the Perth Articles—Popular feeling in Edinburgh—John Cameron, Principal of the College of Glasgow—Death of Andrew Melville—His character—Death of John Welsh—English Service introduced at St. Andrews—Dr. William Forbes—His teaching at Aberdeen—His removal to Edinburgh—His dispute with the Puritans there—His return to Aberdeen—Death of King James—His character and ecclesiastical policy, ... 320

CHAPTER XLVII.

From the death of King James VI. in March, 1625, to the ratification of the Book of Canons in May, 1635.

Accession of Charles I.—Ecclesiastical instructions issued by the King—Arrangement in regard to Tithes—David Dickson—Religious movement in the West of Scotland—Robert Blair—John Livingstone—Voyage of Blair and Livingstone—The King's Journey to Scotland—His Coronation—Meeting of Parliament—Service at the Chapel Royal—Foundation of the see of Edinburgh—Dr. William Forbes, Bishop of Edinburgh—His sermon before the King—His death—His character and opinions—His writings—Archbishop Spottiswood appointed Chancellor of Scotland—Patrick Forbes, Bishop of Aberdeen—His diocesan administration—His restoration of the University of Aberdeen—His illness and death—His character—Ratification of the Book of Canons, ... 335

CHAPTER XLVIII.

From the ratification of the Book of Canons in May, 1635, to the Act of the Privy Council regarding the Book of Common Prayer in December, 1636.

State of the Scottish Church—Its Government, Ritual, and Doctrines—The Cathedral and parish churches—The Book of Canons—Objections to the Canons—The Ordinal of 1636—New warrant for the Court of High Commission—Alleged Diocesan Commission Courts—Samuel Rutherford—Andrew Boyd, Bishop of Argyll—John Durie's attempt to unite the Lutherans and the Reformed—Judgment of the Theological Faculty of Aberdeen on this subject—The divines of Aberdeen—Dr. Alexander Scroggie—Dr. William Leslie—Dr. James Sibbald—Dr. Alexander Ross—Dr. Robert Baron—Dr. John Forbes—Education of Dr. John Forbes—His ordination—His theological teaching—Publication of his Irenicum—Act of the Privy Council regarding the Book of Common Prayer, . . 359

CHAPTER XLIX.

From the act of the Privy Council regarding the Book of Common Prayer in December, 1636, to the three Proclamations of 17th October, 1637.

Difficulties in the introduction of a Liturgy—Alleged abandonment of such a design by King James—Proposal to introduce the English Liturgy—Resolution to prepare a Liturgy for Scotland—Delays in its publication—Supposed differences of opinion among the Bishops—The Scottish Service Book—The Communion Office—The reading of the Service Book—The tumult at Edinburgh—The authors of the tumult—Proceedings of the Privy Council—Diocesan Synod of Glasgow—Petitions against the Service Book—Conversation between the Primate and the Earl of Rothes—Increased agitation—Proclamations of the Seventeenth of October, ... 375

CHAPTER L.

From the three Proclamations of 17th October, 1637, to the Proclamation of 19th February, 1638.

Gillespie's Book against the English Ceremonies—Objections to the Liturgy—Unreasonable expectations of the King—Causes of the opposition to the Liturgy—Opinions of the Clergy—Conduct and Character of the Bishops—The Nobility—Riot at Edinburgh—Complaint against the Bishops—Proceedings of the Privy Council—The King's determination to adhere to the Service Book—Proclamation of the Nineteenth of February, 395

ECCLESIASTICAL HISTORY OF SCOTLAND.

CHAPTER XXVIII.

FROM THE DEATH OF ARCHBISHOP FOREMAN IN 1521, TO THE DEATH OF ARCHBISHOP JAMES BEATON IN 1539.

Government of James V.—James Beaton, Archbishop of St. Andrews—Attempted Reform of the Cistercian Order—Foundation of St. Mary's College—John Mair, Provost of St. Salvator's College—Alexander Mylne, Abbot of Cambuskenneth—Succession of Bishops—John Bellenden, Archdeacon of Murray—Gavin Dunbar, Bishop of Aberdeen—Introduction of Lutheran Doctrines into Scotland—Patrick Hamilton, Abbot of Ferne—His Opinions—His Death—Death of Henry Forrest and others—School of Reforming Divines within the Church—John Winram, Sub-Prior of St. Andrews—Gavin Logie, Principal of St. Leonard's College—Robert Richardson, Canon-Regular of Cambuskenneth—Friar Alexander Seaton—Friar William Airth.

WHEN the Duke of Albany finally returned to France, the king's person and the government of the realm were for some time under the entire control of the Earl of Angus. In 1528, James escaped from the thraldom of the Douglases, and assumed the actual exercise of sovereignty, being at that time in his seventeenth year. The young king was animated by the desire, which had uniformly been shewn by the princes of his house, to protect the people from oppression, and to enforce an impartial administration of the laws. The more effectually to attain these objects, he instituted the College of Justice, the establishment of which was completed in 1532. On the first of January, 1537, James was married to Magdalen of France, daughter of Francis I. Magdalen died within a few months, and in the following year James was united to Mary of Lorraine.

The see of St. Andrews, which was vacant by the death of Archbishop Foreman, was filled in the course of the year 1522 by the translation of James Beaton from the Church of Glasgow. The new primate was much more of a statesman than an ecclesiastic. In the former capacity he acted with firmness and integrity, assisting his sovereign to throw off the tyranny of the Douglases, and successfully opposing the insidious attempts of the English king against the independence of Scotland. Archbishop Beaton died in the autumn of the year 1539.[1]

In June, 1535, an act of the three estates was passed, by which it was ordained that a provincial council should meet within the church of the Black Friars at Edinburgh, on the first day of March next to come, and that the Archbishop of St. Andrews should be called upon to hold the same—failing which the king was to request authority from the Pope for any two of the bishops to hold it. The Archbishop of Glasgow protested that, while he agreed to this for the common weal of the nation, it should be without prejudice to the rights of his see. The council was held, but no distinct account of its proceedings has been preserved.[2]

Towards the end of the fifteenth century, a visitation of the Scottish Cistercian monasteries had taken place by order of the general chapter of Citeaux, and three abbots had been deposed. In the years 1533 and 1534, a more vigorous reformation was attempted. Commissioners were appointed by the general chapter, with instructions to prohibit the many infringements of the strict rule of the order which had long been prevalent. The monks of Melrose, Newbottle, and

[1] Keith's Catalogue, pp. 36, 37.
[2] Acts of the Parliaments of Scotland, vol. ii. p. 342. Hailes, vol. iii. p. 229. Diurnal of Remarkable Occurrents in Scotland, p. 20.

Balmerino, were particularly referred to as transgressing the Cistercian institute. The delinquents stopped the proceedings for some time by an appeal to the general chapter, and it does not appear what further was done.[1]

An additional college was founded by Archbishop Beaton within the University of St. Andrews. It was called St. Mary's College, and was intended to promote the cultivation of Divinity, the Civil and Canon Law, Natural Philosophy, Medicine, and other liberal studies. The foundation was confirmed by Pope Paul III. in February, 1538. Archbishop Beaton's erection was renewed and extended by Archbishop Hamilton, in 1554.[2]

In the year 1533, John Mair was appointed Provost of St. Salvator's College, an office which he held till his decease in 1550. He was a doctor of the Sorbonne, and, before he came to St. Andrews, was for some time principal regent of the college at Glasgow. In his own day, Mair was famous for his theological and philosophical writings. The only work of his which now attracts any attention is his History of Scotland, but he is probably still better known as the master of Knox and Buchanan. By some modern authors he he has been praised, by others he has been severely censured, for the opinions which he has expressed regarding the relative duties of sovereigns and subjects. Both the praise and the censure might have been considerably abated, if the writers alluded to had been better acquainted with the political views prevalent among many of the ecclesiastics of the middle ages.[3]

During the whole period of Beaton's episcopate, Alexander Mylne was abbot of the Augustinian monastery of Cambuskenneth, in the diocese of St. Andrews. This distinguished churchman was for some time a canon of Aberdeen, and afterwards of Dunkeld. When the latter diocese was divided by Bishop Brown into four rural deaneries, Mylne, as already

---

[1] Morton's Monastic Annals of Teviotdale, pp. 238, 240-242.

[2] Appendix to the Report of the University Commissioners, pp. 388, 389. Evidence taken by the University Commissioners, vol. iii. p. 357-367. Lyon's History of St. Andrews, vol. ii. p. 255-262.

[3] Mackenzie's Lives of Scottish Writers, vol. ii. preface, p. vii. Life of Mair by George Crawford, prefixed to the edition of his History published at Edinburgh in 1740. Knox, vol. i. p. 37. M'Crie's Life of Knox, 6th ed. pp. 4-6, 381, 382. Lyon's History of St. Andrews, vol. i. p. 281-283.

mentioned, was appointed dean of Angus, and he succeeded Patrick Panter, as abbot of Cambuskenneth, in 1516. He was the first president of the College of Justice—a dignity which was conferred upon him on the institution of the court by King James V. As abbot of Cambuskenneth, Mylne zealously endeavoured to restore discipline and the love of learning among the canons of his order. For that purpose, carrying out a design formerly entertained by his predecessor Patrick Panter, in the year 1522 he entered into a correspondence with the abbot and canons of St. Victor, near Paris, and made arrangements to send thither for education the most promising novices of his monastery. He cultivated literature himself, and wrote the Lives of the Bishops of Dunkeld. Mylne died about the year 1548.[1]

Soon after the death of Bishop Douglas, Robert Cockburn, Bishop of Ross, was translated to the see of Dunkeld. In 1526, George Crichton succeeded Bishop Cockburn as Bishop of Dunkeld.[2]

James Hepburn, Bishop of Murray, was succeeded by Robert Shaw, Abbot of Paisley, in 1524. Bishop Shaw died in 1527. The next bishop was Alexander Stewart, Abbot of Scone, son of Alexander, Duke of Albany, who held the see till his death in 1534. Bishop Stewart's successor was Patrick Hepburn, Prior of St. Andrews, son of the Earl of Bothwell. This prelate held also the abbacy of Scone in commendam.[3]

During the episcopate of Bishop Patrick Hepburn, the archdeaconry of Murray was conferred on John Bellenden, the well-known translator of Boece's History. Bellenden's biographers have been unable to ascertain the precise date

[1] Tytler's Life of Sir Thomas Craig, p. 46-51. Brunton and Haig's Historical Account of the Senators of the College of Justice, p. 5-10. Epistolæ Regum Scotorum, vol. i. pp. 275, 335-337. Preface to the Lives of the Bishops of Dunkeld, ed. 1831, p. i.-v. Preface to the Chartulary of the Collegiate Church of St. Mary and St. Anne, and the Charters of the Black Friars, at Glasgow, p. lvii.

[2] Leslie, p. 394. Keith's Catalogue, p. 94. Brunton and Haig's Senators of the College of Justice, pp. 44, 45.

[3] Keith's Catalogue, p. 148-150. Brunton and Haig's Senators of the College of Justice, p. 80. Preface to the Chartulary of Murray, p. xv. Bishop Stewart was the son of Alexander, Duke of Albany, by his wife Catherine Sinclair; but the marriage between his parents was afterwards dissolved, on account of their being within the forbidden degrees of consanguinity.

of his promotion to the archdeaconry; that point, as well as the other circumstances of his life, being involved in much obscurity.[1]

Bishop Gavin Dunbar ruled the diocese of Aberdeen for thirteen years. Next to Elphinstone, he was the most illustrious of the line of prelates who filled the chair of St. Machar. He completed several of the works begun by his great predecessor, and, by his encouragement, Alexander Galloway, the friend and executor of Elphinstone, was enabled to carry out effectually the bequests of that prelate. On the twenty-third day of the month of February immediately before his decease, Bishop Dunbar founded an hospital for the reception of twelve poor beadsmen. He recites in the preamble to his grant that the prelates of the Church are not the lords, but the guardians and stewards of the patrimony of the Redeemer, and that they are bound to bestow on the poor, and for pious uses, whatever they derive from thence, beyond what is required for the Church, and the necessary support of life. The history of his episcopate shews that with him these were not mere words of form. Bishop Dunbar was at Edinburgh when he signed the deed 'of foundation of the hospital. Soon after he proceeded homewards, but died at St. Andrews on the tenth of March, 1532. He was buried in his own cathedral, within the southern transept, which he himself had erected, and where his ruined monument may still be seen.[2]

During the lifetime of Bishop Dunbar, George, Prior of Pluscardine, was appointed his coadjutor and successor in the see. The bishop probably survived his coadjutor, since, on the decease of the former, William Stewart, Provost of Lincluden, was appointed to the see of Aberdeen. This prelate

[1] See Irving's Lives of Scottish Poets, vol. ii. p. 119-127, and his Lives of Scottish Writers, vol. i. p. 12-22. See also the Biographical Introduction to Bellenden's Boece, p. xxxvi.-xlii.

[2] Regist. Episcopat. Aberdon. vol. i. p. 401-406; vol. ii. pp. 211, 249; and preface, p. lii.-lvi. Boece, Aberdon. Episcop. Vitæ, pp. 84, 85. Keith's Catalogue, pp. 120, 121. Orem's History of Old Aberdeen, ed. 1791, p. 97-100. Knox says (vol. i. p. 43) that Bishop Dunbar had an illegitimate daughter. The morals of many of the Scottish ecclesiastics at the time were such that, even in the case of so good a man as the Bishop of Aberdeen, we cannot at once reject a statement of this kind as improbable. But there is no authority for it beyond Knox's own assertion, made in connection with one of those ribald stories which he takes too much pleasure in relating.

was bishop-elect in May, 1532, and was consecrated in the following year.[1]

Keith states that Robert Cockburn, Bishop of Ross, died in 1521. This is undoubtedly a mistake. Bishop Cockburn, as already mentioned, was translated to Dunkeld. His successor in the diocese of Ross was James Hay, who was bishop-elect in February, 1525, and who still held the see in March, 1538.[2]

Andrew Stewart was Bishop of Caithness during the primacy of Archbishop Beaton. The diocese of Caithness was in as lawless a state as it had been before the time of St. Gilbert, and its bishop was now, not the victim, but the promoter of strife. According to Sir Robert Gordon, Bishop Stewart instigated the clan Gunn to slay the laird of Duffus. In retaliation, the dean of the cathedral church, brother of the murdered baron, seized the vicar of Farr, one of the bishop's dependants, and kept him prisoner in the house of Duffus. The bishop was obliged to retire to Atholl for some time, and the matter was afterwards compromised.[3]

John Hepburn was Bishop of Brechin during the whole time of Archbishop Beaton's primacy.

James Chisholm was still Bishop of Dunblane in June, 1526. In the following year he is said to have resigned the see in favour of his half-brother, William Chisholm, retaining, however, the administration of the temporalities till his death in 1534. William Chisholm, we are told, was consecrated at Stirling on the fourteenth of April, 1527. He was certainly bishop in May of that year.[4]

Robert Maxwell, provost of the collegiate church of St. Patrick, at Dunbarton, succeeded Thomas in the see of Orkney. He was bishop-elect in June, 1526, and still held the see in 1540, when King James visited the Islands.[5]

---

[1] Regist. Episcopat. Aberdon. vol. i. p. 394, and preface, p. liii.-lvi. Acts of the Parliaments of Scotland, vol. ii. p. 334. Keith's Catalogue, p. 121.

[2] Acts of the Parliaments of Scotland, vol. ii. pp. 289, 352. Keith's Catalogue, p. 190

[3] Keith's Catalogue, p. 215. History of the Earldom of Sutherland, pp. 102, 103.

[4] Acts of the Parliaments of Scotland, vol. ii. p. 300. Keith's Catalogue, p. 179. Registrum Nigrum de Aberbrothoc, p. 462.

[5] Acts of the Parliaments of Scotland, vol. ii. p. 307. Leslie, p. 427. Keith's Catalogue, p. 223.

On the translation of Archbishop Beaton to St. Andrews, Gavin Dunbar, Prior of Whithorn, was appointed Archbishop of Glasgow. He was nephew of the Bishop of Aberdeen, and had been preceptor to King James. He is mentioned as bishop-elect in 1524, and was consecrated at Edinburgh on the fifth of February, 1525. Three years afterwards he was appointed chancellor of Scotland, an office which he retained till 1543. In 1536, he received the abbacy of Inchaffray in commendam.[1]

David Arnot, Bishop of Galloway, died in 1526, and was succeeded by Henry, whose surname is said to have been Wemyss. On the seventh of February, 1531, within the chapel of Archbishop Dunbar's residence in Edinburgh, Henry, Bishop of Candida Casa, took the oath of canonical obedience to the archbishop as his metropolitan, saving his rights as bishop of the Chapel Royal. Henry was still Bishop of Galloway in December, 1540.[2]

David Hamilton, Bishop of Argyll, was probably succeeded by Robert Montgomery, parson of Kirkmichael, a son of the Earl of Eglinton. Bishop Robert is mentioned as elect and confirmed in February, 1531.[3]

As formerly stated, John was elect of the Isles in February, 1525. He was still elect in November, 1526, and in September, 1528. In 1530, Ferquhard M'Lachlan was appointed Bishop of the Isles, and Commendator of Iona.[4]

Nothing has yet been said regarding the most important event in the primacy of Archbishop Beaton—the beginning of the great religious movement which led to the subversion of the ancient Church.

In Scotland, as in the other kingdoms of Western Europe, the doctrinal corruptions which were prevalent, and, still more, the general immorality of the clergy, had occasioned a deep-rooted feeling of dissatisfaction with the established ecclesiastical order. Reference has already been made to the influence

---

[1] Keith's Catalogue, pp. 257, 258. Preface to the Chartulary of Glasgow, p. li.

[2] Acts of the Parliaments of Scotland, vol. ii. p. 405. Regist. Episcopat. Glasguen. p. 542. Keith's Catalogue, p. 278.

[3] Regist. Episcopat. Glasguen. p. 542. Keith's Catalogue, p. 289.

[4] Acts of the Parliaments of Scotland, vol. ii. pp. 288, 308, 321. Keith's Catalogue, p. 306.

exercised by the opinions of Wickliffe and the Lollards. Although these met with considerable sympathy, their adherents were not sufficiently numerous or powerful to cause much apprehension to the rulers in Church and State. It was otherwise when the effects of Luther's preaching began to be apparent. Scotland was now in constant intercourse with the chief continental states, and the new doctrines of the German Reformer soon became known to our countrymen.

Patrick Hamilton is generally referred to as the first preacher of the Lutheran opinions in Scotland. He was the first who suffered death on that account, but it is known that some of Luther's disciples had prepared the way for his labours. As early as the year 1525, an act of the Scottish parliament was passed, forbidding the importation of Lutheran books into the kingdom, and the propagation of the Reformer's tenets; and it appears that even in the northern diocese of Aberdeen there were persons, both natives of the kingdom and strangers, who favoured these opinions. Hamilton was related, though by a descent of doubtful legitimacy, both to the royal house and to the family of Arran. He was born in the year 1504, and in early youth, according to the custom of the time, was appointed commendator of the abbey of Ferne. The date of this promotion is not mentioned, but it is conjectured to have been about the year 1518, on the decease of Andrew, Bishop of Caithness, who held the abbacy of Ferne in commendam. There is no direct evidence, beyond an assertion of the English reformer Frith, that Hamilton was ever ordained a priest. Being under suspicions of holding the new opinions, he went abroad, in order to avoid enquiry, and to prosecute his studies in the schools of Germany. At Wittenberg and Marburg he became personally acquainted with Luther, Melancthon, and Francis Lambert, and his intercourse with them soon led to the entire adoption of their views. He returned to Scotland and began to promulgate the Lutheran doctrines, but was soon apprehended, and committed a prisoner to the castle of St. Andrews. Being brought before the ecclesiastical court, he was found guilty of affirming, publishing, and teaching divers erroneous and heretical opinions—such as, that man hath no free-will; that man is in sin so long as he liveth; that children, immediately after their baptism, are sinners; that all Christians who are worthy to be called Christians do know that they are in grace; that no man is justified by works, but by faith only; that good works make not a good man, but a good man doth make good works; that faith, hope, and charity, are so knit, that he that hath the one hath the rest, and he that wanteth the one of them wanteth the rest. He was condemned to be deprived of all his dignities, orders, and benefices, and to be delivered over to the secular power. This sentence was pronounced by the primate, within the metropolitan church of St. Andrews, on the last day of February, 1528, in presence of the Archbishop of Glasgow, the Bishops of Dunkeld, Brechin, and Dunblane, the Prior of St. Andrews, and others of the clergy. On the same day he was led forth to the place of execution, in front of St. Salvator's College, where he suffered death at the stake, enduring protracted torments with the greatest constancy.[1]

The circumstances connected with Hamilton's trial and punishment appear to have been communicated soon afterwards to the University of Louvaine, by Alexander Galloway, canon of Aberdeen. On the twenty-first of April, the masters and professors of theology in that university wrote to Archbishop Beaton, congratulating him on the event, and expressing their hope that his vigorous measures would stop the farther growth of heresy in Scotland.[2] The doctors of Louvaine declared what was undoubtedly the general belief among ecclesiastics in regard to the result which was expected from putting the laws against heresy into execution, but the actual consequences were far otherwise. The cruel persecution of the Abbot of Ferne, and the patience with which he bore his

[1] Knox, vol. i. p. 14-35, and appendix, p. 500-515. Lorimer's Life of Patrick Hamilton, pp. 5, 63, 64, 142-155. Leslie, p. 407. Spottiswood, vol. i. p. 124-127. Keith's History of the affairs of Church and State in Scotland, Spottiswood Society ed. vol. i. pp. 13, 14, 329-332. Acts of the Parliaments of Scotland, vol. ii. p. 295. Extracts from the Council Register of Aberdeen, from 1398 to 1570, pp. 110, 111. It appears from a statement in the Accounts of the Scottish Treasurer that Hamilton had a daughter; and Mr. David Laing, who first noted the entries in the accounts, took it for granted (Knox, vol. i. p. 515) that she was illegitimate. She no doubt was so, as the law then stood, but it is ascertained that the Abbot of Ferne was married; see Lorimer's Life of Hamilton, pp. 123, 124.

[2] Knox, vol. i. appendix, p. 512-514.

sufferings, excited deep sympathy, and led to the more extensive diffusion of the condemned doctrines. The popular feeling was characteristically expressed in the advice given by a Scottish gentleman to the primate, to put no more heretics to death, or, if he did, to burn them in cellars, since the smoke of Patrick Hamilton had infected all on whom it blew.

The new opinions continued to acquire adherents, and the rulers of the Church persevered in the attempt to check them by violence. The next person who suffered on account of religion seems to have been Henry Forrest, a Benedictine monk, who was burned at St. Andrews. The precise date of his death is uncertain, but it was probably in 1533. About a year after this event, a gentleman named David Straton, and Norman Gourlay, a priest, were tried before James, Bishop of Ross, acting as commissary for the primate. The trial took place in presence of the king. The accused were condemned, and were burned at Greenside, near Edinburgh, on the twenty-seventh of August, 1534.[1]

On the first of March, 1539, Thomas Forret, a canon-regular of Inch-Colm, and vicar of Dollar, two black friars, named Kello and Beveridge, Duncan Simson, a priest at Stirling, and Robert Forester, a layman of the same place, were burned at Edinburgh. King James was present also on this occasion.[2] In the same year, Jerome Russell, a Francis-

---

[1] Knox, vol. i. p. 58-60, and appendix, p. 516-520. Spottiswood, vol. i. p. 129-131. Keith, vol. i. pp. 15, 16.

[2] Knox, vol. i. pp. 62, 63. Spottiswood, vol. i. p. 132. Keith, vol. i. pp. 16, 17. There is a story told by Foxe (Acts and Monuments, Seymour's ed. p. 621, and appendix to Knox, vol. i. pp. 521, 522), in which the Bishop of Dunkeld is made to reprove Thomas Forret for preaching every Sunday, it being enough to do so when he found any good epistle, or good gospel, which set forth the liberty of Holy Church ; and to thank God that he never knew what the Old and New Testament were. I have no doubt that the vicar of Dollar was censured for his frequent preaching. The prelates neglected that duty themselves, and some of them may have been angry with those of their clergy who attended to it. But the statement about the Old and New Testament can hardly be received in its plain meaning. The bishop, who was a good-natured, careless person, and who wished to convince Forret of the absurdity of getting into danger on account of what he esteemed a very useless practice, remarked, probably, that he himself never looked into his Bible. Such a story, at least, was repeated at the time. It is apparently to this saying that Archibald Hay alludes in his Panegyric on Cardinal Beaton (ff. xxxi. xxxviii.), which was written soon after the death of Forret :—"Qui cum ecclesiæ præfuerunt multis annis, censum am-

can friar, and a young layman, named Kennedy, were brought before the Archbishop of Glasgow on a charge of heresy. The archbishop was reluctant to proceed to extremities, but was urged on by his assessors. Sentence was pronounced, and both Russell and Kennedy were burned.[1]

Besides those whose names have been mentioned, some other individuals are known to have suffered on charges of heresy, during the primacy of Archbishop Beaton. Many likewise were compelled to abjure their opinions, and a considerable number retired from the kingdom to avoid persecution. Among the latter were several persons who afterwards rose to distinction as scholars or divines. Alexander Aless had been led to embrace the Lutheran doctrines by the conversation which he had with Patrick Hamilton, during his confinement. He fled from Scotland in 1529, and subsequently became professor of divinity at Leipzig. John M'Alpine, or Machabæus as he is styled in Latin, was prior of the Dominican monastery at Perth. He went to England, probably in 1535, and finally became a professor at Copenhagen. Among the exiles was also George Buchanan, who escaped from prison, and fled, first to England, afterwards to the Continent.[2]

The condition of the Scottish Church, at this time, was peculiarly unhappy. The persecution appears to have been encouraged or allowed by all the prelates and chief ecclesiastics, and, on the other hand, those who suffered seem to have maintained various opinions contrary to the faith of the Universal Church. But there were, notwithstanding, several theologians who endeavoured to pursue a middle course, and to restore a purer doctrine and discipline, without introducing novel views of their own. Some of these adhered all along to the communion of Rome; while others, finding a true reformation apparently hopeless, were induced to acquiesce in what

plissimum præceperunt, nullam se literam Novi Testamenti attigisse gloriantur, dira comminantes aliis omnibus qui sensum Domini in Scripturis sanctis diligentissime scrutantur."

[1] Knox, vol. i. p. 63-66. Spottiswood, vol. i. pp. 132, 133. Keith, vol. i. p. 18.

[2] Knox, vol. i. pp. 55, 56, and appendix, p. 526-529. Buchanan, vol. i. p. 277. Pitcairn's Criminal Trials, vol. i. part i. p. 297. M'Crie's Life of Knox, pp. 389-393, 395, 396.

they thought was the best which, under the circumstances, could be obtained. It is to be regretted that so little is known of the personal history of this portion of the clergy, and of the extent of the influence which they exercised; but here, and in the course of the narrative afterwards, it will be an object of peculiar interest to trace all that can be ascertained regarding them.

Among the divines referred to, may justly be reckoned John Mair, Provost of St. Salvator's College. We are told by Knox that his word at this time was held as an oracle in matters of religion; and we know that he did not hesitate to give his open support to the efforts for reformation which were made by those who adhered to the Church's communion.[1]

Another of those divines was John Winram, who was appointed sub-prior of St. Andrews some time before the decease of Archbishop Beaton. He was suspected of secretly favouring the Reformed opinions, and of encouraging their more open supporters. His name will often occur in the course of the subsequent narrative.[2]

Gavin Logie, Principal of St. Leonard's College, belonged probably to the same class. The students of the university, particularly those of his own college, became attached to the new opinions by means of his teaching. This was carried so far, that it was commonly remarked of any one inclined to Lutheranism, that he had drunk of St. Leonard's well. Less cautious than Winram, he was obliged to leave Scotland, probably about the year 1535. His subsequent history has not been ascertained.[3]

Another of the same school was Robert Richardson, a canon-regular of Cambuskenneth. In 1530, he published at Paris an Exegesis on the Rule of his order. This work was dedicated to Alexander Mylne, Abbot of Cambuskenneth, and, at the time when he composed it, Richardson was evidently attached to the ancient doctrine and constitution of the Church, though anxious for the correction of abuses. He speaks of Mylne, who was a firm adherent of the Roman communion, in terms of the highest commendation, while he denounces the

---

[1] Knox, vol. i. p. 37.
[2] Knox, vol. i. pp. 36, 150. M'Crie's Life of Knox, p. 19.
[3] Knox, vol. i. p. 36. M'Crie's Life of Knox, pp. 19, 394, 395.

intemperate habits prevalent among the monks, and the scandalous and immoral lives of many of their superiors. Whether it was that the opinions of Richardson became more inclined to Lutheranism, or that the ecclesiastical rulers were resolved to tolerate no attacks on their own conduct, he was obliged to retire to England about the end of Beaton's primacy. Under the year 1538, Calderwood mentions that Robert Logie, a brother or kinsman of the Principal of St. Leonard's, canon of Cambuskenneth, and teacher of the novices there, and *John* Richardson, also a canon of the same monastery, fled to England. "John" is perhaps a mistake for "Robert"; at all events we know that Robert Richardson, a Scottish priest, returned from England to his native country in 1543, and preached the Reformed doctrines there, till he was again obliged to flee in order to escape from the persecution of Cardinal Beaton, who disliked him, both on account of his religious opinions, and as an agent of the English king. It seems almost certain that this Robert Richardson was the canon of Cambuskenneth ; and, as he still retained his priestly office and title, it is probable that he had adopted the belief which at that time was established in the Church of England.[1]

Among those divines may also be reckoned Alexander Seaton, a Dominican friar, and confessor to King James. During a Lenten season, he preached against the prevalent corruptions, censuring particularly the conduct of the bishops. He was so popular, and was held in such esteem by the king, that the Archbishop of St. Andrews was afraid to proceed against him. After some time, however, James was inclined to change the opinion which he entertained of his confessor, and Seaton, afraid of the consequences, left Scotland, still wearing the habit of his order. On his arrival at Berwick, he addressed a letter to the king, explaining the cause of his flight, and pointing out what he thought was the proper course to be adopted by James in regard to the disputes about religion. The exact date of Seaton's flight is not mentioned, but it is

[1] Knox, vol. i. appendix, p. 530. Calderwood, Wodrow Society ed. vol. i. p. 124. Sadler's State Papers, vol. i. pp. 210, 217, 344. Lorimer's Life of Patrick Hamilton, pp. 171, 172. M'Crie's Life of Knox, p. 397. Brunton and Haig's Senators of the College of Justice, pp. 7, 8. Preface to the Chartulary of the Collegiate Church of St. Mary and St. Anne, and the Charters of the Black Friars, at Glasgow, pp, li. lvi-lviii.

supposed to have been in 1535, or 1536. He remained in England, conforming to the established Church of that country. In 1541, Gardiner, Bishop of Winchester, prevailed on him to retract at St. Paul's cross certain doctrines which he had taught. He is said to have died within a year afterwards, in the house of Charles Brandon, Duke of Suffolk, where he officiated as chaplain.[1]

From the account which Knox gives of a friar named William Airth, it is reasonable to infer that he also may be classed with those who have been mentioned. In a sermon preached at Dundee, about the year 1534, he censured the licentious lives of the bishops, and spoke strongly against false miracles, and the abuses of excommunication. Having been severely rebuked for this discourse by his diocesan, the Bishop of Brechin, he repaired to St. Andrews, and, encouraged by the support which he received from the Provost of St. Salvator's, preached the same sermon in the parish church of that city. Among his hearers, besides Mair himself, were Patrick Hepburn, Prior of St. Andrews, the Abbot of Cambuskenneth, and George Lockhart, Provost of the collegiate church of Crichton. It does not appear that he incurred any farther censure on this account. He was afterwards obliged to flee to England; but his steadfast attachment to the communion of the Church is shewn by the fact that he was imprisoned by King Henry for defending the authority of the Pope.[2]

---

[1] Knox, vol. i. p. 45-55, and appendix, p. 531-533. Keith, vol. i. pp. 15, 332-334. Spottiswood, vol. i. p. 127-129.

[2] Knox, vol. i. p. 36-41. Calderwood, vol. i. p. 83-85. I have been unable to find any farther information regarding Airth than what is given by Knox and repeated by Calderwood. The latter writer calls him Friar William Archbishop.

CHAPTER XXIX.

FROM THE DEATH OF ARCHBISHOP JAMES BEATON IN 1539, TO THE DEATH OF CARDINAL BEATON IN 1546.

Death of James V.—Accession of Mary—Regency of the Earl of Arran—Cardinal David Beaton, Archbishop of St. Andrews—Succession of Bishops—Gavin Dunbar, Archbishop of Glasgow—Persecution of the Protestants—Condemnation of Sir John Borthwick—The Protestants favoured by the Regent—The Scriptures allowed to be read in the vulgar tongue—Persecution renewed—War with England—The Border abbeys destroyed by the English—George Wishart—His residence in England—His return to Scotland—His trial—His death—Death of Cardinal Beaton—His character.

HENRY VIII. attempted to induce the King of the Scots to follow his example in transferring the ecclesiastical supremacy to the crown. His persuasions were disregarded. James knew well that the prelates of his kingdom, however unworthy in some respects, were his wisest counsellors, and the firmest supporters of the royal authority; and, besides this, lax as his own personal conduct was, there is no reason to doubt his conscientious attachment to the doctrines of the Church. King Henry could ill brook opposition to any of his designs, and, when repeated proposals of a similar kind were rejected by James, a war between the two kingdoms was the result. Unfortunately, great disaffection prevailed among the Scottish barons. They were jealous of the royal prerogative, and hated the clergy on account of their influence with the king. A few of them, it is probable, had sincerely embraced the Reformed opinions, but many more coveted the possessions of the Church, and were desirous of partaking in its spoils after the example which had been given them in England. The dissensions or the treason of the nobles led to the rout of Solway, and King James was unable to endure the disgrace. He died heartbroken at Falkland, on the thirteenth of December,

1542, in the thirty-first year of his age, and was buried at Holyrood.

Mr. Tytler mentions some points of similarity between the character and fortunes of the first and fifth James. The comparison is so far just, but in one most important respect there was a marked difference between them. The earlier sovereign was distinguished by the purity of his personal conduct, and by his anxiety for the welfare of the Church. James V. was dissolute and immoral, and, while he refused to sanction any scheme for confiscating ecclesiastical property, continued the traffic in ecclesiastical patronage which his immediate predecessors had begun. Among other instances, he bestowed some of the most important abbacies on his own illegitimate children, one of whom became the deadliest enemy of the Church which had tolerated so shameless an abuse without a word of remonstrance.

Mary, the only surviving lawful child of James, was five days old at the time of her father's decease. She was immediately acknowledged as Queen of the Scots, and the usual contests began for the administration of government. An attempt was made by Cardinal Beaton, founded on an alleged will of the late king, to assume the office of regent, but it was defeated by the nobles, who raised to that dignity James, Earl of Arran, head of the powerful house of Hamilton, and next heir to the throne. On Sunday the ninth of September, 1543, the young queen was crowned at Stirling by the Archbishop of St. Andrews.

On the death of Archbishop James Beaton, his nephew, David Beaton, was appointed his successor in the primacy. This famous ecclesiastic was a son of John Beaton of Balfour, in the county of Fife, and is said to have been born in the year 1494. He was educated for some time at St. Andrews, and afterwards at Paris, and his first benefice was the chancellorship of the Church of Glasgow, to which he was presented by his uncle, who was then archbishop of that see. When the elder Beaton became archbishop of St. Andrews, he resigned the abbacy of Arbroath to his nephew, reserving one half of the revenues to himself during his lifetime. In the year 1528, David Beaton was appointed keeper of the Privy Seal. While ambassador for King James in France, he obtained the favour of Francis I., and was presented to the bishopric of Mirepoix in that kingdom, to which he is said to have been consecrated on the fifth of December, 1537. On the twentieth of December, in the following year, a still higher dignity was bestowed upon him. He was appointed a cardinal priest by Paul III., under the title of St. Stephen in the Cælian Hill. On the fourth of May, 1540, the cardinal wrote to Pope Paul, mentioning that, on account of the burden of secular affairs which was laid upon him, he was unable to devote the requisite attention to his ecclesiastical duties, and requesting, in order to relieve him in part within the diocese of St. Andrews, that William Gibson, Dean of Restalrig, should receive episcopal consecration, and be appointed his suffragan. It is said that the Pope acceded to his petition, and that Gibson was raised to the episcopate, as bishop of Libaria in partibus infidelium. In December, 1543, the primate was created chancellor of Scotland, and, on the thirtieth day of January following, he was appointed legate a latere by the Pope.[1]

George Crichton, Bishop of Dunkeld, died on the twenty-fourth of January, 1544, and was succeeded, after some delay caused by the opposition of Robert Crichton, nephew of the late bishop, by John Hamilton, Abbot of Paisley, an illegitimate brother of the regent.[2]

William Stewart, Bishop of Aberdeen, died in April, 1545. A short time before his decease, the Pope had been requested to appoint a coadjutor, and William Gordon,

---

[1] Crawfurd's Officers of State, pp. 77, 78. Keith's Catalogue, pp. 36, 37. Lyon's History of St. Andrews, vol. i. pp. 286, 287; vol. ii. pp. 352, 356-358. Epistolæ Regum Scotorum, vol. i. p. 340-342; vol. ii. p. 66-69. Sadler's State Papers, vol. i. p. 15. Burnet's History of the Reformation, Nares' ed. vol. iv. p. 342-348. Hay, Panegyricus, f. xiii.-xviii. The work last mentioned is a remarkable composition. It was written on the occasion of Beaton's elevation to the dignity of cardinal, and was printed at Paris in 1540. The author, Archibald Hay, was a kinsman of the primate, residing at that time at Montague College, in the University of Paris. It is not easy to say whether his praises of the cardinal are serious or ironical. He was zealous for the purity and well-being of the Church, and denounces, in the strongest language, the ignorance and vices of the Scottish clergy.

[2] Keith's Catalogue, pp. 94, 95. Brunton and Haig's Senators of the College of Justice, p. 73. Epistolæ Regum Scotorum, vol. ii. pp. 158, 159, 174-177, 183-187, 225-228.

chancellor of the cathedral of Murray, son of Alexander, Earl of Huntly, was recommended for the office. Nothing farther was done in this respect in consequence of Bishop Stewart's death, and the chancellor of Murray was then appointed his successor. William Gordon was bishop-elect in July, 1546, and was consecrated in the following year.[1]

James Hay, Bishop of Ross, was succeeded in 1539 by Robert Cairncross, Abbot of Holyrood. On his appointment to the see, Bishop Cairncross resigned the great abbacy which he held, but received soon afterwards that of Ferne in commendam. He died in the year 1545. The next bishop was David Panter, secretary to the regent.[2]

On the death of Andrew Stewart, Bishop of Caithness, which seems to have taken place in 1541, Robert Stewart, brother of Matthew, Earl of Lennox, was appointed to the see. He was at that time very young, and had only received the tonsure. It is probable that he was never ordained or consecrated.[3]

In the year 1541, Robert Reid, Abbot of Kinloss, succeeded Robert Maxwell, as bishop of Orkney, and was consecrated in the course of the same year.[4]

The see of Glasgow continued to be held by Archbishop Dunbar. He strenuously maintained the independence of the Church of St. Kentigern. While admitting the superior dignity of St. Andrews, he resisted the attempts of its archbishops to extend their primatial rule over his province. On one occasion this controversy gave rise to an unseemly brawl. When the papal legate, Contarini, Patriarch of Venice, came over, soon after the appointment of Arran to the regency, he was honourably entertained at Glasgow by the Scottish bishops. A dispute arose between the two arch-

[1] Keith's Catalogue, pp, 122, 124. Preface to the Chartulary of Aberdeen, p. lvii.-lx. Leslie, p. 456. Acts of the Parliaments of Scotland, vol. ii. p. 467. Epistolæ Regum Scotorum, vol. ii. pp. 250, 251. There seems to be no good reason for doubting that the William Gordon recommended as coadjutor to Bishop Stewart was the same person who afterwards succeeded him.

[2] Keith's Catalogue, p. 190-192. Brunton and Haig's Senators of the College of Justice, pp. 45, 46. Leslie, p. 456. Epistolæ Regum Scotorum, vol. ii. p. 104.

[3] Keith's Catalogue, p. 215. Epistolæ Regum Scotorum, vol. ii. p. 222-223.

[4] Brunton and Haig's Senators of the College of Justice, p. 16. Epistolæ Regum Scotorum, vol. ii. p. 112-115. The Stirlings of Keir, p. 400.

bishops—the cardinal contending that, in virtue of his legatine and primatial authority, he was entitled to take precedence even within the cathedral of Glasgow. The attendants of Archbishop Dunbar, indignant at an attempt to enforce this claim, attacked the primate's crossbearer, and the tumult was only stopped by the intervention of the regent.[1]

Archbishop Dunbar died on the thirtieth of April, 1547, and was buried within the chancel of his cathedral. He was a learned, accomplished, and pious prelate, stained by no crime, except that of yielding, against his own judgment, to the persecuting spirit of the day.[2]

On the sixteenth of January, 1546, Malcolm, Lord Fleming, chamberlain of Scotland, with consent of Archbishop Dunbar and the chapter of Glasgow, founded the collegiate church of St. Mary, at Biggar. The foundation provided for the maintenance of a provost, eight prebendaries, four choristers, and six poor beadsmen.[3] In the end of the following year, Lord Fleming was slain at Pinkie.

Henry, Bishop of Galloway, was succeeded in the year 1541 by Andrew Durie, Abbot of Melrose.[4]

Ferquhard, Bishop of the Isles and Commendator of Iona, finding himself unable, from advanced years, to discharge his ecclesiastical duties, resigned the see and the abbacy in the year 1544 in favour of Roderick Maclean, archdeacon of the diocese.[5]

The proceedings against heretics during the primacy of

[1] Regist. Episcopat. Glasguen. pp. 550, 551, 553-556. Leslie, pp. 445, 448, 449. Knox, vol. i. pp. 146, 147. The dispute mentioned by Leslie, and that described by Knox with characteristic glee, probably refer to the same occasion, but there is an apparent discrepancy in the date. The establishment of two metropolitan sees in Scotland, with privileges not always clearly defined, led to contests similar to those which had so often taken place between the two English archbishops.

[2] Keith's Catalogue, p. 257-259. Brunton and Haig's Senators of the College of Justice, p. 3-5. Buchanan (vol. i. p. 270) speaks of Dunbar as "vir bonus et doctus, sed in quo nonnulli civilem prudentiam desiderabant." His beautiful poetical commemoration of the archbishop's accomplishments is well known.

[3] Deed of foundation—Miscellany of the Spalding Club, vol. v. p. 296-308, and preface to that volume, p. 26-30.

[4] Keith's Catalogue, p. 278. Brunton and Haig's Senators of the College of Justice, p. 68. Epistolæ Regum Scotorum, vol. ii. p. 115-120.

[5] Keith's Catalogue, pp. 306, 307. Epistolæ Regum Scotorum, vol. ii. p. 219-221. Calendar of State Papers relating to Scotland, vol. i. p. 53.

Archbishop James Beaton, had been carried on with the full approbation of the cardinal, and, on the accession of the latter to the see of St. Andrews, no change took place in the policy of the Scottish rulers. In May, 1540, Sir John Borthwick, a younger son of William Lord Borthwick who fell at Flodden, was summoned to appear before the cardinal and other prelates at St. Andrews. Before the trial came on, Beaton himself had embarked with the king on his voyage to the Western Isles, but there were present the Archbishop of Glasgow, the Bishops of Aberdeen, Galloway, Brechin, and Dunblane, and the heads of many of the monastic houses, and other ecclesiastics, besides some of the chief temporal nobles. Borthwick having fled to England, evidence was brought regarding his opinions, and sentence was pronounced against him in the cardinal's name. After the establishment of the Reformed religion, he returned to Scotland, and obtained a reversal of his condemnation.[1]

The Earl of Arran, on his appointment to the regency, went so far in his opposition to the cardinal, as openly to favour the new doctrines. He entertained in his service two Protestant preachers, Thomas Williams and John Rough, both of whom had been Dominican friars, and he encouraged others to spread their opinions in various parts of the kingdom. On the fifteenth day of March, 1543, upon the motion of Lord Maxwell, one of the prisoners taken at Solway, who had been permitted to return by King Henry, an act of parliament was passed, allowing the Holy Scriptures of the Old and New Testament to be translated into the English or Scottish tongue, and read by the people. Against this the Archbishop of Glasgow, chancellor of the kingdom, for himself, and in name of all the prelates then present as one of the three estates, entered his protest, until a provincial council could be held for the purpose of considering whether such a step was necessary.[2]

[1] Knox, vol. i. appendix, pp. 533, 534. Leslie, p. 430. Spottiswood, vol. i. pp. 138, 139. Calderwood, vol. i. p. 114-123. Keith, vol. i. pp. 20, 21, 335-341. Dr. John Lee's Lectures on the History of the Church of Scotland, vol. i. p. 327-334.

[2] Acts of the Parliaments of Scotland, vol. ii. p. 415. Regist. Episcopat. Glasguen. pp. 559, 560. Knox, vol. i. pp. 95, 96, 100. Keith, vol. i. p. 89-91. Extracts from the Council Register of Aberdeen, from 1398 to 1570, p. 189.

Almost from the introduction of the Protestant doctrines into Scotland, the maintenance of those opinions was mixed up with the political intrigues of the party which was opposed to the French alliance, and willing to sacrifice the independence of their country to the English supremacy. The great body of the Scottish people were not yet prepared to renounce the communion of the Church, and, with the exception of those of the nobility who had bound themselves to Henry, almost all were opposed to the selfish designs of the English king. It was the object of that prince to obtain the real sovereignty of the Scottish kingdom by means of a marriage between the young queen and Edward, Prince of Wales. The cardinal was at once the chief enemy of the new doctrines, and the head of the political party hostile to England. By the assistance, as is supposed, of John Hamilton, Abbot of Paisley, Arran's illegitimate brother, he induced the regent to abandon his connection with England, and to abjure the Protestant opinions.

The first two years of the new reign appear to have been unstained by the infliction of capital punishment for heresy; but, strengthened by the support of Arran, the cardinal recommenced the persecution. In January, 1544, a considerable number of persons, accused of various offences connected with religion, were summoned before the regent and the cardinal at Perth. Four men and one woman, all of humble rank, were put to death—the men by hanging, the woman by drowning; and others were banished from the kingdom.[1]

The Scottish clergy now began to experience the effects of the line of policy adopted by King Henry in England. Open war had again broken out between the two kingdoms, and a powerful army, under the Earl of Hertford, entered Scotland. The monasteries, which had generally been spared in former invasions, were now the chief objects of attack. Their wealth allured the spoilers, and the sanctity of ecclesiastical buildings was as little regarded by King Henry's nobles, as it had been of old by the heathen Danes. It was not to be expected that they, who in their own land appropriated to sordid uses the most venerated abodes of piety, would shew

[1] Knox, vol i. pp. 117, 118. Spottiswood, vol. i. pp. 147, 148. Keith, vol. i. pp. 98, 100.

more reverence in the country of an enemy. During Hertford's invasion, and in a series of inroads which continued for some time, the great abbeys of Holyrood, Melrose, Dryburgh, Kelso, and Jedburgh, with many other churches and monasteries, were given to the flames. The conduct of the English was wantonly cruel and destructive. At Melrose they defaced the tombs of the Douglases, and the Earl of Angus was recalled by this outrage to the duty which he owed to his country. The spoilers were defeated, and two of their most rapacious leaders slain at Ancrum Moor.[1]

Some of the most important events in Scottish history now become mixed up with the personal fortunes of George Wishart, one of the Protestant preachers. Wishart is supposed to have been a son of the house of Pitarro in the Mearns. His early life is involved in obscurity. Most of our writers speak of his residence at Montrose, and of his having fled from that town to escape the persecution of the Bishop of Brechin for teaching the Greek New Testament. But these circumstances are not mentioned by any contemporary authority, and seem to be founded on a wrong interpretation put on some of the statements made at his trial. He left his native country, probably on account of religion, and appears to have resided for some time in England, and on the Continent. About 1543 he was at Cambridge, and connected with Corpus Christi College in that University, where he was highly esteemed for his piety, charity, and ascetic devotion. In the autumn of that year, and before the southern abbeys had suffered from Hertford's invasion, the first domestic attack was made on the monastic houses in Scotland. This has been attributed to the preaching of Wishart, but it is not certain that he had left England at the time. Of the event itself there can be no doubt. The letter of an English agent mentions that the work of reformation had begun at Dundee by the destruction of the monasteries of the Black and Gray Friars; that afterwards the abbey of Lindores on the opposite side of the Frith of Tay had been sacked, and the monks turned out; and that a similar

[1] Tytler, vol. v. pp. 314-317, 330, 331. Morton's Monastic Annals of Teviotdale, pp. 36, 100, 243, 301. Preface to the Charters of Holyrood, pp. lxxiii. lxxiv.

attack had been made on the monastery of the Black Friars at Edinburgh, but that it had been repelled by the citizens.[1]

George Wishart was in Scotland probably before the end of 1544. His sermons had a great effect on the people, and he found powerful protectors in some of the nobility and gentry. Among those who attended upon him and listened to his discourses was John Knox, who bore for some time a two-handed sword which was usually carried before the preacher. While Wishart was residing at Leith, the regent and the cardinal came to Edinburgh. The latter was aware that plots had been formed against his life, which were encouraged by the English king, and in which some of Wishart's protectors were deeply implicated. Whether it was that he suspected Wishart to be cognisant of the plots, or that he was merely desirous of seizing one of the chief teachers of the new opinions, is uncertain; at all events he endeavoured to apprehend him. The preacher escaped from Leith, but, on the sixteenth of January, 1546, was taken at Ormiston, in East Lothian, by the Earl of Bothwell, and delivered to the primate, who caused him soon afterwards to be conveyed to St. Andrews.

On the twenty-eighth of February, Wishart was brought to trial in the cathedral church of St. Andrews, before the cardinal, the Archbishop of Glasgow, and other ecclesiastical judges, the regent declining to take a part in the proceedings. On

[1] Knox, vol. i. appendix, pp. 534, 535. Miscellany of the Wodrow Society, vol. i. pp. 5, 6. M'Crie's Life of Knox, pp. 399, 400. Calderwood, vol. i. p. 184-186. Keith, vol. i. pp. 103, 104. Chalmers's Life of Mary, Queen of Scots, vol. ii. pp. 403, 404. Diurnal of Occurrents, p. 29. Tytler, vol. v. pp. 341, 342. Wishart's excommunication by the Bishop of Brechin appears to have taken place after his return to Scotland. The statement that he was a schoolmaster at Montrose, and that he fled from that town in 1538 to escape the persecution of the bishop, rests exclusively, so far as I am aware, on the authority of a traditional story told by Petrie in his Church History, p. 182. It has frequently been asserted, on the authority of an extract from the records of the city of Bristol, printed by Dr. M'Crie (Life of Knox, p. 401), that in the year 1539 Wishart preached at Bristol against the opinions then generally received regarding the merits of the Blessed Virgin, and that he made a public recantation when brought before Archbishop Cranmer and others of the English prelates. Dr. Lorimer has shewn (Scottish Reformation, p. 93-96) that this is a mistake arising from a wrong reading of the MS. record, and that the heresy which was retracted was a denial of the merits of our Lord. Perhaps the George Wishart who preached at Bristol was a different person from the reformer.

this occasion, Winram, the sub-prior, preached to the congregation, taking his text from the parable of the tares in the thirteenth chapter of St. Matthew. He said that heresy was the evil seed, and he defined it to be a false opinion, clearly opposed to the word of God, and pertinaciously defended. He shewed that heresy was caused by the ignorance of those who had the cure of men's souls, whose duty it was to have the true understanding of the word of God, that they might be able to win again the teachers of heresy with the sword of the Spirit which is the word of God; and thereupon he quoted St. Paul's account of the duties of a bishop. Heresies, he added, might be known by an undoubted touchstone, the true, sincere, and undefiled word of God. He defended the lawfulness of punishing heretics by the temporal sword, and attempted to reconcile it with the text, "Let both grow together till the harvest."

When the sermon was finished, the charges against Wishart were read. These were chiefly the following: That he had preached after being forbidden to do so by the ecclesiastical and civil authorities; that he had denied there were seven sacraments; that he had taught that auricular confession was not a sacrament; that he had affirmed that the sacrament of the altar was only common bread; that he had stated that every layman was a priest, and that the Pope had no more power than any other man; that he had denied Free-will, Purgatory, and the lawfulness of prayer to the saints, and that he asserted that priests might lawfully marry. These charges were specifically answered by Wishart. Some he denied altogether, complaining that his language had been misrepresented; others he held to be doubtful points, as to which a positive opinion could not be laid down, except in so far as they were sanctioned by the word of God. He expressed himself cautiously in regard to the sacraments and the invocation of saints, denying that he had directly contradicted the teaching of the Church, but professing his inability to believe farther than was agreeable to the word of God. He admitted that he did not hold any distinction to exist between the clergy and the laity, appealing to the texts of St. John and St. Peter which speak of Christians as kings and priests unto God, and as a royal priesthood.

Notwithstanding his defence, he was found guilty of heresy,

and condemned to death. When he was carried back to the castle, two gray friars came to him, and expressed their readiness to hear his confession. He answered, "I will make no confession to you; go fetch me yonder man that preached this day, and I will make my confession to him." The sub-prior accordingly came. What passed between them was never known. On the following morning, Winram again visited him, and asked if he wished to receive the Holy Eucharist. "Willingly," he said, "if it be administered under both kinds, according to our Saviour's institution." The sub-prior went to the bishops and mentioned his request, but was told that it was not reasonable that an obstinate heretic, condemned by the Church, should partake of the Church's blessings. In the meantime the governor of the castle invited Wishart to take breakfast with himself and his attendants. He accepted their hospitality, and, during the meal, acting on the opinion which he entertained in regard to the priestly office, after discoursing for sometime on the Passion of our Lord, and on the duty of mutual charity and forgiveness, he took bread and wine, and, partaking of both himself, gave also, to those who were present, exhorting them to remember the death of Christ. He then retired to his chamber.

When the fire was prepared, he was led forth. Having implored mercy of his Saviour, and commended his soul to His keeping, he addressed the people, beseeching them not to be offended with the word of God, on account of the sufferings to which they saw him exposed. "For the word's sake," he said, "and the true Gospel which was given me by the grace of God, I suffer this day by men, not sorrowfully, but with a glad heart and mind. For this cause I was sent, that I should suffer this fire for Christ's sake. Consider and behold my visage, ye shall not see me change my colour. This grim fire I fear not; and so I pray you for to do, if that any persecution come unto you for the word's sake; and not to fear them that slay the body, and afterwards have no power to slay the soul. Some have said of me that I taught that the soul of man should sleep until the last day; but I know surely, and my faith is such, that my soul shall sup with my Saviour this night ere it be six hours, for whom I suffer this." He concluded by praying that all those who had passed sentence upon him and were assisting in his death might be forgiven. He was then fastened to the gibbet, and was burned to ashes.[1]

It has been maintained by various writers that Wishart was aware of the conspiracy which had been formed against the life of Beaton. This question, like some others of a similar kind in the history of the Scottish Reformation, is attended with considerable difficulty. I cannot see, however, that there is evidence of Wishart's guilt. An individual of the same surname was undoubtedly implicated in the plot, but there is hardly anything beyond this to identify him with the preacher. Suspicion certainly arises from Wishart's intimate connection with several of the chief conspirators, and from the prophetic denunciations of the evils about to befall his enemies which have been attributed to him. These denunciations have probably been exaggerated; but, if otherwise, he had seen enough of Brunstone and the other partizans of England to be aware that Scotland was threatened with foreign invasion, and that the leading statesmen on the opposite side were exposed to great danger from their domestic enemies, without its being necessary to infer that he was an accomplice in the plot against them. In such a question also, it is most unjust to keep out of view the gentle disposition and stainless character of Wishart. Had he resembled in his language and demeanour some others of the reformers, the accusation would not have been so improbable. But it is unreasonable to suppose that the man, whose private life at Cambridge was so exemplary, and who died with the words of meekness and forgiveness on his lips, could have taken an active part in the designs of a body of plotters and murderers.[2]

[1] Knox, vol. i. p. 125-171, and appendix, pp. 535, 536. Foxe's Acts and Monuments, p. 622-627. Buchanan, vol. i. p. 292-294. Spottiswood, vol. i. p. 150-162. Calderwood, vol. i. p. 186-219. Keith, vol. i. p. 101-106. Tytler, vol. v. p. 343-349. The proceedings of Wishart on the morning of the day on which he died are related by Buchanan, who also states that they took place immediately after the visit from the two friars, and the request to send for Winram. This last statement is opposed to the narrative of Knox, and I have adopted in the text what seems the most natural explanation. Buchanan mentions that the cardinal looked on while Wishart suffered at the stake. Knox is silent as to this, but it is to be feared that there is nothing improbable in the circumstance. What Buchanan adds as to Wishart's prophecy of the cardinal's death is much more doubtful.

[2] On this point, see Mr. David Laing's appendix to Knox, vol. i. pp 536, 537; Keith, vol. i. p. 109, and Mr. Lawson's notes, pp. 103-105, 110; note by

Soon after the death of Wishart, the cardinal went over to Angus in order to be present at the marriage of one of his illegitimate daughters with the Master of Crawford, and thence returned to St. Andrews.[1]

No single event during the persecutions in Scotland seems to have caused such a deep feeling in the popular mind as the burning of Wishart. Before that time the Protestant opinions were not generally received with favour, even among the inhabitants of the towns, and the cardinal was held in estimation on account of his opposition to the English alliance;[1] but now the general feeling appears to have undergone a great and sudden change, which can only be explained by something peculiar in the character and conduct of the sufferer, and in the proceedings connected with his persecution. The cardinal became an object of hatred to a large proportion of the people, and those who held the new opinions increased in number and influence. The personal and political enemies of Beaton were encouraged to proceed with their designs against him. He was at this time residing in his castle at St. Andrews, where some new buildings were in the course of being erected. At day-break on the twenty-eighth of May, 1546, Norman Leslie, Master of Rothes, his uncle, John Leslie, William Kirkaldy of Grange, and some other gentlemen, with a few attendants, contrived to obtain admission into the castle. The household retainers were seized one by one and dismissed. The cardinal, awakened by the noise, attempted to escape by a private postern, but, finding it guarded, returned to his apartment, and with the assistance of his page barricaded the door. The threat of applying fire compelled him to open it. The conspirators rushed in, and some of them struck him. He cried out, "I am a priest, you will not slay me." James Melville, one of the assassins, reproved his companions for their violence,

---

Bishop Russell, in his edition of Spottiswood, vol. i. pp. 230, 231; Lyon's History of St. Andrews, vol. i. p. 296, and vol. ii. p. 358-366; and Tytler's Life of Craig, p. 333-343, and his History, vol. v. p. 376-391.

[1] See Knox, vol. i. pp. 174, 175; Keith, vol. i. pp. 112, 113; and Lord Lindsay's Lives of the Lindsays, vol. i. p. 201. Some writers, favourable to the cardinal's memory, have attempted to show that he was a widower when he entered into holy orders, and that his children were born in wedlock; but their arguments and authorities appear to be very inconclusive.

telling them that the judgment of God ought to be executed with more gravity. Then, alluding to Wishart's death, and saying that they were sent by God to avenge it, he repeatedly passed his sword through the body of the archbishop, who fell on the ground and immediately expired. The citizens of the town were by this time alarmed, and gathering close to the castle ditch demanded admission, and insisted on being allowed to speak with the cardinal. The murderers hung the dead body over the wall, and the frightened townsmen dispersed.[1]

Such was the awful death of Cardinal Beaton. Whether it was caused by private vengeance, by political and religious hatred, or by paid assassins doing the work they were employed to perform, it was a most inhuman and wicked act. The character of the murdered prelate has been estimated very differently by writers of different opinions; but the truth can be ascertained without much difficulty. His abilities were undoubtedly great. As a statesman, he distinguished himself by a fearless assertion of his country's independence, and the maintenance of its real interests, in opposition to a selfish and powerful faction of the nobility. As an ecclesiastic, he pursued rigorously and without remorse those cruel measures for the repression of the Protestant doctrines, which almost all the adherents of the Roman Church held to be both a duty and an imperative necessity. Had the personal character of Beaton been pure, his memory would have been respected as that of a prelate endowed with many high and noble qualities, though stained with a crime in which all parties then partook in a greater or less degree. But, while he punished with relentless severity the maintenance of opinions opposed to those which the Church of that day taught, he made no attempt to reform the abuses which gave such weight to the arguments of her opponents; and his own manner of living resembled that of the rude nobles by whom he was hated and feared. In the popular belief of Scotland vices and offences have been attributed to him of which he was not guilty; but there is sufficient evidence to shew that his life was secular and irreligious, and in no way regulated by those principles which ought to govern the conduct of a Christian bishop.

[1] Knox, vol. i. p. 174-179. Spottiswood, vol. i. p. 163-165 Keith, vol. i. pp. 108, 109. Tytler, vol. v. p. 353-355.

CHAPTER XXX.

FROM THE DEATH OF CARDINAL BEATON IN 1546, TO THE END OF THE
EARL OF ARRAN'S REGENCY IN 1554.

*Regency of the Earl of Arran—John Hamilton, Archbishop of
St. Andrews—James Beaton, Archbishop of Glasgow—
Succession of Bishops—John Knox—His residence in the
Castle of St. Andrews—His call to be a Protestant minister
—His controversies with the clergy—Council at Edinburgh
in 1549—Members of the Council—Canons enacted—Persecution of the Protestants—Death of Adam Wallace—
Council at Edinburgh in 1552—Publication of a Catechism—Alleged dispute about the Paternoster.*

THE murder of Cardinal Beaton was applauded by the more vehement of the Protestant leaders, and openly abetted by the political faction which was connected with England. The assassins kept possession of the castle of St. Andrews, where they were soon joined by many of their friends, and by John Rough, who had formerly been chaplain to the regent. At a subsequent period, John Knox took up his residence among them. The regent was called upon by the party in alliance with France, and by the clergy, and all the zealous supporters of the Church, to take immediate steps for punishing the sacrilegious crime which had been committed. The castle was accordingly besieged, but was vigorously defended by the garrison. The siege was tedious, and might have been unsuccessful, if a French fleet had not arrived to assist the regent. The garrison was finally obliged to capitulate in the end of July, 1547. The assassins of the cardinal and their chief supporters were conveyed to France, and detained in various fortresses, or in the galleys.

In the autumn of the same year, the Earl of Hertford, now Duke of Somerset, and protector during the minority of Edward VI., again invaded Scotland. The regent sent the fiery cross through the kingdom, and advanced against the English with a numerous army, accompanied by a body of priests and monks who marched under a white banner bearing an emblematic figure of the afflicted Church. They met at Pinkie on the ninth of September, and the Scots were defeated with great slaughter. This victory was of little avail to Somerset, who was recalled to England by the necessity of attending to his own political interests. Hostilities continued for some time without any decisive result, but the national feeling was so embittered against the English, that the three estates, which met at Haddington in July, 1548, unanimously agreed that the young queen of the Scots should marry the Dauphin Francis, and that, in the meantime, she should be entrusted to the care of his father, King Henry II. Peace was not restored between England and Scotland till April, 1550. In April, 1554, the regent was induced by the queen dowager and the court of France to resign his office, the duchy of Chatel-herault being conferred upon him by King Henry, and his title as heir to the crown of Scotland being solemnly recognised. Mary of Lorraine was appointed regent by a commission from the queen her daughter, and her authority was acknowledged by the estates of the kingdom.

After the death of Cardinal Beaton, the see of St. Andrews remained vacant for some time, but finally, John Hamilton, Bishop of Dunkeld, brother of the Earl of Arran, was raised to the primacy. The exact date of his appointment has not been ascertained. He had been consecrated while bishop of Dunkeld, probably in the beginning of 1546, and his formal translation took place in 1549. He continued to retain the abbacy of Paisley.[1]

Archbishop Hamilton's successor at Dunkeld was Robert Crichton, nephew of the former bishop, George Crichton. He is said to have been promoted to the see in 1550.[2]

David Panter remained abroad for seven years after his nomination to the see of Ross. He returned to Scotland in 1552, and was consecrated at Jedburgh, in presence of the regent and a large concourse of the nobility.[3]

On the decease of Gavin Dunbar, Alexander Gordon,

---

[1] Keith's Catalogue, p. 95. Evidence taken by the University Commissioners, vol. iii. p. 367. Lyon's History of St. Andrews, vol. ii. p. 262.

[2] Keith's Catalogue, p. 96.

[3] Keith's Catalogue, p. 192. Leslie, p. 477.

brother of George Earl of Huntly, was chosen archbishop of Glasgow, but his election was disputed, and, in 1551, James Beaton, Abbot of Arbroath, was appointed to the see. The abbot was at that time in his twenty-seventh year, and was not yet ordained. He was raised to the four minor orders and ordained sub-deacon at Rome, on the sixteenth of July, 1552 ; on the seventeenth and twentieth days of that month he was ordained deacon and priest; and on Sunday, the twenth-eighth of August, he was consecrated bishop.[1]

In the year 1549, William was bishop elect and confirmed of Argyll. He is said to have been a brother of the Earl of Glencairn. It is not known at what time he succeeded Bishop Montgomery.[2]

Roderick Maclean died about the year 1553, and Alexander Gordon was promoted to the see of the Isles. This prelate had been named to the administration of the diocese of Caithness during the time that its titular bishop, Robert Stewart, was under forfeiture for treason. As some recompense for his disappointment at Glasgow, the Pope also conferred upon him the nominal dignity of Archbishop of Athens.[3]

After the death of Cardinal Beaton, the clergy seem to have dreaded that attempts would be made to destroy the ecclesiastical and monastic buildings. On the eleventh of June, 1546, an act of the Privy Council was passed, and was subsequently ratified by parliament, denouncing the forfeiture of life, land, and goods, against all who should be guilty of this or similar outrages.[4]

At Easter, 1547, John Knox, accompanied by his pupils, the sons of the lairds of Ormiston and Langniddry, repaired to the castle of St. Andrews. Knox was born near Haddington in 1505. He was educated at the University of Glasgow, and when about twenty-five years of age was ordained a priest. It is said that he embraced the Protestant doctrines in 1542,

[1] Keith's Catalogue. p. 259. Regist. Episcopat. Glasguen. p. 562-577, and preface, p. iii.
[2] Keith's Catalogue, p. 289. Wilkins's Concilia, vol. iv. p. 46.
[3] Keith's Catalogue, p. 307. Brunton and Haig's Senators of the College of Justice, pp. 128, 129. Gordon's History of the Earldom of Sutherland, pp. 111, 290. Epistolæ Regum Scotorum, vol. ii. p. 223-225. Origines Parochiales Scotiæ, vol. ii. part i. p. 293.
[4] Epistolæ Regum Scotorum, vol. ii. pp. 345, 346. Acts of the Parliaments of Scotland, vol. ii p 470. Keith, vol. i. pp. 144, 145.

but he first became known as a disciple of George Wishart, in the year 1545. It is probable that, after the murder of Cardinal Beaton, Knox's opinions exposed him to danger; and he himself asserts that his residence in the castle was necessary for his safety. His avowed sympathy with the act of the assassins would prevent any scruple about the propriety of joining himself to their company.

During the intervals of the siege, a Protestant congregation had been established in the city, and from them, about the end of May or beginning of June, Knox accepted a call to be their minister. The circumstances connected with this proceeding shew how entirely the doctrine of holy orders was rejected by the Scottish reformers. Knox had already declined an invitation to become a preacher, but his friends were determined to overcome his objections. On an appointed day, Rough preached a sermon, in which he explained the power of the congregration, however small in number, provided they were more than two or three, to call to the office of the ministry any one in whom they perceived the suitable gifts, and the duty of the person so invited to obey the call. When this discourse was finished, turning to Knox, he charged him not to refuse the office to which he was now called by the people. After some hesitation, Knox obeyed the summons. No laying on of hands or other ceremony was used, and no allusion was made to the priestly ordination which he had already received. The solemn, deliberate choice of the people was held to be the only authority requisite for conferring the ministerial office.[1]

The ability of Knox was soon displayed in defence of the Protestant opinions. His colleague Rough had been unable to encounter the controversial skill of John Annand, Principal of St. Leonard's College, a zealous maintainer of the Roman doctrines. Knox, according to his own account, refuted the arguments of the principal, and compelled him as a last resource to appeal to the authority of the Church, which had already settled the questions at issue by condemning Lutheranism and heresies of every description. The reformer met this statement by denying that the Church of Rome was the true Church, and by asserting that it was the synagogue of Satan,

Knox, vol. i. p. 184-188.   M'Crie's Life of Knox, pp. 1-9, 25-33.

and that the Pope was the Man of Sin, and Antichrist. He maintained these opinions in a sermon preached in the parish church of St. Andrews. Among his hearers were Winram the sub-prior, John Mair, and other ecclesiastics. The primate-elect, being informed of what had taken place, wrote to the sub-prior, who was the acting vicar-general of the diocese, expressing his surprise that such doctrines were allowed to be taught without answer. Winram sent for Rough and Knox, and offered to reason with them on certain articles drawn from their sermons. A conference took place, relating mainly to the power of the Church to ordain ceremonies, in which Knox, on the one side, and, on the other, Winram, and a Franciscan friar named Arbuckle, took part. Neither party was convinced by the arguments of its opponents. From this time the clergy began a course of sermons, every Sunday, in the parish church, in which they avoided points of controversy; Knox continued his discourses on week days; and the result appeared in the increasing numbers of those who adopted the new opinions. The progress of the Reformation at St. Andrews was interrupted by the renewal of the siege. Rough had previously retired to England, where he was burned in the reign of Mary. Knox remained to the last, and was carried prisoner to France.[1]

In Lent, 1547, a provincial council was held at Edinburgh, at which, or at some former council, a canon was enacted enjoining that in every cathedral church a doctor or licentiate in theology, bound to preach the word of God to the people, should be appointed a member of the chapter.[2]

In August, 1549, a provincial council was held at Linlithgow, at which certain canons were enacted.[3] A few months afterwards another council met at Edinburgh. The proceedings of this synod are interesting, both from their own importance, and as being the first of which a full record has been preserved. The Archbishop of St. Andrews, as primate and legatus natus, summoned the council, and presided at its

[1] Knox, vol. i. p. 188-206. M'Crie's Life of Knox, p. 36-42.
[2] Regist. Episcopat. Aberdon. vol. ii. pp. 317, 318.
[3] Wilkins's Concilia, vol. iv. p. 209. This seems to have been a council entirely distinct from that which met at Edinburgh in the following November, though our writers speak of the one as an adjournment of the other; compare Concilia, vol. iv. p. 46.

meetings. It was convened within the church of the Black Friars, on Wednesday, the twenty-seventh of November, and was attended by the chief prelates, and many other ecclesiastics. The names of those present have been preserved, and we are thus able to know who at this time composed the provincial synod of the Scottish clergy. There met on the appointed day William, Bishop of Aberdeen, Patrick, Bishop of Murray and Commendator of Scone, Andrew, Bishop of Galloway and of the Chapel Royal, William, Bishop of Dunblane, Robert, Bishop of Orkney and Commendator of Kinloss, William, elect and confirmed of Argyll, and the Deans of Glasgow and Dunkeld, as vicars-general during the vacancy of these sees. There were also present James, Commendator of the Priory of St. Andrews, afterwards Earl of Murray, at that time only eighteen years of age, James, Commendator of Kelso and Melrose, also an illegitimate son of the late king, George, Commendator of Dunfermline and Archdeacon of St. Andrews, the Prior of Whithorn, Quintin Kennedy, Abbot of Crossraguel, the Abbots of Cupar, Glenluce, Newbottle, Dundrennan, and Deer, the Commendator of Culross, the Priors of Pluscardine and Monymusk, John Winram, Sub-prior of St. Andrews, Alexander Anderson, Sub-principal of the College of Aberdeen, John Greyson, Provincial of the Black Friars, John Paterson, General Minister of the Gray Friars of the Observance, the Deans and Provosts of several cathedral and collegiate churches, and various members of the cathedral chapters, of the monastic orders, and of the universities. John Mair, and another doctor in theology, named Martin Balfour, both of whom were advanced in years and in infirm health, appeared by their procurators. The prelates and clergy of both provinces met together in one house, and hence those synods were sometimes styled provincial-general councils.

After the celebration of mass, the members of council left the church and repaired to the refectory of the monastery. They then took the seats allotted, and all persons who had no right to be present having been excluded, a sermon was preached, and the proceedings commenced. The synod had been called for the correction of those evils by which the Church was overwhelmed, and the preamble to its acts sets forth that the two main causes of these calamities were the corrupt morals and the ignorance of the clergy of all ranks. Fifty-seven canons were enacted, which were chiefly designed to correct the prevalent abuses, and were in themselves well calculated for that purpose; but the evil was now too deeply rooted to admit of an easy remedy. It was agreed that another provincial council should meet on the fourteenth day of August, next ensuing, in the same place, or at St. Andrews, or Linlithgow.[1]

The first person who suffered death for heresy during Archbishop Hamilton's primacy seems to have been Adam Wallace. He was a layman, a native of Ayrshire, apparently of humble rank and little learning, but zealous and courageous in maintaining the opinions which he had embraced. In the autumn of 1550, he was brought before a court composed both of ecclesiastics and of temporal peers, among whom were the regent and the primate. He refused to abjure the doctrine which he held regarding the Eucharist and other points, and was condemned to death. After sentence was pronounced, the Bible, which hitherto had been his constant companion, was taken from him, but, as he had learned the Psalter by heart, he spent the night which followed in singing psalms. Although he declined to receive the instructions of two gray friars who were sent to him, he willingly entered into religious conversation with John Sinclair, Dean of Restalrig, afterwards Bishop of Brechin, and stated that he was much comforted by it. The place of execution was the Castle-hill of Edinburgh. When the fire was lighted, he lifted up his eyes to heaven, and said to those who were present, "Let it not offend you that I suffer death this day, for the truth's sake. The disciple is not above his Master."[2]

It is probable that another synod was held, as had been appointed, on the fourteenth of August, 1550; but we have no record of its proceedings. The Scottish clergy again met in provincial council at Edinburgh, on the twenty-sixth day

---

[1] Wilkins's Concilia, vol. iv. p. 46-60. The acts of this council and of the others to be afterwards referred to, were preserved among the MSS. of the Royal Library at Paris, and were sent to Wilkins by Thomas Innes. See also Hailes, vol. iii. p. 231-236.

[2] Foxe, pp. 627, 628. Knox, vol. i. pp. 237, 241, and appendix, p. 543-550.

of January, 1552, under the presidency of Archbishop Hamilton. Seventeen canons were enacted, chiefly enforcing the orders of the synod of 1549. The last two referred to the publication and use of a catechism which was appointed to be taught in the Scottish Church. The preamble sets forth, that the inferior ecclesiastics, and the prelates for the most part, were not sufficiently learned to be able, without assistance, to instruct the people in the Catholic faith, and in other points necessary to their souls' health; and it was therefore ordained that a book, written in the Scottish tongue, and approved by the wisest prelates and most learned divines and ecclesiastics present at the synod, should be put into the hands of parsons, vicars, and curates, as well for their own instruction, as for that of the Christian people committed to their charge. This book, containing a catechism on the Ten Commandments, the Creed, the Seven Sacraments, the Lord's Prayer, and the Angelical Salutation, was ordered to be printed and circulated; the primate being enjoined to deliver the requisite number of copies to the clergy of his own diocese, and also to the ordinaries of other dioceses for distribution among their parsons, vicars, and curates; the rest to remain in his keeping for after use. The clergy were warned not to shew the book to the laity, except with the advice of their diocesans, but permission was given to the ordinaries to supply copies to such discreet laymen as would wish to examine them for the sake of instruction rather than of curiosity. The parochial ministers were enjoined to read the catechism to their congregations for half-an-hour every Sunday and holy-day, unless when there was a sermon, and, in order to do this the better, they were directed to prepare themselves for the task before hand.[1]

The catechism printed by order of the synod contains a summary of the doctrines then taught by the Scottish Church, expressed in plain and moderate language. It has sometimes been confounded with a much smaller compilation, issued by a subsequent council, and popularly called the Twopenny

---

[1] Wilkins's Concilia, vol. iv. p. 69-73. Hailes, vol. iii. p. 235-240. Several of our writers have mistaken the true date of this council. Even Hailes is inaccurate. It was undoubtedly held in January, 1552, and the catechism, which was printed in August of that year, was thus issued within seven months after the council; see Keith, vol i. pp. 5, 6.

Faith. The author of the catechism is not known; but there is considerable probability in the conjecture which attributes it to Winram, Sub-prior of St. Andrews.[1]

It is asserted by Foxe, and the statement is repeated by Spottiswood and almost all our ecclesiastical historians, that a dispute arose at this time in the Scottish Church, whether the Pater Noster could properly be addressed to the saints. We are told that Richard Marshall, an Englishman, and Prior of the Black Friars at Newcastle, denied that such a practice ought to be allowed, but that its lawfulness was maintained by a Scottish Franciscan, named Cotes, in a sermon preached at St. Andrews, on the feast of All Saints, 1551; that the university was divided in opinion; and that it became necessary to call a provincial council to settle the question. It is added that, when the council convened at Edinburgh, they also differed in opinion, but that a compromise was finally effected, and a definition adopted which was drawn up by the sub-prior Winram. It is possible that some of the ignorant clergy may have entertained such a notion, and that discussions may even have taken place in the University of St. Andrews; but it is utterly incredible that there was any serious dispute on the point, or that it was formally brought before a provincial synod. Much better evidence than the unsupported statement of Foxe would be required in attestation of the fact. Dr. M'Crie states that the council of 1549 employed Winram " to draw up the canon intended to settle the ridiculous dispute, which had been warmly agitated among the clergy, whether the Pater Noster should be said to the saints or to God alone." But the narratives of Foxe and Spottiswood can apply only to the council of 1552, although the canons of that council make no allusion to the subject. The forty-second and forty-ninth canons of the council of 1549 provide for the continuance of the ancient usage of repeating the Pater Noster and the Ave Maria at the commencement or

---

[1] See Keith, vol. i. pp. 5, 6, 149; Hailes, vol. iii. p. 237-240; M'Crie's Life of Knox, p. 416-420; Cook's History of the Reformation in Scotland, vol. i. p. 363-367, vol. iii. appendix, p. iii.-ix. Lord Hailes has exaggerated the obstacles to the knowledge of the catechism caused by the decrees of the council. It was intended to be a manual for the clergy, and to be systematically read by them *to* the people, but to be read *by* the people only under certain precautions.

the conclusion of sermons; and we know that both Marshall, who was a doctor of theology in the University of St. Andrews, and Cotes, were members of that synod. Some dispute as to this practice may have given rise to the story. Knox is silent on the point; but, had such a discussion really taken place, he would hardly have omitted to mention a matter so prejudicial to his opponents, and the details of which possessed such attractions for his peculiar humour.[1]

A provincial synod was held at Linlithgow, probably in the autumn of 1552, at which the decrees of the Council of Trent were accepted, and additional canons were enacted for reforming the manners of the clergy. In the end of the same year, or the beginning of 1553, another council met at Edinburgh, but the canons there enacted have not been preserved.[2]

During the year 1552, Archbishop Hamilton recovered from a lingering disease by which he had been enfeebled, and his cure was ascribed to the skill of the famous Cardan, who had come from Italy at his request. It was probably while the primate was prevented by illness from attending to his duties, that Gavin Hamilton, Abbot of Kilwinning, was appointed coadjutor in the see of St. Andrews—an office which he is known to have held for some time.[3]

[1] Foxe, pp. 628, 629. Calderwood, vol. i. p. 273-277. Spottiswood, vol. i. p. 180-182. M'Crie's Life of Knox, p. 419. Compare Wilkins's Concilia, vol. iv. pp. 57, 58; Hailes, vol. iii. p. 238-240. Dr. Lee, who was ready enough to believe anything to the discredit of the Church of Rome, (if it be fair to judge of him by his Lectures published after his decease,) nevertheless denies, or at least doubts, the truth of this story; see his Lectures on the History of the Church of Scotland, vol. i. p. 76.

[2] Leslie, pp. 476, 477. Hailes, vol. iii. pp. 240, 241. See Wilkins's Concilia, vol. iv. p. 209, where reference is made to councils held at Edinburgh both in 1551 and in 1552. That of 1551 is evidently the synod of January, 1552, as the year is now reckoned.

[3] Lyon's History of St. Andrews, vol. i. p. 320-322. Tytler, vol. vi. p. 379. Calendar of State Papers relating to Scotland, vol. i. p. 177. M'Crie's Life of Knox, p. 442. The ridiculous story of the precise mode of the archbishop's cure rests on the authority of a letter from Randolph to Cecil, written nine years after the event.

CHAPTER XXXI.

FROM THE END OF THE EARL OF ARRAN'S REGENCY IN 1554, TO THE COUNCIL OF EDINBURGH IN 1559.

Regency of Mary of Lorraine—Succession of Bishops—David Panter, Bishop of Ross—Robert Reid, Bishop of Orkney —Return of John Knox—The effects of his preaching— His letter to the regent—His departure from Scotland— His condemnation and appeal—Bond subscribed by the Protestant leaders—Resolutions agreed to by them—Trial and death of Walter Mylne—Provincial councils in 1558 —Toleration conceded to the Protestants—Advice given to the Bishop of Aberdeen by his chapter—Council at Edinburgh in 1559—Articles of Reformation laid before the Council—Remonstrance presented to the Council—Canons enacted—Conclusion of the Council.

MARY of Lorraine was a princess of great ability and of considerable experience in government. Assisted by the power of France, and steadily pursuing, for the most part, the true interest of her adopted country, she succeeded for some years in preserving the tranquillity of the kingdom, and acquiring the favour and respect of the turbulent factions into which it was divided. In April, 1558, the marriage of the Dauphin Francis and the young Queen of the Scots was celebrated with the utmost splendour in the cathedral of Notre Dame at Paris. A treaty had previously been concluded between the two kingdoms, by which the independence of Scotland was to appearance amply secured. These transactions were ratified by a parliament which met at Edinburgh in the month of November. England and Scotland became involved in the war between France and Spain, but the peace of Chateau Cambresis, in May, 1559, was soon followed by a treaty between the two British kingdoms.

John Hepburn, Bishop of Brechin, died in the end of August, or beginning of September, 1558. Donald Campbell, Abbot of Cupar, son of Archibald, Earl of Argyll, was chosen in his place, but the election was not confirmed by the Pope, in consequence, as is said, of the abbot's favourable disposition towards the new opinions; and the see remained vacant for some years.[1]

The decease of Andrew Durie, Bishop of Galloway, took place almost at the same time. His successor was Alexander Gordon, Bishop of the Isles and Archbishop of Athens. The archbishop held the abbacy of Inchaffray in commendam with the bishopric of Candida Casa, but was never confirmed in the see.[2]

Alexander Gordon was succeeded in the diocese of the Isles by John Campbell, who was never either confirmed or consecrated. Like his predecessors, he was commendator of Iona and Ardchattan.[3]

The decease of the Bishops of Brechin and Galloway was soon followed by that of a more eminent prelate, David Panter, Bishop of Ross. Bishop Panter was distinguished both as a scholar and as a statesman. To him, and to Patrick Panter, Abbot of Cambuskenneth, his predecessor in the office of royal secretary, we are indebted for the series of Latin letters, written in the name of the kings and regents of Scotland. Bishop Panter's successor was Henry Sinclair, Dean of Glasgow, and President of the Court of Session.[4]

But the greatest calamity which Scotland sustained at this time was the sudden death of Robert Reid, Bishop of Orkney.

[1] Keith's Catalogue, p. 165. Brunton and Haig's Senators of the College of Justice, p. 69. Leslie, p. 498. Acts of the Parliaments of Scotland, vol. ii. p. 525. In the parliament of August, 1560, Donald is styled Abbot of Cupar, not Bishop-elect of Brechin.

[2] Keith's Catalogue, pp. 278, 279. Brunton and Haig's Senators of the College of Justice, p. 129. Acts of the Parliaments of Scotland, vol. ii. p. 525. Leslie, p. 498. Knox, vol. i. pp. 261, 262. Gordon's History of the Earldom of Sutherland, p. 290.

[3] John, elect of the Isles, and commendator of Iona and Ardchattan, sat in the parliament of 1560 (Acts of the Parliaments of Scotland, vol. ii. p. 525). Keith (Historical Catalogue, p. 307) says that his surname was Campbell, and that he was of the family of Calder; and such was no doubt the case: see Book of the Thanes of Cawdor, p. 186, where reference is made to this bishop by one of his successors of the same name.

[4] Keith's Catalogue, p. 192-194. Brunton and Haig's Senators of the College of Justice, pp. 58, 59. Leslie, p. 498. Knox, vol. i. pp. 262, 263, 274; vol. ii. p. 398. Epistolæ Regum Scotorum, vol. ii. p. v.-vii. Tytler's Life of Craig, p. 83-85.

Hardly any of our prelates deserve higher praise than the eminent churchman who filled the remotest of the Scottish dioceses during the worst days of the falling hierarchy. Robert Reid was the son of a gentleman who fell at the battle of Flodden. He studied at the College of St. Salvator, in the University of St. Andrews, and completed his education at the University of Paris. On his return to Scotland, he was appointed sub-dean, and afterwards official, of Murray; in 1526, he was promoted to the abbacy of Kinloss; and, in 1530, he received the priory of Beaulieu in commendam. He was nominated a senator of the College of Justice by King James, and, in the end of 1549, or the beginning of 1550, succeeded Alexander Mylne, as president of that court. He was employed on frequent embassies to England, France, and Italy, and was distinguished for his diplomatic ability. Himself an accomplished scholar, he loved to encourage learning wherever he found it. Soon after his appointment to Kinloss, he prevailed on Ferrerius of Piedmont to accompany him to Scotland, where that writer composed the Lives of the Abbots of his patron's monastery.

As formerly mentioned, Reid succeeded Bishop Maxwell in the see of Orkney, in 1541. Notwithstanding his numerous avocations, he ever kept in mind that his diocese was entitled to his chief care, and he devoted himself with unwearied energy to its improvement. He enlarged the church of St. Magnus, and founded a school at Kirkwall for the instruction of the youth of the Islands. He made a new erection of the cathedral chapter, appointing seven dignitaries, the first of whom was styled, not Dean as in other secular chapters, but Provost, the rest being an Archdeacon, a Precentor, a Chancellor, a Treasurer, a Sub-dean, and a Sub-chanter. The foundation included seven other prebendaries, thirteen chaplains, a sacristan, and six choristers. The charter of erection was granted on the twenty-eighth of October, 1544, and was confirmed by Cardinal Beaton, on the thirtieth of June, 1545. The Bishop of Orkney was one of the commissioners present at the marriage of Mary with the Dauphin, and, while preparing to return home, died at Dieppe, on the sixth of September. As three others of the commissioners died at the same time, suspicions were entertained that they had been poisoned by the princes of the house of Lorraine, whose ambitious designs they had opposed; but, beyond their sudden decease, there is no evidence to justify such a charge. By his last will the bishop bequeathed eight thousand merks Scots for building a college at Edinburgh for the education of youth. The money was for some time appropriated by the regent Morton, but was afterwards recovered, and applied in terms of the donor's bequest.[1]

Bishop Reid was succeeded in the see of Orkney by Adam Bothwell, who was put in possession of the temporalities on the eleventh of October, 1559.[2]

James Hamilton, an illegitimate brother of the Duke of Chatel-herault, was appointed to the see of Argyll about the year 1556.[3]

It was the policy of the queen dowager to tolerate the Protestants so long as they conducted themselves quietly towards the State, and for some years we hear of no attempt to inflict capital punishment on account of heresy. Even the preachers who fled from England, to escape the persecutions of Mary's reign, found refuge in the northern kingdom. Among them were two natives of Scotland, William Harlaw and John Willock. The former had been originally a tailor in Edinburgh, and had been ordained a deacon in the English Church during the reign of Edward VI. The latter had been a Dominican or Franciscan friar at Ayr; had been chaplain to the Duke of Suffolk in England; and, after leaving that kingdom,

[1] Keith's Catalogue, p. 223-226. Brunton and Haig's Senators of the College of Justice, p. 14-19. Leslie, p. 497. Knox, vol. i. pp. 264, 265. Gordon's History of the Earldom of Sutherland, p. 137. Mackenzie's Lives of Scottish Writers, vol. iii. p. 46-51. Pinkerton, vol. ii. pp. 422, 423. Tytler's Life of Craig, p. 51-62. The charter of erection of the chapter of Orkney, and Cardinal Beaton's confirmation, are inserted in the appendix to Peterkin's Rentals of Orkney, p. 18-30. Knox relates the death of the Bishops of Galloway, Ross, and Orkney, in language which would be unbecoming, even if the circumstances mentioned were true. According to his narrative, the first was a card-player, the second a glutton and a drunkard, the third a miser; and each of them at the hour of his death was thinking only of his favourite vice: see History of the Reformation, vol. i. p. 261-265. The utter falsehood of the charge against Bishop Reid may well make us suspect the correctness of what he tells us of the other two.

[2] Register of the Privy Seal, quoted by Mr. Mark Napier, in a note to the Spottiswood Society edition of Spottiswood's History, vol. ii. p. 72.

[3] Keith's Catalogue, pp. 289, 290. Origines Parochiales Scotiæ, vol. ii. part i. p. 24.

had practised medicine in Friesland, whence he was sent on a political mission to the queen dowager. During the year 1555, the Protestants were encouraged by the exhortations of these preachers, though they did not yet venture to assemble in public. In the autumn of that year a far more formidable adversary of the Church returned to his native land.[1]

John Knox, after a captivity of nineteen months in the French galleys, had been released along with other prisoners taken at St. Andrews, through the intercession of Edward VI. of England. He was restored to freedom in February, 1549, and lost no time in repairing to the court of his benefactor. The statesmen and divines who had the chief direction of ecclesiastical matters in England gave a commission to Knox to act as one of the preachers employed at that time to disseminate the Protestant opinions. By their order he went to Berwick-on-Tweed, where he continued for two years, preaching zealously against the Roman doctrines. In April, 1550, he appeared before an English court—probably the council of the North—to which he had been summoned at the instance of Cuthbert Tunstall, Bishop of Durham, on account of the language he had used regarding the Eucharist. He vigorously defended his tenets, and, if we are to trust Bale, Tunstall was unable to answer him. In 1551, he was removed to Newcastle, and in December of that year was appointed by the Privy Council one of King Edward's chaplains in ordinary. Knox was much esteemed by the young king. He was offered the bishopric of Rochester, but declined to accept it, because he held the episcopal office to be destitute of divine authority. He was consulted in regard to the revision of the Articles of Religion, and it appears to have been at his suggestion that in October, 1552, the Declaration on the subject of kneeling at the Communion was inserted in the second Prayer Book of King Edward. He was at London when Edward died. When Mary was proclaimed queen, he retired to the north, but during the summer of 1553 again itinerated as a preacher in the centre and south of England.

The laws against heresy having been re-enacted, Knox's residence in England became very unsafe, and in January, 1554,

[1] Knox, vol. i. p. 245. Keith, vol. i. p. 150. M'Crie's Life of Knox, pp. 104, 105. Miscellany of the Wodrow Society, vol. i. p. 261-263.

he embarked for Dieppe. During that year he visited various places in France and Switzerland, and remained for some time at Geneva, where he contracted an intimate personal acquaintance with Calvin. While he abode in that city, he received an invitation to become one of the ministers of the English congregation at Frankfort-on-the-Maine, and after some hesitation accepted the call. The disputes which arose at Frankfort regarding the use of the Book of Common Prayer belong to the ecclesiastical history of England rather than that of Scotland, and need not be more particularly alluded to here. One chief cause of the strong feeling which prevailed against Knox arose from the publication of his Faithful Admonition to the Professors of God's Truth in England. In this work he used language of the most violent description respecting Queen Mary, and her chief counsellors. The treatise was condemned in strong terms by some of the exiles themselves, and was undoubtedly one of the most conspicuous in that class of works, published on the Continent by the British Protestants, which provoked, though they could not justify, the cruel persecution in England. In March, 1555, Knox left Frankfort, and, returning to Geneva, ministered to the English congregation there. Encouraged by the intelligence which he received regarding the favourable position of the Protestants in Scotland, he left Geneva in August, and, embarking at Dieppe, landed near Berwick in the month of September. After a short stay in the north of England, he repaired to Edinburgh. It has been supposed that about this time he solemnised a marriage which he had previously contracted with Marjory Bowes, daughter of Richard Bowes, an English gentleman of good family.[1]

The zeal and ability of Knox were well known, and many of those who were attached to the Protestant opinions began to resort to his lodgings, in order to obtain the benefit of his teaching. Among the most distinguished of these were John Erskine of Dun and William Maitland of Lethington. For some time after his arrival in Edinburgh, several of the Protestants continued to attend mass, and to join in the public

[1] Knox, vol. i. pp. 231, 232; vol. iii. pp. 79, 80, 253, 256, 334. M'Crie's Life of Knox, pp. 47-98, 105, 106, 406, 407. Tytler's England under the reigns of Edward VI. and Mary, vol. i. p. 295; vol. ii, p. 140-142. Hardwick's History of the Reformation, p. 148.

worship of the Church. Knox vehemently opposed this course of proceeding, and a conference was held in Erskine's house for the discussion of the question. The lawfulness of the practice was defended by Maitland; the contrary opinion was maintained by Knox and Willock. The advice of St. James and the elders of Jerusalem to St. Paul was referred to by the former. Knox answered that the two questions were very different, the paying of vows being sometimes commanded, and never being idolatrous as the mass was; and also, that he greatly doubted whether the command of James and the obedience of Paul proceeded from the Holy Ghost, but was not rather worldly-wise counsel, justly punished by the evils which followed it. The arguments of Knox prevailed, and Maitland admitted that he was in the wrong.

Soon after this conference, Knox, at the request of Erskine, accompanied that baron to his house of Dun in Angus, where the chief persons of the neighbourhood came to hear him. When he returned to the south, he abode for the most part at Calder, in West Lothian, the residence of Sir James Sandilands; and among his hearers there were some nobles of high rank, the Lord James, Prior of St. Andrews, Lord Erskine, and Lord Lorn, eldest son of the Earl of Argyll. During the early part of the winter he was generally at Edinburgh, and after Christmas went to various places in Ayrshire, where he preached, and occasionally administered the communion. Some time before Easter, 1556, he administered the communion at the Earl of Glencairn's residence on the Clyde, and afterwards at the house of Dun, on which occasion most of the barons of the Mearns adopted the Protestant opinions.

The bishops were now alarmed by the effects of Knox's preaching, and summoned him to appear in the church of the Black Friars at Edinburgh, on the fifteenth of May. Either on account of some informality in the proceedings, or from a fear of resorting to extreme measures, the citation was abandoned, and, on the day on which he should have appeared as a criminal, Knox preached at Edinburgh with more publicity than ever. Lord Glencairn brought the Earl Marischal to hear him, and, at the request of these noblemen, Knox wrote a letter to the queen regent, in defence of his conduct, and of the Protestant doctrines. This letter was delivered into the queen's own hand by the Earl of Glencairn; and a day or two afterwards she gave it to the Archbishop of Glasgow, saying, "Please you, my lord, to read a pasquil." These words were reported to Knox, and were the cause, as he himself tells us, of the additions which he made to the letter, when two years subsequently it was reprinted at Geneva. The careless remark of Mary of Lorraine annoyed Knox more than might be expected in a person of his character. He mentions the circumstance in his History; and, in the second edition of the letter, his allusions, in connection with it, to the prophet Jeremiah and King Jehoiakim, to Elias and Jezabel, would be ludicrous, if they were not arrogant and profane.[1]

The letter itself is a remarkable production. As originally written, though stern, it can scarcely be called disrespectful in tone. Attention has frequently been drawn to the fact that, in the preamble to the second edition, Knox appeals from the unjust sentence of the bishops to a lawful general council. There is no reason, however, to suppose that the reformer would have submitted to the adverse decision of any synod whatever. Deference to ecclesiastical authority was repugnant to his whole principles and practice, and it is idle to draw conclusions as to his serious opinions from expressions which were mere words of form or of policy.[2]

Soon after these transactions, Knox received a call from the English congregation at Geneva to resume the pastoral office among them. He complied with their request, and left Scotland in July. The reasons which induced him to go away, at a time when his presence seemed so important to the cause of reformation, have given rise to much discussion. It is generally supposed that his life was in danger, and that his retirement for a season was necessary in order to his safety. Had such been the case, there are few who would be entitled to censure him severely. But he does not himself allude to any immediate danger prior to his leaving Scotland, although, if it had existed, he would probably have referred to it, as he did in the case of his retreat to the castle of St. Andrews; nor

[1] Knox, vol. i. p. 245-252. M'Crie's Life of Knox, p. 106-114.
[2] The Letter to the Lady Mary, Regent of Scotland, with the additions, is printed in the appendix to M'Gavin's edition of the History of the Reformation, and in the fourth volume of Knox's Works.

is it likely that those who were ready to defend him in May would have been unable to do so in July. The supposition of immediate danger is indeed inconsistent with the deliberate steps which he took before his departure, going round and bidding farewell to the several congregations among which he had preached, sending off his mother-in-law and his wife before him, spending some time with the Earl of Argyll at Castle Campbell, and, in answer to the entreaties that he would remain in Scotland, declaring that he must once again visit Geneva, but, if his friends continued in godliness, whensoever they were pleased to command him, that they should find him obedient. Timidity was not among his faults, and mere apprehension of danger would never have made him leave. His departure was probably owing to some cause, sufficient in his own opinion, but which he was not willing to make public, and which we have now no means of ascertaining.[1]

Immediately after his leaving Scotland, Knox was again summoned by the bishops, and, when he did not appear, sentence was pronounced against him, and his effigy was burned at the cross of Edinburgh. On receiving intelligence of these proceedings, he drew up a document in defence of his conduct, which was printed in 1558, under the title of " The Appellation of John Knox from the cruel and most unjust Sentence pronounced against him by the false Bishops and Clergy of Scotland, with his Supplication and Exhortation to the Nobility, Estates, and Community of the same Realm:" In it he maintained two propositions, first, that his appeal was lawful and just, secondly, that the estates of the kingdom were entitled and bound to hear it. He asserted that he had just cause to appeal from the sentence pronounced against him, because he was not within the jurisdiction of the Scottish prelates when summoned by them, because no intimation of the summons was made to him, because on account of their tyranny he had no free access to Scotland at that time, and because they could not be competent judges, inasmuch as prior to the citation he had accused them of various crimes which he was ready to substantiate. He further contended that it was lawful to God's prophets and the preachers of Christ to appeal from the judgment of the

[1] Knox, vol. i. p. 252-254. M'Crie's Life of Knox, p. 115-117.

visible Church to the temporal magistrate, and that the magistrate was bound to hear their cause, and to defend them from tyranny. Knox did not merely seek to prove that the civil power was bound to protect him against an unjust ecclesiastical sentence, so far as it affected his life or property; he maintained that the temporal rulers were bound to see that those subject to them were instructed in the true religion, and that they were called upon to remove from honour, and punish with death, if the crime so required, those who deceived the people, or defrauded them of the food of their souls, God's living word. If the sovereign should withold his consent, the estates of the realm were bound to discharge those duties, and, in so far as idolatry, blasphemy, and such like crimes were concerned, not only kings and rulers, but the whole body of the people, and every member of the same, according to his vocation and opportunity, were bound to punish them when manifestly known.[1]

The condemnation of Knox did not stop the progress of the Protestant doctrines. John Willock had returned to the Continent, but William Harlaw, and John Douglas, formerly a Carmelite friar, and now residing with the Earl of Argyll, preached in Edinburgh and the neighbourhood. Paul Methven, who at one time had been a baker, taught at Dundee; and other individuals propagated the same opinions in various parts of Angus and Mearns. Several of these preachers were summoned before the regent at the instance of the bishops. They prepared to obey the citation, but the queen, dreading a tumult, commanded all persons who were at Edinburgh without authority to repair to the seat of war on the Border. The proclamation was disregarded. A number of the Protestants, headed by Chalmers of Gadgirth, forced their way into the regent's presence, and in the most outrageous manner threatened violence to the bishops. Mary, with some difficulty, persuaded them to depart. At this time Chatel-herault, Huntly, and other great nobles, refused to assist the regent in carrying the war into England, and, obliged to rely on the political

---

[1] Knox, vol. i. p. 254. M'Crie's Life of Knox, pp. 116, 117. The Appellation is printed in M'Gavin's appendix, and in the fourth volume of Knox's Works.

support of the Protestants, she was under the necessity of conniving at the insult which she had received.

On the tenth of March, 1557, a letter was addressed to Knox by the Earl of Glencairn, the Lords Erskine and Lorn, and the Prior of St. Andrews, mentioning that the cause of the Reformation continued to prosper, that the friars were falling into disrepute, and that no farther acts of cruelty had been committed, and earnestly requesting his return to Scotland. Knox, after consulting with Calvin and other ministers, intimated his intention of complying with their request, and accordingly set out for Dieppe, but, on arriving there on the twenty-fourth of October, received letters of a contrary tenor, and in consequence returned to Geneva. He wrote, however, to his friends in Scotland, rebuking them in sharp language for their want of zeal and courage; and his admonition had such an effect that the Protestant leaders determined to come forward more boldly in defence of their opinions. In order to secure the aid and co-operation of all who were favourable to the cause, a bond was drawn up and signed at Edinburgh, on the third of December, by the Earls of Argyll, Glencairn, and Morton, the Lord Lorn, Erskine of Dun, and other chief men of the party. This bond was no doubt suggested by the documents so common in the fifteenth and sixteenth centuries, by which the Scottish barons entered into leagues of mutual defence and support, and it became the model of the more formidable covenants of after years. The subscribers bound themselves to maintain and set forward, with all their might, the most blessed word of God, and his Congregation, declaring that they joined themselves thereto, and renounced the Congregation of Satan, with all the superstitious abominations and idolatry thereof. Its words seem to bear reference to the baptismal vow, but they were now used as the symbol of hatred and strife. If the Protestants were the Congregation of Christ, and the adherents of Rome were the Congregation of the Devil, all hope of unity or peace was at an end.[1]

[1] Knox, vol. i. pp. 256, 258, 267-274. Leslie, p. 496. M'Crie's Life of Knox, pp. 121-124, 139, 140. Keith is of opinion (vol. i. p. 153) that the name of "Erskine," attached to the letter of tenth March, is the signature not of Lord Erskine, but of Erskine of Dun, because the former had not yet joined the Protestants. Lord Erskine, however, was among Knox's hearers at the house

The first step of the associated lords and barons, after frequently meeting in council, was the adoption of the following resolutions:—" First, it is thought expedient, devised, and ordained, that in all parishes of this realm the Common Prayers be read weekly on Sunday, and other festival days, publicly in the parish kirks, with the lessons of the New and Old Testament, conform to the order of the Book of Common Prayers; and, if the curates of the parishes be qualified, to cause them to read the same, and, if they be not, or if they refuse, that the most qualified in the parish use and read the same. Secondly, it is thought necessary that doctrine, preaching, and interpretation of Scriptures, be had and used privately in quiet houses, without great conventions of the people thereto, till afterward that God move the prince to grant public preaching by faithful and true ministers." It was long disputed whether the Common Prayer here referred to was the English Book of Common Prayer, or the Service Book of Knox's congregation at Geneva. The most learned writers of the present day are now agreed that the former was meant. But it would be a mistake to suppose that the second Book of King Edward VI. was adopted as a whole; the resolutions bear reference only to the order for Morning and Evening Prayer, so far as applicable to Sundays and Holydays, and say nothing whatever of the other portions of the English formulary.[1]

In furtherance of these proceedings, the Earl of Argyll requested John Douglas to preach in his house, and, his example having been followed by others, the Archbishop of St. Andrews, on the twenty-fifth of March, 1558, wrote to the earl, entreating him to put away the heretical teacher whom he entertained, and promising to send in his place a wise instructor, who would teach nothing contrary to the Catholic faith. The primate farther mentioned that he was himself much blamed for his remissness in allowing such practices to continue unchecked, and that he was bound, both

---

of Calder, and, in connection with the meetings there, is mentioned by Knox, along with the other three noblemen who signed the letter. See History of the Reformation, vol. i. p. 249.

[1] Knox, vol. i. pp. 275, 276. Sage's Works, Spottiswood Society ed. vol. i p. 164-168. Keith, vol. i. pp. 154, 155. M'Crie's Life of Knox, pp. 141, 425-427.

in honour and conscience, to put a stop to them. The earl answered the various points contained in the archbishop's letter in a document of some length, in the composition of which we may conjecture that he had at least the assistance of Douglas. It contained a denial of the charge of false teaching; rejected all submission to the authority of general councils, appealing to that of Scripture alone; and, under the form of a defence of the preacher's doctrine, made a vehement attack on the archbishop's practice. "He preaches against idolatry: I remit to your lordship's conscience if it be heresy or not. He preaches against adultery and fornication: I refer that to your lordship's conscience. He preaches against hypocrisy: I refer that to your lordship's conscience. He preaches against all manner of abuses and corruptions of Christ's sincere religion: I refer that to your lordship's conscience. My lord, I exhort you, in Christ's name, to weigh all these affairs in your conscience, and consider if it be your duty also, not only to endure this, but in like manner to do the same." No notice appears to have been taken of this answer, and the Earl of Argyll died soon afterwards.[1]

The queen-regent had hitherto discouraged all violent measures, and there is reason to believe that the primate also was sincere in his aversion to persecution. Whatever may have led to a change in those respects, within a month after the date of the archbishop's letter to the Earl of Argyll, an act was committed, which proved as disastrous in its results, as it was in itself wicked and cruel. Among those who had adopted the Protestant doctrines was a priest named Walter Mylne, who had been vicar of Lunan. Having been apprehended at Dysart, he was imprisoned in the castle of St. Andrews, and on the twentieth of April was brought before the ecclesiastical court. There were present, in the metropolitan church, the Primate, the Archbishop of Athens, the Bishops of Murray, Brechin, and Caithness, the Abbots of Dunfermline, Lindores, Balmerino, and Cupar, John Winram, Sub-prior of St. Andrews, John Greyson, Provincial of the Black Friars, William Cranstone, Provost of St. Salvator's, and others of the clergy. Mylne was accused of erroneous doctrines regarding the marriage of priests,

[1] Knox, vol. i. p. 276-290.

the seven sacraments, particularly the sacrament of the altar, the office of a bishop, pilgrimages, and other points. He was an old, decrepit man, but, when he rose to speak, the church rang with the clear sound of his voice. He avowed the opinions attributed to him, retorting the charge of false doctrine, with some asperity, on his accusers. When he was asked to make a recantation, he answered, "I am accused of my life: I know I must die once, and therefore, as Christ said to Judas, Quod facis, fac citius. Ye shall know that I will not recant the truth, for I am corn, I am no chaff; I will not be blown away with the wind, nor burst with the flail, but I will abide both." Sentence was pronounced that he should be delivered over for punishment to the temporal judge. The people's hearts were so moved by the defence which he had made that the proper officers refused to execute the sentence, and he was carried to the stake by some of the primate's retainers. As he was raised up on the pile, he said, " Introibo ad altare Domini;" and, being allowed to address the multitude, he thus spoke, " Dear friends, the cause why I suffer this day is not for any crime laid to my charge (albeit I be a miserable sinner before God), but only for the defence of the faith of Jesus Christ, set forth in the New and Old Testament unto us, for which, as the faithful martyrs have offered themselves gladly before, being assured, after the death of their bodies, of eternal felicity, so this day I praise God that He hath called me of his mercy among the rest of his servants to seal up his truth with my life which, as I have received it of Him so willingly I offer it to his glory. Therefore, as you will escape the eternal death, be no more seduced with the lies of priests, monks, friars, priors, abbots, bishops, and the rest of the sect of Antichrist, but depend only upon Jesus Christ, and his mercy, that ye may be delivered from condemnation." Walter Mylne was burned on the twenty-eighth day of April, 1558. He was the last person who suffered death in Scotland for the Protestant opinions.[1]

In the summer of 1558, a provincial synod met at Edinburgh. On this occasion a number of persons convicted of heresy were allowed to escape from farther punishment, on condition of

---

[1] Foxe, pp. 629, 630. Knox, vol. i. pp. 307, 308, and appendix, p. 550-555. Buchanan, vol. i. p. 310. Pitscottie, p. 517-523.

making a public recantation on the first of September following, being the festival of St. Giles, the patron of the city. It was part of the usual ceremonial of that day to have a solemn procession through the streets, at which a wooden image of St. Giles was carried. In the course of the previous year this statue had been stolen by the Protestants, but another was obtained for the festival of 1558. The queen-regent was present during the early part of the day, but, when she retired, a tumult was raised by the supporters of the Protestant party, the image was cast down and destroyed, and the convicted persons were rescued.[1]

Another provincial synod met in the church of the Black Friars at Edinburgh, on the eighth of November. Paul Methven was summoned before it, and, as he did not appear, a sentence of banishment was pronounced against him.[2]

In the meantime the Protestants continued to increase in number and zeal. Aware of their own strength, they began to contemplate the more public profession of their belief. In this they were much encouraged by Willock, who again came over from Friesland in the month of October. They were now known by the name of the Congregation, and it was agreed among them that they should express their wishes in a petition to the queen-regent. In this document, referring to the permission formerly given by parliament to read the Scriptures, they requested leave to assemble, publicly or privately, at the Common Prayers in the vulgar tongue, and that the sacraments of Baptism, and the Lord's Supper under both kinds, might be ministered to them in the same language. They farther desired that the hard places of Scripture might be interpreted in their assemblies, and that the wicked lives of the prelates and of the ecclesiastical estate should be reformed. This petition was presented to the queen by an ancient knight, one of the most esteemed of the Congregation, Sir James Sandilands of Calder. The clergy were willing to allow the Prayers to be offered, and Baptism to be administered, in the vulgar tongue, provided the same were done privately, and also on condition that the doctrines of the Church respecting

---

[1] Knox, vol. i. pp. 256, 258-261, and appendix, p. 558-561. Buchanan, vol. i. p. 310. Leslie, pp. 496, 497. Hailes, vol. iii. p. 241.

[2] Buchanan, vol. i. p. 311. Hailes, vol. iii p. 241.

the Mass, Purgatory, Prayers for the Dead, and Invocation of the Saints, were received. The Protestants indignantly rejected this compromise; but, nevertheless, the queen-regent, anxious, as has been supposed, to prevent opposition to the parliamentary ratification of her daughter's marriage, promised to tolerate them in the ministry of the Prayers and Sacraments, provided they abstained from holding public assemblies in Edinburgh and Leith. The Congregation were so much satisfied with this arrangement that they silenced Douglas, who wished to preach openly at Leith. For their farther protection they presented a letter to the regent, desiring that it might be laid before the parliament which was to meet in November. In this letter they requested that all laws against heresy might be suspended till the whole questions at issue should be decided by a general council, and that certain other privileges might be given to the Protestants. As the queen did not think it advisable to lay this request before parliament, a protestation was drawn up and tendered to the estates, but it was not inserted in their books.[1]

It was now evident to all that a struggle was approaching between the two parties which divided Scotland. The clergy were well aware that the strongest arguments against the Church were drawn from their own evil lives. An important document has been preserved, which shews what was going on in the diocese of Aberdeen; and there can hardly be a doubt that a similar state of matters existed in other parts of the Church. The Bishop of Aberdeen having requested the advice of his chapter in regard to reformation, and the suppression of heresy, the dean and canons, on the fifth of January, 1559, gave him counsel accordingly. They desired their ordinary to cause the churchmen of his diocese reform their scandalous manner of living, and put away their concubines, under the penalties enacted by the provincial synods; and the members of the chapter were themselves exhorted to do the like. It was requested that provision should be made for at least one sermon to be preached in every parish church, between the date of the meeting and Fasten's-even, and again between Fasten's-even and Easter; that all who were absent

---

[1] Knox, vol. i. p. 298-314. Buchanan, vol. i. p. 311. M'Crie's Life of Knox, pp. 144, 145, 427, 428.

from their own parish churches, especially from the sacrifice of the mass, should be cited before the ecclesiastical judges, and that those who took part in the burning of the church of Echt, or in the casting down of images in any churches within the diocese, should be admonished to reveal the same to the bishop or his commissaries. In order that the advice given should have better effect, the bishop himself was entreated to shew a good example, especially by removing from his company the gentlewoman through whom he caused great scandal, and by shunning the company of those suspected of heresy. To this counsel are attached the signatures of the dean and treasurer of the cathedral, of the sub-chanter, of Alexander Anderson, sub-principal of King's College, and of John Leslie, parson of Mortlach, afterwards Bishop of Ross.[1]

On the first of March, 1559, the clergy met in provincial council at Edinburgh, and continued their sittings till the tenth of April. The synod was convened with great formality. The Primate, on the thirty-first of January, addressed a letter to the Archbishop of Glasgow, by which he summoned a Provincial-General Council to meet in the monastery of the Black Friars at Edinburgh, on the first of March next ensuing, with continuation of days, and required the archbishop to appear in person, at eight o'clock of the morning, on the day and at the place appointed. He also required the archbishop to summon to the same effect his suffragan bishops, and the abbots, priors, commendators, deans, and provosts, and as many of the most discreet and learned of the canons, clergy, and regulars, of his diocese and province, as he might think fit. A like general citation was no doubt given by the primate to the bishops and clergy of his own province. Each bishop or vicar-general of a diocese addressed special mandates to the several rural deans, enjoining them to summon the clergy within their respective jurisdictions.

When the council met, certain articles of reformation, which had been presented by the Protestants to the regent, were, at her request, laid before the clergy by the Earl of Huntly,

[1] See this document, as transcribed from a copy of the original made by Thomas Innes, in Keith, vol. i. p. cxx.-cxxiii., and in the preface to the Chartulary of Aberdeen, p. lxi.-lxv.; and, as copied directly from the original, in Cook's History of the Reformation, vol. iii. p. x.-xiii., and in the Miscellany of the Spalding Club, vol. iv. p. 57-59.

chancellor of Scotland. The chief of these were the following :—That the prayers should be said and the sacraments administered in the vulgar tongue; that the bishops should be chosen with the consent of the nobility and barons of the diocese, and the parish priests with the consent of the parishioners; that those who were unfit for the pastoral office should be removed, and others appointed in their place, who could preach regularly to the people; that in time to come all persons of indifferent morals, or insufficient learning, should be excluded from the ministration of the sacraments and other functions of the Church.

There was considerable discussion in the synod as to these points, but the following answer was finally returned :—That to celebrate the prayers and sacraments in any other than the Latin tongue was plainly repugnant to the tradition of the Church for many ages, and could not be allowed; that the rules of the canon-law must be observed in regard to the election of bishops and parish priests, and besides, that as the election of prelates belonged to the crown, with consent of the Pope, nothing affecting that privilege could lawfully be done during the queen's minority; and in regard to the other two articles, that the ancient canons and the regulations of the Council of Trent should be adhered to, and that all bishops, abbots, priors, deans, archdeacons, parish priests, and the regulars of every order, should within six months either perform their duties in person, or lose their benefices.

Besides these articles from the Protestants, a remonstrance was presented to the synod urging earnestly the duty of reformation in various important particulars. This document, which is in the English language, has been preserved among the acts of the council, but we are not told from whom it came. It undoubtedly expressed the wishes of the large party among the laity who were well affected to the Church, but who were anxious for the correction of abuses. It is divided into thirteen heads, embracing the following points :—1st. Referring to the intentions of the late king, and the efforts of various provincial synods to reform the lives of the prelates and clergy, which hitherto had produced no good effect, the remonstrants earnestly urged this duty on the members of the council. 2nd. They requested that sermons should be

preached in every parish church on all Sundays and holy-days
—at the least on Christmas-day, Easter-day, Whitsunday,
and every third or fourth Sunday. 3rd. That before any one
were admitted to preach in public, he should be examined as
to his life and doctrine. 4th. That in time to come no one
should be admitted as curate or vicar of a parish, unless
sufficiently qualified to minister the sacraments of the Church,
and to read the catechism. 5th. That before the sacraments
of the Eucharist, Baptism, and Marriage, were celebrated in
church, an explanation of the nature of these sacraments
should be made to the people in the English tongue. 6th.
That the Common Prayers and Litanies in the vulgar tongue
should be said in parish churches on all Sundays and other
holy-days, after the celebration of Mass; and that the Evening
Prayers should also be said in the afternoon. 7th. That inasmuch as corpse presents, Easter offerings, and the like,
which were originally given freely by the faithful, were now
demanded as of right by the clergy under the pain of excommunication, the same in time to come should be abolished, or
at all events brought back to their former voluntary use.
8th, 9th, 10th. That the forms of process in the consistorial
courts should be shortened, and a remedy provided for the
abuse of allowing appeals to Rome in every case, however
small; that relief against appeals to Rome should be given to
the feuars of church lands; and that the acts of parliament in
the reign of James IV., regarding the privileges granted by
the Roman see to the Church and kingdom of Scotland,
should be put in execution. 11th. That no person should be
allowed to speak irreverently of the sacrament of the Body
and Blood of Christ, and that no dishonour should be done to
the divine service of the Mass. 12th. That the sacraments
of Marriage, Baptism, and the Eucharist, should be celebrated
as before set down, and by such persons as were duly admitted and ordained to the administration of the same. 13th.
That no persons should be allowed to burn, spoil, or destroy
churches, chapels, religious places, or their ornaments; and
that no innovations should be made in the rites and ceremonies of the Church, but that they should continue as before,
until farther order were taken by the sovereign and the ministers of the Church.

This remonstrance is a very important document. It shews that the reforming party within the Church had objects in view similar to those which prevailed among persons of the like opinions in other parts of Christendom, especially in England. Had the members of the council been heartily desirous of carrying out its recommendations, the Scottish Church might even yet have been preserved. They did partially adopt them, but such half measures were insufficient to avert the storm which was gathering round.

Thirty-four canons were enacted by the synod. Some of the more important points embraced in them may be mentioned. The former regulations against ecclesiastics keeping concubines were renewed. In order to shew an example of obedience to the canons, the two archbishops agreed to submit themselves to the counsel and admonition of six members of the synod—the Bishop of Dunkeld, the Bishops-postulate of Galloway and Ross, the Dean of Restalrig, the Provincial of the Black Friars, and the Sub-prior of St. Andrews. The provisions in regard to frequent preaching, and episcopal and archidiaconal visitations, were also re-enacted, and made more stringent. The preachers were especially enjoined to exercise themselves and instruct the people in regard to the Traditions of the Church, the Invocation of Saints, the right use of Images, the existence of Purgatory, the true presence of our Lord in the Eucharist, the lawfulness of lay communion under one kind, the profit of the Sacrifice of the Mass both to the living and the dead, and the necessity of Holy Orders to give the power of consecrating the Eucharist. Certain exhortations respecting the right use of the sacraments were appended to the acts of the council, and were enjoined to be read by the parish priests to the people before the celebration of the Eucharist, and by the bishops and confessors in ministering Confirmation, Orders, and Penance. These exhortations have not been preserved. Rules were made to guard against the admission of unfit persons to ecclesiastical benefices. Several reforms were ordered in the proceedings of the consistorial courts, and in regard to tithes, mortuaries, and Easter offerings. The thirty-third canon refers to some changes introduced into the administration of baptism by the Protestant preachers. The nature of these changes is not explained, but, to ensure the validity of the sacrament, it was enacted that infants so baptized should receive conditional baptism from the parish priest or other lawful minister. The thirty-fourth canon prohibited all persons from ministering or receiving the sacraments of the Eucharist and Matrimony, except according to the established ritual of the Church, and that under the pain of excommunication.

It was agreed that the next synod should meet at the same place, on Septuagesima Sunday, in the following year, that it might then be ascertained whether the canons had been duly executed, and in order to advise as to any farther points which might occur.[1]

The provincial council of the Scottish Church never met again.

[1] Wilkins's Concilia, vol. iv. p. 204-217. Leslie, pp. 504, 505. Buchanan, vol. i. pp. 311, 312. Hailes, vol. iii. p. 242-244. M'Crie's Life of Knox, p. 153-155. Lord Hailes is mistaken in supposing that the canons alluded to by Knox are those of 1549: they are evidently the canons of 1559; see Annals, vol. iii. p. 234-236, and History of the Reformation, vol. i. pp. 291, 292. The error was owing to the great similarity of several of the canons enacted at the councils of those years. Hailes remarks that Knox's account of the canons "is exceedingly partial and erroneous."

CHAPTER XXXII.

FROM THE COUNCIL OF EDINBURGH IN 1559, TO THE PARLIAMENT OF AUGUST, 1560.

Quintin Kennedy, Abbot of Crossraguel—Publication of his Compendious Tractive—Summary of its argument—Reply by John Davidson, Principal of the College of Glasgow—Correspondence between Quintin Kennedy and John Willock—The Regent's Proclamation against the Protestants—Arrival of Knox in Scotland—His sermon at Perth—Destruction of the monasteries there—Spoliation of the Cathedral of St. Andrews—Destruction of the Abbey of Scone—Civil War—Queen Elizabeth assists the Protestants—Destruction of the monasteries at Aberdeen—Death of Mary of Lorraine—Treaty of Edinburgh—Protestant ministers appointed to the chief towns—John Row, minister at Perth—Alleged imposture at the Nunnery of St. Catharine of Sienna—Improbability of the story—Appointment of Superintendents—Parliament at Edinburgh—Confession of Faith presented by the Protestants—Feeble opposition to it—Its ratification—The authority of the Pope taken away—The Mass proscribed—Conclusion of the Parliament.

WHILE the provincial council continued its sittings at Edinburgh, one of the most learned of the Scottish ecclesiastics, Quintin Kennedy, Abbot of Crossraguel, was endeavouring by his personal exertions to arrest the progress of the Reformed opinions in the West. Kennedy was a younger son of Gilbert, Earl of Cassillis, and was educated at St. Andrews and Paris. His first benefice was the vicarage of Girvan, in the deanery of Carrick. He was afterwards appointed Abbot of Crossraguel, and was present, in that capacity, at the council of Edinburgh, in November, 1549. In 1558, he published "A compendious Tractive, conform to the Scriptures of Almighty God, reason, and authority, declaring the nearest and only way to establish the conscience of a Christian man in all matters which are in debate concerning faith and religion." This work was written at the request of his nephew, Gilbert, Master of Cassillis, to whom it was dedicated.

The author of the Tractive begins by stating that all errors and disputes on the points referred to have chiefly proceeded from a wrong understanding of the Law and Scripture of Almighty God. In order, he says, to the due understanding of God's word, it is necessary to know what judge is to determine between the right and the wrong interpretation. The Holy Scripture is the faithful witness to the truth, according to the words of St. John's Gospel, " Search the Scriptures —They are they which testify of me ;" but for that very cause it cannot also be the judge. The Bible, experience, reason, and authority, point to the Church of God as the only judge, whose duty it is to pronounce sentence according to the Scripture, the true and faithful witness of the will and mind of the Lord. It is therefore necessary to know what is the Church. The word Church has various senses in Scripture. Sometimes it means the whole congregation of Christians, young and old, rich and poor, learned and ignorant, good and bad, all who are not heretics or excommunicated, united together in one faith by baptism, forming one mystical body of which Christ is the head. But the Church in this sense can never be gathered together to take order in matters of faith. This it can only do by means of those who are specially appointed for that purpose ; and such power was accordingly given to the apostles and elders, and after them to those who succeeded in their place, who, duly assembled in general council, and representing the Universal Church, had the same power as if all the members of the congregation had been joined with them.

He proceeds to prove these statements by testimonies drawn from the history of the Church in all ages, beginning with the first council at Jerusalem. Paul and Barnabas, though inspired apostles, did not venture individually to pronounce judgment. That was reserved to the apostles and elders collectively, and to them alone ; and their decision was binding on the whole congregation. The question in dispute was moved in the congregation ; the Scriptures were appealed to as witnesses ; but the apostles and elders were the judges—" My sentence is "—" It seemed good to the Holy Ghost and to us." Thus, as under the old law recourse was to be had to the priests of the tribe of Levi and to the judge that was in those days, not to the Scriptures, so, under the new law, the apostles and elders and their successors, in general council assembled, are the sole judges regarding the interpretation of the mysteries of Scripture, and the apostolic council at Jerusalem was the model for synods in succeeding times.

But, he continues, there is now a common saying, Why should not every man read the Scripture and seek out his own salvation? Has not Christ bought us at as high a price as bishop or abbot, prior or pope? Must not every man bear his own burden? Neither monk, friar, nor priest, will answer for my soul, but myself only. This saying is very true, if well understood. It is as important for a poor Christian man to know all things necessary to his salvation, as for those in highest dignity; and there is one duty common to all—to love God above all things, and their neighbours as themselves. But, for this, provision is made in the Creed, wherein are contained all things necessary for a Christian man's belief; in the Ten Commandments, which comprehend the way to please God and to do our duty to our neighbours; and in the Lord's Prayer, appointed by the Lord God to be said daily to Him, wherein are contained all things necessary to be desired, both for soul and body. To the direct question—whether the lay people should read the Scriptures for themselves, he answers, that the point has not been determined by the Church, but, in his opinion, they may do so with much profit for the correction of their lives and conversation, but not for curiosity regarding mysteries such as the Sacraments, Predestination, Free Will, and Justification.

He answers the ordinary objection drawn from the evil lives of ecclesiastics against the authority of their office, by reference to Judas and Caiaphas, and to the declaration of our Lord, "The Scribes and Pharisees sit in Moses' seat: all therefore whatsoever they bid you observe, that observe and do; but do not ye after their works, for they say and do not." He defends the rules of the Church in regard to Fasting at appointed times, the Invocation of Saints, and the forbidding of Marriage to the priests, by an appeal to the authority of St.

Jerome and St. Augustine, Cyprian, Origen, and Chrysostom. He admits the grievous abuses which then existed in connection with ecclesiastical patronage, and the lives, learning, and manners of the clergy; indignantly denounces the avarice of great men and others which led to these evils; and appeals to those in authority to do their duty. "I beseech the living God," he says, "that they who are already ministers in the Church of God, especially those who occupy the place of apostles by office and authority, call to remembrance the severe and rigorous sentence of the apostle, saying, 'Woe is unto me if I preach not the Gospel,' and also the words of the prophet, saying, 'Woe be to the shepherds of Israel that do feed themselves. Should not the shepherds feed the flocks.' Whereby, the pastors doing their debt and duty to the simple people committed to their cure, all heresies, wickedness, and vice, should be suppressed, the Church freed from scandal, and God honoured, to whom be glory for ever."

We are told that the treatise of the Abbot of Crossraguel was held in high esteem, and that many persons were induced by his arguments to remain in the communion of the Church. It continued unanswered till 1563, when, at the instance of the Earl of Glencairn, a reply was published by John Davidson, Principal of the College of Glasgow. This reply bears special reference to an abstract of the Tractive, prepared by the abbot for circulation among the Protestants, containing a rash promise—not uncommon among controversialists of that day—that, if any one part of his book were refuted, he would hold the whole to be disproved, and embrace the Reformed opinions. Davidson's answer is much inferior to the Tractive, as well in learning and ability, as in style and expression. Both are written in becoming language, and in a mild and charitable spirit. The authors had in youth been fellow-students, and it is pleasing to find Davidson alluding to "the old Parisian kindness that was betwixt them," and speaking of the Archbishop of Glasgow as his "good master and liberal friend, howbeit for religion they were now separated, as many fathers and sons were in these their days."[1]

---

[1] Kennedy's Tractive and Davidson's Answer are printed in the Miscellany of the Wodrow Society. See also Keith, vol. iii. p. 405-412; M'Crie's Life of

In March, 1559, John Willock was residing at Ayr, where he had been a friar before he adopted the Reformed opinions. He preached against the mass, asserting that it was idolatrous, and maintaining that the texts of Scripture which he brought forward in proof of this were expounded by him in conformity with the interpretation of Irenæus, Chrysostom, Hilary, Origen, and Tertullian. On Easter Eve, the twenty-fifth of March, the Abbot of Crossraguel came to Ayr. Hearing of Willock's sermons, and of the line of argument adopted in them, he entered into a correspondence with him regarding the points in dispute. In his first letter, he maintained that whoever asserts the mass to be idolatrous is himself a heretic; and he offered to prove this by the express word of God, according to the judgment of the most ancient and godly doctors, and that in presence of twelve persons to be chosen by each of the disputants. Willock accepted this challenge, and proposed that the discussion should take place publicly in the church of St. John the Baptist; but, on the abbot expressing his apprehension of a tumult arising if the meeting were open to all, it was agreed that it should be held in a private house. The disputation, however, did not take place. Willock having declared that he was content to be judged by the word of God, Kennedy answered that, as they were sure to differ about the interpretation of Scripture, there must be some judge between them, and the most competent judges were the ancient fathers and doctors whose authority the preacher himself had appealed to. Willock, in reply, stated that he consented to abide by the authority of the ancient doctors, but so far only as they were in accordance with the Holy Scriptures. As they could not agree on this point, the correspondence ended. On the seventh of April, Kennedy, who was then at Maybole in the immediate vicinity of his own abbey, sent an account of the whole proceedings to the Archbishop of Glasgow, at whose request, it would appear, he had gone to Ayr.[1]

Knox, pp. 241-242; M'Crie's Life of Melville, vol. i. p. 453-456; and Mr. David Laing's prefatory remarks on the two treatises in the Wodrow Miscellany.

[1] See the correspondence, published from the papers in the Scots College at Paris, in Keith, vol. iii. p. 393-404; and reprinted in the Miscellany of the Wodrow Society. See also M'Crie's Life of Knox, p. 242, and Mr. Laing's remarks in the Wodrow Miscellany, pp. 93, 261-263.

The feast of Easter, in the year 1559, was kept with great solemnity by Mary of Lorraine and her court. About that time a proclamation was issued, forbidding any persons to preach, or to administer the sacraments, except with the authority of the bishops. The Reformed preachers paid no attention to this injunction, and several of their number were summoned to appear before the Justiciary Court at Stirling, on the tenth of May. The Congregation were determined to support their ministers, and assembled at Perth in great numbers. At this very time John Knox returned to Scotland.[1]

From the time that he left Scotland in 1556, Knox had resided for the most part at Geneva, where he and Whittingham, afterwards Dean of Durham, were joint ministers to the English congregation. In the year 1558, he published the " First Blast of the Trumpet against the monstrous Regiment of Women." The object of this work is expressed in the opening sentence : " To promote a woman to bear rule, superiority, dominion, or empire, above any realm, nation, or city, is repugnant to nature, contumely to God, a thing most contrarious to his revealed will and approved ordinance; and finally, it is the subversion of good order, of all equity and justice." It was chiefly directed against Mary of England, but its arguments and allusions were equally applicable to the government of the young Queen of the Scots and her mother. It has already been mentioned that an invitation to return to Scotland was sent to Knox by some of the Protestant leaders, but that he stopped short in his journey, in consequence of receiving subsequent letters of a contrary tenor. After the subscription of the bond in December, 1557, he was again requested to come back, and the Congregation wrote to Calvin, soliciting his influence in persuading Knox to comply. The letters containing these requests were not received at Geneva till November, 1558. In that month Mary of England died. The exiles began to return home, and Knox acceded to the request which had been made. He left Geneva in January, 1559, and, on arriving at Dieppe, learned that an application which he had made for permission to pass through England was refused. This was chiefly owing to his treatise on female

[1] Knox, vol. i. p. 315-318. History of the Estate of Scotland—Wodrow Miscellany, vol. i. pp. 56, 57. M'Crie's Life of Knox, p 155-158.

government, the opinions expressed in which, now that Elizabeth was on the throne, were disavowed even by the exiles. He sailed direct for Scotland in the end of April, and on the second of May landed at Leith. As soon as his arrival became known to the government, he was proclaimed an outlaw; but, without giving his enemies an opportunity of seizing him, and remaining only two nights at Edinburgh, he hastened to Dundee, where several of the Protestant barons were assembled for the purpose of accompanying the accused preachers to their place of trial. Knox received a joyful welcome, and went with his friends to Perth.[1]

Had it been in the power of the Reformed to arrange beforehand the precise time for the return of their great preacher, they could not have done so more auspiciously for their cause. The citation of the Protestant ministers by the queen-regent brought the struggle between the two parties to a crisis, which both must have foreseen, but for which neither seems to have been prepared. The Protestants were evidently acting in concert, yet there is no appearance of any formal plan of proceeding having been drawn up, or of any thing having been resolved on beyond a determination to maintain the open profession of their opinions, and the exercise of their worship. Neither, on the other side, was the regent in a position to suppress any strong movement against her authority, although she had avowed her intention of prohibiting the public exercise of the Reformed worship, and punishing all tumultuous opposition to the established Church. How far it was contemplated, on the one hand, to assail the privileges of the hierarchy and the power of the crown, or, on the other, to prevent the maintenance by individuals of the new opinions, we have no sufficient means of knowing. The course of events hurried on the adoption of measures which probably neither party could have anticipated.

The Protestants who assembled at Perth were unarmed, it is said, but this expression can hardly apply with accuracy to the barons and their feudal retainers. They may not have been prepared for actual hostilities, but the avowed object of the assemblage was to overawe the government by their presence at the trial, and to protect the accused, as they had

[1] Knox, vol. i. pp. 274, 318. M'Crie's Life of Knox, p. 120-158.

formerly done by similar demonstrations. Some, however, were reluctant to bring matters to extremity. Erskine of Dun, desirous of promoting moderate counsels, went on to Stirling, and endeavoured to effect an accommodation with the regent. Hoping to succeed in his desire, he prevailed on the Reformed to remain at Perth. When the accused preachers did not appear on the tenth of May, those who had become sureties for their presence, among whom was Erskine himself, were fined, and the ministers were outlawed. The laird of Dun, finding that his efforts were fruitless, returned to his friends at Perth.[1]

While Erskine was vainly endeavouring to promote tranquillity, the preachers at Perth were declaiming against the mass, and enlarging on the divine command to destroy the monuments of idolatry. The feelings of the multitude were excited by the intelligence which they received of the condemnation of their ministers, and, on the day after the sentence of outlawry had been pronounced, Knox roused their passions still farther by a vehement sermon against idolatry, which he preached in the parish church of St. John the Baptist. Soon after the conclusion of the sermon, a priest appeared in the chancel, and, preparing to celebrate mass, opened a magnificent tabernacle which stood on the high altar. What his motives were can only be conjectured. He may have intended simply to perform the usual service at whatever individual hazard, or he may have hoped to win back the affections of the people by an appeal to what they had once been taught to reverence. However this may have been, the result was most disastrous.

[1] Knox, vol. i. p. 317-319. Buchanan, vol. i. p. 313. Leslie, p. 505. History of the Estate of Scotland—Wodrow Miscellany, vol. i. p. 57. Pitcairn's Criminal Trials, vol. i. part i. pp. 406, 407. Spottiswood, vol. i. p. 271. Keith, vol. i. pp. 187, 188. Tytler, vol. vi. pp. 98, 99. It is not easy to ascertain the true history of the events at Perth and Stirling. Knox mentions that the queen promised to Erskine that, if the multitude were stayed, she would take some better order in regard to the ministers, and that, at Erskine's request, both people and preachers remained at Perth. Buchanan states that the queen sent for Erskine, and that the greater number of the Protestants, relying on her promises, actually left Perth, though their leaders remained. The narrative, as given by Spottiswood, Keith, and Tytler, assumes the deceit of the queen, and the consequent dispersion of the great body of the Protestants. Yet this is more than Knox asserts, and is not supported by the account given by Bishop Leslie, and by the author of the History of the Estate of Scotland.

A number of persons had continued to linger in the church. One of these, a young man or boy, cried out, "This is intolerable, that when God in his word hath plainly condemned idolatry we shall stand and see it used in despite." The indignant priest gave the boy a blow, and he, taking up a stone and throwing it at the priest, struck the tabernacle and broke one of the images. The others immediately took up stones, and dashed in pieces the tabernacle and all the ornaments of the church. When this was known through the city, a disorderly rabble assembled from every quarter, and attacked the Dominican, Franciscan, Carmelite, and Carthusian monasteries. The work of spoliation and destruction continued for two days, and so effectually was it accomplished, that only the bare walls of the monastic buildings and churches remained. It does not appear that any of the inmates sustained personal injury. The Charter-house was a magnificent erection, and was the burial place of its founder, King James I. In the monastery of the Black Friars, the Scottish sovereigns had frequently kept their court, and parliaments and provincial synods had met within it. But when more solemn restraints had been thrown aside, it was hardly to be expected that recollections such as these would have any effect upon the people. As soon as the proceedings at Perth became known at Cupar in Fife, the inhabitants of that place followed the example which had been given, and destroyed all the altars and images in the parish church.[1]

These excesses were noted at the time as an evil commencement of the movement in favour of reformation, and ever since they have frequently been referred to in the same unfavourable manner. Attempts have been made to apologize for the riot at Perth. It has been spoken of as purely accidental, and it has been asserted that Knox and his friends did their best to prevent it. For this last statement there is no evidence, except one vague remark of Knox himself, and it is contradicted by the facts of the case; the outrages of the multitude could not have continued two days successively, had the nobles and preachers been really anxious to check them. The commencement of the tumult on this particular occasion seems to have

---

Knox, vol. i. p. 320-324. Buchanan, vol. i. p. 313. Leslie, p. 506. Spottiswood, vol i. pp. 271, 272.

been accidental, but when the feelings of an excited populace have been systematically roused, when at the very time exhortations to violence are ringing in their ears, when the act itself is neither checked nor punished, it is obvious that the multitude are not the worst criminals. Among the more violent of the Reformed the destruction of the monasteries appears to have been deliberately planned. The example had been given fifteen years before by the inhabitants of Dundee. The monks, and still more the friars, had long been the objects of the most outrageous invective, and in the month of January, 1559, a warning, in language borrowed from the ordinary legal forms, had been fixed on the gates of the monasteries of the friars, commanding them, in name of the poor, the maimed, the widows, and the orphans, whose houses and property they occupied, to depart forth therefrom before the ensuing term of Whitsunday, in order that the true owners might enter on possession, and afterwards enjoy the benefits of which they had been unjustly deprived.[1]

The queen-regent received an account of the riot at Perth with deep indignation. She dwelt particularly on the destruction of the royal foundation of the Charter-house, and threatened to take severe vengeance on the guilty parties. The Reformed began to fortify the town, and, at the same time, addressed a letter to the regent, in which they stated plainly that they would resist with the sword, if farther attempts were made to molest them in the exercise of their religion. This communication was written in a tone of defiance, hardly veiled under words of seeming deference and humility. They wrote in a similar strain to the nobility who adhered to the queen, asserting that whatever they had done was by the command of God, who plainly enjoins all idolatry and the monuments thereof to be destroyed. After some interval of time they put forth a declaration, bearing the following superscription :—" To the generation of Anti-Christ, the pestilent prelates and their shavelings within Scotland, the Congregation of Christ Jesus within the same, sayeth—." The tenor of this document corresponded with the title. The opponents of the Congregation were told that, if they did not alter

[1] Knox, vol. i. pp. 291, 320, 321. History of the Estate of Scotland—Wodrow Miscellany, vol. i. pp. 57, 58.

their conduct, the same treatment would be measured to them which they had meted to others; and they were threatened with the same war which God had commanded Israel to wage against the Canaanites.

The queen-regent prepared to march against Perth. The Reformed, in the meantime, had been encouraged by the arrival of the Earl of Glencairn, and a large number of their friends from the West, with whom was John Willock the preacher. Before actual hostilities commenced, an accommodation was effected by means of the Earl of Argyll and the Prior of St. Andrews, who accompanied the regent. The Reformed agreed, on certain conditions, to depart from Perth, and, on the twenty-ninth of May, the queen entered the town with her army. According to Knox and Buchanan, the articles of capitulation were broken by Mary, who declared that no faith was to be kept with heretics, and that princes were not to be too strictly bound by their promises. How far these statements are to be relied on is very doubtful, but the Earl of Argyll and the Prior, alleging that the queen had broken her promises, openly joined her opponents. By these two lords the Congregation were requested to assemble at St. Andrews. Knox accompanied the barons of Angus, and on his way preached at Crail and Anstruther. His hearers destroyed the altars and images in the churches, and the reformer announced his intention of preaching at St. Andrews on Sunday the eleventh of June. The archbishop attempted to defeat this intention, but, finding that the Protestants were determined to resist, he retired with his followers. The sermon was accordingly delivered. Its subject was the casting of the buyers and sellers out of the Temple. Knox compared the state of Jerusalem to that of Scotland, and pointed out the duty of those to whom God had given power and zeal for the work. The provost and magistrates, and the community of the city, proceeded deliberately to execute the prescribed task. The cathedral and other churches were spoiled, and the Dominican and Franciscan monasteries were destroyed.[1]

[1] Knox, vol i. p. 324-350. History of the Estate of Scotland—Wodrow Miscellany, vol. i. p. 58-60. Buchanan, vol. i. p. 313-315. Leslie, pp. 506, 507. Spottiswood, vol. i. p. 272-277. Keith, vol. i. p. 193-206. M'Crie's Life of Knox, pp. 160-164, 486, 487. Lyon's History of St. Andrews, vol. i. p. 335-

The Congregation soon became so powerful that the regent was unable to keep the field against them. The abbey of Lindores, which had already suffered so much, was now thoroughly reformed. The altars were overthrown, and the images, vestments, and liturgical books, were burned in presence of the monks, who were commanded to throw aside the habits of their order. Similar proceedings took place at the neighbouring monastery of Balmerino.[1]

On the twenty-fifth of June, the queen's troops retired from Perth, and the Congregation again obtained possession of the town. The abbey of Scone, in the immediate vicinity, was held by its commendator, the Bishop of Murray. The lords of the Congregation wrote to him, that, unless he joined them, they could not preserve his monastery from destruction. It is said that he offered to comply with their request; but, without waiting for his answer, a multitude of persons belonging to the towns of Dundee and Perth commenced an attack on the monastery. They were persuaded to give up their purpose for a time, but on the following day the assault was renewed, and the magnificent abbey and palace, the residence of the Scottish sovereigns, and the place of their inauguration, were set on fire, and reduced to a heap of blackened ruins.[2]

While these events took place at Perth, the Earl of Argyll and the Prior of St. Andrews went southwards to Stirling and Linlithgow. There also the monasteries were destroyed. The regent abandoned Edinburgh at their approach, and on the twenty-ninth of June they entered the capital. The friars in that city had hitherto been protected from the populace by

---

337. A tradition of very general reception connects the destruction of the cathedral of St. Andrews with Knox's sermon there. I have found no written evidence of this. The reformer himself, in his History, and in a letter written at the time, makes no express reference to the cathedral church. The language of Bishop Leslie, and of the author of the History of the Estate of Scotland, is vague and ambiguous; and Buchanan speaks only of the spoiling of the churches and the destruction of the monasteries. It is certain, however, that the primatial church sustained such injuries at the time of the Reformation that the archbishops of the following century did not even attempt to restore it. There is great probability in the conjecture that it was partially ruined in June, 1559, and that its destruction was completed when the abbey churches were systematically demolished two years afterwards.

[1] M'Crie's Life of Knox, p. 487. Leslie, p. 507.
[2] Knox, vol. i. p. 350-362. Buchanan, vol. i. p. 316. Leslie, p. 508.

Lord Seaton, the provost. All restraint was now at an end; the monasteries were demolished, the churches were spoiled of their ornaments, and the palace of Holyrood was pillaged. About the same time, the Earl of Glencairn and other gentlemen of the West reformed Glasgow according to what was become the established model. Some weeks afterwards a sort of truce was arranged between the contending parties, and the queen resumed possession of the palace of Holyrood.

On the eighth of July, Henry II., King of France, died, and Francis, the husband of the Queen of the Scots, succeeded to the crown. The princes of the house of Lorraine immediately acquired the chief direction of the government, and made vigorous efforts to restore the authority of their sister in Scotland. More troops were sent over, and, towards the end of September, Nicholas de Pellevé, Bishop of Amiens, afterwards cardinal archbishop of Sens, arrived at Leith. He held a commission as apostolic nuncio, with the authority of legate a latere, and was accompanied by three doctors of the Sorbonne, of great reputation for their learning. According to Leslie, their exhortations had the effect of confirming the minds of many who were wavering in their attachment to the Church.

There was no true reconciliation between the queen and the Reformed, and both only waited an opportunity of renewing the war with advantage. The insolence and exactions of the French soldiers excited deep dislike among the Scots, and did Mary's cause more injury than the advantages derived from their courage and discipline could compensate. The feeling of the people was much divided. Appeals were made to them by proclamations on either side, and Knox seems to admit that those of the queen had considerable effect. The Duke of Chatel-herault joined the Congregation, and, though several Protestants of high rank still adhered to the regent, the Earl of Huntly, the most powerful nobleman in the communion of the Church, began to waver in his political principles, and his eldest son, the Lord Gordon, openly allied himself with the Reformed. Encouraged by the support of the house of Hamilton, the lords of the Congregation burned the altars and images in the abbeys of Paisley and Kilwinning; and Dunfermline, which seems hitherto to have escaped, now shared the same treatment. A decisive step was finally taken. The Reformed again occupied Edinburgh, and, on the twenty-first of October, a meeting was held there for the purpose of discussing the question, whether the regent ought to be longer allowed to administer the government. Different opinions were expressed, and the judgment of the preachers was requested. Both Willock and Knox advised that she should be deprived of her office. This resolution was accordingly adopted, and the deprivation was embodied in a formal act, and proclaimed at the market-cross. They sent a letter to the regent, by the Lion King-at-Arms, by which, in name of their sovereign lord and lady, they intimated the suspension of her commission, being assured, they said, that her proceedings were contrary to their sovereigns' will. At midnight of the same day on which this letter was sent, Knox announced the event to one of the English agents. "The queen-regent," he wrote, "with public consent of the lords and barons assembled, is deprived of all authority and regiment among us. . . . The authority of the French king and queen is yet received, and will be, in word, till they deny our most just requests." [1]

This proceeding was the prelude to open war between the Congregation and the regent. The Congregation were at first much less successful than they anticipated, and, on the sixth of November, were compelled to abandon Edinburgh, and retreat northwards to Stirling. If they had been obliged to rely on their own efforts alone, there is every reason to believe that the insurrection would have been suppressed, but they now obtained effectual assistance from another quarter.

From the time of her accession to the throne, Queen Elizabeth had anxiously watched the state of matters in Scotland. She disliked the political principles and peculiar ecclesiastical opinions of the northern reformers, and was at first reluctant to give them any support. At an early period of the contest, negociations had commenced between the leaders of the Congregation and Elizabeth's ministers, and, after the act sus-

---

[1] Knox, vol. i. p. 362-451. History of the Estate of Scotland—Wodrow Miscellany, vol. i. p. 61-69. Buchanan, vol. i. p. 316-319. Leslie, p. 508-518. Sadler's State Papers, vol. i. pp. 464-470, 680, 681. Tytler, vol. vi. p. 115-147. Keith, vol. i. p. 211-237. Spottiswood, vol. i. p. 280-304.

pending the authority of the regent, the application to the English government for assistance was urged more strongly. In these proceedings on the part of the Scots, the most active political agent was Knox. He spared no exertions, and cheerfully exposed himself to the greatest personal danger, travelling with rapidity from one part of the kingdom to another, in order to encourage the supporters of the Reformation, or to hold conferences with the English envoys. His written correspondence appears to have been unceasing, and, having no doubts as to the goodness of the cause which he was supporting, he was not restrained by any scruples in regard to the means for promoting it. On the twenty-fifth of October, under the feigned name of John Sinclair, he wrote to Sir James Crofts, the English commander at Berwick, urging him to send troops to the assistance of the Congregation; mentioning that this would be no infraction of the treaty of peace between England and France, because it was free to the soldiers to serve any prince or nation for their wages; and suggesting, if this were not sufficient, that Sir James might declare them rebels to their sovereign so soon as he was assured that they had joined the Scots. About the beginning of the same month, the Prior of St. Andrews received a letter, written as if from France, containing an account of the great preparations making in that country to aid the regent, and advising the Reformed to seek assistance from England. Queen Elizabeth's envoy, Randolph, suspected Knox of being the real author of this letter.

The supposed political necessity of checking the French ascendency in Scotland finally outweighed other considerations in the mind of Elizabeth. She yielded to the advice of her ministers, and resolved to support the cause of the Congregation. From that time she carried out towards the northern kingdom the line of policy which had long been familiar to English statesmen. It was apparently justified in this case by expediency, and by a due regard to the interests of her people; but in itself it was wicked and unjust, and, though apparently successful, was fraught with evils which produced results fatal to the happiness and well-being of both kingdoms. On the twenty-seventh of February, 1560, a convention was signed at Berwick between the Duke of Norfolk,

Lieutenant in the North, on behalf of the Queen of England, and the Prior of St. Andrews and others, commissioners for the Duke of Chatel-herault and the lords of the Congregation, by which a league of amity and mutual defence against France was concluded. The act of the Scottish commissioners was afterwards ratified by their constituents, among whom were the Earl of Huntly, the Lords Borthwick and Somerville, the Bishop of Galloway, the Lord Robert Stewart, Abbot of Holyrood, the Preceptor of the Knights of St. John, the Abbots of Kinloss and Culross, and the Commendators of Arbroath, Kilwinning, and Inch-Colm. This treaty refers to political reasons alone for its motives and justification. A direct reference to religious differences was probably avoided by the Duke of Norfolk, and would certainly have prevented its ratification by some of the Scottish nobles. The opposition to the regent at this time assumed the appearance rather of a political combination, than of an ecclesiastical movement.[1]

In the beginning of the year 1560, the barons of the Mearns, distinguished all along for their zeal in the cause of the Reformation, crossed the Dee and entered Aberdeen, where they destroyed the Dominican and Carmelite monasteries, and were proceeding to attack those of the Franciscan and Trinity Friars, when they were prevented by the citizens. The work of destruction, however, so far as the monasteries were concerned, was completed by the townsmen themselves, and the cathedral was saved only by the exertions of Bishop Leslie, then official of the diocese, and the assistance of the Earl of Huntly.[2]

After the conclusion of the treaty between the Duke of

---

[1] Knox, vol. i. p. 451-473 ; vol. ii. p. 3-56. History of the Estate of Scotland—Wodrow Miscellany, vol. i. p. 69-80. Buchanan, vol. i. p. 319-321. Leslie, pp. 518, 519. Sadler's State Papers, vol. i. p. 499. Spottiswood, vol. i. p. 304-314. Keith, vol. i. pp. 241-262, 395, 396, 398. M'Crie's Life of Knox, p. 174-181. Tytler, vol. vi. p. 147-159.

[2] Leslie, pp. 520, 521. Kennedy's Annals of Aberdeen, vol. i. pp. 112, 113. Extracts from the Council Register of Aberdeen, from 1398 to 1570, pp. 315-323, 325, 326. It has frequently been stated that the chancel of the cathedral was demolished at the same time with the monasteries. This is inconsistent with the narrative of Leslie, who could not have been mistaken as to the facts, and who was certainly not disposed to palliate the excesses of the reformers, but there can be no doubt that it was destroyed within a year or two after this date ; see James Gordon's Description of both towns of Aberdeen, p. 22.

Norfolk and the lords of the Congregation, an English army entered Scotland, and advanced towards Edinburgh. The royalists and the French were unable to keep the field against the united forces of the Congregation and their English allies. The war, however, continued to be carried on with various success. In the meantime, the queen-regent, wearied with care, and sinking under bodily illness, sought refuge in the castle of Edinburgh, which the governor, Lord Erskine, had refused to deliver up to either party. Her disease rapidly increased, and on the ninth of June she requested the leading nobles on both sides to visit her. They attended at her call. She exhorted them to consult the true interests of their country and their sovereigns, and asked their forgiveness for anything wherein she had offended them. The Reformed entreated her to receive the instructions of one of their preachers, and she allowed Willock to be sent for. She listened to his exhortations, professed that her only hope of salvation was in the merits of her Saviour, and was silent when he spoke against the superstition of the mass. Early on the morning of the eleventh of June, Mary of Lorraine expired, being then in the forty-fifth year of her age. The Congregation refused to allow her Christian burial in Scotland according to the ritual of the Church, and, after considerable delay, her body was carried to France, and interred in the monastery of St. Peter at Rheims, of which her sister was then abbess.[1]

Before the death of Mary, some of the most eminent of the clergy had deserted the Church, and joined the Protestants. Among these were three of the six persons who had been appointed advisers to the Archbishops of St. Andrews and Glasgow at the last provincial council. Alexander Gordon, Archbishop of Athens and Bishop of Galloway, had gone along with the head of his house in ratifying the convention of Berwick, but he went beyond him in adopting the ecclesiastical principles

---

[1] Knox, vol. ii. pp. 56-72, 160, 161, and appendix, p. 590-592. Buchanan, vol i. p. 321-324. Leslie, p. 519-526. Spottiswood, vol. i. p. 314-321. Keith, vol. i. p. 263-285. Tytler, vol. vi. p. 159-165. The character of the queen-regent, as given by Buchanan, is not unfair in itself, nor incapable of being reconciled with the description of Bishop Leslie. The manner in which Knox speaks of her, especially in connection with the circumstances of her death, has frequently been commented on, and never more severely than it deserves.

of the Reformed. John Winram, Sub-prior of St. Andrews, had for many years acknowledged the corruptions of the Church, and had laboured to bring about a peaceful reformation in doctrine and discipline. We are not told what finally led him to despair of success, but he now openly united himself to the Protestants. John Greyson, Provincial of the Black Friars, likewise conformed. On the seventeenth day of March, 1560, he made a public and formal recantation in the parish church of St. Andrews. This document is valuable as throwing light on the nature and extent of that change of opinion which had become so prevalent; and it probably shows how far the Protestant doctrines were at this time adopted by those who belonged to the reforming school within the Church. It is as follows:—

"Here, in presence of Almighty and Everlasting God, and of this holy congregation, I grant and confess that in time by-past I have maintained and defended divers kinds of superstition and idolatry, contrary to the laws and ordinances of Almighty God, and have remained too long in the opinion and defence of such things; and I repent the same from the bottom of my heart, and am content in time to come to institute and conform my life to the word and doctrine of the eternal God, set forth, explained, and declared by his prophets, and the apostles of our only Saviour, Christ Jesus, in the Old Testament and the New, and think that the Church and Congregation of God may be sufficiently instructed to eschew sin, death, and hell, and how they may come to everlasting life, by those things which are revealed to us by the Holy Ghost in the New and Old Testament; and therefore I reject, renounce, and abhor all other doctrines and traditions of men, which are contrary to God's holy word, and were set out to bind men's conscience to obey them under the pain of deadly sin.

"And in especial, I renounce the Pope to be the head of the Church, and also I renounce him and all his traditions and laws repugnant in any sort, or making derogation to God's laws and the liberty of the same.

"Also, I renounce the Mass, as it has been used in times by-past, and the feigned and invented Purgatory, as pestiferous and blasphemous things, and as contrary to the merits, and passion, and omnisufficient sacrifice offered upon the cross by our Saviour Christ for the redemption of mankind.

"Also, I grant that no graven image should be made and worshipped in the Church of God, and that no honour should be given thereto, and that all exhibition of such honour, exhibited or to be exhibited to such stocks or stones, is very idolatry, and against the express command of God.

"Also, I grant that we have no command of God bidding us pray to any saints that are departed, but only to Him who is Saint of all saints, Christ Jesus, our only Saviour, Mediator, and Advocate, everliving, and perpetually making intercession to his Father for his faithful people and members of his body; and so also I grant that we have no command to pray for them that are departed.

"Also, as I grant that to them that have the gift of chastity it is good and godly to live in chastity, even so I grant, according to St. Paul's doctrine, that it is lawful to all men and women to marry, who have not the gift of chastity, notwithstanding any vow made to the contrary; but if they be vexed and wearied with the urgent appetites of the flesh, they are bound by the commandment of the Lord to marry.

"Also, I deny all Transubstantiation in the sacrament of the Body and Blood of our Saviour Christ Jesus, and that Auricular Confession is necessary for the salvation of man.

"The foresaid and all other ungodly opinions and inventions of men, which are contrary to God and his holy word, I detest, abhor, and renounce for now and ever. And of my long adherence to the same, I ask God mercy, and this holy congregation forgiveness." [1]

The country was miserably wasted by the contending armies, but the ecclesiastics were the chief sufferers. The Bishops of Ross, Dunkeld, and Dunblane, were driven from their palaces, and deprived of their estates. Many monasteries were pillaged, and the abbeys of Melrose, Kelso, and Dunfermline, are particularly mentioned as having again been exposed to the ravages of the spoiler. The property of the clergy was seized, and their rents were sequestrated, special officers being ap-

---

[1] See Greyson's recantation, printed from the records of the Kirk Session of St. Andrews, in Dr. Lee's Lectures on the History of the Church of Scotland, vol. ii. pp. 107, 108.

pointed to collect and take account of them. All parties, however, were weary of the war, and commissioners having arrived from England and France, negotiations were begun, which led to the establishment of peace between these kingdoms. The French commissioners, notwithstanding instructions which they had received to the contrary, also agreed to certain articles of accommodation between the King and Queen of the Scots, and the party in arms against their authority. These were drawn up in the form of concessions by the sovereigns to the nobility and people of Scotland. One of the most important of the stipulations was, that a parliament should be held on the tenth of July, to be adjourned for the despatch of business to the first of August, and that, during the interval, the king and queen should be advertised of the concessions, and humbly requested to confirm the same; and it was farther agreed that the parliament should be as valid, in all respects, as if summoned by the express command of the sovereigns, provided always nothing were treated of prior to the first of August. The government, during the queen's absence, was to be carried on by a council of twelve—seven to be selected by the sovereigns, and five by the estates, out of twenty-four to be named by the estates. Touching the articles of religion presented by the nobility and people, it was agreed that, inasmuch as this was too important a matter to be settled by the commissioners, deputies should be chosen at the ensuing parliament, who should repair to France in order to effect an arrangement with the sovereigns.

On the eighth of July this treaty, known as the treaty of Edinburgh, was proclaimed at the market-cross of the Scottish capital, and a few days afterwards the French and English troops left the kingdom. The Reformed were now the predominant party in Scotland. A species of ecclesiastical discipline had already been set up by them in some places, but ministers were at this time formally appointed to the chief towns, and persons, under the name of Superintendents, were entrusted with the charge of various districts. The successful result of the struggle had greatly added to the power of the Congregation. That body was able not only to protect its own adherents, but to proscribe and punish its opponents; and those who hitherto had secretly favoured the Reformed doctrines, or who did not possess the principle and courage required in the adherents of a falling cause, now hastened to proclaim their adoption of the Protestant opinions. Some of those that conformed were persons whose learning and ability were of great assistance, and their merits were not forgotten in the distribution of the newly created offices.

The following ministers were appointed to the chief towns—John Knox to Edinburgh, Christopher Goodman to St Andrews, Adam Heriot to Aberdeen, John Row to Perth, Paul Methven to Jedburgh, William Christison to Dundee, David Ferguson to Dunfermline, and David Lindsay to Leith. Goodman, an Englishman by birth, was the associate of Knox in ministering to the congregation at Geneva, and like him was notorious on account of the theories which he promulgated regarding the relative duties of subjects and sovereigns. When he afterwards returned to England, he was obliged to retract his political opinions. Heriot was an Augustinian canon at St. Andrews, much esteemed for his learning, integrity, and eloquence as a preacher. Having embraced the Reformed opinions, he was now appointed to the chief city of the North, where the Church had still many adherents; and the prudence and moderation which he subsequently displayed justified the wisdom of the choice. Of a similar character was David Lindsay, a younger son of the house of Edzell, who had lately returned home after finishing his education on the Continent.[1]

The circumstances which are said to have produced the conversion of John Row require more particular detail. Row was educated at the University of St. Andrews, and practised for some time as an advocate in the consistorial court of that city. He was employed by the Scottish clergy to act as their agent at Rome. During his residence in Italy, which continued for about eight years, he took the degree of doctor of laws at Padua.

The following is the generally received account of the next events in the life of Row.—He was in great favour with the Pope, but, having fallen into bad health, was advised by his

[1] Knox, vol. ii. p. 72-87. Buchanan, vol. i. p. 326. Leslie, p. 527-529. Spottiswood, vol. ii. pp. 197, 198; vol. iii. p. 220. Keith, vol. i. p. 286-311. Tytler, vol. vi. p. 166-175.

physicians to return to his native country. The Pope having given his consent, he received a commission as legate, with authority to check the innovations which were then commencing. He left Rome on the twentieth of May, 1558, and landed at Eyemouth, on the twenty-ninth of September. On his arrival, he opposed the progress of the Reformation, by disputing with the preachers and otherwise. At that time the chapel of our Lady of Loretto, near Musselburgh, was a famous place of pilgrimage, and was held in great reverence by the adherents of the Roman Church. Taking advantage of this superstitious feeling, the bishops and clergy endeavoured to strengthen their influence by the performance of a false miracle. A fit person had been carefully trained for the purpose. In his youth, while in the service of the nuns of the monastery of St. Catharine of Sienna, near Edinburgh, he had learned to turn up his eyes in such a manner as to have the appearance of one who was entirely blind. The sisters communicated this singular faculty of their servant to some of the clergy at Edinburgh, and by their advice he was kept concealed in the vaults of the nunnery for seven or eight years, till it was forgotten that such a person existed. At the end of that period he was brought out, and, having been taken bound by a solemn oath to obey his instructions, was led through the country as a blind beggar. After some time, it was announced that a great miracle would be performed at the chapel of Loretto. The man was led forth in presence of a multitude of people, and, when certain ceremonies had taken place, it was proclaimed that he had been restored to sight.

Among those who witnessed the cure was a gentleman of Fife, known by the name of Squire Meldrum, who had embraced the Reformed opinions. Doubting the truth of the miracle, he induced the man to accompany him to his lodgings at Edinburgh, and, when he was there, compelled him by the threat of immediate death to confess the imposture. Meldrum farther persuaded him to proclaim the whole story to the people at the market-cross of the city; and, as soon as this was done, they both left Edinburgh, and crossing the Queen's Ferry landed in Fife, where the lords of the Congregation were in arms against the regent. Meldrum returned to his own house of Cleish, and soon afterwards John Row came thither, on a visit to the lady of the mansion, who adhered to the Roman Church. Row and Meldrum entered into discourse concerning matters of religion, and reference was made to the wonderful cure lately performed at Loretto. The latter explained the true nature of the transaction, and produced the man himself in confirmation of his account. Row listened in amazement, and was soon afterwards converted to the Reformed religion.

This narrative calls for a more careful examination than it appears to have yet received. No writer of the time, or of the period immediately succeeding, makes any allusion to the pretended miracle at Loretto, or to the conversion of Row by such means. The silence of Knox on such a subject is a strong negative argument against the truth of the story. Archbishop Spottiswood gives an account of Row, and says nothing of the miracle, but refers to the counsel of the Prior of St. Andrews, and the persuasions of Knox, as inducing him to remain in Scotland and become a minister in the Reformed communion. The only authority for the narrative is an appendix to the supplement or concluding portion of the History of the Kirk, by John Row, minister of Carnock, son of John Row the reformer. The younger Row was not twelve years old at the time of his father's death, and his History was written when he was far advanced in years. There is no evidence that the appendix was composed by him at all, though it seems to have been the work of some of the family; and the manuscript from which it was printed was not written till about the year 1670. The author of the appendix gives the name of Squire Meldrum to the person who discovered the imposture, confounding him apparently with the well-known hero of Sir David Lindsay's poem. This is corrected in the manuscript, by the insertion, in another hand, of the name of Robert Colville, to whom Meldrum's estate of Cleish belonged in the year 1559. The story itself bears no date, but the events must have taken place while Mary of Lorraine was in possession of Edinburgh, and the Congregation were in arms in Fife. Although the narrative states that Row returned to Scotland in September, 1558, we know from a letter written by him to Donald, Abbot of Cupar, that he was still at Rome in May, 1559. The alleged miracle must have been performed during the autumn of the latter year, but this can hardly be reconciled with the circumstance that the nunnery of St. Catharine, along with the other monasteries in Edinburgh, was demolished in the end of June. There are other parts of the story which do not seem very probable, such as the detention of the young man for eight years in the vaults of the monastery, and his acquiescence in the subsequent proceedings, and the holding of the office of legate by Row. On a review of the whole circumstances, there does not appear to be sufficient evidence for the narrative, while there are strong indications of wilful fabrication, or of extreme credulity.[1]

It has been mentioned that superintendents of districts were appointed at the same time with the ministers of the towns. Willock was named to Glasgow; the laird of Dun, though not exercising the functions of a preacher, and in all respects a layman, was appointed to Angus and Mearns; and John Carsewell, parson of Kilmartin, to Argyll and the Isles. The superintendency of Lothian was conferred on John Spottiswood. The father of Spottiswood—a descendant of the ancient family of that name in the Merse—was slain at Flodden. The son, left an orphan at four years of age, was educated at the University of Glasgow, and afterwards went to England, where he became intimate with Archbishop Cranmer, and embraced the Reformed opinions. He was presented to the parsonage of Calder by Sir James Sandilands, but it is not stated whether he had ever received holy orders; it would rather seem that he had not. The superintendency of Fife was bestowed on John Winram.[2]

The articles agreed to by the royal commissioners regarding the calling of a parliament were not very clearly expressed, and admitted of different interpretations. The commissioners seem in this respect to have exceeded their powers, and the concession was not ratified by Francis and Mary. The estates of the kingdom, however, in terms of the previous adjournment, met in the tolbooth of Edinburgh, on the first of

[1] Compare Row's History of the Kirk of Scotland, Wodrow Society ed. p. 447-455, and Mr. David Laing's preface, pp. vii.-ix. xiv. xv. xvii. lxii.; Spottiswood, vol. ii. pp. 273, 274; and M'Crie's Life of Knox, pp. 197-199, 213, 214, 442, 443.

[2] Knox, vol. ii. p. 87. Spottiswood, vol. ii. p. 336. Keith's Catalogue, p. 307.

August. All were invited who were entitled by law or ancient custom to be present, and there was in consequence a large attendance. The ecclesiastical members were—the Archbishop of St. Andrews, the Bishops of Dunkeld, Dunblane, and Argyll, the Bishops-elect of Galloway and the Isles, the Prior of St. Andrews, the Prior of the order of St. John, the Abbots of Lindores, Cupar, New-Abbey, Kinloss, and Ferne, the Commendators of Arbroath, Holyrood, Jedburgh, Newbottle, Dundrennan, Dryburgh, Inch-Colm, Culross, Kilwinning, and Deer, the Postulate of Cambuskenneth, the Commendators of Coldingham and St. Mary's Isle, the Sub-prior of St. Andrews, and the Minister of Failford. Many of these were ecclesiastics only in name, and in religious opinions and political principles were among the leading men in the Congregation. A number both of the spiritual and temporal peers declined to attend, and several zealous supporters of the hierarchy were absent, from various causes. The Archbishop of Glasgow and Lord Seaton were in France. The Earl of Huntly excused his absence on the ground of ill health. We hear nothing of the Abbot of Crossraguel, but his influence may probably be discerned in the line of conduct adopted at the convention by the Earl of Cassillis.

In the absence of the Earl of Huntly, the chancellor, William Maitland of Lethington was appointed to preside. The objections to the legality of the meeting were overruled, and, in the choice of the Lords of the Articles, the temporal nobles secured a majority, by electing those only of the ecclesiastical estate who were favourable to the cause of the Congregation. A petition was presented to the parliament in name of the barons, gentlemen, burgesses, and others professing the Protestant religion, craving reformation in regard to doctrine, discipline, and the administration of the sacraments, the power of the Pope, and the patrimony of the Church. No notice was taken of the reference to ecclesiastical property, but the Reformed were requested to lay before parliament a summary of the doctrines which they proposed to establish. Within four days, a document was presented, containing "the Confession of the Faith and Doctrine believed and professed by the Protestants of the

Realm of Scotland." This confession was read over, first to the Lords of the Articles, and afterwards before the whole parliament. Some of the ministers were present to defend it if necessary, and the members were desired to make objections to it, if they had any. None appear to have been stated at this time, and a day was fixed for taking the votes.

These proceedings on the part of the Reformed were contrary to the previous stipulations, in terms of which the whole subject of religion was to be submitted to the king and queen by commissioners to be chosen at the convention. But the conduct of the primate and other bishops was also deserving of censure. They were probably right in attending parliament, notwithstanding the doubts as to its lawfulness, but, being there, they were bound to defend to the utmost the faith which they professed, and the institutions which it was their solemn duty to maintain. It might not be easy for them to determine what precise line of conduct they should adopt, but under no circumstances could their silence be justified. It encouraged their enemies, and entirely disheartened their friends among the laity. The excuse has been made, that it was unsafe to provoke by opposition a party already irritated by past wrongs, and now forming a triumphant majority. It has even been said that the primate was threatened with death by his own brother, the Duke of Chatel-herault; but this statement is erroneous, and, however violent the language of some of the preachers may have been, it does not appear that the lives of the clergy were then in danger. Even had it been otherwise, this was not the time for caution or timidity. Those who felt no hesitation in putting their fellow Christians to death for not believing as they themselves did, should have been prepared to peril their own lives in defence of their faith. It is to be feared that the bishops' chief anxiety was for the restitution of their sequestrated estates, and that they had no adequate conception of the important nature of the change in religious belief which was the subject of discussion.

On the seventeenth of August, it was put to the vote in parliament whether the new confession should thenceforth be the established creed of the Scottish kingdom. It was again read over, one article after another. Now at last the primate, and the Bishops of Dunkeld and Dunblane, made some opposition. They do not seem, however, to have argued against the doctrines of the confession. The Earl Marischal thus spoke: " It is long since I have had some favour unto the truth, and since that I have had a suspicion of the Papistical religion; but, I praise my God, this day has fully resolved me in the one and the other. For seeing that my lords the bishops, who for their learning can, and for the zeal that they should bear to the verity, would, as I suppose, gainsay anything that directly impugns the verity of God; seeing, I say, my lords the bishops here present speak nothing to the contrary of the doctrine proponed, I cannot but hold it to be the very truth of God, and the contrary to be deceivable doctrine. And therefore, so far as in me lieth, I approve the one and condemn the other: and do further ask of God that not only I, but also all my posterity, may enjoy the comfort of the doctrine that this day our ears have heard. And yet more, I must vote, as it were by way of protestation, that if any persons ecclesiastical shall after this oppose themselves to this our confession, they have no place or credit, considering that they having long advisement and full knowledge of this our confession, none is now found, in lawful, free, and quiet parliament, to oppose themselves to that which we profess. And therefore, if any of this generation pretend to do it after this, I protest he be repute rather one that loveth his own commodity and the glory of the world, than the truth of God and the salvation of men's souls." Besides the three bishops who have been mentioned, the Abbot of Kilwinning voted against the confession. Of the temporal peers, the Earls of Atholl, Crawford, Caithness, Cassillis, and Eglinton, and the Lords Home and Gray, had refused to attend. The Lords Somerville and Borthwick opposed the formulary, giving as their reason, " We will believe as our fathers believed." All the other members of the three estates supported the confession, and it received the formal sanction of the parliament.[1]

[1] Acts of the Parliaments of Scotland, vol. ii. p. 525-534. Knox, vol. ii. p. 87-122. Keith, vol. i. p. 311-322 ; vol. iii. p. 4-7. Tytler, vol. vi. p. 175-184. See also a letter from Lethington to Cecil, dated 18th August, 1560, quoted by

On the twenty-fourth of August, three other acts were passed. By the first of these, the authority and jurisdiction of the Pope within the realm of Scotland were taken away, and all bishops and other prelates were forbidden to do anything in his name; by the second, all former acts of parliament, contrary to God's word, and the Confession of Faith now ratified, were declared to have no effect in time to come; and by the third, on the preamble that the sacraments of Baptism and the Body and Blood of Christ had been corrupted by the Church of Rome, and that, notwithstanding the reformation already made, there were some who persevered in their wicked idolatry, saying mass and baptizing in secret places according to the Roman ritual, it was ordained that no one, in time to come, should administer the sacraments, openly or secretly, except those who were admitted, and had power to that effect, and all persons were forbidden to say or hear mass, under pain of confiscation of their goods and personal punishment at the discretion of the judge for the first offence, banishment from the kingdom for the second, and death for the third.

In terms of one of the articles of the treaty, several prelates supplicated the parliament to restore their sequestrated estates. Their petitions received no answer till the last day of the session, and were then rejected, on the pretence that no one appeared to support them. An express enactment was even made, by which all rights to tithes, granted subsequently to the sixth of March, 1559, by the Archbishops of St. Andrews and Glasgow, the Bishops of Murray, Dunkeld, and Dunblane, the Abbots of Dunfermline and Crossraguel, the Priors of

Dr. Lorimer, Scottish Reformation, p. 246. Knox mentions that the only temporal peers who opposed the confession were the Earl of Atholl, and the Lords Somerville and Borthwick. Randolph, the English envoy, states in a letter to Cecil, as quoted by Mr. Tytler, that the lords who opposed it were the Earls of Cassillis and Caithness. In relating the proceedings of the parliament, I have chiefly relied on the authority of a letter sent by the primate to the Archbishop of Glasgow on the day after the vote was taken, which was preserved among the archives of the Scots College at Paris, and is printed by Keith. Archbishop Hamilton could hardly be mistaken, and had no motive to give a wrong account to his brother-prelate. The primate mentions, in the commencement of his letter, that he writes, more for the sake of friendship, than that he had any matter of importance to communicate. This remark shews how little weight he attached to the parliamentary sanction of the new confession.

Whithorn and Pluscardine, and certain other of the chief opponents of the Congregation, were declared to be of no avail. On the twenty-fourth of August the parliament rose.[1]

Such were the acts concerning religion passed by the convention of estates which met at Edinburgh, in August, 1560. By these statutes, the parties then possessing the temporal authority in Scotland set up a new rule of faith; threw off the supremacy of the Roman see; abolished the offices and ceremonies formerly used at Baptism and the Eucharist; and forbade the celebration of the sacraments themselves by the clergy of the Church. Nothing was yet said regarding the mode by which lawful ministers were to be admitted, or the source whence their authority was to be derived; and, so far as the mere words of the statutes went, the hierarchy, though bound to adopt a new creed, and forbidden to obey the Pope, or to minister the sacraments according to the ancient ritual, might still have been supposed to be the only body entitled to exercise ecclesiastical jurisdiction in the kingdom.

[1] Acts of the Parliaments of Scotland, vol. ii. pp. 534, 535. Knox, vol. ii. p. 123-125. Keith, vol. i. p. 322-326; vol. iii. p. 7-11. It is stated by Tytler and others that the parliament rose on the twenty-seventh of August. The twenty-fourth of that month is the day given by Thomas Archibald, in a letter to the Archbishop of Glasgow, written from Edinburgh on the twenty-eighth of August; see Keith, vol. iii. p. 8.

CHAPTER XXXIII.

FROM THE PARLIAMENT OF AUGUST, 1560, TO THE RETURN OF QUEEN MARY TO SCOTLAND, IN AUGUST, 1561.

The Confession of Faith—The compilers of the Confession— The Book of Discipline—The Book of Common Order— The Superintendents—First General Assembly—Proposed alteration in the law of Marriage—Convention of the Estates—Aberdeen clergy summoned before the Estates— Act for demolishing abbey-churches and cloisters—Commissioners sent by the Estates, and by the Roman Catholic nobles, to Queen Mary—Return of Mary to Scotland.

THE Confession of Faith, ratified and approved by the parliament of August, 1560, consisted of twenty-five chapters. Beginning with the belief in One God, Father, Son, and Holy Ghost, it set forth the Creation of man; his Fall, whereby the image of his Maker was utterly defaced; the promise of a Saviour; the continuance of the Church from Adam to the coming of the Messiah; the Incarnation of Christ, very God and very man, united in one person—condemning the heresies of Arius, Marcion, Eutyches, Nestorius, and all others who deny the eternity of his Godhead, or the verity of his human nature; his Passion, Death, and Burial; his Descent into hell; his Resurrection and Ascension; his Session at the right hand of God, from which He shall visibly return at the Judgment of the last day; and faith in the Holy Ghost, who is equal with the Father and the Son.

After explaining whence good works proceed, and in what they consist, it defined the Church to be a company of men, chosen of God, who rightly worship and embrace Him by true faith in Christ Jesus, its only Head; Catholic, as containing the elect of all ages, the Communion of Saints, out of which there is neither life nor eternal felicity; invisible, known only to God, who alone knows whom He has chosen. The notes whereby the true Church is known from the false one are neither antiquity, usurped title, lineal descent, place appointed, nor multitude of men approving an error; but, first, the true preaching of the word; secondly, the right administration of the sacraments; and, thirdly, ecclesiastical discipline, uprightly ministered. When controversy arises as to the meaning of any part of Scripture, or for the reformation of any abuse in the Church of God, regard should not so much be given to what men have before said or done, as to what the Holy Ghost uniformly speaks in the Scriptures, and what Christ Himself did and commanded to be done. The decrees of General Councils are not to be received without due examination. Such councils were convened, not to make any perpetual law or new articles of belief, but partly for the confutation of heresies, and partly for the good policy and order of the Church. But no policy, or order in ceremonies, can be appointed for all times and places; for as ceremonies, such as men have devised, are but temporal, so they may and ought to be changed when they foster superstition, rather than conduce to edification.

The sacraments were next defined. There are only two under the Gospel, Baptism and the Supper of the Lord. They are utterly to be condemned who affirm that the sacraments are nothing but naked and bare signs. By Baptism we are ingrafted into Christ Jesus, to be made partakers of his righteousness, by which our sins are covered and remitted; and in the Supper, rightly used, Christ is so joined with us, that He becomes the very nourishment and food of our souls. To the right administration of the sacraments two things are necessary; first, that they be ministered by lawful ministers, who are only those that are appointed to the preaching of the word, or into whose mouths God has put some sermon of exhortation, they being lawfully chosen thereto by some Church; secondly, that they be ministered in such elements, and in such sort, as God has appointed. Baptism appertaineth to the infants of the faithful, as well as to those who are of age and discretion; but the Supper of the Lord to those only who, being of the household of faith, can try and examine themselves, as well in their faith, as in their duty towards their neighbours.

The power of the Civil Magistrate is declared to be God's ordinance. Such persons as are placed in authority are to be loved, honoured, feared, and held in most reverent estimation, as being God's vicegerents, to whom also chiefly pertain the reformation and purgation of religion.[1]

The compilers of the Confession were Knox, Winram, Spottiswood, Willock, Row, and John Douglas, rector of the University of St. Andrews. Winram was not concerned only in drawing it up: to him and to Maitland of Lethington commission was given, apparently by some of the temporal lords, to revise it before publication. They modified many words and sentences, and, in particular, recommended the leaving out of a chapter on the obedience and disobedience of subjects towards their magistrates. It is probably allowable to trace in the language and character of the formulary the influence of the conciliatory opinions of Winram; and, if the conjecture formerly mentioned, as to the share which that divine had in preparing the catechism agreed to in the council of 1552, be correct, it is singular that the statements of doctrine put forth both by the Roman Catholic and by the Reformed Church should have been composed or modified by the same individual. It was no doubt owing to the recommendation of Lethington and Winram that the chapter in the Confession on the Civil Magistrate was drawn up in the language finally adopted—language which gives no encouragement to the political theories of the school of Knox and Goodman.[2]

After the dissolution of parliament, the same five persons who had been entrusted by the Protestants with preparing a confession of their doctrine were also empowered to draw up a statement of the discipline which they proposed to establish. A draft of such a work had been prepared before the parliament met, and it was now revised and completed. The volume was submitted to a convention of the nobility, which met at Edinburgh in January, 1561, and various opinions were expressed regarding it. Some approved of it, and were desirous that it should receive the authority of law; others, who feared the censures which their own evil lives might

---

[1] See Acts of the Parliaments of Scotland, vol. ii. p. 526-534, and Knox, vol. ii. p. 95-120.

[2] Knox, vol. ii. p. 128. Letter, Randolph to Cecil, dated 7th September, 1560, as quoted by Mr. Tytler, vol. vi. p. 183, and by Dr. Lorimer, Scottish Reformation, p. 245. See also Calendar of State Papers relating to Scotland, vol. i. p. 162.

provoke, or who had partaken largely in the spoils of the Church, opposed it altogether, styling it in mockery a devout imagination. It received the support, however, of many of the nobility, and, though not formally sanctioned by the convention, was subscribed on the twenty-seventh of January by the Duke of Chatel-herault, his son the Earl of Arran, the Earl Marischal, the Earls of Argyll, Glencairn, Monteith, Morton, and Rothes, the Lords Yester, Boyd, Ochiltree, and Lindsay, the Bishop of Galloway, the Prior of St. Andrews, the Commendator of Culross, the Dean of Murray, and others. They added a proviso to their subscriptions, that the bishops, abbots, priors, and other prelates and beneficed persons who had joined the Congregation, should enjoy their ecclesiastical revenues during their lifetime, under the burden of sustaining the ministers of the word and sacraments.[1]

The Book of Discipline was divided into nine heads.

The first head declared it necessary that the Gospel should be truly and openly preached, and that all doctrine repugnant thereto should be utterly suppressed. By the Gospel, it was added, is meant not only the New, but the Old Testament; and by the contrary doctrine are understood all laws, counsels, or constitutions, imposed on the consciences of men, without the express command of God's word, among which are specified vows of chastity, superstitious observance of fasting days, prayer for the dead, and keeping holy-days commanded by man, such as the feasts, as they are styled, of Apostles, Martyrs, Virgins, of Christmas, Circumcision, Epiphany, the Purification, and other feasts of our Lady.

The second head declared that there were only two sacraments, Baptism and the Holy Supper of the Lord. In Baptism the element of water alone is to be used, and all additions to it are forbidden. At the Supper, sitting at a table is declared to be most convenient, because our Lord Himself sat with his disciples. The error of the Papists in defrauding the people of the cup is condemned. The minister is to break the bread, and distribute it to those next to him, commanding the rest, every one with reverence and sobriety, to break with each other. During this action, some comfortable places of Scrip-

---

[1] Knox, vol. ii. p. 128-130.

ture, bringing to mind the death of Christ, are to be read at the discretion of the minister.

The third head required the utter suppression of idolatry, and all the monuments thereof, such as abbeys, monkeries, friaries, nunneries, chapels, chantries, cathedral churches, canonries, and colleges, other than those then used as parish churches or schools, and excepting also the palaces, mansions, and dwelling places adjacent thereto, with the gardens and orchards.

The fourth head related to Ministers and their lawful election. No one ought to preach or administer the sacraments, till he is regularly called to the office. Ordinary vocation consists in Election, Examination, and Admission. It appertaineth to the people and to every several congregation to elect their own minister. Examination is to be in public, by the ministers and elders of the Church. Admission is also to be public. A sermon is to be preached by some specified minister touching the duties of the office, and an exhortation is to be given, both to the minister to be admitted and to the people. It is declared that no other ceremony is necessary besides the approbation of the people, and declaration of the chief minister that the person there presented is appointed to serve his particular church; for albeit the Apostles used the imposition of hands, yet, as the miracle has ceased, the using of the ceremony is judged not to be necessary. In those churches where no ministers can be had, Readers are to be provided, able to read distinctly the Common Prayers and Scriptures, who afterwards, if duly qualified, may be raised to the degree of ministers.

The fifth head related to the provision for the ministers, and the distribution of the rents and possessions of the Church. These provisions were to vary according to the rank and condition of the persons on whom they were bestowed; larger sums being required for the superintendents than for other ministers, and for ministers than for readers, the readers getting an increase of their salaries when they were able to act as exhorters. The Exhorters were recognised as a sort of middle order between the common reader and the minister. It was further declared that, if all the ministers were appointed to fixed places, the greatest part of the realm would be destitute of doctrine. It was therefore thought expedient for that time, that, from the whole number of godly and learned men, so many should be selected, with power to plant and erect churches, and to appoint ministers within the bounds of their several jurisdictions. The districts and places of residence proposed to be assigned to the superintendents were mentioned. The Superintendent of Orkney was to reside at Kirkwall, and to have for his diocese Orkney, Zetland, Caithness, and Strathnaver. The Superintendent of Ross was to reside at Canonry of Ross, and to have for his diocese Ross, Sutherland, Murray, and the isles of Skye and Lewis. The diocese of the Superintendent of Argyll was to comprehend Argyll, Kintyre, Lorn, Lochaber, the South Isles, Arran, and Bute, and he was to reside in Argyll. The Superintendent of Aberdeen was to reside at Old Aberdeen, and to have for his diocese the counties of Aberdeen and Banff. The Superintendent of Brechin, whose residence was to be in that city, was to have Angus and Mearns for his diocese. The Superintendent of St. Andrews, who was to reside in that city, was to have for his diocese the sheriffdoms of Fife and Perth, and Fothric as far as Stirling. The Superintendent of Edinburgh was to reside in that city, and to have for his diocese the Lothians, Merse, Lauderdale, Wedale, and the sheriffdom of Stirling to the south of the Forth. The Superintendent of Jedburgh was to reside in that town, and to have for his diocese Teviotdale, Tweeddale, Liddisdale, and Ettrick Forest. The Superintendent of Glasgow was to reside in that city, and to have for his diocese Clydesdale, Renfrew, Monteith, Lennox, Kyle, and Cunningham. The Superintendent of Dumfries, whose residence was to be in that town, was to have for his diocese Galloway, Carrick, Nithsdale, Annandale, and the other dales in the West. If the superintendent were negligent of his duties, he was to be deprived, without respect to his person or office. Rules were laid down for the election of superintendents, similar to those established in the case of ministers. Other ceremonies than examination, approbation of the ministers and superintendents, and the public consent of the elders and people, were not allowed.

Under the same head, provision was made for education. Every church situated in a town of any size was to have a

Schoolmaster attached to it; in other places, the reader or minister was to instruct the youth in the catechism contained in the Book of Common Order. In every large town, especially where a superintendent resided, there was to be a college for teaching the arts and languages. The universities were to be continued as before at St. Andrews, Glasgow, and Aberdeen, and the course of study there was pointed out.

The sixth head related to the rents and patrimony of the Church, from which it was declared that the ministers, the schools, and the poor, should be supported.

The seventh head referred to Ecclesiastical Discipline, especially to the rules established in regard to Excommunication.

The eighth head related to the election of Elders and Deacons. These office-bearers were to be chosen yearly in each congregation. The elders were to assist the minister in all the public affairs of the Church, in judging of causes, and in admonishing licentious livers. They were also to take heed to the life, manners, diligence, and study of the minister himself, to admonish and correct him, and, where necessary, with consent of the Church and superintendent, to depose him. The office of the deacons was to receive the rents, and gather the alms of the Church, and to keep and distribute them as should be appointed. They were also to assist in judgment with the ministers and elders, and might be admitted to read publicly, if required, and found fit for that duty. The elders and deacons were to receive no stipend, because their office was only from year to year, and because their services did not prevent them from attending to their own private business.

The ninth head related to the Policy of the Church. It was declared that there were two sorts of Policy, one absolutely necessary, as that the word be truly preached, the sacraments rightly administered, common prayers publicly made, children and ignorant persons instructed in the chief points of religion, and offenders corrected and punished, without which things there is not even the face of a visible Church; the other, profitable but not necessary, as, that Psalms should be sung, that certain places of the Scripture should be read when there is no sermon, and that the Church should assemble on this or that number of days during the week. In matters of the latter sort, every particular Church was allowed to prescribe its own rules. It was thought expedient that in great towns there should be either Sermon or Common Prayer every day, with some exercise of reading the Scriptures. On the days when there was a public sermon, it was neither required nor greatly approved that the Common Prayers should be used, lest the people should be fostered in superstition who came to the Prayers as they came to Mass, or else occasion be given to suppose that those were no prayers which were made before and after the sermon. In all towns the Sunday was to be regularly kept, the word being preached, the sacraments administered, and marriage solemnized, in the forenoon, and the children taught the catechism in the afternoon. Baptism might be administered whenever the word was preached. Four times a year was thought sufficient for the administration of the Lord's Table, in which the superstition of seasons, such as Easter, was to be avoided, and none were to be admitted to that mystery who could not say the Lord's Prayer, the Belief, and the Ten Commandments.

It was thought expedient that in all towns, where there were schools and learned men, one day every week should be appointed for the exercise which St. Paul calls Prophesying. These exercises were declared to be most necessary at that time for the Church of God in Scotland, and rules were laid down for their proper and becoming observance. Marriage, as a general rule, was to be solemnized publicly on Sundays before sermon, the banns having previously been duly proclaimed. Marriage was only to be dissolved on account of adultery; and the Civil Magistrate was exhorted to inflict on adulterers the punishment of death. To prevent superstition, it was judged best that neither singing nor reading should be allowed at Burials. Churches were ordered to be kept in proper repair, and each was to be provided with a bell to summon the people together, a pulpit, a basin for baptism, and tables for the ministration of the Lord's Supper. It was declared that papistical priests have neither power nor authority to minister the sacraments of Christ, because that in their mouth is not the sermon of exhortation; and it is neither the clipping of crowns, the crossing of fingers, the blowing of the dumb dogs, called the bishops, neither yet the laying on of their hands, which maketh true ministers of Christ Jesus, but the Spirit of God, first inwardly moving the heart to seek God's glory and the good of the Church, and thereafter the nomination of the people, the examination of the learned, and public admission, as before mentioned.[1]

The Book of Discipline has several references to the mode of worship observed at that time among the Reformed in Scotland, and makes special mention of the Book of Common Order, called the Order of Geneva. In the beginning of the religious movement, and while the contest between the queen-regent and the Congregation was yet undecided, the English Book of Common Prayer was used by many of the Scottish Protestants. But, when the struggle was over, and the Reformed had acquired ascendency, the preference was naturally given to a formulary much more in accordance with the opinions and tastes of their leaders, and the English Order was gradually superseded by that of Geneva. The latter was originally compiled for the use of the English congregation at Geneva, while Knox was their minister.

The Book of Common Order contained a form of prayer for the ordinary assemblies of the congregation. It began with a Confession of Sins, said by the minister alone, but the people were enjoined to follow in their hearts the tenor of his words. The people then sung a psalm to a plain tune, after which the minister, having first prayed for the assistance of God's Holy Spirit in words of his own selection, proceeded to the sermon. When the sermon was over, the minister said the appointed prayer for the whole state of Christ's Church, concluding with the Lord's Prayer. A short prayer followed for continuance and increase in faith, and after it the Apostles' Creed was repeated. The people then sung another psalm, and the minister pronounced a short blessing, either in the form contained in the sixth chapter of the Book of Numbers, or in that in the thirteenth chapter of the Second Epistle of St. Paul to the Corinthians, the first person plural being substituted for the second in the words of blessing. Forms were also prescribed for the administration of the sacraments. Baptism was forbidden to be administered by women, or in

[1] Knox, vol. ii. p. 181-260. Spottiswood, vol. i. p. 331-372.

private. After an exhortation by the minister, the father or godfather was ordered to rehearse the Apostles' Creed, the meaning of which was explained by the minister. A prayer followed, concluding with the Lord's Prayer. The name of the child was then asked, and baptism was administered by sprinkling water on its forehead, in the Name of the Father, and the Son, and the Holy Ghost. The service was finished by the minister giving thanks to God. In the form of administering the Lord's Supper, the minister first recited St. Paul's account of its institution, from the First Epistle to the Corinthians. He then proceeded to an exhortation on the subject of the sacrament, after which he came down from the pulpit, and seated himself at the table with the congregation. He next took bread, and gave thanks in the form prescribed; and this done, he broke the bread, and delivered it to the people, who distributed and divided it among themselves: and so also in regard to the cup. During this time, certain places of the Scripture, setting forth the death of Christ, were ordered to be read. A prayer of thanksgiving was then said by the minister; the people sung the hundred-and-third psalm; and one of the benedictions before-mentioned was recited.

A form of Marriage was also given, and a prayer to be said at the Visitation of the Sick. The Book concluded with some instructions on the order of Ecclesiastical Discipline.

The systems of doctrine and church government laid down in the Confession of Faith and the Book of Discipline are sufficiently distinct, and require little illustration. The Scottish reformers adopted no doctrines, except what they held to be revealed in the Scriptures; and in the interpretation of the Scriptures they rejected all authority whatever, except the text of the Bible itself, neither the ancient nor the existing Church being appealed to as a witness or interpreter of the faith. The Church itself was held to exist, not in virtue of any life of its own, derived from its Lord through the Apostles, but in consequence of the belief of its members in the system of doctrine revealed in the Scriptures. The visible Church was not tied down to any one rule of divine polity. Government and discipline in themselves were necessary, but no particular form was prescribed. As to this the Congregation could judge what was best. As all religious truth was derived from the Scriptures, so all ecclesiastical power proceeded from the people; and from them directly, not from any divine commission or descent, the office-bearers of the Church derived their authority. Ordination of ministers by the laying on of hands was rejected as needless and superstitious.

As the primitive doctrine of the Christian ministry was thus utterly thrown aside, so also the old ritual in which the Church had commemorated the life and actions of our Saviour was renounced. There was no distinction of seasons; even the great feast of Easter was no longer observed. The Sunday alone remained, and was ordered to be kept as a day of religious worship; but it does not clearly appear in what light it was viewed at the commencement of the Reformation, and at the time of its first establishment by the civil power. At the date of the Confession of Faith and the Book of Discipline, it was still known by its ancient name, and it is probable that the gradual adoption of the new title of Sabbath marked a change in the opinion which was taking place regarding it.

Both in faith and in ritual, the change was a mixture of good and evil. The papal supremacy, and, with it, many erroneous opinions and superstitions, usages and ceremonies, were abolished; the Bible was made freely accessible; and the common prayers were offered in a language understood by the people. But, on the other hand, in matters of doctrine, the ancient truth was obscured or disregarded in various ways; and, in ritual, the daily service and the frequent communion, the hallowed buildings, the return of fast and festival, the ordered hierarchy, and the consecrated priesthood, found no place.

It has been contended by some writers that, in two important points, the difference between the old and the new system was more apparent than real—that the episcopal government of the Church was kept up in the persons of the superintendents, and that the liturgical offices were continued under another form. This opinion seems to be erroneous. The superintendent scheme was never fully carried out, and doubts have been raised whether it was regarded by its promoters as more than a temporary arrangement; but, had it been otherwise, it bore only a faint external resemblance to the hierarchy. Unordained themselves, the superintendents could not ordain others; appointed by the ministers and people, and liable to be deposed by them, they neither possessed nor claimed distinct independent jurisdiction. So also it was in regard to liturgical forms. Except in name, the new service bore little resemblance to the old. There was no distinction of morning or evening, of day or season; no alternation of suffrage and response, psalm, and hymn, and lesson; no absolution, or consecration, or authoritative blessing: even the form, such as it was, partook more of the character of a directory than of a liturgy. The minister was not restricted to the words of the book before him, but was expressly allowed to substitute his own language where the alteration might seem desirable.

Such were the changes in belief, and discipline, and ritual, which marked the commencement of the Reformation. The practical bearings of those changes on the condition of the Scottish people will be learned from the course of events which followed.

On the twentieth day of December, 1560, the ministers and commissioners of the Reformed communion met at Edinburgh. This meeting is generally referred to as the first General Assembly. A considerable number of lay commissioners appeared; of the superintendents, Erskine alone was present; the only persons bearing the name of ministers were Knox, Goodman, Row, Lindsay, Harlaw, and Christison.

On the twenty-first of December, two resolutions were agreed to. By the first, the people of the parish of Restalrig were ordered to resort to Leith for the ministry of the word and sacraments, and the church of Restalrig was appointed to be cast down and utterly destroyed, as a monument of idolatry. Restalrig was a collegiate church for secular priests, entirely unconnected with the monastic orders; and no reason can be given for its demolition which would not equally apply to any parish church in the kingdom. It was perhaps singled out on this occasion, because its dean, John Sinclair, was one of the ablest opponents of the Reformation. The second resolution declared that, by the law of God, marriage might be solemnized between parties being of the second, third, and fourth degrees of consanguinity or affinity, and all others not expressly forbidden by the Scriptures; and the estates were requested to interpose their authority to this ordinance. Of the many practical abuses prevalent in the Scottish Church at the time of the Reformation, none was attended with worse results to the morals of the people than the enforcement of the rules of the canon law regarding consanguinity and affinity in marriage, and the liability of marriages contracted within the forbidden degrees to be dissolved as absolutely null. This rule, strict in appearance, led in reality to the most shameful laxity, and to an almost unlimited freedom of divorce to those who were able to afford the expense of an action in the consistorial court. The decree of the assembly of 1560, and the rule regarding divorce contained in the Book of Discipline, were the first steps towards the restoration of greater domestic purity.

On the twenty-seventh of December, it was agreed to petition parliament to punish as idolaters certain persons who celebrated mass, or were present at its celebration. The individuals named resided in Nithsdale, Galloway, Kyle, Carrick, Cunningham, Ettrick Forest, East Lothian, and Fife; and among them were the Earls of Eglinton and Cassillis, the Abbot of Crossraguel, and the Prior of Whithorn. It is stated that mass was openly said in the parish churches of Maybole, Girvan, Kirk-Oswald, and Dailly.

The assembly was adjourned to the fifteenth of January, at which time parliament was to meet.[1]

On the fifteenth of January, 1561, a convention of the estates, or at least of the nobility, met at Edinburgh, and it is probable that the ministers and commissioners of the Congregation assembled at the same time, though no record of their meeting has been preserved. It was to this convention, as already mentioned, that the Book of Discipline was presented. Several members of the Roman Church were summoned to appear before the estates, four from the diocese of Aberdeen being particularly specified—Alexander Anderson, Principal of the King's College, John Leslie, Official of the diocese, Patrick Myrton, Treasurer, and James Strachan, one of the canons of the cathedral. These divines were questioned as to their faith, especially in regard to the mass, by Knox, Willock, and Goodman. According to Leslie's

[1] Book of the Universal Kirk, Peterkin's ed. p. 1-5. Keith, vol. iii. p. 25-31.

narrative, Anderson discoursed with such learning on the sacrifice of the altar, that the Catholics were confirmed in their opinions, and the Protestants were unable to gainsay him. Knox, on the other hand, mentions that Anderson denied a propitiatory sacrifice in the mass, affirming that there was one of commemoration only, but was unable to defend even the latter proposition, while Leslie declined to offer any argument whatever. Knox not only claims the advantage in controversy, but, as usual, ridicules the personal character of his opponents. With more reason, he appeals to this conference as a proof that the Reformed, although they now had the ascendency in the state, were not unwilling to listen to the arguments of their adversaries.[1]

Another assembly of the Reformed met within the Tolbooth at Edinburgh, on the twenty-seventh of May. The names of the members present are not mentioned. The record bears that a complaint was laid before the privy council, and the convention of the estates, touching the suppression of idolatry and other points. The document bore, that the pestilent generation of the Roman Antichrist were endeavouring anew to erect their idolatry; and it craved that such attempts should be repressed, otherwise the brethren would be obliged to take the sword themselves for that purpose. The lords of the council made an act agreeing to their request.[2]

In the convention of the estates which met in May, an act was passed for demolishing such abbey churches and cloisters as yet remained. Its execution was intrusted, in the West, to the Earls of Arran, Argyll, and Glencairn; in the North, to the Prior of St. Andrews; and, in other parts of the kingdom, to various nobles. Paisley was burned, its commendator, the Archbishop of St. Andrews, escaping with difficulty; and Failford, Kilwinning, and Crossraguel, were wholly or partially demolished. Spottiswood mentions that, under colour of this act, a miserable devastation ensued of all churches without distinction, the multitude readily following the example which had been given them by persons in au-

---

[1] Leslie, p. 530. Knox, vol. ii. p. 138-142. Keith, vol. iii. p. 31-33. Diurnal of Occurrents, p. 63.

[2] Book of the Universal Kirk, pp. 5, 6. Knox, vol. ii. p. 161-164. Keith, vol. iii. p. 33-36.

thority. The buildings themselves were destroyed; their whole furniture, the holy vessels, and bells, and whatever else could be made gain of, were sold; books and registers were burned; and even the graves of the dead did not escape violation.[1] It was probably at this time that St. Andrews, and the other churches in the midland counties, which had formerly escaped, or only been partially injured, were entirely ruined. The act could not be strictly enforced in the remote provinces of the North and West, where some of the great nobles yet maintained the ancient ritual.

During all these events, the members of the hierarchy seem to have abstained from any open assertion of their authority. The only proper ecclesiastical act, mentioned at this time, is the nomination of William Chisholm, as coadjutor and successor to his uncle of the same name in the see of Dunblane. The brief of Pope Pius IV., by which the appointment took place, was dated on the second of June, 1561.[2]

After the dissolution of the parliament of August, 1560, Sir James Sandilands, Prior of the Knights of St. John, was sent to France, to give an account of what had been transacted to the King and Queen of the Scots. His reception was such as was probably anticipated. The Cardinal of Lorraine expressed the feeling of the French court in a conversation with the English ambassador, Throckmorton. "I will tell you frankly," he said, "the Scots, the king's subjects, do perform no part of their duties; the king and the queen have the name of their sovereigns, and your mistress hath the effect and the obedience. They would bring the realm to a republic, and say in their words, they are the king's subjects." The Prior of St. John was received personally with courtesy, but Francis and Mary refused to ratify the treaty of Edinburgh.

The death of Francis, in the beginning of December, materially altered the position of matters in Scotland. The interests of the widowed queen were no longer necessarily bound up with those of France, and there was reason to be-

---

[1] Buchanan, vol. i. p. 328. Knox, vol. ii. pp. 167, 168. Spottiswood, vol. i. pp. 372, 373. Spottiswood is evidently mistaken in ascribing this act to the same convention to which the Book of Discipline was submitted—that is, the convention of January, 1561. Knox states that the act was passed by the privy council.

[2] Keith's Catalogue, p. 180.

lieve that many who had opposed her mother, and courted the English alliance from the dread of French supremacy, would now heartily return to their allegiance. This opinion was fondly cherished by Mary herself. In the month of February, commissioners arrived in Scotland, intrusted with a conciliatory message from the queen to the estates, assuring them of her forgiveness for all that was past, and announcing her speedy return. They were also the bearers of a commission to the Duke of Chatel-herault, the Primate, the Earls of Atholl, Huntly, Argyll, and Bothwell, and the Prior of St. Andrews, containing authority to summon a parliament in the queen's name.

At the meeting of the convention in January, the Prior of St. Andrews had received instructions to repair to the queen, and tender to her their duty and allegiance. He passed through England, and on the way had an interview with Elizabeth and Cecil. John Leslie, Official of Aberdeen, left Scotland about the same time, intrusted with a message to the queen from the Earls of Huntly, Atholl, Crawford, and Sutherland, the Bishops of Murray and Ross, and other chief persons of the nobility and clergy, opposed to the ruling party in the convention. Leslie anticipated the Prior in obtaining an interview with Mary. On the fourteenth of April, he was admitted to her presence at Vitry, in Champagne. On the part of Huntly and his associates, he warned her to beware of the Prior of St. Andrews, advising her to detain him in France till after her arrival in Scotland; at all events that she herself should land at Aberdeen, where her faithful subjects in the North would meet her with an army of twenty thousand men, and conduct her to Edinburgh. The queen received Leslie kindly, but refused to accede to his proposals. She was anxious to secure the obedience of all her subjects, and was determined not to be the mere sovereign of a party. She also suspected the fidelity of Huntly, knowing the doubtful policy which he had pursued during the contest between her mother and the Congregation. On the following day, the Prior of St. Andrews met her at St. Dizier. He was welcomed by his sister with great affection, and soon admitted to her confidence, but she still peremptorily refused to ratify the treaty of Edinburgh. Mary's trust was ill repaid. Her designs were betrayed by the Prior to Elizabeth, and, when preparing to sail for Scotland she applied to the English queen for a passport, her request was refused, and secret preparations were made to intercept her on the voyage. She embarked at Calais, and, escaping from the English ships, arrived in safety at Leith, on the nineteenth of August.[1]

[1] Leslie, p. 531-535. Knox, vol. ii. p. 125-143. Spottiswood, vol. i. p. 328-331. Keith, vol. ii. p. 1-62. Tytler, vol. vi. p. 191-235. I have followed the narrative of Leslie himself, in regard to the proceedings connected with his mission to France. Spottiswood mentions (vol. i. p. 329) that the letter which he carried was subscribed by the Archbishop of St. Andrews, and the Bishop of Aberdeen, as well as by the other peers and prelates named in the text, and with this, Keith (vol. ii. p. 13), and Tytler (vol. vi. p. 207), agree. The statement may be correct, but I am not aware of any earlier authority for it than that of Spottiswood.

CHAPTER XXXIV.

FROM THE RETURN OF QUEEN MARY TO SCOTLAND, IN AUGUST, 1561, TO THE REASONING BETWEEN THE ABBOT OF CROSSRAGUEL AND JOHN KNOX, IN SEPTEMBER, 1562.

Difficulties of Queen Mary—Her prudent government—Her interview with Knox—Efforts of the Protestant ministers to obtain a competent maintenance—John Craig, minister at Edinburgh—Controversial discussions between the clergy and the ministers—Ninian Winzet, schoolmaster at Linlithgow—His Tractate addressed to the Queen—His eighty-three questions delivered to Knox—He is obliged to leave Scotland—Reasoning between Quintin Kennedy and John Knox.

WHEN Mary Stewart returned to assume in person the government of her kingdom, she was only in her nineteenth year. The enthusiastic welcome, which she received from her subjects on her arrival at Edinburgh, seemed to warrant a hope that the factions into which Scotland was divided were to be united in one feeling of attachment to their young sovereign. A few days, however, showed that any expectations of this kind were fallacious. Other difficulties in the queen's position might have been overcome, but one was insurmountable. Mary, by education and conviction, was zealously attached to the Church of Rome; the most numerous and influential portion of her subjects were determined to maintain the principles of the Reformation. The first untoward circumstance which occurred arose from this difference in religion.

The queen had been accompanied to Scotland by three of her uncles, princes of the house of Lorraine, by a son of the Constable Montmorency, and other nobles and gentlemen of France, and by a Parisian doctor of the Sorbonne, besides her own ladies and domestics. On the Sunday after her arrival, being St. Bartholomew's day, preparations were made to celebrate mass in the queen's private chapel at Holyrood. This proceeding was denounced by the more zealous of the

Reformed. Some said, "Shall that idol be suffered again within the realm?" And the Master of Lindsay exclaimed, "The idolatrous priest shall die the death, according to God's law." The Prior of St. Andrews, placing himself before the chapel door, succeeded in preventing violence, and, when the service was over, got the officiating priest conveyed away in safety. In the afternoon, the Reformed, assembling before the abbey in great numbers, repeated their threats of vengeance, and the terrified attendants of the queen began to speak of returning to France, since their religion was not tolerated in Scotland.

The privy council having assembled on the following day, proclamation was made, that the queen was soon to take the advice of the estates in regard to the differences in religion, but, in the meantime, that no one should attempt to alter what was at present established. Farther, all persons were forbidden to disturb her majesty's domestic servants, or those who had come from France, on any pretence whatever. The privy council was at this time composed exclusively of Protestants, and this act indicated the line of conduct which its leading members had resolved to adopt—the protection of the Reformed religion as established by the convention of the preceding year, and toleration to the queen and her attendants to worship God agreeably to the ritual of their Church. According to a fashion not unusual in Scotland, and which in after times became very common, the Earl of Arran publicly protested against the royal proclamation, declaring that the queen's servants who were guilty of idolatry were no more to be tolerated than if they were guilty ot murder. This open defiance of authority encouraged other chief men of the Congregation to resort to Edinburgh, for the purpose of giving their assistance in the same cause; but the queen's measures were so prudent, and her conduct was so conciliatory, that no outrage took place. Many even of the Reformed leaders were won over to submission. "My lord," said Campbell of Kingzeancleuch, a zealous Protestant, to the Lord Ochiltree, "You are come and almost last of all, and I perceive you are yet warm; but, when the holy water of the court is sprinkled upon you, you will become temperate like the rest. I have been here five days, and at first 1 heard every man say, 'Hang the priest;'

but after they have been twice or thrice at the abbey, all their fervency is past. I think there be some enchantment whereby men are bewitched." Knox, who relates this, adds, that the queen's flattering words, ever crying, "Conscience, conscience, it is a sore thing to constrain the conscience," and the pretences of her chief supporters among the Reformed that she might be won to their opinions, kept the people in quietness.

Alarmed at the turn which affairs were taking, Knox himself attempted to rouse the multitude to a sense of what he believed to be their duty. On the following Sunday, he preached against idolatry; affirming that one mass was more fearful to him than the landing of ten thousand armed enemies to suppress religion. Whether by the advice of her counsellors, or hoping that her persuasions might win the reformer, as they had gained the nobles, Mary sent for him, and admitted him to an interview, none being present except the Prior of St. Andrews, and two of her ladies. Knox has left an account of what took place. The queen charged him with stirring up her subjects against her mother, and with writing his book against the government of women. Knox answered that, if to rebuke idolatry was to stir up subjects against their princes, then he had done wrong. He defended the doctrine of his book. An Englishman, he understood, had written against it; but he thought himself better able to maintain what was there affirmed, than any ten in Europe to confute it; and he added that, if the realm found no inconvenience from her government, he would be as content to live under her grace, as St. Paul was to live under Nero. The queen asked how his doctrine could be from God, seeing he had taught the people to receive another religion than that which their princes allowed, although God commands subjects to obey their princes. Knox answered that, as religion did not derive its authority from princes, so subjects were not bound to frame their religion according to the appetite of their sovereigns. Had it been otherwise, Daniel and the three Children would have been of the religion of Nebuchadnezzar and Darius, and the Apostles of that of the Roman emperors. "But," added the queen, "none of these men raised the sword against their princes." "Madam," said Knox, "you cannot deny but that they resisted; for those that obey not the commandments which are given in some sort resist." "But yet," said the queen, "they resisted not by the sword." "Madam," replied Knox, "God had not given unto them the power and the means." "Think you," said Mary, "that subjects, having power, may resist their princes?" "If princes," answered Knox, "exceed their bounds, and do against that for which they should be obeyed, no doubt, they may be resisted even by power. For there is neither greater honour nor greater obedience to be given to kings or princes, than God has commanded to be given to father or mother. But so it is, Madam, that the father may be stricken with a frenzy, in the which he would slay his own children. Now, Madam, if the children arise, join themselves together, apprehend the father, take the sword or other weapon from him, and, finally, bind his hands and keep him in prison till his frenzy be overpast; think you Madam, that the children do any wrong, or think you that God will be offended with them that have stayed their father from committing wickedness? It is even so, Madam, with princes that would murder the children of God that are subject unto them. Their blind zeal is nothing but frenzy, and therefore to take the sword from them, to bind their hands, and to cast them into prison till they be brought to a more sober mind, is no disobedience against princes, but just obedience, because it agrees with the will of God."

The queen stood for some time amazed. On the conversation being resumed, Knox alluded to God's command that kings should be nursing fathers of the Church, and queens its nursing mothers. "Yes," said Mary, "but ye are not the Church which I will nourish. I will defend the Church of Rome, for I think it is the true Church of God." Knox asserted that the Roman harlot was not the true and immaculate spouse of Christ. The queen answered that the Scriptures were interpreted one way by the Pope and cardinals, and another by the reformers. "Whom shall I believe, and who shall be judge?" Knox replied, "Ye shall believe God that plainly speaketh in his word; and farther than the word teaches you, ye neither shall believe one nor the other."

After some farther remarks they parted, Knox saying, as he

went away, " I pray God, Madam, that ye may be as blessed within this commonwealth of Scotland, if it be the pleasure of God, as ever Deborah was in the commonwealth of Israel." What Knox's real mind was regarding the queen, appears from the answer which he himself tells us he gave to one who asked the question : " If there be not in her a proud mind, a crafty wit, and an indurate heart against God and his truth, my judgment faileth me."[1]

The nobility having met at Edinburgh, a new privy council was formally constituted on the sixth of September. The members were the Duke of Chatel-herault, the Earls of Huntly, Argyll, Bothwell, Errol, Marischal, Atholl, Morton, Montrose, and Glencairn, the Prior of St. Andrews, the Lord Erskine, and the Treasurer, Secretary, Clerk-Register, and Justice-Clerk. Several of these were Roman Catholics, but neither the primate nor any of the bishops were members, and it was soon observed that the chief direction of affairs was intrusted to the prior, and the secretary, Maitland. The queen could only expect to govern quietly by conciliating the Protestants, and this line of policy was further necessary for obtaining, what for some time had been her most cherished object, the recognition of her right of succession to the English crown, failing the lawful issue of Elizabeth. In the endeavour to attain that wish, the prior and the secretary served their mistress with zeal and fidelity, and the negotiation appeared so hopeful, that the two parties in the Scottish kingdom most opposed to each other became alarmed. The zealous adherents of the Roman see were afraid that the queen would forsake her religion, in order to gain the object of her ambition, and the Reformed ministers, apprehensive that the change would be of a kind for which they were by no means anxious, began to denounce the English Church in the same language which they had formerly applied to that of Rome.[2]

During the month of September, the queen went on a progress to Linlithgow, Stirling, Perth, Dundee, and St. Andrews; all which places, Knox tells us, she polluted with her idolatry.

---

[1] Knox, vol. ii. p. 267-286. Keith, vol. iii. p. 39-43. Tytler, vol. vi. p. 236-241.

[2] Knox, vol ii. p. 286. Keith, vol. ii. pp. 78, 79. Tytler, vol. vi. p. 243-254. Calendar of State Papers relating to Scoland, vol. i. p. 178.

The statement evidently means that the rites of her religion were celebrated in her own presence, during her journey. The Congregation were indignant, and when, after her return to Edinburgh, mass was said at Holyrood on the feast of All Saints, another effort was made to prohibit it. Some of the leading persons among the Protestants met at the house of Makgill, the clerk-register, to discuss the question, whether subjects were entitled to suppress the idolatry of their prince. The ministers argued in the affirmative, but the Prior of St. Andrews, the secretary, the Earl of Morton, and other statesmen, maintained that they could not lawfully do so. It was finally resolved to refer the matter to the Church of Geneva. Knox offered his services to write for an answer, but the secretary said he would do so himself.[1]

The general assembly of the Reformed Church met at Edinburgh, for the third time, in the month of December. The members of the queen's council and their friends among the barons declined to attend, and questioned the lawfulness of such conventions without the sovereign's permission. The assembly requested that the Book of Discipline should be ratified by the queen, but this was refused. A supplication was thereupon presented to the privy council by the lay commissioners, craving that idolatry should be suppressed, the churches planted with true ministers, and some fixed provision made for the preachers. This last request was judged reasonable, and the council, after advising with the nobility and clergy, finally enacted that one third of the ecclesiastical benefices should be bestowed on the ministers and the crown, the other two thirds remaining with the beneficiaries.[2]

A moiety of one third of the revenues of the Church would have been amply sufficient for the needs of the small number of superintendents, ministers, exhorters, and readers of the new establishment, but they never received even that propor-

---

[1] Knox, vol. ii. pp. 291, 292. Buchanan, vol. i. p. 332. It appears that Knox had already written to Calvin on the subject; and, as he does not mention the fact in his History, it may be presumed that the answer was unfavourable to his views. See the letter, as quoted from the Papers edited for the Bannatyne Club by M. Teulet, in the Scottish Ecclesiastical Journal, vol. vii. p. 40.

[2] Knox, vol. ii. p. 294-313. Keith, vol. iii. p. 45-47. See also Keith's appendix, vol. iii. p. 360-390.

tion, and they long vainly importuned their friends among the laity to make some better provision for them. The state of ecclesiastical property at this time was very singular. During the civil war, considerable portions of it had been made over by the prelates and other beneficiaries to their own friends and dependants, and part had been appropriated, without any title whatever, by the most powerful of the nobility and barons. What still nominally belonged to the Church was in the hands of the bishops, abbots, priors, deans, provosts, parsons, and other holders of ecclesiastical benefices; many of whom had never received holy orders at all, or had embraced the Reformed opinions. These were the parties who were now allowed to retain two thirds of their revenues. It may easily be supposed that the account given of the other third to the royal collectors was not a very faithful one; and, when the proportion falling to the sovereign was deducted, little remained for the Reformed ministers, and that little was dealt out to them in the most niggardly manner by the Protestant barons to whom its distribution was intrusted.

The general assembly again met at Edinburgh, on the twenty-ninth of June, 1562. The five superintendents, Winram, Willock, Spottiswood, Carswell, and Erskine, and Knox, Lindsay, Goodman, and other ministers and commissioners, were present. The members continued their sittings till the fourth of July.

A petition was presented to this assembly by the Bishop of Galloway, in which he craved to be recognized as the superintendent of his diocese. The assembly answered, that they were not aware he had been named to that office, either by the privy council, or by the province of Galloway, and, in any event, that the order appointed in regard to the election of a superintendent had not been observed by him, and therefore, at present, he could not be recognized in that capacity; but they offered their assistance, if the churches in Galloway should solicit his appointment, and the lords of the council should grant him a presentation. He was at the same time called upon to subscribe the Book of Discipline, but it is not stated whether he did so.

As Galloway was not by itself one of the districts assigned to a superintendent, but formed part of the district of Dumfries, it would rather seem that Bishop Gordon claimed the office of superintendent of Galloway, as being bishop of the diocese. Having embraced the Protestant opinions, he probably thought that his former ecclesiastical appointment entitled him, without any other election or formality, to a similar position in the Reformed Church.

At this assembly John Craig was appointed to assist Knox as minister at Edinburgh.[1]

Knox's new colleague soon became a leading person in the Congregation. He was born in the beginning of the century, and, like many eminent Scotsmen of that day, was left an orphan by the death of his father on Flodden field. After completing his education at St. Andrews, he resided for some time in England, and, on his return to his own country, joined the Dominican order. Being suspected of holding heretical opinions, he was cast into prison, but, having cleared himself of the charge, he again went to England, and afterwards to Italy, where he acquired the favour of Cardinal Pole, by whose recommendation he was appointed master of the novices in the Dominican convent at Bologna. His diligence and attention to his duties attracted the notice of his superiors, and he was intrusted with the management of various important matters, among others, with a commission to reform a monastery of the order in the isle of Chios. On his return to Italy, he was led to doubt the doctrines of his Church, by perusing a copy of Calvin's Institutions. Having expressed his opinions too freely, he was delated of heresy, and, after a confinement of some weeks, was tried by the Inquisition at Rome, and condemned to be burned. The day appointed for his execution was the nineteenth of August, 1559. On the evening before, Pope Paul IV. died; and the people, who detested his stern rule, broke out into tumult, set fire to the buildings of the Inquisition, and liberated the prisoners. Craig escaped with the rest, and with great difficulty reached the dominions of the Emperor. After residing for some time at Vienna, where he was favourably noticed by the Archduke Maximilian, he returned through Germany and England to his native country. He at once joined himself to the

[1] Book of the Universal Kirk, p 8-11. Knox, vol. ii. p. 337-345. Calderwood, vol. ii. p. 183-194. Keith, vol. iii. p. 51-59.

Reformed, but was at first, on account of his long residence abroad, unable to preach in his mother tongue. He therefore preached in Latin, in St. Magdalen's chapel at Edinburgh, and was afterwards minister of the Canongate for a short time previous to his appointment as colleague to Knox.[1]

While the Reformed, in their assemblies and by their individual efforts, were endeavouring to confirm the ascendency which they had acquired, the Roman Catholic prelates, content with securing the greater portion of their estates, appear to have made no systematic effort to regain the influence they had lost, or to supply the ordinances of the Church to those who still adhered to it. There was, no doubt, some danger in the attempt, and they were not disposed to incur much risk. So far indeed as theological controversy was necessary, few of them were qualified to take any part in it. Some exceptions, however, there were, even among the prelates; and, in the ranks of the inferior clergy, a considerable number were not deterred by the apathy of their rulers, or by the hazards to which they were exposed, from exerting themselves in defence of their Church. The conference between the Protestant ministers and the clergy of Aberdeen has already been referred to. Other controversial discussions took place at various times, though the details, in most cases, have not been preserved. A short time before the queen's return, there was a public disputation at Edinburgh on the sacrament of the altar, between Willock and a Dominican named John Black. It lasted two days, but without any advantage on either side. In the course of the same year, Ninian Winzet, a priest and schoolmaster at Linlithgow, disputed in that town, first with

---

[1] Spottiswood, vol. iii. p. 91-94. Craig appears to have told marvellous stories about his adventures subsequent to his escape from the Inquisition. These are singular enough, as related by Spottiswood on the authority of persons to whom Craig was in the way of mentioning them; but the archbishop's narrative is surpassed by that of the author of the Coronis to Row's History, and the latter again by what is stated in the additions to the Coronis in the same work. The marvels become greater at every stage; yet Dr. M'Crie smooths away small difficulties, harmonises the whole narrative, and expresses no disbelief as to any part, beyond quoting an expression of doubt by Spottiswood. See Row, pp. 415-417, 457-461; and Life of Knox, p. 237-240. It is worth observing that the author of the most wonderful edition of the story of the dog and the purse of gold, by whose assistance Craig effected his escape, is also the sole voucher for the conversion of Row by means of the pretended miracle at Loretto.

Knox, and afterwards with Spottiswood and a minister named Kinlochy; and another schoolmaster, Robert Maxwell, encountered Willock at Glasgow. About the end of the year, a discussion took place at Edinburgh, between the Reformed ministers and a doctor of the Sorbonne, in attendance on the queen.[1]

Ninian Winzet was undoubtedly the most able controversial writer on the Roman side. He was born at Renfrew in the year 1518, and was appointed master of the grammar school at Linlithgow, about the year 1551. He himself tells us that, after spending about ten years of his most flourishing age in the discharge of the duties of this office, he was expelled from his "kindly town," because he refused to subscribe the new Confession. This event took place soon after his dispute with Spottiswood and Kinlochy. He appears to have subsequently resided at Edinburgh, where he devoted himself to the composition of a series of works in defence of the Roman Catholic Church.

On the fifteenth of February, 1562, Winzet presented to the queen a Tractate addressed to her Majesty, the Prelates, and the Nobility. In this treatise, he asks the queen's license to propose in writing to the Protestant ministers certain articles touching doctrine, order, and manners. He then addresses himself to the bishops, and other pastors of the Church, and denounces in the strongest terms their evil lives and erroneous doctrines, whereby they had wellnigh destroyed the flock intrusted to their keeping.

It was no ordinary ignorance and neglect which could have called forth such language as the following, from one who had laboured faithfully, and was prepared to suffer patiently, in the cause of his Church:—" Your dumb doctrine, in exalting ceremonies only without any declaration of the same, and, far more, keeping in silence the true word of God, necessary to

---

[1] Leslie, pp. 533, 538. Keith, vol. ii. p. 124. The last mentioned dispute is referred to in a letter from Randolph to Cecil, dated 7th December, 1561. The doctor of the Sorbonne was, no doubt, René Benoist, who accompanied the queen to Scotland. In December, 1561, Benoist addressed a letter to Knox, which was translated from the Latin by a Scottish friar, and answered by David Ferguson, minister of Dunfermline; see Life of Winzet, prefixed to the Maitland Club edition of his Tractates, as quoted by Dr. Irving, in his Lives of Scottish Writers, vol. i. p. 106.

all men's salvation, and not resisting manifest errors, to
world is known. What part of the true religion, by
slothful dominion and princely estate, is not corrupted
obscured? Have not many, through lack of instructior
mad ignorance misknown their duty, which we all owe to
Lord God, and so in their perfect belief have sorely stumbl
Were not the sacraments of Christ Jesus profaned by igno
and wicked persons, neither able to persuade to godlines:
learning nor by living? Of the which number we cor
the most part of us of the ecclesiastical state to have beer
our ignorant and inexpert youth, unworthily by you admi
to the ministration thereof. If these things most spe
through ignorance and avarice, be brought from their pu
what marvel is it that matters of less price, as of Images,
Invocation of Saints to pray for us, the Prayer for the s
departed, and many such like things in sobriety and lear
simplicity lawful, be at this time corrupted and profaned f
the mind of our ancient elders by the same vices? Wer
commanded in vain of God by the mouths of his Prophets
Apostles to watch carefully and continually on your flock,
know diligently the same by face? Or gave the prince
the earth to you yearly rents, (as the disciples in the be
ning sold their land and gave the prices thereof to
Apostles,) to the end that every one of you might spend
same upon his dame Dalila, and base-born offspring?
albeit it chance oft to the infirmity of man, that he fall as
when he should chiefly watch, and be given to pastime w
he should most diligently labour, yet, O merciful God, w
deadly sleep is this that has oppressed you, that in so g
uproar, tumult, and terrible clamour, ye waken not fort
your dream, and in so great danger of death ye have
regard of your own lives or others? Awake, awake, and
to your hands stoutly to save Peter's ship; for He nei
sleeps nor slumbers who beholds all your doings, and
your thoughts, but shall require the blood at your ha
of the smallest one that shall perish through your ne
gence."

Then addressing himself to the nobles in a like indign
strain, he attacks the simoniacal abuse of ecclesiastical patr
age which had prevailed for the last hundred years, the cor

...iences of which, he tells them, were now visited on them-
...lves: for some great houses had of late been utterly ruined;
...hers of the nobility lived like Epicureans without faith in
...od, or love for man; and others, who gloried in the name of
...ospellers, made of the Gospel a craft, urging a reformation
...om idolatry, but making no attempt to reform themselves
...om the idolatry of avarice.

About the twentieth of February, Winzet delivered to
...nox a treatise containing eighty-three questions touching
...ctrine, order, and manners. Among the questions put are
...e following:—Whether the Protestants believe the judg-
...ent of the Holy Church to be set forth most truly by the
...imitive doctors and general councils, or by John Calvin and
...s associates? Why they have taken away the true meaning
... the article of the Creed, that Christ descended into hell, sub-
...tuting for it Calvin's private opinion that the words signify
...ly the anguish which Christ suffered? Why they make
...eir two sacraments signs only of salvation whereby men are
...sured of God's grace, and not rather efficacious means where-
... God works his grace in them? Why, since they admit of
... ceremonies except such as are expressly commanded in
...ripture, they notwithstanding refuse to baptize children,
...less their father holds them up before the pulpit; why
...ey baptize in the church only, and not in the field, or by a
...er side, like St. John the Baptist and St. Philip; why they
...ptize not, unless the child then receive a name; why their
...ble is covered with a white cloth at the communion; why
...ey cause others than the minister to distribute the bread and
...e wine, when our Saviour alone did so to the Apostles, com-
...nding them as his ministers to do the same; why they
...ke their communion before dinner, when the sacrament was
...tituted after supper; why they refuse to solemnize matri-
...ony, unless the banns are first proclaimed; why they cause
...rsons about to be married take each other by the hand, and
...netimes a ring to be given? Why they say that in the
...nmunion nothing is present except bread and wine, when
...e Saviour says expressly, "This is my Body; This is my
...ood?" Why they do not minister the communion to the
...k before they depart out of this life? Why, when their
...ereign lady, Mary, has shown such humility, gentleness,

and wisdom, as should soften the heart of every true Scot, they exhort her subjects so fervently to rebellion, unless she accept the opinions of Calvin? Since by elders in the New Testament are meant bishops and priests, whose office it is to preach and minister the sacraments, why they have invented a new order of elders, who are forbidden to discharge those offices? Since the sacrament of Confirmation was used by the Apostles, why do they esteem it a thing of no importance, and but Papistical superstition? Since the priests of the Church should come to the sick and anoint them with oil, and pray for them, as our Saviour teaches by the mouth of St. James, why have they abolished Extreme Unction, and deprived it of the name of a sacrament? Although it is well known that in the primitive Church married persons were ordained bishops, priests, and deacons, where was it ever heard in that Church, that men, unmarried at the time of their ordination, were allowed to marry afterwards, without reproof? Since in the Scriptures we read of care bestowed on the funerals of the Patriarchs, of our Lord, of St. John the Baptist, and of St. Stephen, why have they dishonoured the bodies and sepulchres of the princes and nobles of Scotland? Since they admit no unwritten tradition, why do they celebrate their Sabbath day with the Catholics on Sunday, and not with the Jews on Saturday? Why do they use, as Catholics do, to sing Glory to the Father, and to the Son, and to the Holy Ghost, at the end of every Psalm, when that godly form was commanded to be sung by Pope Damasus for the rebuke of heretics? What can they shew expressly written to confute the Anabaptists of error, who deny that children should be baptized in infancy? What Scripture have they for receiving so many Gospels and Epistles in the New Testament, and no more? If the Church be invisible, how can men shew their complaints to the Church, according to our Saviour's command, and how in that case can the Church be the pillar and ground of the truth? Since Fasting was practised by Moses, Elias, and the Ninevites, by St. John the Baptist, and by our Saviour, who also foretold that his disciples should fast when the Bridegroom was removed, why is the Church guilty of idolatry in observing the yearly fast of Lent, and the weekly fasts of Friday, and Wednesday or Saturday? Why have they rejected the monastic life, which was held in such estimation by the primitive Church; why have they thrown down the monasteries which by a godly reformation might have nourished men given to prayer, and been colleges of learning for the support of poor students; or, if the monasteries were polluted with idolatry, why have they not destroyed wholly, as they have actually done in part, the parish churches and cathedrals? Since the Scriptures mention the frequent prayers of our Lord and his Apostles, of David, and of Daniel, was it not a godly rule of the Church that prayers should be sung or read seven times daily by able ministers chosen thereto, and why do they in their reformed order pray only by one minister, once only every day in the best churches, in many places thrice a week, and in far more not once in a month?

These eighty-three questions were delivered to Knox privately, through one of the Reformed, who had exhorted the adherents of Rome to unite with the Protestants; and a private answer in writing was requested. Knox gave no written answer, but discussed them in his public sermon, alluding particularly to three of the questions which referred to the lawful calling of himself and the Protestant ministers; and to these three Winzet again directed his special attention, in a letter dated the third of March. They were the following: —" Since we read that none should take the honour of the ministration of God's word and sacraments on him, except he be lawfully called thereto, either by God immediately, or by men having power to promote him to that office, and since we read of none called by God only, except such as shew their power given to them by Him by the power of the Spirit, or in signs and wonders; therefore if you John Knox be called immediately by God, where are your marvels wrought by the Holy Spirit? For the marvels of overturning of realms to ungodly sedition and discord we number not to be of his gifts. But if you be called by men, you must shew them to have had lawful power thereto, as the Apostles ordained St. Paul and Barnabas, albeit chosen by God before, and they such like others, in the fourteenth of the Acts; and as St. Paul ordained Timothy and Titus, giving them power and command to ordain others; wherein appears the lawful ordination of ministers. Your lawful ordination by one of these two ways we desire you to shew, since you renounce and esteem that ordination null, or rather wicked, by the which sometime you were called Sir John."

"If he cannot shew himself a lawfully ordained bishop, not merely a priest or inferior minister, how can you superintendents, or other inferior preachers, ordained and elected by him not having power thereto, judge yourselves to be lawful ministers in the Church of God?"

"If John Knox and you affirm yourselves lawful by reason of your knowledge, and that you are permitted, if you be not admitted, by those Churches which you serve, why have you taught manifestly a great error and schism in your Congregation, contending with tooth and nail, (as is the proverb,) that some lords and gentlemen have grievously erred in ministering your communion in times by-past to their own household-servants and tenants; since the said lords and gentlemen, being men of knowledge by their own judgment, in that case were permitted by their said servants to that office, who affirm themselves to be a Church of God?"

Winzet's next letter to Knox was written on the tenth of March. The reformer had, in the interval, attempted to defend his calling by appealing to the example of the prophet Amos. Winzet's reply was, that Amos had been sent by God to deliver a special message, and that he had not usurped the authority of the high-priest at Jerusalem, as Knox did that of the primate of Scotland. He farther requested his opponent to notice three things—first, the terrible punishment of Korah, Dathan, and Abiram, who said, "All the congregation are holy every one of them, and the Lord is among them;" just as he said, "Thou hast made us unto our God kings and priests:" secondly, "that the wisdom, which is from above, is first pure, then peaceable, gentle, and easy to be entreated, full of mercy and good fruits, without partiality, and without hypocrisy;" "and the servant of the Lord must not strive, but be gentle unto all men, apt to teach, patient, in meekness instructing those that oppose themselves:" and, thirdly, to shew at once some proof of his vocation, either mediate or immediate, for otherwise his own scholars will think that one mistuned string confounds all his harmony.

In a third letter, dated the twelfth of March, Winzet again exhorted Knox to give a proof of his calling, or else to renounce his usurped office.

At Easter, some disturbances took place in Edinburgh, caused by an attempt of the magistrates to prevent the observance of the festival. Winzet wrote a short treatise on the subject, not for publication, but as an exercise, he tells us, such as he used to teach his scholars in his happy days at Linlithgow. Copies of this paper were distributed without his knowledge, and, on the twenty-fourth of May, he admitted it to be his, explaining the true circumstances of its composition, and adding that he had nothing to regret in its being made public, except that it had not been more carefully prepared. It is a defence of the ecclesiastical festivals against the arguments of Knox, who denounced them as superstitious and idolatrous. He refers to the example of the Jewish Church, the feast of the Dedication of the Temple by King Solomon, and the thanksgiving for the deliverances from Holofernes and Haman; asks on what principle the observance of the Sunday can be required, if other festivals are abolished; and appeals to the natural feelings of the human heart, and the universal practice of mankind. "O madman and most foolish," he exclaims, "would he persuade a faithful Christian that the whole Universal Church is more unthankful and less mindful of the birth of her Spouse and King, the Son of God, than any realm is of its temporal king, whose day of nativity no country forgets during his lifetime? But our King and most sweet Spouse lives for ever. Wherefore ever shall the day of his blessed Nativity, Circumcision, Passion, Resurrection, Ascension, and his Manifestation to the world called the Epiphany, in despite of the devil and all his furious members, (who ever have laboured to abolish his name out of this world,) be in fresh memory of his dear beloved spouse, his Holy Church Universal."

His repeated challenges called forth no answer from Knox, and, about the end of July, Winzet sent to the press another work, called "The last Blast of the Trumpet of God's word against the usurped authority of John Knox, and his Calvinian brethren." Unable, or unwilling to meet him in argument, the leaders of the Reformed had recourse to other weapons.

The Edinburgh magistrates caused the printing office to be forced open, seized and imprisoned the printer, and carried off all the copies of the work which they could find. It was intended to apprehend Winzet himself, but he was leaving the house at the very time the officers entered, and succeeded in making his escape. He retired to the Low Countries, and appears to have resided for some time at Louvaine and Antwerp. At the latter city, his book of eighty-three questions was published in October, 1563.

Winzet was never allowed to return to his native country. In December, 1563, he published at Antwerp a Scottish translation of the Commonitorium of Vincent of Lerins, which he dedicated to Queen Mary. He seems also to have translated into the same language portions of the works of Tertullian and St. Optatus. In 1565, he published at Paris a translation of René Benoist's treatise on the "Method of composing discords in Religion." In the year 1576, he was, on the recommendation as is supposed of Bishop Leslie, appointed by Pope Gregory XIII. abbot of the Scottish Benedictine monastery of St. James at Ratisbon, and after his elevation to that office he wrote in Latin his "Flagellum Sectariorum," to which was appended an answer to Buchanan's treatise "De Jure Regni apud Scotos." Winzet died at Ratisbon, on the twenty-first of September, 1592, being then seventy-four years of age.[1]

In the assembly of June, 1562, commission was given to George Hay to preach in Carrick and Cunningham, while Knox was sent to Kyle and Galloway. The former, having proceeded to the scene of his labours, was encountered by the Abbot of Crossraguel. A controversy took place between them, and a book, which was written by Kennedy on the

---

[1] See Winzet's Exhortation to the Queen, Letters to Knox, Address to the Magistrates of Edinburgh, and Book of four-score and three Questions, in the appendix to Keith, vol. iii. p. 413-507. See also Leslie, p. 538-540; Mackenzie's Lives of Scottish Writers, vol. iii. p. 148-156; M'Crie's Life of Knox, pp. 249, 250, 453, 454; and Irving's Lives of Scottish Writers, vol. i. p. 98-121. Some interesting details are given by Irving from a manuscript in the Advocates' Library, containing an account of the monastery of Ratisbon, written by a Scotsman, named Boniface Strachan. Winzet's earlier works were reprinted for the Maitland Club in 1835, with a Life of the author prefixed.

subject of the Mass, was answered by Hay, in a work published in the course of the following year.[1]

In the beginning of September, Knox was at Ayr. The queen had already set out on her northern expedition; rumours were abroad that the Hamiltons were preparing to assist Huntly in an attempt to overthrow the existing establishment; and, conscious how much the influence of the Reformed opinions was dependent on the political supremacy of those by whom they were held, Knox persuaded many of the barons of Kyle, Cunningham, and Carrick, to unite in a bond, by which they solemnly engaged to assist each other, and to maintain the preaching of the Gospel and its ministers against all persons, power, and authority, that should oppose the same. From Ayr he went to Nithsdale and Galloway on a similar errand, using his endeavours successfully to prevent a rising among the friends of the Gordons.[2]

The districts which Knox visited at this time still contained numerous adherents of the Roman Church, who were encouraged to preserve their allegiance by the exertions of the zealous abbot of Crossraguel. During the year 1561, Kennedy had published a work bearing the following title:— "An Oration in favour of all those of the Congregation, exhorting them to espy how wonderfully they are abused by their deceitful preachers." In this treatise, he alluded, among other points, to the argument of the preachers, that because God commanded the Israelites to destroy idolaters and the places wherein idols were had in reverence, therefore all places, wherein mass had been said, were to be destroyed by the Congregation. The abbot maintained that Christian men never built a temple, church, or place of prayer, but for the purpose that the living God should be worshipped therein; and even if those places were any way profaned, the abuse was to be corrected without destruction of the buildings, even as our Saviour purified the Temple without destroying it. Had this, he said, been rightly understood, such proceedings as lately had brought disgrace on Scotland would never have occurred, and the antiquities and monuments of the realm,

---

[1] Leslie, p. 540. Knox, vol. ii. pp. 347, 352. M'Crie's Life of Knox, pp. 242, 452, 453. Miscellany of the Wodrow Society, vol. i. p. 94.

[2] Knox, vol. ii. p. 347-351.

which in other kingdoms are so highly prized, would not have been shamefully destroyed.

On Sunday the thirtieth of August, 1562, the abbot delivered a controversial discourse in the church of Kirk-Oswald—the parish in which Crossraguel is situated—and this he promised to continue on the following Sunday, and to maintain against all opposition. Knox, hearing what had taken place, repaired to Kirk-Oswald on the sixth of September, with the intention of answering the arguments of Kennedy. The latter, dreading a tumult, did not appear, but wrote to Knox, proposing that on the Sunday after they should discuss the points in dispute in any house he might name at Maybole, with a limited number of persons present on each side, and assuring him, in his own name, and that of his nephew and chief, the Earl of Cassillis, that he would receive a fair and gentle hearing. Knox's answer was expressed in terms of sufficient courtesy. Refusing to the abbot the title of lord in respect of his office, he willingly conceded it by reason of his birth, stating that he doubted not the earl's word, but that he was in the hands of the Almighty, and feared nothing for himself. He then proposed that the conference should be in the church of St. John the Baptist, at Ayr, rather than in a private house, and mentioned that he could not attend on the day named, because he was about to visit Nithsdale and Galloway. The Earl of Cassillis dissuaded them from going on with the discussion, as being likely to produce no good; but neither party was willing to draw back, and it was finally agreed that the disputation should take place on the twenty-eighth of September, at the house belonging to the provost of the collegiate church of Maybole.

They met accordingly, and the discussion was carried on during three days. Knox began the proceedings with a prayer, with which, it is said, the abbot was at first offended, but afterwards remarked, "By my faith, it is well said." Kennedy then desired one of his scribes to read a paper, in which he protested that, while ready to speak on the points in question, he did not hold them really disputable, inasmuch as they were already determined by the Church. To this protestation Knox afterwards gave in a written answer, in which he denied the authority of the Church to be of more avail among Christians, than it was among the Jews of old. "If my lord thinketh," he said, "that the Holy Catholic Church is sufficient assurance for his conscience, let him understand that the same buckler had the false prophets against Jeremiah, for they cried, 'The temple of the Lord, the temple of the Lord, the temple of the Lord!' But as he with one stroke did burst their buckler asunder, saying, 'Put not your trust in lying words,' so say we, that how Catholic, that is, universal, their Church hath ever been, holy are they never able to prove it, neither in life, making of laws, nor in soundness of doctrine, as in my answer given by mouth I have more plainly shown." He then proceeded to state that, as Elijah, Jeremiah, Amos, and the rest of the prophets, had been raised up in former times, so those whom the abbot called heretics were now raised up. "But," he added, "my lord perchance requireth miracles to prove our lawful vocation, for so doth Winzet, procurator for the Papists. To both I answer, that a truth by itself, without miracles, hath sufficient strength to prove the lawful vocation of the teachers thereof, but miracles, destitute of truth, have efficacy to deceive, but never to bring to God. But this, by the grace of God, shall be more fully entreated in the answer to Winzet's questions thereupon."

Having proceeded to discuss orally the chief question in dispute—that regarding the Mass—the abbot, being asked by Knox to define it, answered, "I define the Mass, as concerning the substance and effect, to be the sacrifice and oblation of the Lord's body and blood, given and offered by Him in the Last Supper." Knox replied, that in the Scriptures various kinds of sacrifices were mentioned—as sacrifices of thanksgiving, of mortification, of obedience, of prayer, and of almsgiving, but there was one sacrifice above all others, called propitiatory, whereby satisfaction was made to the justice of God; and he desired to know under which description of sacrifices the Mass was to be reckoned. Kennedy answered, that he held the sacrifice upon the cross to be the only sacrifice of redemption, and the Mass to be the sacrifice of commemoration of Christ's death and passion. Knox observed, "So far as I can conceive of my lord's answer, he maketh no sacrifice propitiatory in the Mass, which is the chief head I intend to impugn. For as for the commemoration of Christ's death and passion, that I grant and publicly do confess to be celebrated in the right use of the Lord's Supper, which I deny the Mass to be." The abbot having referred to the offering of Melchisedec in proof of his proposition, Knox denied that Melchisedec made any sacrifice of bread and wine unto God. The abbot referred for proof to the text of the Scriptures, and asked, if the bringing forth of the bread and wine was not for sacrifice, what its purpose really was. Knox said that he was not bound to answer this question, because the Scripture was silent, but if conjecture were allowable, it was to refresh Abraham and his weary soldiers. He also denied that Christ in the Last Supper made any sacrifice of his Body and Blood, under the forms of bread and wine, to God the Father.

Some farther arguments and illustrations were brought forward on each side, but the conference terminated without any definite result.[1]

The discussion between the abbot and Knox was conducted by both parties with temper and courtesy. The reformer had the advantage in the argument. Kennedy, believing devoutly what was taught by his Church, was yet unable to explain and defend it with sufficient clearness to others—perhaps had hardly realized its precise import to himself. Knox, on the other hand, spoke like one who had fully mastered his subject, meeting his opponent's arguments fairly, and putting forward his own views without ambiguity or hesitation.

It had been proposed by Kennedy and Knox to renew the controversy at Edinburgh, if the consent of the queen and the privy council should be obtained. It does not appear that farther discussion took place, or that the abbot again came forward in any public disputation. He was advanced in years before he became known as an author or a controversialist; and the fatigues and anxieties of that harassing time exhausted his strength. He was threatened with prosecution by the

[1] In 1563, Knox published at Edinburgh an account of the conference, under the title of "The Copy of the Reasoning which was betwixt the Abbot of Crossraguel and John Knox in Maybole, concerning the Mass, in the year of God 1562." It was reprinted by Sir Alexander Boswell, to whom we are also indebted for an impression of Kennedy's Oration. Both the Oration and the Reasoning are inserted in the appendix to M'Gavin's edition of Knox's History. See also Knox, vol. ii. pp. 351, 352; Leslie, p. 540; and M'Crie's Life of Knox, p. 242-249.

Reformed, but his nephew's rank and influence were still sufficient to protect him. He died in peace at his own monastery, on the twenty-second of August, 1564.[1]

Had all the Scottish prelates possessed the learning and the virtues of the last consecrated abbot of Crossraguel, the reformation of the Church might have been effected in a very different manner.

[1] Miscellany of the Wodrow Society, vol. i. p. 94.

CHAPTER XXXV.

FROM THE REASONING BETWEEN THE ABBOT OF CROSSRAGUEL AND JOHN KNOX, IN SEPTEMBER, 1562, TO QUEEN MARY'S MARRIAGE WITH DARNLEY, IN JULY, 1565.

Rebellion of the Earl of Huntly—Second Interview of Mary with Knox—Meeting of the General Assembly—Excommunication of Paul Methven—Prosecution of the Primate and other ecclesiastics—Knox's sermon on the Queen's marriage—Riot at Holyrood—Knox summoned before the Council—Discussion between Lethington and Knox—Marriage of Mary with Darnley.

THE Earls of Huntly, the chiefs of the house of Gordon, had for many years occupied the foremost place among the nobility of the north of Scotland. The power of that great family had been still farther increased by George, the fourth earl, who held the office of chancellor of the kingdom, and ruled with an authority, virtually independent, most of the provinces beyond the Dee. His conduct, as already mentioned, had been very suspicious during the contest between the queen-regent and the Congregation, and had lost him the confidence of his sovereign, without securing the good-will of the successful party. He was both feared and disliked by the Protestants, and it could hardly have been otherwise; for, however he may have wavered in his political measures, there is no reason to suspect the consistent sincerity of his religious belief, which he had shewn by maintaining the cause of the Church, and upholding its ritual, at a time when few others dared even avow their opinions. It has been seen that his offer to restore the ancient system, if Mary would unite her cause with his, was rejected by the queen, and, though he had since occupied a high rank in her government, he had never in reality been trusted.

During the year 1562, various circumstances occurred which excited the indignation of Huntly. The earldom of Murray, of which he was in possession, was taken from him, and bestowed on the rival who filled the place in the counsels of his sovereign, which he himself, as the chief of the Roman Catholic nobility, had expected to hold. In the course of the summer, his son, Sir John Gordon, was thrown into prison on account of a feudal affray with the house of Ogilvie, and, when he effected his escape, was exposed to the penalties of forfeiture. The fidelity of the earl was suspected, and Mary, with a view, perhaps, of preventing any outbreak, chose this time for a progress to the northern parts of her kingdom.

Just before she set out, a foreign bishop arrived at Edinburgh, sent by the Pope with a secret message to the queen. It was with difficulty that Lethington succeeded in bringing him into her presence, and, when it was ascertained that such an envoy was within Scotland, the Protestants determined to put him to death, and were only prevented from doing so by the exertions of the Earl of Murray. It was supposed that he had been sent to keep the queen firm to her religion, and to ascertain whether she would send an ambassador to the Council of Trent. Nothing more is mentioned regarding this matter, which is only known to us through a letter of Randolph's. Whatever may have been the object of the envoy, the result shewed that his mission had no effect in altering the line of policy adopted by the queen.

Mary left Edinburgh on the eleventh of August, and on the twenty-seventh of that month arrived at Aberdeen, where Huntly met her. He entreated her to visit him at his castle of Strathbogie; but she refused to honour him so far, and proceeding westward through Strathisla reached Inverness on the eleventh of September. The castle of Inverness was held by one of Huntly's vassals, who refused to admit the queen, but was obliged to surrender, and was put to death as a rebel. After some vain attempts to conciliate his sovereign, Huntly actuated as it would seem by a sudden impulse of resentment, appeared openly in arms against the royal authority. Mary had returned to Aberdeen, where she remained, while her army, under the Earl of Murray, advanced to attack Huntly at Corrichie. The Gordons were defeated, and their chief perished in the battle. The authors of the rebellion were severely punished. Sir John Gordon was immediately beheaded at Aberdeen; his eldest brother, the Lord Gordon, was thrown into prison; and, in a parliament held at Edinburgh in May of the following year, the deceased earl, his kinsman the Earl of Sutherland, and eleven barons of the house of Gordon, were attainted, and their estates forfeited to the crown.[1]

The forfeiture of the Earl of Huntly was the just and legal punishment of an undeniable crime, but the queen's conduct, in utterly destroying the power of his family, was at once harsh and imprudent. His insurrection was the first act of open treason which Mary had encountered. Had she known all that her most trusted counsellors had already done, could she have suspected what they were soon to do, the punishment of the Gordons would have been less severe, and their ruin less complete.

The queen returned to Holyrood on the twenty-first of November. The fall of their most dreaded enemy did not tend to make the Protestant ministers more mild and tolerant. On Sunday the thirteenth of December, Knox in his sermon denounced the ignorance, vanity, and hatred of all virtue, for which princes were distinguished, and made particular allusion to the queen's indulgence in excessive dancing. Mary, disliking such liberties, again sent for the reformer. The Earls of Murray and Morton, and the secretary, were present at the interview. She accused Knox of endeavouring to bring her into hatred and contempt with the people. He answered, that the stubborn of this world often hear false reports to their own great displeasure. "I doubt not," he said, "but that it came to the ears of proud Herod, that our master, Christ Jesus, called him a fox; but they told him not how odious a thing it was before God to murder an innocent, as he had lately done before, causing to behead John the Baptist to reward the dancing of a harlot's daughter. Madam, if the reporters of my words had been honest men, they would have reported my words and the circumstances of the same." In reference to his denunciations of the queen's conduct, he explained that,

---

[1] Knox, vol. ii. pp. 345, 346, 352-360, 380, 381. Buchanan, vol. i. p. 334-339. Keith, vol. ii. p. 154-173. Tytler, vol. vi. p. 262-268. Perhaps the statements of Buchanan (p. 336), in regard to communications from the Pope and the Cardinal of Lorraine to the queen, are founded on the mission of the Papal envoy mentioned in the text.

while he disliked dancing, he did not condemn it absolutely, but only when indulged in to the neglect of proper duties, and for pleasure in the calamities of God's people. This was an allusion to the reports which had lately come of the successes of the princes of Lorraine in their contest with the Huguenots. The queen said, "Your words are sharp enough, as you have spoken them, but yet they were told to me in another manner. I know that my uncles and you are not of one religion, and therefore I cannot blame you, albeit you have no good opinion of them. But if ye hear anything of myself that mislikes you, come to myself and tell me, and I shall hear you." "Madam," said Knox, "I would be glad to do all that I could to your grace's contentment, provided that I exceed not the bounds of my vocation. I am called to a public function within the Church of God, and am appointed by God to rebuke the sins and vices of all. I am not appointed to come to every man in particular to shew him his offence; for that labour were infinite. If your grace please to frequent the public sermons, then doubt I not but that ye shall fully understand both what I like and mislike, as well in your majesty as in all others. Or, if your grace will assign unto me a certain day and hour when it will please you to hear the form and substance of doctrine which is proponed in public to the churches of this realm, I will most gladly await upon your grace's pleasure, time, and place. But to wait at your chamber door or elsewhere, and then to have no farther liberty but to whisper my mind in your grace's ear, or to tell you what others think and speak of you, neither will my conscience, nor the vocation whereto God hath called me, suffer it. For albeit, at your grace's commandment, I am here now, yet cannot I tell what other men shall judge of me, that at this time of day am absent from my book, and waiting upon the court." The queen remarked, "You will not always be at your book," and so turned away. As Knox was departing "with a reasonable merry countenance," some of the courtiers exclaimed, "He is not afraid." "Why," said he, "should the pleasing face of a gentlewoman affray me? I have looked in the face of many angry men, and yet have not been affrayed above measure."[1]

[1] Knox, vol. ii. p. 330-335.

The general assembly met at Edinburgh on the twenty-fifth of December. Reports were abroad seriously affecting the moral character of Paul Methven, minister at Jedburgh, and commission was given to Knox and certain others to repair to the residence of the accused, and investigate the matter. After careful enquiry, it was ascertained that Methven had been guilty of adultery; and he was in consequence excommunicated, and deprived of his office.[1] Methven had been one of the most eminent of the Reformed preachers, and his offence necessarily produced great scandal, and called for severe punishment. On this occasion the Protestants shewed that their rebukes of immorality, and their censures of one of the worst vices of the Roman clergy, had been called forth by a sincere hatred of sin, and that they were determined, so far as lay in their power, to prevent the occurrence of such offences among themselves.

In the spring of 1563, the scattered adherents of the Roman communion still attempted to keep up the solemnities of the Paschal season. Their priests ventured in a few places to appear in the churches, but they were now obliged, for the most part, to celebrate the holy rites in private houses, or in the forests, apart from any human dwelling. Even there they were followed by the persecution of the triumphant Protestants. Some ecclesiastics of high station came forward more boldly in the West, hoping, probably, that their rank and noble birth would protect them. The primate himself, the Abbot of Crossraguel, and Malcolm Fleming, Prior of Whithorn, are particularly mentioned. The Reformed apprehended some of the priests, and intimated to others that they would not trouble themselves by complaining to the queen in council, but would, at their own hand, execute the punishments ordered by God to be inflicted on idolaters. Mary, alarmed for the safety of those who held her own religious opinions, and indignant that her authority in putting the laws in execution should be invaded, again sent for Knox.

---

[1] Book of the Universal Kirk, p. 11-13. Knox, vol. ii. p. 363-367. Calderwood, vol. ii. p. 205-210. Keith, vol. iii. p. 61-68. Methven retired to England, but came back in 1566, and, at his own entreaty, it was agreed that the excommunication should be removed, on his performing public penance. He went through part of the penance, but before it was finished again left Scotland.

She was at this time residing at Lochleven Castle, and there her interview with the reformer took place. She requested him to use his influence with the people and the gentlemen of the West not to put to their hands to punish any one simply on account of religion. Knox answered, that if she would take care that the laws should be enforced, he could promise quietness, but not otherwise. "Will you," she said, "allow that they shall take my sword into their hands?" "Madam," replied Knox, "the sword of justice is God's, and is given to princes and rulers for one end, which, if they transgress, sparing the wicked and oppressing innocents, they that in the fear of God execute judgment where God has commanded offend not God, although kings do it not; neither yet sin they that bridle kings from striking innocent men in their rage. The examples are evident; for Samuel feared not to slay Agag, the fat and delicate king of Amalek, whom King Saul had saved. Neither spared Elias Jezebel's false prophets and Baal's priests, albeit that King Ahab was present. Phineas was no magistrate, and yet feared he not to strike Cosbi and Zimri in the very act of filthy fornication. And so, Madam, your grace may see that others than chief magistrates may lawfully punish, and have punished, the vice and crimes which God commands to be punished. And in this case, I would earnestly pray your majesty to take good advisement, and that your grace should let the Papists understand that their attempts will not be suffered unpunished. For power by act of parliament is given to all judges within their own bounds to search mass-mongers or the hearers of the same, and to punish them according to the law. And therefore it shall be profitable to your majesty to consider what is the thing your grace's subjects look to receive of your majesty, and what it is that ye ought to do unto them by mutual contract. They are bound to obey you, and that not but in God. You are bound to keep laws unto them. You crave of them service; they crave of you protection and defence against wicked doers. Now, Madam, if you shall deny your duty unto them, (which especially craves that you punish malefactors,) think you to receive full obedience of them? I fear, Madam, you shall not."

The queen left Knox in displeasure, but next morning the

reformer again met her while she was hawking near Kinross. She cautioned him against trusting in the Bishop of Galloway, who wished to be chosen superintendent. In this, Knox tells us, the queen was not deceived, for the bishop had attempted to gain the office by bribery, but was unsuccessful in the attempt. Mary, in parting, declared that she would cause all offenders against the laws to be summoned, and so let it be seen that she would minister justice.

The royal promise was faithfully kept. On the nineteenth of May, the Archbishop of St. Andrews, the Prior of Whithorn, and forty-six other persons, were tried before the Court of Justiciary at Edinburgh, on charges of hearing auricular confession, and assisting at the celebration of mass. The accused, for the most part, submitted to the queen's mercy, and were committed to ward in various places. The proceedings against the Roman Catholics at this time must have been very severe, since we find Randolph writing to Cecil, on the third of June, that the priests were fleeing for refuge to England[1]

While the parliament, which met in May, was sitting, Knox preached before the assembled nobles, and took the opportunity of alluding to the negotiations which were then going on with various foreign princes relative to the queen's marriage. "My lords," he said, "I hear of the queen's marriage. Dukes, brethren to emperors, and kings, strive all for the best game; but this will I say, (note the day and bear witness after,) whensoever the nobility of Scotland, professing the Lord Jesus, consent that an infidel, (and all Papists are infidels,) shall be head to your sovereign, ye do so far as in you lieth to banish Christ Jesus from this realm; ye bring God's vengeance upon the country, a plague upon yourselves, and perchance ye shall do small comfort to your sovereign." Both Protestants and Papists, he himself tells us, were offended by his discourse, and he was once more summoned before the queen.

Knox, on this occasion, was accompanied by Erskine of Dun. Mary reproached him with the language which he

[1] Knox, vol. ii. p. 370-380. Keith, vol. ii. p. 197-199. Tytler, vol. vi. p. 278-280. Pitcairn's Criminal Trials. vol. i. part i. p. * 427-* 431. Diurnal of Occurrents, p. 75. Calendar of State Papers relating to Scotland, vol. i. p. 190.

had used, and burst into tears. "What have you to do with my marriage," she asked, "and what are you within this commonwealth?" "A subject born within the same, Madam," answered Knox, "and albeit I neither be earl, lord, nor baron, yet has God made me (how abject that ever I be in your eyes) a profitable member within the same. Yea, Madam, to me it appertains no less to forewarn of such things as may hurt it, if I foresee them, than it does to any of the nobility; for both my vocation and conscience crave plainness of me. And therefore, Madam, to yourself I say that which I speak in public place. Whensoever that the nobility of this realm shall consent that ye be subject to an unfaithful husband, they do as much as in them lieth to renounce Christ, to banish his truth from them, to betray the freedom of this realm, and perchance shall, in the end, do small comfort to yourself." Mary again wept. Erskine endeavoured to soothe her, and, after a pause, Knox continued, "Madam, in God's presence I speak; I never delighted in the weeping of any of God's creatures; yea I can scarcely well abide the tears of my own boys whom my own hand corrects, much less can I rejoice in your majesty's weeping. But seeing that I have offered to you no just occasion to be offended, but have spoken the truth, as my vocation craves of me, I must sustain, albeit unwillingly, your majesty's tears, rather than I dare hurt my conscience, or betray my commonwealth through my silence."

Knox was ordered to retire to the ante-chamber, and Erskine and the Prior of Coldingham remained in consultation with the queen. While he waited the issue of their deliberations, he conversed with the ladies of the court who were in attendance. "O fair ladies," he said, "how pleasing were this life of yours if it should ever abide, and then in the end that we might pass to heaven with all this gay gear. But fie upon that knave Death, that will come whether we will or not. And when he has laid on his arrest, the foul worms will be busy with this flesh, be it never so fair and so tender; and the silly soul, I fear, shall be so feeble, that it can neither carry with it gold, garnishing, pearls, nor precious stones." Mary's wrath, as usual, was soon appeased, and no farther steps were taken against the reformer.[1]

[1] Knox, vol. ii. p. 384 389.

On the twenty-fifth of June, the general assembly met at Perth. Commission was given to the Bishops of Galloway, Orkney, and Caithness, to plant churches within the bounds of their dioceses. Similar commissions were granted to John Hepburn, minister at Brechin, for Murray, Banff, and the adjacent districts; to Robert Pont, for Inverness; and to Donald Munro, for Ross. All these commissions were to last only for a year. It was ordained that no work touching on religion should be set forth in print, or published in manuscript, until it was approved by the superintendent of the diocese, and such persons as he might call to his assistance.[1]

On Sunday, the fifteenth of August, while the queen was at Stirling, a disturbance took place in her chapel at Holyrood. The Protestants of Edinburgh, indignant that some of their Roman Catholic fellow-citizens had resorted thither to mass on the previous Sunday, burst open the doors, and found the altar covered, and the priest ready for the celebration. One of the rioters, Patrick Cranston, exclaimed, "The queen's majesty is not here. How dare you then be so malapert as openly to do against the law?" A French lady, the mistress of the maids, hastened to the comptroller, Wishart of Pitarro, who was attending sermon at St. Giles', and implored his protection. Pitarro and the magistrates of the city immediately went to the abbey, and prevented farther disturbance.

An enquiry regarding this occurrence was instituted by the queen's order, and the proceedings which followed mark the even-handed justice which hitherto had uniformly distinguished the reign of Mary. Cranston and another of the rioters were ordered to appear and answer for their offence, but, at the same time, twenty-two persons, several of whom were females, were prosecuted on the charge of attending mass on the eighth of August. The parties accused of the latter offence were evidently inhabitants of the city, who had no right to participate in the special immunity conferred on the queen's household. Knox, displeased that two of his friends should be called to account for what he held to be a religious and

---

[1] Book of the Universal Kirk, p. 14-16. Calderwood, vol. ii. p. 223-229. Keith, vol. iii. p. 71-77.

commendable act, wrote and circulated letters requesting the presence of the Reformed at Edinburgh on the day appointed for the trial. They prepared to obey the call, but the trial was postponed, and no farther record of the judicial proceedings has been preserved.

A copy of Knox's letter having fallen into the hands of Henry Sinclair, Bishop of Ross, and President of the Court of Session, it was shewn by him to the queen, and the reformer was summoned before the council on a charge of illegally convocating the lieges. He appeared before them about the middle of December, accompanied by a large body of his supporters who crowded the passages and stairs of the council-chamber. He was asked if he acknowledged the letter to be his, and he at once admitted it. "You have done more than I would have done," was the remark of Lethington. He was then asked if he was sorry for having written it. He answered that his offence in doing so must first be explained. "If there were no more," said Lethington, "than the convocation of the queen's lieges, the offence cannot be denied." "Remember yourself, my lord," said Knox, "there is a difference betwixt a lawful convocation, and an unlawful. If I have been guilty in this, I have oft offended since I came last to Scotland; for what convocation of the brethren has ever been to this day to which my pen served not. Before this, no man laid it to my charge as a crime." "Then was then," said Lethington, "and now is now. We have no need of such convocations as some times we have had." Knox answered, "The time that has been is even now before my eyes; for I see the poor flock in no less danger than it has been at any time before, except that the devil has got a visor upon his face. Before, he came in with his own face, discovered by open tyranny, seeking the destruction of all that had refused idolatry: and then, I think you will confess, the brethren lawfully assembled themselves for defence of their lives. And now, the devil comes under the cloak of justice, to do that which God would not suffer him to do by strength." The examination went on, and Knox was finally acquitted, the queen and Lethington expressing great indignation at the result. According to his own account, the sentence was unanimous, even the Bishop of Ross concurring, and the nobles praising God for his modesty, and for his plain and sensible answers.[1]

The council, sitting almost in the sight of Knox's ardent adherents, could hardly have pronounced an unbiassed judgment. But the chief motive which influenced them was probably the consciousness of the good reason that Knox had to appeal to their former proceedings in justification of his conduct. The nobles present were the Duke of Chatelherault, the Earls of Argyll, Murray, Glencairn, and Marischal, and the Lord Ruthven. They had not the assurance to concur in the reasoning of the secretary.

The usual half-yearly meeting of the general assembly took place at Edinburgh, on the twenty-fifth of December. At its first session, Knox, with evident allusion to his recent appearance before the queen, asked whether he had received charge from the whole Church convened at Edinburgh, after the beginning of the Reformation, to advertise the brethren to assemble and give counsel when any of their number should chance to be troubled. The Lord Lindsay, several of the barons and ministers, the Superintendents of Angus, Fife, Lothian, Glasgow, and Galloway, and the majority of the members, answered in the affirmative. It was agreed at this meeting that a moderator should be appointed to keep order in the assembly, and John Willock, the Superintendent of Glasgow, was the first who was named to that office.

In the fourth session a circumstance occurred, which, though relating rather to a civil than an ecclesiastical matter, deserves to be noticed, as marking the first communication between the assembly and the authorities of the English Church. One of the members having complained that his wife had deserted him and fled to England, the assembly ordered letters to be directed to the Archbishops of Canterbury and York, subscribed by the Superintendent of Lothian, and Knox and Craig, requesting the archbishops to cause the wife to be cited to appear before the Superintendent of Lothian, and the session of the church of Edinburgh.

At the same assembly, Robert Ramsay was accused of

---

[1] Knox, vol. ii. p. 393-412. Pitcairn's Criminal Trials, vol. i. part i. pp. *434, 435. Keith, vol. ii. pp. 210, 211. Knox takes no notice of the proceedings against the Roman Catholics for attending mass.

entering the ministry within the bounds of the Superintendent of Angus, without election, or admission by the superintendent, and of having affirmed that there was a midway between Papistry and the religion now established. For these, and other charges of borrowing money to buy books without repaying it, he was suspended from the ministry till further trial should be taken.[1] This was the first open avowal, in the new establishment, of a wish for that middle way which afterwards so many sought to find. The person referred to could hardly, even at this time, have stood alone in cherishing such a wish. It must have been entertained by others of that numerous party, which, while within the Roman Church, earnestly desired a reformation, and, though now belonging to the Protestant communion, could not be satisfied with the many changes that had been adopted.

In the interval between the assembly of December, 1563, and June, 1564, John Knox contracted a second marriage. His first wife, Marjory Bowes, had died in the end of the year 1560, and in March, 1564, he was married to Margaret Stewart, the youthful daughter of Lord Ochiltree, one of his chief supporters among the nobility.[2]

The general assembly met at Edinburgh, on the twenty-fifth of June. None of its proceedings call for particular notice, with the exception of a discussion between Lethington and Knox, in regard to language used by the latter in his prayers and speeches about the queen, and his doctrine as to the duties of subjects and sovereigns. This discussion took place at a conference between the lords of the council and some of the members of the assembly. Knox justified his words and opinions, by appealing to the language used by the prophets to the sovereigns of Israel, and by referring to the slaughter of King Joash, and of King Amaziah, by their subjects, as righteous acts; and argued that, while by the ordinance of God authority and government are to be maintained, the persons

---

[1] Book of the Universal Kirk, p. 17-19. Knox, vol. ii. p. 412-415. Calderwood, vol. ii. p. 241-247. Keith, vol. iii. p. 79-89.

[2] Knox, at the time of his marriage, was in his sixtieth year. More than a twelvemonth before, Randolph, in a letter to Cecil, referred to Knox's approaching marriage "to a young lass of sixteen." (Calendar of State Papers relating to Scotland, vol. i. p. 187.)

by whom the authority is administered may lawfully be resisted, and, if the sovereign be an idolater, he ought to die the death at the hands of his own people.[1]

The ministers were allowed without much opposition to preach what doctrines they pleased, but their efforts to obtain a larger share of the Church's spoils were successfully resisted by the Protestant nobles. They had still no more than the portion of the thirds which they could rescue from the comptroller, although the holders of ecclesiastical property were daily becoming farther secularized. It was remarked by John Craig, that the abbot could no longer be distinguished from the earl, nor the nun from the noble-woman. It was no consolation to the ministers that individuals among their supporters were enriched. In October, 1564, George Buchanan received from the queen a grant of the temporalities of the abbacy of Crossraguel, lately vacant by the death of Quintin Kennedy.[2]

The general assembly met at Edinburgh, on the twenty-fifth of December. It was enjoined that every minister, exhorter, and reader, should have a copy of the Psalm-book lately printed at Edinburgh, and use the order contained therein in Prayers, Marriages, and the administration of the Sacraments.[3] This was the Book of Common Order, which, it is probable, now entirely superseded the English Book of Common Prayer. The assembly again met at Edinburgh on the twenty-fifth of June, 1565. The usual remonstrances were made regarding the toleration of idolatry, and the poverty of the ministers.[4]

The attention of the Scottish people was now chiefly directed to the approaching marriage of their sovereign. Within a short time after her return from France, the expediency of such a step became obvious to her wisest counsellors, and Mary herself affected no indifference towards it. The difficulty was in the choice of a husband. She would fain

---

[1] Book of the Universal Kirk, p. 19-24. Knox, vol. ii. p. 421-461. Calderwood, vol. ii. p. 250-282. Keith, vol. iii. p. 89-96.

[2] Keith, vol. ii. p. 242. Irving's Life of Buchanan, p. 135.

[3] Book of the Universal Kirk, p. 24-27. Knox, vol. ii. p. 471. Calderwood, vol. ii. p. 282-285. Keith, vol. iii. p. 97-102.

[4] Book of the Universal Kirk, p. 27-32. Knox, vol. ii. p. 484-486. Calderwood, vol. ii. p. 287-291. Keith, vol. iii. p. 105-115.

have consulted at once her own inclinations, and the wishes of Elizabeth, whose approbation was of so much importance in relation to the succession to the English crown. But Elizabeth's policy, in this as in every thing else regarding Scotland, was selfish and insincere. She would have prevented Mary's marriage altogether, had it been in her power: finding herself unable to accomplish this, she threw obstacles in the way of every match which would have brought her kinswoman again into connection with the royal houses of the Continent. When the queen of the Scots rejected the Earl of Leicester, who had been recommended by Elizabeth, and fixed her affections on her own cousin, Henry Stewart, Lord Darnley, son of the Earl of Lennox, it has been conjectured, with great probability, that the English sovereign was not at heart ill pleased. In several respects the choice of Mary appeared to be a good one, but the advantages which might have been expected from her union with a husband of illustrious descent, personal and intellectual accomplishments, and common religious belief, were never realized. The weakness and vices which marred the character of Darnley were unknown to Mary, or were disregarded by her; and, notwithstanding the opposition of Elizabeth, and the urgent remonstrances of the Earl of Murray, who dreaded the loss of the political influence which he had hitherto enjoyed, the marriage was formally resolved on.

William Chisholm, Bishop-coadjutor of Dunblane, had been sent to Rome, to obtain the papal bulls which were necessary in consequence of the relationship between Mary and Darnley. On his return, the marriage was celebrated, according to the ritual of the Roman Church, by John Sinclair, Dean of Restalrig, within the chapel at Holyrood, on Sunday the twenty-ninth of July, 1565.[1] On the following day, Darnley, who

---

[1] Letter from Randolph to the Earl of Leicester—Robertson's History of Scotland, 20th ed. vol. iii. p. 307-311. Knox, vol. ii. p. 495. Keith, vol. ii. pp. 320, 344-347. The chapel at Holyrood, where the marriage was celebrated, and in which divine service had been performed according to the Roman ritual from the time of the queen's return from France, was not the abbey church, as some writers have supposed, but a private chapel in the palace. This would appear probable from the various circumstances mentioned in connection with the attempts of the Protestants to suppress the Roman service, and is rendered certain by what is mentioned in a letter of Randolph to Cecil, dated 24th July, 1565, in

had now received the royal title, was proclaimed King of the Scots, at the market cross of Edinburgh.

which he makes a marked distinction between the abbey church and the queen's chapel. After having mentioned that the banns were proclaimed in St. Giles's church, he adds, "Upon Sunday next, without all doubt, the marriage goeth forward, but yet uncertain whether it shall be in the church where the banns were asked, in the abbey church, or in her own chapel." (Ellis's Original Letters, 2d ed. vol. ii. p. 199.) The abbey church, as well as that of St. Giles, was in possession of the Protestants.

CHAPTER XXXVI.

FROM QUEEN MARY'S MARRIAGE WITH DARNLEY IN JULY, 1565, TO HER ABDICATION IN JULY, 1567.

Rebellion of the Earl of Murray—Knox's sermon at St. Giles' —Attempts of the Queen to restore the Roman Church— John Sinclair, Bishop of Brechin—John Leslie, Bishop of Ross—Murder of Riccio—Question as to Knox's participation in the crime—Proposal to send a Nuncio to Scotland—Baptism of Prince James—Murder of Darnley— Meeting of Parliament—The Queen's Marriage with Bothwell—Her Imprisonment—Her Abdication.

THE marriage of the queen was the signal of open revolt to a powerful faction of the nobility. Murray and his friends saw that their political ascendency was at an end; the Hamiltons hated their feudal rivals of the house of Lennox; and, encouraged by the promised assistance of Elizabeth, the Duke of Chatel-herault, the Earls of Murray, Argyll, Glencairn, and Rothes, the Lords Boyd and Ochiltree, Kirkaldy of Grange, and other barons, assembled their followers, and appeared in arms against their sovereign. They attempted to gain the support of the people by representing that the Protestant religion was in danger, and their efforts were zealously seconded by the ministers, but the great body of the nation remained faithful to the queen. Mary appeared in person at the head of her troops, and her vigorous measures compelled the insurgent leaders to seek refuge in England. Parliament was summoned to meet, and the rebel lords were ordered to appear and answer on a charge of treason. The Duke of Chatel-herault, with some difficulty, obtained a pardon on condition of his retiring to France, but the others remained exposed to all the penalties of an attainder.[1]

During these proceedings, Knox continued at his post in the capital, and made no secret of his sympathy with the

[1] Knox, vol. ii. p. 496-515. Keith, vol. ii. p. 348-381. Tytler, vol. vii. p. 1-13.

rebels. On Sunday, the nineteenth of August, Darnley attended the Protestant service in the church of St. Giles. The conduct of the young king, in regard to the external observances of religion, was deficient in the consistency and firmness which his consort had shewn in that respect. At his marriage he retired before mass was celebrated, and he now sought to conciliate the good wishes of the Reformed by frequenting their churches. Knox preached on this occasion, and took for his text the words of Isaiah, "O Lord our God, other lords beside Thee have had dominion over us." "Whereupon," as he himself tells us in his History, "he took occasion to speak of the government of wicked princes, who, for the sins of the people, are sent as tyrants and scourges to plague them. And amongst other things he said, 'That God sets in that room, for the offences and ingratitude of the people, boys and women.' And some other words which appeared bitter in the king's ears, as 'That God justly punished Ahab and his posterity, because he would not take order with that harlot Jezebel.'" In consequence of this language, Knox was summoned before the council. The answer which he made to the charge was characteristic of the man, and of the principles on which he professed to act. He said, "That he had spoken nothing but according to the text, and, if the Church would command him either to speak or abstain, he would obey so far as the word of God would permit him." The only censure which he incurred was an injunction to abstain from preaching for some days.[1]

The general assembly met at Edinburgh, on the twenty-fifth of December. At its fourth session, the question was put whether Baptism administered by a Roman Catholic priest was to be reiterated. It was agreed that such baptism was valid, inasmuch as it was celebrated with water, and the due form of words; but persons so baptized were ordered, when they attained the proper age, to be instructed in the true religion, and to make a public renunciation of the corruptions of Popery before being admitted to communion.[2]

Knox tells us that in the months of November and Decem-

---

[1] Knox, vol. ii. pp. 497, 498.
[2] Book of the Universal Kirk, p. 32-42. Calderwood, vol. ii. p. 294-310. Keith, vol. iii. p. 118-133.

ber the queen began more openly to shew her favour to the Papists. The Earls of Lennox, Atholl, Cassillis, and others, went to mass in her chapel, and certain friars requested her license to preach, which was granted to them. At Christmas, the king and queen went to mass and the friars preached publicly, which they had not done during the seven years before. Knox adds that they were so little esteemed that their preaching did not continue long.[1]

There is probably no exaggeration in the statements of Knox, so far as they refer to the queen's more open avowal of her attachment to her own religion, and the marks of favour which she bestowed on those who adhered to it. The rebellion and banishment of Murray and his associates had weakened the influence of the Protestants, and the violent language of the preachers had brought discredit on their cause. Supported by some of the most powerful of the nobility, and urged on by her relatives of the house of Lorraine, there can hardly be a doubt that Mary was considering the best method of securing a legal position for the ancient Church, perhaps a restoration of some of its former privileges. She had uniformly refused to ratify the proceedings of the convention of 1560; and the Reformed system had no other legal sanction than the royal proclamations securing in the meantime the execution of those laws which were in force at the queen's return. The whole ecclesiastical constitution might be reviewed and altered at the ensuing parliament.

One of the most effectual means of restoring the Roman Church was the filling up of the vacant sees with prelates of character and ability, attached from conviction to the doctrines of their communion, and invested with the proper apostolical authority. Several of the bishops had openly joined the Reformed, but, as they retained the political dignity which their ecclesiastical office had given them, no change could be made in the government of their dioceses so long as they lived. Two sees, however, were vacant at this time. Donald Campbell, Bishop-elect of Brechin, had died about the end of the year 1562; and a much more distinguished prelate, Henry Sinclair, Bishop of Ross, and President of the Court of Session, having gone to France to obtain medical advice for a

[1] Knox, vol. ii. p. 514-516.

painful disease, died at Paris on the second of January, 1565. On the thirteenth of November, John Sinclair, Dean of Restalrig, was appointed to succeed his brother, as President of the Court of Session, and his nomination to the see of Brechin appears to have followed soon afterwards. Emulating his predecessor's merits as a judge, the new prelate was equally fitted for the discharge of his episcopal duties. For many years he had taken a leading part in the counsels of the Church. He belonged to the ecclesiastical party which was anxious for a reformation of abuses, and had shewn his moderation and charity in his intercourse with the Protestant martyr, Adam Wallace. He had exerted himself to win back the affections of the people by his sermons, and had been misconstrued on both sides to such a degree, that the Reformed said he was not far from the kingdom of God, and some of the friars asserted that if he took not heed to his doctrine, he would be the destruction of the whole estate of the Church. The queen had testified her regard for the Dean of Restalrig, by selecting him to celebrate her marriage with Darnley, and she now expected, from his zeal and ability, the most effectual assistance in the promotion of her designs.[1]

The successor of Bishop Henry Sinclair in the diocese of Ross was John Leslie, Official of Aberdeen. Leslie had for some time held a distinguished place among the defenders of the hierarchy. His origin has not been clearly ascertained, but it is supposed that he was the illegitimate son of a priest. He was born in the year 1527, and in 1550 was a prebendary of the cathedral church of Aberdeen. His dispute with the Reformed ministers at Edinburgh, and his mission to the queen previous to her return to Scotland, have already been mentioned. In 1565, he was promoted to the abbacy of Lindores, and it is probable that he was appointed to the see of Ross about the end of that year, although some months elapsed before he was put in possession of the temporalities.[2]

There does not seem to be any record which mentions the

---

[1] Knox, vol. i. pp. 265, 266, 274, 275; vol. ii. p. 398. Keith's Catalogue, pp. 165, 194. Tytler's Life of Craig, p. 74-87. Diurnal of Occurrents, p. 79.

[2] Keith's Catalogue, pp. 194, 198-200. Knox, vol. ii. appendix, pp. 600, 601. Irving's Scottish Writers, vol. i. p. 122-127.

consecration either of Bishop John Sinclair, or of Bishop Leslie. That the latter was consecrated is certain from the subsequent events of his life; and it is probable that the former also was duly ordained to the episcopate. The want of positive information is easily explained by the peculiar position of Scotland at that time. The temporal rank and emoluments of the episcopal office might be openly conferred; but the religious rite could be celebrated only in private.

That Mary was contemplating some design for restoring the Church or relieving its members from the penalties to which they were exposed may therefore be held as certain; but it has been frequently stated that for this purpose she had asked the assistance of the great Roman Catholic powers on the Continent, and that she had actually joined the League which they had formed against the Protestants. I have seen no proof of this beyond the assertion of Randolph, who does not mention the source of his information, and whose individual word, in a matter of this kind, is not much to be relied on. What the English envoy states in one letter is contradicted in another, and there is the distinct evidence of the papal nuncio, the Bishop of Mondovi, afterwards Cardinal Laurea, that Mary had either never joined the League, or had refused to regulate her proceedings in accordance with its objects.[1]

The correspondence carried on between the Queen of the Scots and her friends in Italy, France, and Spain, was probably conducted by David Riccio, who acted as her French secretary, and his services in this matter were known or suspected by the Protestant leaders. They were aware that he had persuaded Mary to refuse her pardon to the exiled lords, and they feared that the forfeiture of those nobles would be the first step towards a restoration of Popery. They were also displeased that a person of Riccio's humble origin should possess any share of that power which they held to be their own exclusive right. The same complaints were heard which had been so common in the reign of James III., and they were now aggravated by the circumstance that the object of

---

[1] Compare Randolph's letter to Cecil, 7th February, 1566 (Robertson, vol. iii. p. 315), with his letter of the 14th of the same month, and the nuncio's letter to the Grand Duke of Tuscany, both quoted by Miss Strickland (Lives of the Queens of Scotland, vol. iv. p. 246, and vol. v. p. 214).

aristocratic hatred and suspicion was a foreigner by birth, and an alien in religion. Mary was aware of these murmurs, but disregarded and despised them. "If the sovereign," she said, "finds a man of low estate, poor in means but generous in mind, faithful in heart, and well adapted to fill an office in his service, will he not dare to intrust him with any authority, because the nobles who already possess power are ever craving for more?"

The meeting of parliament had been postponed from February to March, and, on the twelfth of that month, it was proposed to carry through the forfeiture of Murray and his associates. There was no way of preventing this result except one of those violent measures which had been too frequent in Scottish history. The friends of the banished nobles and the zealous supporters of the Reformation might have been unable to execute their plans had they not found an ally in Darnley, who was jealous of Riccio's influence with the queen, and indignant that she had refused him the crown-matrimonial. A conspiracy was formed by those various parties, and bonds were interchanged, according to the Scottish fashion, by which they engaged to put Riccio to death, to confer the crown-matrimonial on Darnley, and to place the queen under restraint. The chief persons concerned, besides Darnley himself, were the Earl of Morton, and the Lords Ruthven and Lindsay, but the plans of the conspirators were approved by Lennox, Murray, Argyll, Lethington, and Grange, and by the Earl of Bedford and Randolph, by whom they were communicated to Elizabeth, Cecil, and Leicester.

A fast had been ordered by the last general assembly, and Knox and Craig had been enjoined to set forth the form of it. It began on Sunday, the third of March, 1566, and the Protestants resorted to Edinburgh in large numbers. The subjects selected from the Scriptures for the prayers and sermons were the slaying of Oreb and Zeb, the death of Sisera, the hanging of Haman, and similar events in the Old Testament history. On Thursday, the seventh, the Lords of the Articles were chosen for the parliament, and everything was prepared for the process of attainder on the twelfth. On the evening of the following Saturday, Riccio was murdered at Holyrood. The queen's friends escaped from the palace, but Black, the Dominican friar who had on several occasions come forward as a champion of the Roman Church, was killed in the tumult. Mary was detained a prisoner in her chamber; and, on Sunday, Darnley caused proclamation to be made, commanding the lords of parliament to leave Edinburgh. On the evening of that day, Murray and the banished nobles arrived in the capital.

It was proposed to imprison the queen until she should agree to confer the crown-matrimonial on Darnley, establish the Reformed religion, and ratify in parliament the proceedings of the nobles, but she prevailed on her husband to separate his cause from that of the conspirators, and to retire with her to Dunbar. There she was soon joined by the Archbishop of St. Andrews, by the Earl of Huntly, who had been restored to his father's title and estates, by the Earls of Bothwell and Atholl, and others. By their advice she pardoned Murray and the banished lords, and turned her whole attention to the punishment of Riccio's murderers. The conspirators, unable to offer any resistance, fled to England, and Knox sought refuge among his supporters in Kyle. The office of chancellor of the kingdom, which had been bestowed on Morton after the battle of Corrichie, was now conferred on the Earl of Huntly.[1]

The circumstances relating to Riccio's murder and the conspiracy which led to it are now for the most part clearly ascertained. One important point remains undecided— whether Knox was aware of the plot. The direct evidence against the reformer was first discovered by Mr. Tytler. It consists of a list of the names of those who were implicated, transmitted by Randolph to Cecil twelve days after the murder. In this list the names of Knox and Craig appear; and, taken along with the other circumstances of the case,

[1] Knox, vol. ii. p. 519-526, and appendix, p. 592-598. Sir James Melville's Memoirs, Bannatyne Club ed. p. 130-149. Keith, vol. ii, p. 380-424; vol. iii. p. 260-278. Tytler, vol. vii. p. 14-36. Labanoff, vol. vii. pp. 298, 299. as quoted in Mignet's History of Queen Mary, English Translation, vol. i. p. 210. The death of Black is mentioned in a letter from Parkhurst, Bishop of Norwich, to Bullinger, dated 21st August, 1566, referred to by Mr. David Laing in his appendix to Knox, vol. ii. pp. 594, 595, and printed in Burnet's History of the Reformation, vol. iv. p. 594, and in the Zurich Letters, Parker Society ed. vol. i. pp. 98, 99, and translation, p. 165-167

it is, in Mr. Tytler's opinion, conclusive as to the ministers' guilt. So far as Knox is concerned, it would not require direct evidence of a very strong description to establish his complicity. The presumptions which go so far to render improbable a similar accusation against George Wishart lean entirely in the opposite way in regard to Knox. It was an opinion of his, and one which he openly avowed, that every idolater should be put to death. He could have little scruple in acting on this in the case of a foreigner whose life was believed to be inconsistent with the safety of the Reformed cause. He formerly boasted that no great attempt in support of the Protestant religion had ever been made without his assistance; and on this occasion his father-in-law, Lord Ochiltree, and his principal friends among the nobility and barons, were cognisant of the plot. His course of proceeding during the fast, and his flight to Kyle—a circumstance so different from his usual bold confronting of danger—are suspicious. The portion of his History of the Reformation, in which the murder is related, cannot be entirely relied on as genuine, but in another passage of undoubted authenticity he thus expresses himself:—" That great abuse of this commonwealth, that poltroon and vile knave, Davie, was justly punished, the ninth of March, in the year of God, 1565, for abusing of the commonwealth, and for his other villany which we list not to express, by the counsel and hands of James Douglas, Earl of Morton, Patrick, Lord Lindsay, and the Lord Ruthven, with other assisters in their company, who all, for their just act, and most worthy of all praise, are now unworthily left of their brethren, and suffer the bitterness of banishment and exile."

Suspicious, however, as these circumstances are, and shewing, as they do, the reformer's deliberate approbation of the murder, I do not think that the evidence brought forward by Mr. Tytler, and the arguments by which he supports it, are sufficient to prove that Knox was aware of the conspiracy. There is no reason to doubt the genuineness of the list transmitted by Randolph, though it is not in his own handwriting; but the information which he received might have been erroneous, and it would seem that the subsequent list, sent to the English council by Bedford and Randolph, in which the names of Craig and Knox do not appear, was the result of more accurate investigation, rather than a document prepared for the purpose of concealing the guilt of the reformers.[1]

John, Bishop of Brechin, died on the ninth of April, 1566, and in him Mary lost one of the wisest and most faithful of her counsellors. The nomination of his successor reflects no credit on the queen. Through the influence of the Earl of Argyll, Alexander Campbell, a young man of the family of Ardkinlas, was appointed to the see on the sixteenth of May. The new prelate was never consecrated. He was a supporter of the Reformed opinions, and fulfilled what was expected of him, by alienating the possessions of the bishopric to his patron the earl.[2]

The district of Carrick had hitherto been one of the strongholds of the ancient Church, but it ceased to be so in the autumn of this year. The Earl of Cassillis, having married a sister of Lord Glammis, by her persuasion became a Protestant, and, as Knox expresses it, caused "reform his churches in Carrick, and promised to maintain the doctrine of the Evangel."[3]

In the month of September, the superintendents and the most influential ministers assembled at St. Andrews, to consider the confession drawn up by the Reformed in Switzerland. This confession was sent by its compilers to the Scottish Protestants, with a request to know whether they agreed with it, because it was alleged that in some points they differed from their brethren on the Continent. After due consultation, the superintendents and ministers, in an answer addressed to Beza, stated that they agreed on all points, except in regard to the observance of festivals: "This one thing, however, we can scarcely refrain from mentioning, with regard to what is written in the twenty-fourth chapter of the aforesaid

---

[1] Compare the statements and arguments in the seventh volume of Tytler, Proofs and Illustrations, p. 353-362, with the remarks of Dr. M'Crie, son of Knox's biographer, appended to his Sketches of Scottish Church History, 4th ed. vol. i. p. 309-320. See also Knox, vol. i. p. 235, and Ellis's Original Letters, vol. ii. p. 220-222.

[2] Knox, vol. ii. p. 528. Diurnal of Occurrents, p. 98. Keith's Catalogue, p. 166.

[3] Knox, vol. ii. p. 533.

confession, concerning the 'festivals of our Lord's Nativity, Circumcision, Passion, Resurrection, Ascension, and sending the Holy Ghost upon his disciples,' that these festivals at the present time obtain no place among us; for we dare not religiously celebrate any other feast day than what the divine oracles have prescribed. Everything else, as we have said, we teach, approve, and most willingly embrace."[1]

During this autumn, a formal attempt was made to induce the queen to consent to the reception of a nuncio in Scotland. Soon after her marriage, Mary had opened a communication with the King of Spain. An English gentleman, named Francis Yaxley, formerly in the service of Queen Mary of England, now in attendance on Darnley, was sent to notify the marriage to Philip, to assure him of their attachment to the Church of Rome, and to ask his assistance in maintaining their rights. Philip gave the envoy a favourable answer, and wrote to the Pope, requesting his co-operation in the cause of the King and Queen of Scotland. Nothing farther seems to have been done during the pontificate of Pius IV., but his successor, Pius V., on the sixteenth of June, 1566, wrote to the queen with a supply of money, recommending the Bishop of Mondovi as nuncio to Scotland, and promising all the assistance in his power to aid her design of bringing back her kingdom to the obedience of the holy see. When the nuncio arrived at Paris, he received a communication from the queen, through the Archbishop of Glasgow, expressing her wish that he might come to Scotland as soon as practicable, but advising delay till matters should be prepared for his reception. The nuncio praised her zeal, sent over a Jesuit named Edmund Hay, to assist her secretly with his counsels, and urged her to dismiss Lethington, who, he said, was a secret adherent of the Earl of Murray.

On the ninth of October, Mary wrote to the Pope, acknowledging his bounty, mentioning that she had succeeded, with considerable difficulty, in obtaining the consent of her nobility to the public baptism of her son according to the ritual of the Church, and expressing a hope that this would be a beginning towards the restoration of the right use of the sacraments in her dominions. Meanwhile, the nuncio again urged her,

[1] Knox, vol. ii. p. 534. Zurich Letters, vol. ii. p. 362-365.

through the Bishop of Dunblane who was then at Paris, to allow of his coming to Scotland. Mary held a secret meeting of the nobles and prelates of her own communion, to consider the propriety of sending Lord Seaton with a convoy of ships to bring the nuncio over. The prelates are said to have offered to defray the whole expense, but Mary still declined to give her sanction, alleging that she could not warrant the nuncio's safety from the violence of the Protestants. Farther proceedings were stopped by the king's murder; and the nuncio, who was prepared to come over at all hazards, severely blamed the queen's lukewarmness, attributing her subsequent misfortunes to her refusal of his visit, and to her not following the counsels of the League. Of Mary's zeal in the cause of her religion there can be no doubt, but these circumstances shew that it was tempered with prudence and discretion. She knew much better than the Italian prelate what dangers would attend the open appearance of a papal envoy in Scotland, and, rather than incur these, she chose to expose herself to the censures and misconstructions of the ardent adherents of Rome.[1]

The baptism of the infant son of Mary and Darnley has been alluded to in the preceding remarks. The Prince of Scotland was born at Edinburgh, on the nineteenth of June, 1566. His baptism was long delayed, probably to enable the queen to make the necessary arrangements for its public celebration. All things having finally been prepared, he was baptized by the name of Charles James by the Archbishop of St. Andrews, in the chapel-royal at Stirling Castle, on the seventeenth of December, in presence of the queen, the Bishops of Dunkeld, Dunblane, and Ross, the Prior of Whithorn, and various nobles who adhered to the communion of Rome. The sponsors were the King of France, the Duke of Savoy, and the Queen of England, who were represented by their several proxies. The Countess of Argyll, who acted

[1] In regard to Mary's negotiations with Spain and Rome, see Mignet, vol. i. p. 191-193, vol. ii. p. 432-437; Burnet's History of the Reformation, vol. iii. p. 487-489; Keith, vol. ii. pp. 600, 601, vol. iii. pp. 311, 341, 342; Miss Strickland's Lives of the Queens of Scotland, vol. v. p. 212-215; and the original authorities referred to by these writers. After her marriage with Bothwell, Mary blamed the nuncio for not coming to Scotland, though, as she said, he was invited by her; but the statement made by her at that time cannot be relied on.

for Elizabeth, was afterwards obliged to do penance for assisting at a Popish sacrament. The English ambassador, the Earl of Bedford, and the Scottish Protestant nobles, remained outside the chapel door. This was the last public ceremonial in which the Scottish bishops of the Roman communion took part.[1]

Soon after the baptism of her son, Mary, yielding to the entreaties of the Earls of Murray and Bothwell, granted a pardon to the Earl of Morton, the Lord Lindsay, and the chief conspirators against Riccio. On the other hand, she restored to the Archbishop of St. Andrews the consistorial jurisdiction which he had lost in the year 1560. This was not now looked upon as an ecclesiastical privilege, but it may have been intended as a beginning towards the re-establishment of other rights.[2]

The general assembly met at Edinburgh on the twenty-fifth of December. The members agreed to present a remonstrance to the privy council against the late grant in favour of the primate. Knox had not resumed his former office in the capital, and, as his sons were pursuing their education in England, he obtained leave from the assembly to go to that country for the purpose of visiting them, and for other business. The assembly furnished him with testimonials of character, and also 'intrusted him with a letter to the English bishops, in which they were requested to deal gently with their brethren who scrupled to wear the ecclesiastical vestments.[3]

The temporary reconciliation between the queen and Darnley had not continued long. The conduct of the latter grew daily more capricious and unbecoming. Mary strove for some time to win her husband to a better disposition, but at last seems to have abandoned him to his own sullen humour and evil courses. Darnley was encouraged in his waywardness by his father, and, deserted by almost all others, sought support among the most bigoted adherents of the

[1] Knox, vol. ii. pp. 536, 537. Diurnal of Occurrents, pp. 103, 104. Keith, vol. i. pp. xcvii. xcviii.; vol. ii. p. 485-489.

[2] Knox, vol. ii. p. 548. Tytler, vol. vii. pp. 56, 57. Laing's History of Scotland, 2nd ed. vol. ii. pp. 75, 76.

[3] Book of the Universal Kirk, p. 46-54. Knox, vol. ii. p. 537-547. Calderwood, vol. ii. p. 328-340. Keith, vol. iii. p. 146-159.

Roman Church, who were offended by the queen's refusal to incur the hazard of an attempt to restore the influence of the papacy. Soon after the baptism of the prince, he went to visit the Earl of Lennox at Glasgow, and while in that city was taken dangerously ill of the small-pox. Mary sent her own physician to attend him, and when he began to recover went herself to Glasgow, where a reconciliation, to all appearance full and sincere, took place between them. In the end of January, Darnley was able to be removed to Edinburgh. A house belonging to the provost of the collegiate church of St. Mary-in-the-Fields was fitted up for his reception. At an early hour in the morning of Monday, the tenth of February, that house was blown up with gunpowder, and the dead body of Darnley, unscathed by fire, was found lying in an adjoining garden.

The immediate agents in this horrible crime were the retainers of the Earl of Bothwell, and, from the first, public suspicion was directed towards them and their master. The queen was earnestly advised by her best friends to use every effort for the discovery and punishment of the murderers. The Archbishop of Glasgow, writing from Paris, did not conceal the reports which pointed to herself as implicated in the conspiracy, and told her plainly that it was better for her to lose life and all, rather than not take vengeance on those who were really guilty. Bothwell was formally accused by the Earl of Lennox, and a day was appointed for his trial, but, as he continued to direct all public proceedings in the queen's name, no one ventured to appear against him, and he was acquitted by the jury. There cannot be a doubt as to Bothwell's guilt. Whether Mary was cognisant of the murder still remains a subject of dispute. The positive evidence against her is quite insufficient to establish her guilt, but her conduct in regard to Bothwell exposes her to very grievous suspicion.[1]

The parliament met at Edinburgh immediately after the trial of Bothwell. The three estates appear under the ancient form. The record bears that the parliament was holden and begun at Edinburgh, on the fourteenth day of April, by the

[1] Knox, vol. ii. p. 549-552. Keith, vol. i. pp. civ. cv.; vol. ii. p. 496-562. Tytler, vol. vii. p. 56-84.

most reverend, and reverend fathers in Christ, John, Archbishop of St. Andrews, Primate of all Scotland, and legatus natus, Alexander, Bishop of Galloway, William, Bishop of Dunblane, Adam, Bishop of Orkney, John, Bishop of the Isles, and by the earls, barons, and others there specified. In the course of the proceedings, the Bishops of Dunkeld, Brechin, Aberdeen, and Ross, and various abbots and priors were also present. The Bishop of the Isles was John Carsewell, the Protestant superintendent of Argyll, who had been nominated to the see of the Isles and the abbacy of Iona on the twenty-fourth day of March preceding, the queen's presentation bearing that he was appointed in the same form, and as freely in all respects as if he had been provided thereto by the court of Rome. Nothing is mentioned respecting the death of Carsewell's predecessor, Bishop John, but it appears that on the twenty-first of May, 1567, a person named Lachlan M'Lean renounced all right which he had to the bishopric of the Isles and abbacy of Iona, and became bound not to molest John Carsewell in the posession of the same. At this parliament various acts were passed ratifying the grants which had been made to several of the nobility and barons, and the repeal of the penal statutes formerly enacted against the Protestants was confirmed.[1]

On the evening of the day on which parliament rose, the Earl of Bothwell entertained a large number of the chief nobility at supper. During the banquet, the guests were requested to subscribe a bond, in which they declared their belief of the earl's innocence of the murder of Darnley, and recommended him as a suitable husband for the queen. It is said that the house was surrounded by his armed retainers, but the subscription of such a paper, under any circumstances, is one of the most disgraceful incidents in Scottish history.

The course of events now hurried rapidly on. The queen was seized by Bothwell on the twenty-fourth of April, and carried to his castle of Dunbar. As he was already married to a sister of the Earl of Huntly, a divorce was urged forward, both in the Protestant consistorial court, and in that of the primate, and on the fifteenth of May he attained the

---

[1] Acts of the Parliaments of Scotland, vol. ii. p. 545-590. Keith's Catalogue, pp. 307, 308. Collectanea de rebus Albanicis, p. 5.

object of his ambition by his marriage with the queen. The ceremony was performed within the presence chamber of Holyrood by the Bishop of Orkney, after sermon, according to the Protestant mode. None of the excuses which have been made for Mary's conduct at this time are of any avail. Whatever threats or violence may have been used, death itself ought to have been welcome to her rather than such dishonour.

During these transactions a powerful confederacy of the nobles, strengthened by the promised support of England and France, was forming against the queen and Bothwell. Mary, finding that she could not rely on the fidelity of her troops, surrendered to Kirkaldy of Grange, on his promise that she would be treated by the associated barons as their sovereign. Bothwell was allowed to depart in safety. The condition agreed to by Kirkaldy was disregarded. Mary was carried to Edinburgh, and, after being exposed to the insults of the soldiers and populace, was shut up in prison within the castle of Lochleven, on the sixteenth of June.[1]

On the twenty-fourth of June, the Earl of Glencairn, accompanied by his own domestics, went to the queen's chapel at Holyrood, and destroyed the altars, images, and other furniture. This act was well-pleasing to the ministers and zealous Protestants, but was not approved of by most of the nobility.[2]

On the twenty-fifth of the same month, the general assembly met at Edinburgh, and George Buchanan was chosen moderator. Buchanan was neither a superintendent nor a minister, and his appointment to preside in the highest court of the Reformed communion shews the privileges possessed by the lay members of that body. It was agreed that another assembly should be held at Edinburgh on the twentieth of July, an endeavour being made in the meantime to prevail on the Earls of Huntly and Argyll, and other Protestant nobles favourable to the queen, to concur with the party of the associated barons in measures for the welfare of the Reformed religion.

---

[1] Knox, vol. ii. p. 552-562. Keith, vol. ii. p. 562-647. Laing, vol. ii. p. 106-115. Tytler, vol. vii. p. 85-113.

[2] Knox, vol. ii. p. 562. Calderwood, vol. ii. p. 366. Keith, vol. ii. pp. 654, 655.

The assembly met on the twenty-first of July, but the queen's lords refused to appear. Among the barons present were the Earls of Morton, Mar, and Glencairn, the Lords Ruthven, Lindsay, and Ochiltree, the secretary, Maitland, and Kirkaldy of Grange. The Earl of Murray had left Scotland a short time before the trial of Bothwell. All the members of the assembly agreed to maintain and confirm the acts in favour of the Protestant religion which were made by the parliament of 1560, to use their endeavours to obtain the patrimony of the Church for the Reformed ministers, to avenge the murder of the late king, to commit the prince to the care of wise and godly men, and utterly to take away all idolatry without respect of place or person. It was also agreed that, in time to come, the sovereign should, before his coronation, take an oath to maintain the true religion now professed in Scotland. The assistance of the ministers was of the utmost importance to Morton and his friends, who were threatened at this time by a powerful combination of the party of Huntly, Argyll, and the Hamiltons, with those who had always remained faithful to the queen. They were therefore ready to make any engagements which the zealous Protestants might desire.[1]

In the meantime, the associated barons were deliberating about the fate of Mary. With few exceptions, they were resolved on her deposition, and several of them proposed to bring her to a public trial and put her to death, as accessory to the conspiracy against Darnley. This last measure was supported by the influence of the Protestant ministers, and vehemently urged on by Knox, who had returned from England before the first meeting of the assembly. The deposition and imprisonment of the queen were finally resolved on, and three instruments were prepared for her signature. By these, she resigned the government in favour of her infant son, conferring the regency, during his minority, on the Earl of Murray, and, till that nobleman's return from France, or in the event of his decease or his declining to act, on the Duke of Chatel-herault, and the Earls of Lennox, Argyll, Atholl, Morton, Glencairn, and Mar. The Lord Lindsay and Sir

[1] Book of the Universal Kirk, p. 54-69. Knox, vol. ii. p. 563-565. Calderwood, vol. ii. pp. 368-371, 377-384. Keith, vol. iii. p. 164-184.

Robert Melville were sent to Lochleven to demand the signature of the queen to these papers. For some time she refused to subscribe them, but, overawed at length by the violence of Lindsay, and the fear of an ignominious death if she persisted in her refusal, she gave her consent. The instruments of Mary's abdication were signed on the twenty-fourth of July, 1567.[1]

[1] Keith, vol. i. p. cx. cxv.; vol. ii. p. 655-716. Tytler, vol. vii. p. 113-138.

CHAPTER XXXVII.

FROM QUEEN MARY'S ABDICATION IN JULY, 1567, TO THE DEATH OF ARCHBISHOP HAMILTON IN APRIL, 1571.

Coronation of James VI.—Regency of the Earl of Murray—Escape of Queen Mary from Lochleven—Her defeat at Langside—Her flight to England—Deprivation of the Principal and regents of King's College, Aberdeen—Negotiations between Murray and Elizabeth—Murder of the Earl of Murray—Regency of the Earl of Lennox—Death of John Hamilton, Archbishop of St. Andrews.

THE associated barons cared little how Mary's abdication was obtained, and proceeded at once to act upon it. They assembled at Stirling for the coronation of the prince, and the place appointed for the ceremony was the parish church of that town. It was the wish of the nobles, on this occasion, to conform as far as possible to ancient usage, and, when Knox and the ministers objected to the unction as a Jewish practice, their scruples were disregarded. The deeds of abdication were read, and Lindsay and Ruthven swore that they were signed by the free act of the queen. Knox preached the sermon; the prince was crowned and anointed by the Bishop of Orkney; and the Earl of Morton, laying his hand on the Bible, engaged on behalf of the infant sovereign, that he would maintain the true Reformed religion as now received within the realm, and extirpate all heresy from his dominions. This inauguration took place on the twenty-ninth of July.[1]

The English ambassador, Sir Nicholas Throckmorton, by order of his mistress, kept aloof from these proceedings. Elizabeth's hatred to Mary was qualified by another feeling which on various occasions affected her policy towards Scotland—a dislike and dread of the example shewn by the associated lords in deposing and imprisoning their sovereign. Throckmorton even interceded in favour of Mary, and in his

[1] Knox, vol. ii. p. 566. Calderwood, vol. ii. p. 384. Keith, vol. ii. p. 719-726. Tytler, vol. vii. pp. 138, 139.

correspondence with Elizabeth he states that, when he did so, the secretary, Lethington, and the comptroller, Tullibardine, answered him with the startling averment that the Earl of Huntly, the Archbishop of St. Andrews, and the Abbot of Kilwinning, were ready to support the barons in all their designs, if they would at once put the queen to death, and so prevent the risk of her marrying again and postponing the claims of the Hamiltons to the crown. This strange statement has met with the too ready belief of Mr. Tytler, by whom the letter in which it is contained was first discovered. Throckmorton's veracity is less suspicious than that of any other of the English envoys, but no reliance can be placed on the unsupported averment of Lethington and Tullibardine. Such a proceeding on the part of the queen's lords is very improbable, and, in regard to the primate particularly, there is nothing which we know of his conduct that would entitle us to judge him so harshly.[1]

The return of Murray was now anxiously expected by all parties. On his arrival, he declined to accept the regency until he should have a personal interview with the queen. At Lochleven he was welcomed by Mary as the only one on whose wish and power to assist her she could now rely. He answered her affectionate entreaties for support by a formal recital of all the evil deeds she had done since her marriage with Darnley, and by setting before her the punishment with which she was threatened by so many of her subjects. The queen was alarmed, and implored him, for her sake, to accept the regency. Murray had now gained his object in the manner which he wished. He returned to Edinburgh, and on the twenty-second of August was proclaimed regent.[2]

A parliament was convened at Edinburgh on the fifteenth of December. The proceedings were very important. The queen's abdication, the coronation of the prince, and the appointment of Murray to the regency, were confirmed. The ecclesiastical acts of the convention of 1560—the abolition of the Pope's authority, the abrogation of all laws opposed to the Reformed religion, and the establishment of the Protestant

---

[1] Tytler, vol. vii. p. 140-141.
[2] Knox, vol. ii. p. 566. Keith, vol. ii p. 730-754. Tytler, vol. vii. p. 144-154.

Confession of Faith, were ratified. It was enacted that all succeeding kings at their coronation should take an oath to maintain the true Church, and to extirpate heresy. These statutes were passed in fulfilment of the promise made to the general assembly in July. The estates also declared that no other ecclesiastical jurisdiction, save that of the Reformed communion, should be acknowledged within the realm; but they still refused to bestow on the ministers a greater share of the patrimony of the Church than that which they had already received, and no notice whatever was taken of the provisions of the Book of Discipline.[1]

The general assembly met at Edinburgh on the twenty-fifth of December. Various charges of neglect in the visitation of churches, and other complaints, were brought against the Superintendent of Fife, and the Bishops of Orkney and Galloway. The Bishop of Orkney was farther accused of celebrating the queen's marriage with Bothwell. This prelate thought, perhaps, that he had sufficiently atoned for his offence by sailing with Kirkaldy to his island diocese in pursuit of the earl, and displaying an eagerness to apprehend him, more befitting a soldier than a priest. He was deprived of his office in the ministry till he should make satisfaction to the assembly.[2]

The government of the regent was conducted with vigour, and, where his own interests and those of his party were not concerned, with justice. The associated barons had taken up arms and dethroned and imprisoned their sovereign, chiefly under the pretext of avenging Darnley's murder. Murray had now the most ample opportunity of ascertaining who were guilty, and of bringing them to punishment. But, instead of doing so, he only proceeded against the subordinate actors, while he connived at the suppression of the evidence against persons of higher rank, and granted a remission to one of those most deeply implicated—Sir James Balfour—as a consideration for the surrender of Edinburgh Castle, with the keeping

[1] Acts of the Parliaments of Scotland, vol. iii. p. 3-25. Calderwood, vol. ii. p. 388-392. Keith, vol. iii. p. 184-186. Tytler, vol. vii. p. 162-167.

[2] Book of the Universal Kirk, p. 70-73. Calderwood, vol. ii. p. 392-401. Keith, vol. iii. p. 186-198. As to the Bishop of Orkney's share in Kirkaldy's expedition, see the interesting narrative of Mr. Mark Napier, in a note to Spottiswood's History, vol. ii. pp. 74, 75.

of which he had been intrusted by Bothwell. These circumstances were openly commented on, and the popularity which the regent had at first enjoyed was fast abating, when the tenure of his office and the authority of his party were brought into most imminent danger by the escape of the queen from Lochleven. That event took place on the second of May, 1568; and within a few days Mary was joined by a large number of the chief nobility, and was at the head of an army of six thousand men. She formally declared her abdication void, as having been extorted by force, and annulled all the proceedings which had taken place in consequence of it. She was not, however, elated by returning prosperity, but made offers of reconciliation to Murray. The regent declined her proposals, and determined to hazard all on the issue of an engagement. The battle of Langside was fatal to the cause of Mary. She fled southwards towards the Solway frith, and, in the dread of her own rebellious subjects, forgetting all which experience might have taught her of the character of Elizabeth, formed the resolution of seeking protection in England. On Sunday the sixteenth of May, she landed at Workington, in Cumberland, and soon afterwards was conducted to Carlisle.[1]

Mary had expected that Elizabeth would not only protect her, but assist in the recovery of her kingdom. When these hopes were dispelled, and when the Queen of England assumed the character of a judge instead of that of a kinswoman, Mary endeavoured to escape from captivity, and appealed for aid to the Roman Catholic subjects of Elizabeth, and to all who were favourable to her cause, whether in England or in Scotland. Her plans were discovered and her hopes of escape frustrated, first, by the ill success of the Rising in the North, and afterwards by the imprisonment and execution of the Duke of Norfolk.

The general assembly met at Edinburgh on the first of July, 1568. It was enacted that no one should have place or vote in that body except superintendents, commissioners appointed for the visitation of churches, and such fit ministers as they might bring with them, and the commissioners for counties, burghs, and universities. A printer, named Thomas

---

[1] Keith, vol. ii. p. 782-823. Tytler, vol. vii. p. 167-182.

Bassandine, was commanded to call in a book printed by him, called "The Fall of the Roman Kirk," in which the king was styled Supreme Head of the Primitive Church. The Bishop of Orkney was restored to the ministry, but enjoined to make public confession of his offence in solemnizing the queen's marriage with Bothwell. The assembly again met, as usual, on the twenty-fifth of December, but on account of the tempestuous weather and the apprehensions of the plague, adjourned to the twenty-fifth of February. None of the proceedings at the latter meeting call for notice.[1]

The assembly of July, 1568, had petitioned the regent to take order for the reformation of the University of Aberdeen, and he had promised to comply with their request. Murray found no opportunity of carrying this into effect till his expedition to the north in June, 1569. At that time he summoned the Principal of King's College and several of the regents before the council, and required them to subscribe an approbation of the Confession of Faith, and the acts concerning religion of the parliaments of 1560 and 1567, and to join themselves to the Reformed Church, and submit to its jurisdiction. They refused to comply with these demands, and were in consequence deprived of their offices. This decree of the civil power was soon followed by an ecclesiastical sentence, in like terms, pronounced by John Erskine of Dun, Superintendent of Angus and Mearns, with the advice and consent of the ministers, elders, and commissioners present on the occasion. The members of the university named in the sentence are Alexander Anderson, Principal of the college, Andrew Galloway, Sub-principal, Andrew Anderson, Thomas Austen, and Duncan Norrie, regents. These proceedings were confirmed by the assembly which met on the fifth of July, 1569. Alexander Anderson, the deprived principal, was distinguished for his learning and virtues. He was succeeded by Alexander Arbuthnot, one of the most accomplished of the Protestant ministers. At the same assembly of July, 1569, John Carsewell was rebuked for accepting the bishopric of the Isles without permission of the Reformed communion, and

---

[1] Book of the Universal Kirk, p 99-111. Calderwood, vol. ii. pp. 421-427, 470, 477-486.

for assisting at the parliament held after the king's murder.[1]

During the regency of Murray, the requests of the assembly were listened to with respect. In this, the earl consulted at once his inclinations and his interest. The Reformed on their part gave his government their most strenuous support, but all the assistance of his friends, and his own ability, were scarcely sufficient to maintain his power. The Hamiltons and the greater part of the nobility were still opposed to him; and to these were now added two of the ablest among the persons who had hitherto acted with him—Maitland and Kirkaldy. His enemies accused him of a design to set the young king aside, and usurp the throne, and, about the beginning of the year 1570, a satirical paper appeared, in which his various projects were alluded to and advocated by Knox and others of his confidential supporters in a series of fictitious speeches. The authorship was not avowed, but it was afterwards known that the paper was written by Thomas Maitland, brother of the secretary, who shared the hereditary genius of his family. The real character of the dialogue is sufficiently obvious, but it is said that at first many persons supposed the speeches to be genuine. Knox, who was always exceedingly sensitive in regard to any remark on himself, was very indignant. In a sermon preached at Edinburgh, he attacked the author of the paper, and foretold that he would perish in a strange land, without a friend to support his head. As Maitland soon afterwards died in Italy, the prediction was believed to be accomplished.[2]

[1] Book of the Universal Kirk, p. 111-117. Calderwood, vol. ii. p. 490-504. Preface to the Fasti Aberdonenses, p. xxvii.-xxxii.

[2] Calderwood, vol. ii. p. 515-525. M'Crie's Life of Knox, pp. 311, 312. Calderwood asserts that this paper came out immediately after the regent's murder, and Dr. M'Crie thinks its object was to blacken his memory, and lessen the odium of the assassination. It is more probable that it was written and circulated before the murder. According to Spottiswood (vol. ii. pp. 121, 122), the judgment denounced on Maitland was caused by a subsequent and less excusable offence against the reformer—his throwing into Knox's pulpit, the day after Murray's death, a paper containing the following words:—" Take up the man whom you accounted another God, and consider the end whereto his ambition hath brought him." When the archbishop recorded the fulfilment of Knox's prophesy, he forgot what he mentions in another place (vol. ii. p. 320), that Maitland was accompanied in his Italian journey by Thomas Smeaton, afterwards Principal of the College of Glasgow. It is possible that Calderwood has confounded two distinct transactions—the circulation of the dialogue prior

The regent endeavoured to secure his authority by persuading Elizabeth to deliver Mary into his hands. He accompanied his request with an assurance that no improper means should be taken to shorten his sister's life. A negotiation was commenced for this purpose, and, on the second of January, 1570, a confidential friend, Nicholas Elphinstone, was sent by Murray to the English court, to urge his proposal, and to offer, if the queen were delivered up, to surrender the Earl of Northumberland, who had fled for refuge to Scotland. On the same day Knox addressed a letter to Cecil, written in the mystical style which he frequently used. "If ye strike not at the root," he said, "the branches that appear to be broken will bud again, and that more quickly than men believe, with greater force than we would wish." It is not clear, however, whether this points to Mary's death, or to some other object.

The regent's proceedings were discovered by Mary's faithful counsellor, the Bishop of Ross, who presented to Elizabeth an indignant protest against what he said was equivalent to the death warrant of his sovereign, and called on the ambassadors of France and Spain to remonstrate on the point. Several of the Scottish nobles also interfered to oppose the base purpose of surrendering Northumberland. The farther progress of the negotiation was stopped by the death of Murray. On the twenty-third of January, while passing through Linlithgow, he was shot by Hamilton of Bothwell-haugh.[1] It is to be feared that the assassination of the regent was not solely the act of private revenge. Many among the nobles were anxious to rid themselves of their most formidable enemy, and were utterly unscrupulous as to the means. As in the case of the conspiracy against Riccio, the crime may have been hastened by the knowledge of negotiations, which, if successful, would be fatal to the existence of their party.

The friends of Mary would now have acquired complete ascendency, had not their opponents been supported by an English army. On the twelfth of July, the Earl of Lennox

to the regent's death, and the placing of the paper in Knox's pulpit immediately after it. It is evident that either his narrative, or that of Spottiswood, is erroneous. Dr. M'Crie attempts to avail himself of both.

[1] Tytler, vol. vii. p. 243-255.

was chosen regent by the lords of the opposite faction, but his authority was disowned and set at defiance by the queen's adherents.

The general assembly should have sat at Stirling on the twenty-fifth of February, but, on account of the troubled state of the country, it adjourned to the first of March, when the members met at Edinburgh. The Bishop of Orkney had been charged with the simoniacal exchange of his bishopric for the abbacy of Holyrood; with leaving off preaching, and giving himself to the office of a lord of Session; with assuming the title of reverend Father in God, which belongs not to a minister of Christ; with negligence in the planting of churches, and in sustaining those already planted; with allowing the buildings of his churches to fall into decay, especially that of Holyrood, although in the times of Popery the Archbishop of St. Andrews sequestrated the whole rents of the abbacy because the glass windows were not kept in repair; and with other offences. In answer to these complaints, the bishop alleged to the assembly that he had been compelled by the violence of Robert, Abbot of Holyrood, to accept of that abbacy in place of his bishopric; he denied that he had left off preaching, justified his acceptance of the office of a temporal judge, and asserted that most of the churches belonging to Holyrood had been pulled down in the beginning of the Reformation, and had never been repaired since. Knox and some others were directed to enquire into these charges.[1]

In the month of August, an act of horrible cruelty was perpetrated, which marks the lawless state of Scotland at this time. A person of the name of Allan Stewart had been appointed commendator of the abbey of Crossraguel by a grant from the queen, while Buchanan still claimed the rights which had formerly been conferred upon him over the same benefice. The Earl of Cassillis, who was popularly styled the King of Carrick, disregarded the pretensions of both, and acted as if the abbacy was his own property. As Stewart refused to give up his rights, the earl caused him to be seized, and imprisoned in the castle of Dunure, where he was roasted over

[1] Book of the Universal Kirk, p. 117-120. Calderwood, vol. ii. p. 529-544.

a fire till he subscribed the papers which were placed before him. Stewart and his friends afterwards complained to the regent, and Cassillis was ordered to find security not to molest either the commendator or Buchanan in person or property; but little other satisfaction was obtained for this outrage.[1]

From the commencement of the war, the castle of Dunbarton had been held for Mary by her faithful adherent, Lord Fleming. On the second of April, 1571, it was surprised by one of the regent's officers. The governor escaped, but among the prisoners was the Archbishop of St. Andrews. In his character of primate, the archbishop was hated by the Reformed; as the real leader of the Hamiltons, and one of the most formidable opponents of the regency, he was feared and disliked by Lennox. Religious and political animosity prompted the measures which followed, but the pretexts used were his alleged knowledge of the conspiracies which led to the murder of Darnley and Murray.

Some contemporary writers assert that he admitted his knowledge of the plot for assassinating Murray, and that he expressed his sorrow on that account. Buchanan tells us that his share in Darnley's murder was known through the evidence of a priest, to whom one of the assassins, a retainer of the primate, had revealed it in confession, and this statement is supported by the account given in the contemporary Diurnal of Occurrents: the archbishop maintained his innocence in this matter to the last. Having been refused a regular trial, he was condemned by the regent, in terms of a former attainder, and was hanged at Stirling on the sixth of April.[2]

---

[1] Bannatyne's Transactions in Scotland, ed. 1806, p. 55-67. Calderwood, vol. iii. p. 68-70.

[2] Buchanan, vol. i. p. 394-397. Bannatyne, pp. 120, 121. Diurnal of Occurrents, pp. 204, 205. Spottiswood, vol. ii. pp. 155, 156. Calderwood, vol. iii. p. 54-59. Cook's History of the Church of Scotland, vol. i. p. 122-129. Tytler, vol. vii. p. 288-291. Buchanan says that the priest who gave evidence against the primate adhered to his statement more than fifteen months afterwards, when about to suffer punishment according to the laws for saying mass a third time. This must mean that the priest was put to death in terms of the act of the convention of 1560, as renewed by the parliament of 1567, imposing capital punishment in such cases; and it shews that the statement made by some writers, that no Roman Catholic in Scotland suffered death by judicial sentence on account of religion, is erroneous. Another instance of capital punishment inflicted for saying mass is mentioned, under the date of 4th May, 1574, in the Diurnal of

Archbishop Hamilton was a prelate of great ability and of respectable learning. His private life, like that of too many of his order, was irregular. He bore a distinguished part in all the remarkable transactions of his time, and, if we could forget that he was primate of Scotland, his conduct would contrast favourably with that of most of the other political leaders. Although strongly attached to the interests of his family, there is no proof that he ever allowed his feelings as a Hamilton to involve him in treasonable attempts against the crown. Sharing in the persecuting measures by which the clergy endeavoured to check the Reformation, it does not appear that he was prominent in urging them on; and under ordinary circumstances he seems to have been mild and generous in his disposition. The sentence by which he died was cruel and unjust, and the manner in which it was executed was disgraceful to Lennox and his supporters.

John Hamilton was the last archbishop of St. Andrews of the ancient line. He had never ceased to assert his ecclesiastical rights, although their exercise had in a great measure ceased since the convention of 1560. The Roman Catholic members of the chapter of St. Andrews made an attempt to fill the vacancy in the primatial throne. An ecclesiastic, named Robert Hay, was elected to the see. He was never consecrated, but it is said that during several years he continued to perform various acts of jurisdiction, not only in his own province but in that of Glasgow. It is not stated that either the Scottish bishops or the see of Rome acknowledged his metropolitan title, and no other endeavour was made to keep up the succession of the hierarchy, or to maintain the metropolitan and diocesan system of the Roman Catholic Church.[1]

Occurrents (p. 341). The name of the priest is not given, and it is possible, making allowance for some inaccuracy in Buchanan's date, that he may have been the same person who bore evidence against the archbishop. That person was called Thomas Robison, and was at one time master of the school of Paisley.

[1] See the preface to Blackhall's Brief Narrative, p. xxvii.

CHAPTER XXXVIII.

FROM THE DEATH OF ARCHBISHOP HAMILTON IN APRIL, 1571, TO THE DEATH OF JOHN KNOX IN NOVEMBER, 1572.

Regency of the Earl of Mar—Letter of Erskine of Dun to the Regent—Erskine's Opinions as to Ecclesiastical Polity and the Episcopal Office—His remonstrances against the usurpations of the State—Ecclesiastical Convention at Leith—Sermon preached at the Convention by David Ferguson—Ecclesiastical Polity agreed to by the Commissioners of the Convention and of the Privy Council—John Douglas appointed Archbishop of St. Andrews—General Assembly at St. Andrews—General Assembly at Perth—Residence of John Knox at St. Andrews—His return to Edinburgh—His illness—His parting interviews with his friends—His death and character.

FIVE months after the capture of Dunbarton Castle, the Earl of Lennox was surprised and slain at Stirling by a body of the queen's adherents, under the command of the Earl of Huntly and Lord Claud Hamilton. On the day following—the fifth of September—the Earl of Mar was chosen regent by the nobles of the king's faction. His rule, like that of his predecessors, was disowned by the other party, who opposed him on equal terms in the southern parts of the kingdom, and in the north obtained a complete predominance under their able leader, Sir Adam Gordon, brother of the Earl of Huntly.

The regency of Mar was of short duration, but it was marked by an infamous attempt on the life of Mary. The proposal came from Elizabeth, and none in England were privy to it except her ministers Burleigh and Leicester, and Killigrew, the envoy sent to Scotland. The English queen offered to surrender Mary to the regent, on condition that she should be immediately put to death. Killigrew found a ready instrument for the actual execution of the deed in Nicholas Elphinstone, the same person who had before been employed by the Earl of Murray to negotiate the surrender of Mary. The consent of

Mar and Morton was next obtained, and the conditions were in the course of being arranged, when the regent became suddenly ill. He died on the twenty-eighth of October, 1572, and, on the twenty-fourth of November, the Earl of Morton was chosen his successor.[1]

In a parliament, which met at Stirling a few days before the death of Lennox, a petition was presented by the commissioners of the general assembly, requesting that benefices should be conferred only on qualified persons, duly admitted by the Church. The petition was rejected, and the Earl of Morton spoke of the ministers with great contempt.[2]

Through the influence of Morton, John Douglas, Rector of the University of St. Andrews and Provost of St. Mary's College there, had been presented to the vacant primatial see, and sat as archbishop in the parliament at Stirling. Other bishoprics were also conferred on various persons without consulting the assembly, and there was reason to apprehend that the higher benefices of the Church, with the right of representing the spiritual estate in parliament and other privileges, would be given to individuals not recognized by those to whom the actual ecclesiastical government was intrusted. This must have led to a separation or hostility between Church and State, and, to guard against such evils, Erskine of Dun, on the tenth of November, 1571, wrote a letter to the regent. The opinions expressed by the Superintendent of Angus are on several accounts worthy of attention. "As to the provision of benefices," he says, "this is my judgment; all benefices of tithes, or having tithes joined or annexed thereto, which are taken out of the people's labours, have the offices joined to them, which office is the preaching of the Gospel, and ministration of the sacraments; and this office is spiritual, and therefore belongs to the Church, which only has the distribution and ministration of spiritual things. So by the Church spiritual offices are distributed, and men received and admitted thereto, and the administration of the power is committed by the Church to bishops or superintendents: wherefore to the bishops and superintendents pertains the examination and admission of men unto benefices and offices of spiritual cure,

[1] Tytler, vol. vii. pp. 296-328, 384-388.
[2] Bannatyne, p. 285. Calderwood, vol. iii. pp. 137, 138.

whatsoever benefice it be, as well bishoprics, abbacies, and priories, as other inferior benefices. That this pertains by the Scriptures of God to the bishop or superintendent is manifest; for the Apostle Paul writes in the Second Epistle to Timothy, second chapter, and second verse: 'The things that thou hast heard of me among many witnesses, the same commit thou to faithful men who shall be able to teach others also.' Here the Apostle refers the examination to Timothy of the quality and ability of the person, when he says 'to men able to teach others.' And also the admission he refers, where he bids 'commit to him the same that is able to teach others.' And in another place, First Epistle to Timothy, fifth chapter, and twenty-second verse: 'Lay hands suddenly on no man, neither be partakers of other men's sins. Keep thyself pure.' By laying on of hands is understood admission to spiritual offices, the which the Apostle will not that Timothy do suddenly, without just examination of their manners and doctrine. The Apostle also writing to Titus, Bishop of Crete, puts him in remembrance of his office, which was to admit and appoint ministers in every city and congregation. And that he should not do the same rashly without examination, he expressed the qualities and conditions of all men that should be admitted, as at length is contained in the first chapter of the Epistle foresaid. The deacons that were chosen at Jerusalem by the whole congregation were received and admitted by the Apostles, and that by laying on of their hands, as St. Luke writes in the sixth chapter of the Acts of the Apostles. Thus we have expressed plainly by Scripture, that to the office of a bishop pertain examination and admission into spiritual cure and office, and also to oversee them that are admitted, that they walk uprightly, and exercise their office faithfully and purely. To take this power from the bishop or superintendent is to take away the office of a bishop, that no bishop be in the Church. There is a spiritual jurisdiction and power which God has given unto his Church, and to them that bear office therein; and there is a temporal jurisdiction and power given by God to kings and civil magistrates. Both the powers are of God, and most agreeing to the fortifying one of the other, if they be rightly used. But when the corruption of man enters in, confounding the offices, usurping to himself what he pleases, nothing regarding the good order appointed by God, then confusion follows in all estates. In the twelfth chapter of the First Book of Kings, it is written that King Jeroboam, in presumption of his authority, made priests in his realm expressly against the order that the Lord in those days had appointed touching the priesthood, whereupon followed destruction of that king and his seed; and likewise of all other kings that followed him in that wickedness. For the better understanding of that matter, Christ has given forth a rule which ought to be weighed by magistrates and by all people, saying, 'Render unto Cæsar the things which be Cæsar's, and unto God the things which be God's.' The Church of God should fortify all lawful power and authority that pertains to the civil magistrate, because it is the ordinance of God: but if he pass the bounds of his office, and enter within the sanctuary of the Lord, meddling with such things as appertain to the ministers of God's Church, as Uzziah, the King of Judah, did (Second Chronicles xxvi. 16), entering into the Temple to burn incense, the which pertained not to his office, then the servants of God should withstand his unjust enterprise, as did the bishop at that time withstand the King of Judah; for so are they commanded of God. The servants of God, when such wickedness occurs, should not keep silence, flattering princes in vain pride, but withstand and reprove them in their iniquity; and who does otherwise is unworthy to bear in God's Church any office. A greater offence and contempt of God and his Church can no prince do, than to set up by his authority men in spiritual offices, as to create bishops and pastors of the Church: for so to do is to conclude no Church of God to be; for the Church cannot it be, without it have its own proper jurisdiction and liberty, with the ministration of such offices as God hath appointed. In speaking this touching the liberty of the Church, I mean not the hurt of the king or others in their patronages, but that they have those privileges of presentation according to the laws; provided always that the examination and admission pertain only to the Church of all benefices having cure of souls.

"As to the question," continues Erskine, " if it be expedient that a superintendent should be where a qualified bishop is, I understand a bishop or superintendent to be but one office, and where the one is, the other is. But having some respect to the case whereupon the question is moved, I answer, the superintendents that are placed ought to continue in their office, notwithstanding any others that intrude themselves, or are placed by such as have no power in such offices. They may be called bishops, but are no bishops but idols (Zechariah, xi. 17), saith the Prophet, and therefore the superintendents, who are called and placed orderly by the Church, have the office and jurisdiction, and the other bishops, so called, have no office or jurisdiction in the Church of God, for they enter not by the door, but by another way, and therefore are not pastors, as sayeth Christ, but thieves and robbers."

On the fourteenth of November, Erskine again wrote to the regent about the oppressive proceedings of the civil power. Mar answered both letters, mentioning that he had redressed one particular grievance of a temporary character, and entreating a charitable construction of the rest of his conduct. "Our meaning was," he says, "and still is, to procure the reforming of things disordered in all sorts, as far as may be, retaining the privilege of the king, crown, and patronage. The default of the whole stands in this, that the policy of the Church of Scotland is not perfect, nor any solid conference among godly men that are well willed and of judgment how the same may be helped. And for corruption which daily increases, whensoever the circumstances of things shall be well considered by the good ministers that are neither busy nor over-desirous of promotion to them and theirs, it will be found that some have been authors and procurers of things that no good policy in the Church can allow. Whereanent we thought to have conferred specially with yourself, and to have yielded to you in things reasonable, and craved satisfaction of other things alike reasonable at your hands, and by your procurement."[1]

It was probably owing to the efforts of the regent himself on the one side, and of his kinsman, the Superintendent of Angus, on the other, that an attempt was made to arrange the differences between the civil and ecclesiastical powers. During the month of December, several conferences were held at Leith, between the regent and council, and the superin-

[1] Bannatyne, p. 279-293. Calderwood, vol. iii. p. 156-165.

tendents and ministers. On the twelfth of January, 1572, a meeting of superintendents, commissioners, and ministers, was held at Leith. This meeting was styled a convention, because those only met who were specially warned to attend, but it was agreed that its acts should have equal authority with those of a proper assembly. The state of feeling prevalent among the members may be judged of from a sermon preached before them by David Ferguson, minister at Dunfermline. Referring to his text from the third chapter of Malachi, the preacher remarked—" The same accusations and complaints that God used of old by his prophets against the Jews, serve this day against them that are like the Jews in transgression; yea, they serve against us. For, this day, Christ is spoiled amongst us, while that which ought to maintain the ministry of the Church and the poor is given to profane men, flatterers in court, ruffians, and hirelings; the poor in the meantime oppressed with hunger, the churches and temples decaying for the lack of ministers and upholding, and the schools utterly neglected. But now to speak of your temples where the word of God should be preached and the sacraments administered, all men see to what miserable ruin and decay they are come; yea, they are so profaned, that in my conscience, if I had been brought up in Germany, or in any other country where Christ is truly preached, and all things done decently and in order, according to God's word, and had heard of that purity of religion which is among you, and for the love thereof had taken travel to visit this land, and then should have seen the foul deformity and desolation of your churches and temples, which are more like sheep-cots than the house of God, I could not have judged that there had been any fear of God, or right religion in the most part of this realm. And as for the ministers of the word, they are utterly neglected, and come in manifest contempt among you. Ye rail upon them at your pleasure. Of their doctrine, if it serve not your turn, and agree not with your appetites, ye are become impatient. And to be short, we are now made your table-talk, whom ye mock in your mirth, and threaten in your anger. This is what moves me (let men judge as they list) to lay before your eyes the miserable state of the poor Church of Scotland, that thereby ye may be provoked to pity it, and to restore the things that unjustly you spoiled it of. Cleanse then your hand of all impiety, specially of sacrilege, whereby ye spoiled the poor, the schools, the temples, and the ministers of God's word, yea Christ Himself. I grant that our fathers, out of their immoderate zeal, besides the tithes and necessary rents of the Church, gave thereto superfluously, and more than enough. What then is to be done, but that the preachers of God's word be reasonably sustained (seeing that there is enough and too much for that purpose), the schools and the poor be well provided as they ought, and the temples honestly and reverently repaired; that the people may, without injury from wind and weather, sit and hear God's word, and participate in the holy sacraments. And if there rest anything unspent when this is done, (as no doubt there will,) in the name of God let it be spent on the most necessary affairs of the commonwealth, and not on any man's private commodity."

The convention having proceeded to business, commission was granted to John Erskine, Superintendent of Angus, John Winram, Superintendent of Fife, William Lundie of that ilk, Andrew Hay, commissioner of Clydesdale, David Lindsay, commissioner of Kyle, Robert Pont, commissioner of Murray, and John Craig, one of the ministers of Edinburgh, to meet with the lords of the council, and, on behalf of the Church, to arrange in regard to the ecclesiastical polity and the sustentation of ministers, and to report to the next assembly. These commissioners accordingly met with a committee of the council, consisting of the Earl of Morton, the Bishop of Orkney, the Commendator of Dunfermline, and others, and agreed as to various points, of which the following are the most important:—

In regard to archbishoprics and bishoprics, it was thought good, in consideration of the present state, that the names and titles of archbishops and bishops, and the boundaries of dioceses, should not be altered, but that the same should continue as before the Reformation of religion, at the least till the king's majesty, on attaining majority, or till the parliament, should otherwise determine; that the persons presented to archbishoprics and bishoprics should be endued, as far as might be, with the qualities mentioned in the examples of Timothy and Titus; that an assembly or chapter of learned ministers should be annexed to every metropolitan or cathedral see; that all archbishoprics and bishoprics, vacant or to become vacant, should within a year and day after the vacancy be filled up with qualified persons, thirty years of age at least; that the dean, or, failing him, the next in dignity in the chapter, should be vicar-general during a vacancy; that archbishops and bishops should in the meantime have no farther jurisdiction than superintendents; that they should be subject to the Church and general assembly in matters spiritual, as to the king in matters temporal, and that they should follow the advice of the best learned of their chapter in the admission to spiritual offices.

In regard to abbacies, priories, and nunneries, it was agreed that no appointment to any vacancies in these benefices should take place, nor any grants be conferred out of the same, till provision were made for the ministers belonging thereto; that the person holding the title, and possessing the remaining fruits thereof, as representing the ecclesiastical estate in parliament, and bearing the style of abbot, prior, or commendator, should be well learned, and qualified for his office, and for that purpose, on the king's letters commendatory, should be tried and admitted by the archbishop or bishop; that, on the failure of the present convents, the ministers of the churches belonging to the abbey or priory should act as the chapter of the commendator in the administration of the temporalities; that persons so named as commendators should be capable of acting as senators for the spiritual estate in the College of Justice, and of serving the king in the affairs of the commonwealth.

In regard to benefices having a cure of souls, it was agreed that the king, the universities, and the lay patrons, should possess their several rights of patronage; that only qualified persons, twenty-three years of age, should be admitted as ministers; that readers, found qualified by the bishop or superintendent, and duly admitted, should be entitled to solemnize marriages, and minister the sacrament of baptism, and to hold vicarages not exceeding the yearly value of forty pounds; that all ministers and beneficed persons should subscribe the Confession of Faith, and acknowledge the king's authority; and that pluralities of such benefices should be forbidden.

In regard to deaneries, provostries of collegiate churches, prebends, and chaplainries, it was in like manner agreed that no appointment to the same should take place, till provision were made for the ministers of their several churches, and that all provostries, prebends, and chaplainries, founded on temporal lands, should be bestowed on students in grammar, the arts, theology, law, and medicine.

As to the manner of creating a bishop, a letter under the great seal was to be directed to the dean and chapter of the cathedral church, setting forth the decease of the last bishop, the king's license to proceed to a new election, and his requisition to choose a faithful pastor, along with a recommendation of a person fit to be elected. The chapter were to meet accordingly, and, in the event of their finding the person nominated and recommended to be duly qualified, were to return their testimonial to that effect, certifying his election, and requesting the king's approbation of the same; but, if they found him to be not duly qualified, the testimonial was to specify the fact, and request the king to make another nomination. On the chapter's certificate of the election being returned, a letter under the great seal was to be directed to the most reverend father in God, the archbishop of the province, or the bishop to whom it appertained, setting forth the election, ratifying the same, and requiring the archbishop or bishop to consecrate the bishop-elect, as bishop and pastor of the church to which he was appointed, and to confirm the election. If the bishop-elect were already a bishop, and translated from another see, the election was simply to be confirmed. The new made bishop was to take the following oath in presence of the king:—" I, A. B. now elected Bishop of S. utterly testify and declare, in my conscience, that your majesty is the only lawful and supreme governor of this realm, as well in things temporal, as in the conservation and purgation of religion; and that no foreign prince, prelate, state, or potentate, hath or ought to have any jurisdiction, power, superiority, pre-eminency, or authority, ecclesiastical or spiritual, within this realm. And therefore I utterly renounce and forsake all foreign jurisdictions, powers, superiorities, and authorities; and promise, that from this forth I shall and will bear faith and true allegiance to your majesty, your heirs and lawful successors; and to my power shall assist and defend all jurisdictions, privileges, pre-eminency, and authorities, granted and belonging to your highness, your heirs and lawful successors, as united and annexed to your royal crown. And further, I acknowledge and confess to have and hold the said bishopric, and possessions of the same, under God, only of your majesty and crown royal of this your realm: and for the said possessions I do my homage presently unto your majesty; and unto the same, your heirs and lawful successors, shall be faithful and true. So help me God." The bishop thereupon was to receive letters under the privy seal, restoring his temporalities.

As several of the deaneries, canonries, and prebends of the cathedral churches, were still possessed by members of the Church of Rome, or by individuals who were not lawful ministers of the Reformed communion, a temporary arrangement was ordered till the chapters should be properly constituted. Rules were also laid down for the admission of abbots, priors, and bursars. All persons admitted to benefices having cure of souls were to promise obedience to their ordinary, and bursars in schools and colleges to the master or principal of the school or college.

These articles and conditions were approved by the regent on the first of February, and it was agreed to obtain a parliamentary ratification of the whole.[1]

The system thus proposed to be established is remarkable for its general resemblance to the external polity of the Church, as it existed before the Reformation in Scotland, and as it was at that time sanctioned by law in England. It was expressly required that bishops should be consecrated, and, in the admission of ministers and readers, it was probably intended that forms of ordination analogous to those previously observed in making priests and deacons should be used. Even the principles and scriptural precedents, by which these ceremonies, and the jurisdiction of the prelates, and the inherent rights and independence of the spiritual power, were supported by Erskine of Dun in his correspondence with the regent, bear a

[1] Calderwood, vol. iii. p. 168-196. Bannatyne, p. 296. See also Book of the Universal Kirk, p. 130; Spottiswood, vol. ii. p. 170-172; and note by Mr. Lyon in Keith's History, vol. iii. pp. 197, 198.

wonderful similarity to the old ecclesiastical teaching. But there was one fatal deficiency, which made the new polity, however outwardly fair and regular, a mere empty form. The persons to whom the office of consecration was intrusted had not themselves the gift which they were required to bestow on others.

No time was lost in carrying out the arrangements made at Leith. The chapter of the metropolitan see was ordered to meet at St. Andrews, on the sixth of February, for the purpose of electing a bishop and pastor for that church, and, on the day appointed, John Douglas was chosen archbishop. His inauguration took place on the following Sunday. An exhortation on the duties of a bishop was made by Winram, from the first chapter of the Epistle to Titus; the questions in the form used at the admission of a superintendent were put and answered; and the archbishop-elect was admitted to his office by the laying on of the hands of the Bishop of Caithness, the Superintendent of Lothian, and David Lindsay, minister at Leith.[1] The Bishop of Caithness, a brother of the late regent, the Earl of Lennox, appears never to have been consecrated, and it is probable that none of the three had even received orders as a priest. This seems to have been the first time at which the laying on of hands in ordination was used by the Reformed in Scotland.

The general assembly met within St. Leonard's College, St. Andrews, on the sixth of March. Winram resigned into their hands the superintendency of Fife, and asked that a successor should be appointed. He was requested, however, to continue the exercise of his jurisdiction in those parts which were not subject to the Archbishop of St. Andrews, and to assist the archbishop in his visitations or otherwise, when required by him. Similar injunctions were given to the Superintendents of Angus and Lothian. Douglas was allowed, in the meantime, to retain his office of provost of St. Mary's, in addition to the rectorship of the university and the archbishopric. Knox,

[1] Bannatyne, p. 321-324. Calderwood, vol. iii. p. 205-207. John Douglas, Rector of the University and Principal of St. Mary's College, has been supposed by Keith and others to be the same person with Douglas the Carmelite friar, who was chaplain for some time to the Earl of Argyll. This mistake is pointed out by Dr. M'Crie (Life of Melville, vol. i. p. 229), and by Mr. David Laing (Knox, vol. i. p. 286).

who had declined to assist at his inauguration, now protested against this accumulation of offices. His objection appears to have been, not to the episcopal office itself, but to its being bestowed on an unfit person, whose duties were already more than he was able to discharge.

The assembly again met at Perth, on the sixth of August. The Superintendent of Angus was chosen moderator. It was declared that the visitation and plantation of churches in the whole diocese of St. Andrews belonged to the archbishop, and to no other superintendent; but the Superintendents of Angus and Lothian, and three other persons, were, at his own desire, appointed to assist him. At this assembly the proceedings agreed to at Leith were reviewed. Objections were made to certain of the ecclesiastical titles which had been recognised on that occasion, as appearing to have a Popish tendency. It was enacted that, so far as the functions of the Church were concerned, the name of Archbishop should not be used, but that of Bishop only; in regard to the names of Chapter, Dean, Archdeacon, and Chancellor, a desire was expressed that they should be changed to others of the same purport—the chapter, for instance, to be called the bishop's assembly, and the dean, the moderator of that assembly; and it was also ordered that some persons should be appointed by the general assembly to consider the nature and extent of the functions of Deans, Archdeacons, Chancellors, Abbots, and Priors, and the propriety of changing their names to others more agreeable to God's word and the practice of the best reformed Churches. A letter and certain articles were addressed to the assembly by Knox, and delivered by his friends, Winram and Pont. In these documents, he exhorted them to contend for the truth, to endeavour to recover the patrimony of the Church, and to petition the regent to have all bishoprics filled up in terms of the agreement at Leith.[1]

John Carsewell, Bishop of the Isles, and Superintendent of Argyll, died in the autumn of this year. He translated Knox's Liturgy into Gaelic, and his work is remarkable as being the first which was printed in that language. In the

---

[1] Bannatyne, pp. 329-331, 364-369. Calderwood, vol. iii. pp. 208-210, 219-223, 765-768. Book of the Universal Kirk, pp. 131-133. Spottiswood, vol. ii. p. 172.

end of 1572, or the beginning of 1573, the bishopric of the Isles was bestowed on John Campbell, uncle of the laird of Calder.[1]

For a considerable time back, Knox had been in feeble health. In October, 1570, he had an attack of apoplexy, which affected his speech for several days, and led to exaggerated stories among his opponents, not unlike some of those which he himself tells about the Roman Catholic prelates. Early in the summer of the following year, when the strife between the two political parties became very much embittered, and his residence at Edinburgh was thought unsafe on account of the enmity of the Hamiltons and the garrison in the castle, he left that city, and retired to St. Andrews. His style of preaching was not so acceptable there as it had been in Edinburgh. The members of the university were a very different audience from the citizens of the capital. Many of them also held political opinions quite contrary to those which were maintained by the reformer, and some, it is probable, secretly adhered to the doctrines of the Roman Church. One of his chief opponents in the university was Archibald Hamilton, who afterwards abandoned the Reformed communion.

While Knox resided at St. Andrews, he published a treatise in defence of the Protestant opinions, which he had formerly composed in answer to a letter written by a Jesuit, named James Tyrie. This letter was addressed by Tyrie to his own brother, a gentleman of good family in the north of Scotland, for the purpose of bringing him back to the Church of Rome. The advertisement to Knox's treatise is dated at St. Andrews, the twelfth of July, 1571. In 1573, Tyrie published a reply at Paris, having his own original letter and Knox's answer prefixed.[2]

When a cessation of hostilities took place between the con-

---

[1] Keith's Catalogue, p. 308. Collectanea de rebus Albanicis, pp. 6, 7. Origines Parochiales Scotiæ, vol. ii. part i. p. 293. Wodrow Miscellany, vol. i. p. 281-283. Book of the Thanes of Cawdor, p. 186-188.

[2] M'Crie's Life of Knox, p. 313-332. Referring to the answer to Tyrie, Bishop Keith remarks (vol. iii. p. 507), "Mr. Knox makes some good and solid observations, from which, in my opinion, the Jesuit has not handsomely extricated himself." Bishop Leslie, as might be expected, gives a very different opinion; see his History, pp. 540, 541. See also on this subject Mackenzie's Lives, vol. iii. p. 424-432.

tending factions in the summer of 1572, Knox was invited back to Edinburgh. He returned thither in the month of August, and resumed his duties as a minister, although, in preaching, his infirmities obliged him to use a smaller church than that in which he had formerly officiated. Neither age nor sickness abated his zeal in the cause of the Reformation, or prevented his unceasing efforts to maintain it. When Killigrew came to Scotland to treat with the regent about the surrender of the queen, he had repeated conferences with Knox. The reformer was deeply affected by the intelligence which had been received of the massacre of the twenty-fourth of August at Paris, and a convention of the Protestants was summoned, in the regent's name, to meet at Edinburgh on the twentieth of October. When the day appointed came, whether owing to Mar's illness or some other cause, not a single nobleman appeared; but the ministers and several commissioners met, and presented certain articles to the regent and council, in which, among various measures, they recommended that a fast should begin on the twenty-third of November, to continue till the end of the month, and proposed that a league should be made with England and other Reformed countries for the maintenance of the true religion. These proceedings were encouraged by the English envoy for the furtherance of his own objects.[1]

On Sunday, the ninth of November, Knox officiated at the installation of James Lawson as his colleague and successor at Edinburgh, and this was the last occasion on which he appeared in public. On the following Tuesday, he was seized with a severe cough, which obliged him to give up his daily readings in the Old and New Testament. On Friday, supposing that it was Sunday, he wished to go to the church and preach, saying that he had been meditating all night on the Resurrection of Christ, which was to have been the subject of his next discourse. On Saturday, he was visited by John Durie, minister at Leith, and by another of his friends. He sat at table for the last time, ordered a hogshead of wine to be pierced, and cheerfully told one of his visitors to send for it so long as it lasted, as he could not tarry till it was consumed.

[1] Bannatyne, p. 385-411. Tytler, vol. vii. p. 316-321. M'Crie's Life of Knox, pp. 333, 334.

On Sunday the sixteenth, forgetting the day appointed for the fast, and thinking it had begun, he declined to take any food, till his mistake was pointed out. On Monday, he sent for his new colleague, Lawson, and the elders and deacons of his congregation, and bade them farewell, protesting that he had taught nothing but true and sound doctrine, and, however he had been against any man, that it was never for hatred of his person, but only for suppression of his wickedness. The Prayer for the Sick, as contained in the Psalm Book or Liturgy used at that time, was then read, and Lawson and the others departed. On Wednesday, he was visited by the Earl of Morton, Lord Boyd, and the laird of Drumlanrig; but what passed between them was not known at the time, no one else being present. Morton afterwards mentioned, that Knox then enquired whether he knew of the design to murder Darnley, and that he exhorted him to use the gifts which God had given him to better purpose than he had done in time past, threatening him with the divine vengeance if he did otherwise. On Thursday, when the Lord Lindsay, the Bishop of Caithness, and others, came to see him, he earnestly advised them to continue in the truth, and to have nothing to do with Kirkaldy and the defenders of the castle. On Friday, he requested his attendant, Bannatyne, to prepare the coffin for his funeral.

On Sunday the twenty-third, being the first day of the fast, he lay quiet for a considerable time, after which he said, " I have been in meditation these last two nights on the troubled Church of God, the spouse of Jesus Christ, despised of the world, but precious in his sight; I have called to God for her, and have committed her to her head, Jesus Christ; I have been fighting against Satan, who is ever ready to assault; yea, I have fought against spiritual wickedness in heavenly things, and have prevailed; I have been in heaven and have possession, and I have tasted of the heavenly joys where presently I am." He then repeated the Lord's Prayer and the Creed, with some words in explanation of the different petitions and articles, and, on saying " Our Father which art in heaven," added, " Who can pronounce so holy words?" After the evening sermon, many came to see him, and he spent the rest of the day in repeating devout prayers and ejaculations.

On Monday morning, he insisted on rising from bed, and sat up for half-an-hour. During the afternoon, he requested his wife to read the fifteenth chapter of the First Epistle to the Corinthians. Other passages of the Scripture, and portions of Calvin's sermons, were also read to him. When the usual evening prayers were said, one of those present asked whether he had heard them. He answered, "I would to God, that you and all men heard them as I have heard them, and I praise God for that heavenly sound." About eleven o'clock, he gave a deep sigh, and Bannatyne, sitting down beside him, reminded him of the comfortable promises of our Saviour which he had so often declared to others, and asked him to make some sign that he heard what was said. He lifted up his hand, and immediately afterwards expired.

Knox died on the twenty-fourth of November, being then in the sixty-seventh year of his age. On the twenty-sixth, he was buried in the church-yard of St. Giles. His funeral was attended by Morton, who had been elected regent on the very day the reformer died. When his body was laid in the grave, the earl said, "Here lieth a man, who in his life never feared the face of man; who hath been often threatened with pistol and dagger, but yet hath ended his days in peace and honour. For he had God's providence watching over him in a special manner when his very life was sought."[1]

The character of Knox, like that of the other leading persons of the age in which he lived, has continued from his own time to the present to be a subject of much discussion. The political and ecclesiastical party in Scotland which looked upon him as the chief supporter of their cause, and those who held similar principles in England, naturally venerated his memory and defended his opinions. But, in the former country, the same veneration, to a certain extent, was entertained for some time by those who, like Archbishop Spottiswood, belonged to a different school. Viewing the Reformation on the whole as a great blessing, they were unwilling to examine minutely the life and character of the man whose name was identified with it in Scotland. This reverence could hardly have existed along with a belief in the genuineness of Knox's his-

[1] Bannatyne, pp. 413-429, 508, 509. Calderwood, vol. iii. p. 230-242. Spottiswood, vol. ii. p. 179-184. M'Crie's Life of Knox, p. 335-347. Dr.

torical work; and that circumstance must never be lost sight of when Spottiswood's panegyric on the reformer is mentioned. Had the primate known, that "the scurril discourses we find in it, more fitting a comedian on the stage than a divine or minister," "the ridiculous toys and malicious detractions contained in that book," were not, as he supposed, the invention of another, but the undoubted composition of Knox himself, he would have found better materials for appreciating his true character than the tradition of the Scottish Protestants.

It is of course by his actions and his authentic writings that we are best able to judge of Knox's character; and these afford ample information for the purpose. The libels of his enemies may be passed by with contempt, but the panegyrics of his friends are equally worthless as evidence. His ability and courage, and the wonderful sway which he exercised over his followers, have never been disputed. His conviction of the truth and importance of the principles for which he contended is equally undeniable. Imputations have been thrown on the purity of his moral character, but no proof, so far as I am aware, has ever been brought of these charges; and on such a point mere suspicion, or the scandalous stories of opponents unsubstantiated at the time, should be absolutely disregarded. His opinions were avowed and acted on with stern uprightness and independence. Neither fear nor favour, flattery nor corruption, ever induced Knox to deviate from what he thought to be the path of duty.

M'Crie states that, when Knox was buried, "the regent emphatically pronounced his eulogium in these words, 'There lies he who never feared the face of man.'" The substitution of this epigrammatic remark, for the whole speech as given by Calderwood, has been almost universal among writers subsequent to the publication of Knox's Life. I have made no allusion in the text to the prophecy of Kirkaldy's death, said to have been made by Knox a week before his own decease. That he predicted the downfall of his old associate is certain, but the details given by James Melville and Spottiswood are not to be relied on. Bannatyne, who mentions the reference to Grange, would hardly have failed to relate the words ascribed to his master had they really been spoken. The subject bears a great resemblance to Wishart's alleged prophecy of the death of Beaton. It is probable that a general denunciation was, after the event, converted into a particular and distinct prediction. Knox, by his first wife, left two sons, who were both educated at Cambridge, and one of whom became a clergyman in the English Church. By his second wife he had three daughters.

On the other hand, believing, as he did, that his opinions were not only true, but essentially necessary for the welfare of the Church and kingdom, he was as ready to compel others to adopt them, as he was prepared himself to suffer for them. The persecuting tenets and assumptions of infallibility, which he denounced in the Church of Rome, he defended and sought to carry out for the maintenance of the Protestant cause. It was the prudence and caution of the nobility, not the toleration of the preachers, which moderated the execution of the penal laws enacted against the Roman Catholics. But Knox had recourse to worse weapons in defence of the Reformation. He corresponded with the rulers of a foreign state; abetted plots and conspiracies against his own sovereign; and did not scruple to postpone the true interests of his country to the supremacy of a party.

Another deep stain in his character was the harsh and uncharitable language, the false and slanderous accusations, which he systematically used against his opponents, and this, not merely in the heat of controversy, but calmly and deliberately in the closet. In some instances his language admits of palliation, if not of excuse. It was not easy for one who had seen his dearest friends put to death for their religious opinions, who himself had pined for many months in the French galleys, to speak with calmness of his persecutors. But in other cases this apology will be of no avail. Mary of Lorraine, if she had sanctioned, had never encouraged persecution, and her unfortunate daughter was scarcely able to obtain toleration for herself; yet towards both Knox cherished a feeling of malignity which no persuasions could appease, and no sufferings in the objects of his hatred could diminish. This feeling could hardly have been caused by political or theological differences alone; some personal injury or slight would rather seem to be connected with it. The angry passions and words of hatred, which he encouraged in himself and in others, were as much opposed to the plain rules of the Gospel, as were the crimes and vices which he so justly rebuked. And the evil of which he was thus guilty lived after him. Some of the worst deeds which stained the history of our country in the following age were justified by an appeal to the principles and example of Knox.

The History of the Reformation in Scotland has been referred to in connection with the character of its author, but it is proper to say a few words in regard to the literary merits of the work itself. The defects which have been alluded to necessarily lessen its value as a correct and impartial narrative of facts. In other respects, its merits have never been estimated at their true worth. Its style is remarkable for clearness and vigour, and its picturesque descriptions, its humourous illustrations of character, its dramatic reports of speeches and conversations, are superior to any thing previously to be found in the prose literature of Britain, and unequalled by any work which appeared in Scotland before the middle of the eighteenth century.

CHAPTER XXXIX.

FROM THE DEATH OF JOHN KNOX IN NOVEMBER, 1572, TO THE RESIGNA-
TION OF THE REGENCY BY THE EARL OF MORTON IN MARCH, 1578.

*Regency of the Earl of Morton—Proceedings of the General
Assembly—Protestant ministers appointed to the vacant
bishoprics—Objections made to the office of Bishop—
Andrew Melville, Principal of the College of Glasgow—
Limitations of the powers of the Bishops—Patrick Adamson,
Archbishop of St. Andrews—Resignation of the Regency
by the Earl of Morton—Ecclesiastical condition of Scot-
land—Intellectual and moral results of the Reformation.*

THE Earl of Morton governed the kingdom with vigour and success. He effected a reconciliation with Huntly and the Hamiltons, who agreed to acknowledge his authority on condition that the forfeitures which had passed against them should be rescinded. Others of the queen's adherents made their submission soon afterwards: in the spring of 1573, the only persons of note who still maintained the cause of Mary were Sir Adam Gordon in the north, and Lethington and Grange in the castle of Edinburgh. Morton resolved to put an end to the contest by obtaining possession of the fortress which had so long overawed the capital. Supported by a body of English soldiers he laid siege to the castle, and, after a desperate resistance, the garrison, fearing an assault, compelled their governor to surrender. The regent rejected the solicitations which were made to him to spare the lives of Lethington and Grange. The former escaped the ignominy of a public execution by dying in prison—as some said, by his own hand, though the report was never sufficiently confirmed. Kirkaldy was hanged on the third of August. Such was the miserable end of the brave soldier, and of the accomplished statesman and scholar, who had long occupied a distinguished place in the Scottish kingdom. Stained as their characters were by many crimes, their death cannot be regarded without pity. Lethington, in particular, appears amid all his treasons to have cherished a sincere admiration for his sovereign, whom he repeatedly shielded from the cruel designs of his associates, and to whose cause his last years were devoted with unswerving fidelity, when almost every one else had forsaken her.[1]

The general assembly met at Edinburgh on the sixth of March, 1573, and David Ferguson, minister at Dunfermline, was chosen moderator. Complaints having been made against the Bishop of St. Andrews for neglect of his duties, that prelate excused himself on account of ill health. The Superintendent of Angus protested that he should not be obliged to visit within the bounds of the diocese of St. Andrews, inasmuch as it was wholly assigned to the bishop, nor within that of Dunkeld, when it should be filled up. The Superintendent of Lothian made a similar protestation, and both the documents were remitted to certain commissioners who were appointed to confer with the regent and council touching the affairs of the Church. Among the members of that commission were the Bishop of St. Andrews, the Superintendent of Angus, Winram, now styled Superintendent of Stratherne, John Row, and David Lindsay. It was ordered that in future no minister should act as a senator of the College of Justice, except Robert Pont, who had already been allowed to hold that office. It was also enjoined that collections for the poor should be made, not during the administration of the communion or in the time of the sermon, but only at the church door.[2]

The next meeting of the assembly began at Edinburgh on the sixth of August. Alexander Arbuthnot, Principal of King's College, Aberdeen, was moderator. A complaint was presented against James Paton, Bishop of Dunkeld, that he used the name without exercising the office of a bishop, and that he had made a simoniacal agreement with the Earl of Argyll in regard to the revenues of his bishopric, and had committed other offences. Paton had been appointed to his see by the civil power in the year 1571, on the forfeiture of the canonical prelate, Robert Crichton, for adherence to the queen. After the agreement at Leith, he was elected

---

[1] Tytler, vol. vii. p. 335-349.
[2] Calderwood, vol. iii. p. 272-281. Book of the Universal Kirk, p. 134-136.

bishop, and a letter was issued to the Archbishop of St. Andrews and the Superintendents of Fife, Lothian, and Angus, enjoining them to proceed with his consecration. In April, 1573, he was restored to the temporalities, being then legally confirmed.

The Bishop of Galloway was accused of intruding himself into the office of the ministry at Edinburgh, and of having acknowledged the queen's authority. He admitted the latter charge, but pleaded in defence the pacification made between the regent and the Earl of Huntly. He justified his preaching at Edinburgh by alleging that he had been elected and admitted to the office by the professors of the word in that city. He was ordered to perform public penance, and failing his doing so to be excommunicated.

Certain articles were laid before the assembly by the regent, in which he promised to redress the complaints that had been made regarding the payment of the ministers' stipends, and to fill up all vacant sees forthwith, the superintendents or commissioners to continue to do the duties so long as there were no bishops; in particular, a day was to be named for filling the sees of Glasgow, Murray, Ross, and Dunblane, and for electing a suffragan to the Bishop of St. Andrews in Lothian.

The arch-diocese of Glasgow and the dioceses of Ross and Dunblane were held to be vacant by the forfeiture of the canonical prelates, Beaton, Leslie, and Chisholm. Murray was vacant by the decease of Bishop Hepburn, which took place at his castle of Spynie, on the twentieth of June preceding. The archbishopric of Glasgow had been bestowed, in 1571, on a minister named John Porterfield, but after the agreement at Leith, this nomination was not confirmed, and the see was now conferred on James Boyd, a kinsman of the Lord Boyd. On the third of November, a letter for his consecration was directed to the Bishops of Dunkeld, Orkney, and the Isles, and the Superintendent of Lothian, and he was afterwards confirmed. Alexander Hepburn was raised to the see of Ross. George Douglas, a natural son of Archibald, Earl of Angus, was promoted to the bishopric of Murray, and after election by the chapter was consecrated in the Protestant manner on the fifth of February, 1574. Andrew Graham, son to the laird of Morphie, was elected and consecrated in the same form to the see of Dunblane, in the summer of 1575.[1]

The general assembly met at Edinburgh on the sixth of March, 1574, and again at the same place on the seventh of August following. The proceedings were of the usual character. Calderwood has preserved the form of a commission given at the latter of these meetings to the persons appointed to visit the counties of Caithness and Sutherland. It is valuable as shewing distinctly what were the duties and powers of such commissioners, and as proving that the general assembly still exercised the right of bestowing the highest ecclesiastical functions on persons who were neither bishops nor superintendents. This particular commission was probably granted because the Bishop of Caithness, though a Protestant and a member of the assembly, had not been admitted as one of the Reformed bishops. Its tenor was as follows:—" At Edinburgh, the eleventh day of August, in the year of God 1574, the whole kirk presently assembled, in one voice and mind, giveth full commission, special power and charge, to their loved brethren, Mr. Robert Graham, Archdeacon of Ross, and Mr. John Robertson, Treasurer thereof, conjointly and severally, to pass to the counties of Caithness and Sutherland, and there to visit kirks, colleges, and schools, and other places needful within the said bounds; and in the same to plant ministers, readers, elders, and deacons, schoolmasters, and other members necessary and requisite for erecting a perfect reformed kirk; suspend for a time, or simpliciter deprive such as they shall find unworthy or not apt for their office, whether it be for crimes committed or ignorance; abolish, eradicate, and destroy all monuments of idolatry; establish and set up the true worship of the eternal God, as well in cathedral and college kirks, as in other places within the said bounds, conform to the order taken and agreed upon in the Book of Discipline; and also to search and enquire the names of all those that possess benefices within the said bounds, and at whose provision they have been; and if any are vacant, or happen to be

---

[1] Calderwood, vol. iii. pp. 287-301, 302, 341, 342, 359. Book of the Universal Kirk, p. 137-139. Keith's Catalogue, pp. 96, 97, 150, 151, 180, 181, 261. Preface to Original Letters relating to the Ecclesiastical affairs of Scotland in the reign of James the Sixth, p. xi.-xiv.

vacant within the commissionary, to confer and give the same to the persons qualified, and being presented by the just patrons of the same, due examination preceding; to reject and refuse such as they shall find unable and not apt thereto, as they will answer to God and the Kirk thereupon; their diligence to be done therein with these presents to report to the next assembly general, where it shall happen to be for the time. Given in the general assembly, and ninth session thereof, subscribed by the clerk of the same, day, year, and place foresaid."[1]

The assembly met at Edinburgh on the seventh of March, 1575, when the Bishop of Glasgow was chosen moderator. It was declared that no dramatic entertainments, founded on the canonical Scriptures, should be allowed in time to come on any day whatever; and it was recommended that other plays should be examined before being performed in public, and should not be acted at all on the Lord's day.[2]

The assembly again met at the same place on the sixth of August, and Robert Pont was moderator. The proceedings shew that certain usages of the ancient Church were still cherished, both by the ministers and the people, in some districts of the country. A complaint was given in against the commissioner of Aberdeen, that the ministers and readers in that diocese kept patron and festival days; and the commissioner of Nithsdale brought a charge against the citizens of Dumfries, that finding neither he nor the reader would officiate at Christmas, they got another reader, who said prayers during the festival.

The meeting of this assembly is remarkable, as being the first occasion on which objections were made to the lawfulness of the episcopal form of government. At the commencement of the proceedings, John Durie protested, that the usual examination regarding the manner in which the bishops discharged their duties should not prejudge the reasons which he and others had against the name and office of a bishop. The question was afterwards formally put, whether the functions of bishops as then existing in Scotland were grounded on the

---

[1] Calderwood, vol. iii. pp. 302-309, 330-339. Book of the Universal Kirk, p. 139-145.

[2] Calderwood, vol. iii. p. 339-346. Book of the Universal Kirk, pp. 146, 147,

word of God, and whether the chapters appointed for electing them should be tolerated in that reformed Church. The members appointed John Craig, now minister at Aberdeen, James Lawson, minister at Edinburgh, and Andrew Melville, Principal of the College of Glasgow, on the one side, and George Hay, commissioner of Caithness, John Row, minister at Perth, and David Lindsay, minister at Leith, on the other, to confer on these questions, and report their judgment to the assembly. They reported that they did not think it expedient at present to answer the first question directly, but that if any bishop were found who had not such qualities as the word of God requires, he should be tried by the assembly anew, and so deposed. They farther reported the following as their joint opinion concerning the office of a bishop :—" The name of bishop is common to all those who have a particular flock over the which they have a peculiar charge, as well to preach the word, as to minister the sacraments, and execute ecclesiastical discipline with consent of their elders. And this is their chief function by the word of God. Also out of this number may be chosen some to have power to oversee and visit such reasonable bounds, besides their own flock, as the general Church shall appoint, and in these bounds to appoint ministers, with consent of the ministers of that province, and with consent of the flock to whom they shall be appointed; also to appoint elders and deacons in every particular congregation where there are none, with consent of the people thereof; and to suspend ministers, for reasonable causes, with consent of the ministers foresaid."[1]

This discussion regarding Episcopacy was contemporaneous with the first appearance of Andrew Melville as a leading member of the assembly, although he had sat in that body at its meeting in the spring preceding; and it was he, according to Spottiswood, who prevailed on Durie to raise the question. Melville was born at Baldovy, near Montrose, on the first of August, 1545. He was the youngest son of Richard Melville, a gentleman of good family, who was slain at the battle of Pinkie. He was only two years old at the time of his father's death, but he was carefully educated at Montrose, under the

---

[1] Calderwood, vol. iii. p. 347-357. Book of the Universal Kirk, p. 148-153. Spottiswood, vol. ii. pp. 200, 201.

superintendence of his mother, and was afterwards sent to St. Mary's College, St. Andrews, where he attracted the attention and regard of John Douglas, rector of the university. Leaving his native country when approaching to manhood, he went to the Continent to pursue his studies, and attended the lectures of the most distinguished teachers in the University of Paris, among others, those of Turnebus and Ramus. He subsequently resorted to Poitiers, for the purpose of acquiring a knowledge of the civil law, and his reputation was already such, that, on his arrival there, he was made a regent in one of the colleges. The disturbed state of the kingdom obliged him to leave France; and, proceeding to Geneva, he obtained the friendship of Beza, by whose recommendation he was appointed professor of Humanity in the academy of that city. While teaching others, he continued to improve himself, particularly in the knowledge of the eastern languages.

In the beginning of 1574, Melville left Geneva along with Alexander Campbell, Bishop of Brechin. After a short residence at Paris, where he had a public dispute with Knox's opponent Tyrie, he embarked at Dieppe, and passing through England arrived at Edinburgh. His character as a scholar soon became known, and the regent would have given him a situation in his own family; but what he most anxiously desired was to pursue the academical career to which he had devoted himself on the Continent. The Scottish universities at this time were by no means in a flourishing condition, and their improvement afforded ample scope for the zeal and ability of Melville. In the autumn after his return, he accepted an invitation to be Principal of the College of Glasgow; and, under his superintendence, and by means of those whom he trained up as his assistants, and imbued with his own ardent love of knowledge, the western university, from being the most depressed of the Scottish schools, became distinguished for the learning and attainments of its members.[1]

The attack on episcopal government having begun, Melville

---

[1] James Melville's Autobiography and Diary, Wodrow Society ed. p. 38-50. M'Crie's Life of Andrew Melville, ed. 1819, vol. i. p. 2-75. There are some inaccuracies in Dr. M'Crie's account of the early life of Melville, owing probably to the circumstance that James Melville's Diary could then be consulted only in manuscript.

was not of a disposition to allow the subject to be forgotten. In private he conversed with the leading persons in the Church, urging his own views upon them with a zeal and learning which they were unable or unwilling to resist; and in every successive assembly he renewed the assault, till the system established in 1572 was finally overthrown.

In the general assembly which met at Edinburgh on the twenty-fourth of April, 1576, John Row was chosen moderator. The Bishops of Glasgow, Dunblane, Murray, and Ross, were censured on various grounds. The Bishop of Dunkeld was charged with dilapidating his benefice, and was deprived, but appealed to the lords of parliament. Spottiswood, the Superintendent of Lothian, was complained of, because he had inaugurated the Bishop of Ross in the abbey of Holyrood. The opinion expressed at last assembly regarding the office of a bishop was formally affirmed, and all the members of that order, who had not yet received the charge of a particular congregation, were enjoined to make choice of one. The cathedral of Dunblane was set apart for the bishop of that see, and the church of Canonry in Ross, which also was the cathedral of the diocese, for the Bishop of Ross. The Bishop of Murray agreed to accept any particular flock which the assembly might point out; and the Bishop of Glasgow made general professions of submission, but did not become bound to confine himself to one charge.[1]

The assembly again met at Edinburgh on the twenty-fourth of October, and John Craig was chosen moderator. The Bishop of Glasgow was asked if he was now ready to accept the charge of a particular flock, and to visit within such bounds as the assembly might point out. He answered by referring them to the agreement between the regent and the assembly at Leith, which was to remain effectual during the king's minority, or at least till parliament should decide otherwise, and stated that, if he opposed the arrangement in virtue of which he had been appointed to his see, he would be guilty of perjury, and liable to be punished by the king's majesty; but he was prepared, without binding himself

---

[1] Calderwood, vol. iii. p. 358-368. Book of the Universal Kirk, p. 153-155. Spottiswood, vol. ii. pp. 201, 202. James Melville's Diary, pp. 54, 55. M'Crie's Life of Melville, vol. i. pp. 161, 162.

in any way or prejudging his episcopal jurisdiction, to take charge of some particular church, while residing in the sheriffdom of Ayr, and of another while at Glasgow. In this the assembly acquiesced till its next meeting.

A discussion also took place regarding the see of St. Andrews. John Douglas had died on the twenty-first of July, 1574, and Patrick Adamson, lately minister at Paisley, was presented to the bishopric by the regent. An ordinance had been made that all bishops should be tried by the assembly, before being admitted by the chapter, and in the present case the chapter of St. Andrews delayed proceeding till the assembly should be satisfied. Adamson, being asked whether he would submit to trial and examination by the assembly, and so receive the office of a bishop, answered that he could not.

At this assembly, a minister, named Thomas Hepburn, was accused of maintaining that no soul is admitted to heaven, where Christ is glorified, till the judgment of the last day. After several of his brethren had been appointed to reason with him, he still declared that he was not satisfied, but said he would abandon his opinion if the assembly condemned it as erroneous and heretical. The opinion was condemned as false and heretical, and repugnant to the plain meaning of the Scriptures.[1]

The next meeting of the assembly was at Edinburgh, on the first of April, 1577. Alexander Arbuthnot was moderator. A question was put as to what should be done with those who would not receive the communion except in Lent, and it was enjoined that their superstition should no way be sanctioned. An order was also made that all ministers and readers who persisted, after due admonition, in reading, preaching, or administering the communion, at Christmas or Easter, during Lent, on Saints' days, or at such superstitious times, should be deprived.

Notwithstanding the proceedings of last assembly, the regent persisted in filling up the see of St. Andrews. The members of the chapter abandoned their scruples, and Adamson was elected in the legal form. He was afterwards con-

---

[1] Calderwood, vol. iii. p. 369-377. Book of the Universal Kirk, p. 155-162. Spottiswood, vol. ii. p. 202.

secrated and confirmed, in virtue of a letter addressed on the twenty-first of December, 1576, to the Bishops of Caithness and Orkney, and other bishops and superintendents. The new archbishop left his ordinary office of the ministry, entered on the discharge of his duties, and claimed the right of visitation within his diocese. The assembly, in consequence, empowered a commission of their number to summon him before them, and examine into the whole matter, with authority also to cite the members of the chapter who had taken part in his inauguration, and to report to the next meeting of their body.[1]

Patrick Adamson, or Constantine, as he was sometimes also called, was one of the most distinguished of the Scottish ministers, irreproachable in his private character, and enjoying as high a reputation as Melville himself for learning and elegant scholarship. He was the son of a burgess of Perth, and was educated at St. Mary's College, St. Andrews. He became a preacher in the Reformed Church, but soon afterwards went abroad, and studied in the universities of France. On his return to Scotland, he practised for some time at the bar, but, having resumed his former vocation in the ministry, acquired the favour of the regent, by whom he was esteemed a fit person to be raised to the archiepiscopal see.

The promotion of Adamson exposed him to the enmity of the party which was now most powerful in the ecclesiastical courts, and most influential among the people. Morton had been accused of obtaining the election of John Douglas in order to secure the revenues of the see of St. Andrews to himself, and the charge of simony was now renewed. It was also subsequently alleged that Adamson accepted an office which, on a former occasion, he had denounced and held up to ridicule. It was said that, having been disappointed of the see when Douglas was elected, he preached a sermon, in which he told the people that there were three sorts of bishops, my lord bishop, my lord's bishop, and the Lord's bishop: "My lord bishop was in the Papistry; my lord's bishop is now, when my lord gets the benefice, and the bishop serves

[1] Calderwood, vol. iii. p. 378-384. Book of the Universal Kirk, p. 162-167. Spottiswood, vol. ii. p. 203. Preface to Original Letters of the reign of James the Sixth, p. xiv.

for nothing but to make his title sure; and the Lord's bishop is the true minister of the Gospel." This statement has been disputed by Mackenzie and others, who maintain that Adamson was not in Scotland at the time. There can be no doubt, however, that he really preached at St. Andrews on the occasion referred to, such circumstance being distinctly related both by Bannatyne and James Melville, the latter of whom was present at the sermon. But Bannatyne makes no allusion to the words which have been mentioned: the only authority for them is Melville, who was then not sixteen years old, and who wrote after an interval of many years, when it was the object of his party to blacken the character of the archbishop, and to make the titular episcopacy as odious as possible. The assertion that Adamson was disappointed of the see rests also on the authority of Melville. If, on the subject of Episcopacy, he held principles similar to those of Erskine, as he probably did, it may easily be understood how words, intended to censure the corrupt system prevalent before the agreement at Leith, were wrested to condemn what the preacher really believed to be a great ecclesiastical reform.[1]

The next assembly was held at Edinburgh, on the twenty-fifth of October. David Lindsay was moderator. The regent was asked to attend in person or by a commissioner. He excused himself in respect of his being otherwise occupied; but, either at this time, or at the assembly held in October in the preceding year, he caused certain questions to be laid before the members for their consideration. These questions related for the most part to the government, discipline, and revenue of the Church. They were apparently intended to perplex the assembly, by bringing under their notice various points of difficulty which would necessarily have to be discussed in any new arrangement of the ecclesiastical system; and it was believed that they had been suggested by the Archbishop of St. Andrews. The questions were referred to a select number of the members, who had for some time been engaged, by order of the assembly, in drawing up a Book of Policy for the Church.

The archbishop presented to the assembly a letter addressed

[1] See Mackenzie's Lives, vol. iii. p. 364-366; M'Crie's Life of Melville, vol. i. pp. 122, 445-448; Bannatyne, p. 323; and James Melville's Diary, pp. 31, 32.

by Queen Elizabeth to Morton, regarding a Protestant synod which was to meet at Magdeburg, with a request from the regent to send some of their members to attend it, if they thought such a step advisable. The assembly approved of the suggestion, and, from among those named by them, Morton selected Melville, Arbuthnot, and George Hay. It was suspected that the regent wished to have Melville and his friends out of the country for some time, but, whether this was the case or not, the parties appointed never left Scotland.[1]

During this and the preceding year, the two bishops of the house of Gordon, who filled the sees of Galloway and Aberdeen, were removed by death. Alexander, Bishop of Galloway, died in 1576. There is no evidence that he was ever consecrated. In the year 1567, he had resigned the see in favour of his son John, afterwards Dean of Salisbury. This resignation does not seem to have taken effect, and another son, George, obtained possession of the benefice, and held the title of Bishop of Galloway after his father's decease. Had it not been for the agreement at Leith, the Scottish bishoprics would probably, as a general rule, have been viewed as patrimonial rights, and descended from father to son like the see of Candida Casa in this instance. William, Bishop of Aberdeen, died on the sixth of August, 1577, and was buried within his cathedral church. David Cunningham, Sub-dean of Glasgow, was nominated to the see by the regent, and, on the eleventh of November, was consecrated at Aberdeen by the Archbishop of St. Andrews, assisted by John Craig and another minister.[2]

While the discussions were going on regarding ecclesiastical government, Lord Glammis, Chancellor of Scotland, a nobleman who was respected by all parties, wrote a letter to Theodore Beza, asking his opinion as to certain doubtful

---

[1] Calderwood, vol. iii. p. 385-393. Book of the Universal Kirk, p. 167-172.

[2] Gordon's History of the Earldom of Sutherland, pp. 143, 172, 181, 290, 291. Original Letters of the reign of James the Sixth, vol. i. pp. 426, 427. Miscellany of the Spalding Club, vol. ii. pp. 46, 47. James Melville's Diary, p. 57. The historian of the Earldom of Sutherland states that William Gordon, one of the sons of the Earl of Huntly who fell at Corrichie, "was designed Bishop of Aberdeen, and died at Paris, in the College of Bons-enfans." The date of his death is not mentioned, and I am not aware of any other notice of this William Gordon. It was perhaps intended that he should succeed his uncle in the see of Aberdeen.

points. His questions, six in number, were the following:—Whether the episcopal function is necessary in the Church, in order that bishops may, as circumstances require, provide that ministers be called to assemblies, admitted to their office, and removed therefrom; or ought rather all the ministers, being equal in power, and subject to no bishop, to choose fit persons, with consent of the patron and people, and correct them and remove them from their office? Whether the general assemblies should be gathered together without the commandment or will of the Prince? By whom, that is, whether by the King or by the Bishops, should ecclesiastical assemblies be convened, and, when convened, on what points are they entitled to make laws? Should Papists be excommunicated as apostates are, or should they be visited with a lighter punishment? For what causes may excommunication be pronounced? What may lawfully be done with property which in former times was dedicated to the Church?

Beza answered the questions put to him, and wrote a treatise entitled, "De Triplici Episcopatu," which was soon afterwards translated into English, and published as "The Judgment of a most reverend and learned man from beyond the seas, concerning a threefold order of Bishops, with a Declaration of certain other weighty points concerning the Discipline and Government of the Church." The threefold order was the Divine, the Human, and the Satanic. The first was that which was recognized in the Scriptures; the second that which the ancient Fathers submitted to, but only as a human invention; the third that which existed under the Papacy, and into which the second was very apt to degenerate.

This treatise seems to have contained an absolute condemnation of the form of episcopal polity then established in Scotland. It was welcomed by the opponents of the bishops, and contributed greatly to the success of Melville in the struggle in which he was engaged. That reformer himself was in frequent correspondence with Beza. One of his letters, written in November, 1579, seems to refer to the points mentioned by Lord Glammis. "For five years," he says, "we have now maintained a warfare against pseudo-episcopacy, and have not ceased to urge the adoption of a strict discipline. We have presented to his majesty and the three estates of the kingdom at different times, and recently at the parliament which is now sitting, a form of discipline to be enacted and confirmed by public authority. The king is favourably inclined to us; almost all the nobility are adverse. They complain that, if pseudo-episcopacy be abolished, the state of the kingdom will be overturned; if presbyteries be established, the royal authority will be diminished; if the ecclesiastical goods are restored to their legitimate use, the royal treasury will be exhausted. They plead that bishops, with abbots and priors, form the third estate in parliament; that all jurisdiction, ecclesiastical as well as civil, pertains solely to the king and his council, and that all the ecclesiastical property should go into the exchequer. In many this way of speaking and thinking may be imputed to ignorance; in more to a flagitious life and bad morals; in almost all to a desire of seizing such of the church property as yet remains, and the dread of losing what they have already got into their possession. They also insist that the sentence of excommunication shall not be valid until it has been approved by the king's council after taking cognizance of the cause. For, being conscious of their own vices, they are afraid of the sentence of the presbytery, not so much from the awe in which they stand of the divine judgment, as from terror of the civil penalties, which, according to the laws and custom of our country, accompany the sentence of excommunication. In fine, while they judge according to the dictates of the carnal mind instead of the revealed will of God, they desire to have everything done by the authority of a single bishop and perpetual overseer of the churches, rather than by the common sentence of presbyters possessing equal authority. May God shew mercy to his Church, and remove these evils."[1]

In March, 1578, an alteration took place in the government of Scotland. The Earl of Morton had never been popular, and for some time back the disaffection towards him had been increasing among all classes. By the advice of the Earls of

[1] See James Melville's Diary, p. 55; Calderwood, vol. iii. p. 397; Spottiswood, vol. ii. p. 221; Sage's Works, vol i. p. 275-278; M'Crie's Life of Melville, vol. i. pp. 199-202, 463. The six questions of Lord Glammis, as given in Saravia's Works, are printed at full length by Bishop Sage's editor. Neither Sage nor his editor had seen Beza's treatise; even Dr. M'Crie had been able to consult it only in the English translation.

Argyll and Atholl, the young king, then in his twelfth year, called on the regent to resign his office; and, finding resistance hopeless, he at once obeyed. The administration was committed to a council of twelve, at the head of which were the two earls who had mainly assisted in bringing about the change.[1]

At the conclusion of Morton's regency, the Scottish Church, as recognized by the state, was still conformed to the model agreed to at Leith in 1572; but, as it was soon to experience another alteration, a brief account may be given of its condition at this time.

The thirteen dioceses of the ancient Church continued to exist in name, and most of them were filled by Protestant ministers, bearing the style of bishops, although none of them, except Adamson and Boyd, and perhaps Cunningham, now ventured to exercise their episcopal jurisdiction. They sat in parliament, managed the cathedral property with the advice of their chapters, and discharged the various duties, partly of an ecclesiastical, partly of a secular character, which devolved on them as prelates. In these respects they differed little from their Roman Catholic predecessors, who had continued to perform the same duties except so far as hindered by individual forfeiture. As late as June, 1577, we find William, Bishop of Aberdeen, giving collation of the vicarage of that city by the symbol of a ring to Walter Cullen, the Protestant reader. The superintendents, Winram, Erskine, and Spottiswood, still presided over the districts, or parts of the districts, to which they had been originally appointed; and the rest of the kingdom was under the inspection of temporary commissioners, named by the assembly, and removable at pleasure. But the real ecclesiastical chiefs were the ministers and teachers most distinguished by their eloquence and ability. Among these Melville already held the foremost place, although he never acquired the supremacy which had been wielded by Knox.

The old parochial divisions also subsisted, and happily no attempt was ever made to effect any alteration in that respect. Through all the changes which took place, they remained the single territorial link connecting the Church of King David's time with the ecclesiastical system of the sixteenth and seventeenth centuries. The parishes were about a thousand

[1] Tytler, vol. viii. p. 22-30.

in number, and it was long after the Reformation before each was supplied with a minister of its own. In 1567, there were only two hundred and fifty-seven ministers, assisted by one hundred and fifty-one exhorters, and four hundred and fifty-five readers. Under the polity established during the regency of Morton, the parochial benefices were arranged in districts, containing generally three or four parishes, having only one minister for the whole, but each provided with a separate reader. The order of exhorters had gradually been given up, or had merged in the common denomination of readers. In the year 1574, there were two hundred and eighty-nine ministers, and seven hundred and fifteen readers. The chief fund from which they were supported was the thirds of the old benefices.[1]

Most of the readers, and a considerable proportion of the ministers, had probably little learning, but they were conscious how much the success of the Reformation had been owing to the ignorance of the Roman clergy, and they zealously endeavoured to promote as high a standard of attainments as the circumstances of the country and their slender endowments would allow. The number possessed of respectable qualifications in this respect was daily increasing, and some of their leading men, especially those educated on the Continent, were persons of erudition, and not unworthy to bear a part in the movement, then in progress among the various portions of the Reformed communion, for the revival of theological learning. Buchanan held an influential position in the state, and was high in the confidence of the ruling ecclesiastical party. The genius of Melville and Adamson was already known beyond the bounds of their own country; and Arbuthnot, Smeaton, and others, had attained considerable fame, or were in the course of acquiring distinction, either by their writings, or by their exertions in the cause of education.

It is more difficult to ascertain what influence the Reformation had on the moral character of the Scottish people. There can be no doubt, however, that a great change had taken place for the better among those classes, and in those parts of the country, where the Protestant doctrines had been generally received. The nobility and the higher ranks of the

[1] Miscellany of the Wodrow Society, vol. i. p. 321-396.

gentry remained, it is to be feared, much the same as before, but, throughout the Lowland districts, the inferior gentry and the burgesses of the towns had wakened to a new spiritual and intellectual life. The Reformed tenets were gladly listened to by them, and, when once thoroughly embraced, were maintained with the fervent devotion which marked the character of the nation. The ministers themselves belonged, for the most part, to those classes, and the austere morality by which they were distinguished was shared by the more earnest portion of their congregations. The vices and crimes which appear so frequently in the records of the time, even in quarters where they could hardly be expected, are no proof to the contrary of what has just been stated. They only shew what would appear at all times, if an equally rigorous inquisition prevailed. In the greater part of the Highlands and Isles the Reformation was less beneficial, or rather led to results of an entirely opposite character. Even the old ecclesiastical system had never been properly established in those districts, and the change of religion and ritual, and the confiscation of church endowments, nearly destroyed whatever discipline or refinement there was. Among the peasantry of the Lowlands also the change appears to have been for the worse. Many years elapsed before the Reformed ministers were able to counteract the mischief caused by the overthrow of the ancient Church, and the suppression of the monastic orders. And when the new doctrines reached this class, they were mingled in many parts of the country with so much superstition, that the ignorance and lawlessness of the Highlanders were hardly more opposed to the true principles of the Christian religion, than the fanaticism which marked a large proportion of the Lowland peasants.

While the Reformed system was acquiring strength and consistency, the Roman Catholic communion had fallen into a state of seemingly hopeless decay. The few bishops who survived had deserted their flocks, or been obliged to abandon them. The Archbishop of Glasgow had remained abroad since the year 1560; the Bishops of Ross and Dunblane were almost constantly employed in the political service of the queen in England or in foreign parts; the Bishop of Dunkeld alone continued to reside in Scotland. The inferior ecclesiastics most distinguished for their learning and zeal had embraced a voluntary exile on the Continent, or had fled thither to escape the persecutions of the Reformed. The greater number of the clergy who remained in Scotland, particularly those of the regular orders, had conformed to the Protestant doctrines, and were frequently to be found discharging the office of readers in the new establishment. Several of the nobles, and a considerable proportion of the higher gentry, still professed allegiance to the Roman see, which had also numerous adherents of all classes in the northern and western districts of the kingdom; but the attachment of the barons seemed to be merely nominal, and the others, without ecclesiastical rulers, and forsaken by their political leaders, disheartened by repeated defeats, and intimidated by persecuting laws, did not venture to come forward openly in defence of their religion.

CHAPTER XL.

FROM THE RESIGNATION OF THE REGENCY BY MORTON IN MARCH, 1578, TO THE RAID OF RUTHVEN IN AUGUST, 1582.

Influence of the Duke of Lennox—His designs in favour of the Roman Church—Roman Catholic Missionaries in Scotland—Sermon of Walter Balcanquhal—Meetings of the General Assembly—General Assembly at Dundee—Condemnation of the titular Episcopacy—Subscription of the King's Confession—Second Book of Discipline—Differences between the First and Second Book of Discipline—The Tulchan bishops—Distinction between them and the titular bishops—Conflict between the Church and the State—List of grievances drawn up by the General Assembly—Andrew Melville at Perth—Raid of Ruthven.

THE government of the nobles, which succeeded that of Morton, was of short duration. By a union with the young Earl of Mar, the late regent recovered his ascendency, and, although he did not again assume his former title, he once more possessed the chief rule in the kingdom. He secured his authority by depriving the Hamiltons of all their possessions, and compelling their leaders, John, Commendator of Arbroath, next heir to the throne, and his brother Claud, Commendator of Paisley, to leave Scotland. In September, 1579, Esmé Stewart, Lord of Aubigny, nephew of the late Earl of Lennox, came over from France, and was affectionately received by the young king. As he had been brought up in the Church of Rome and professed to belong to that communion, he was suspected of being an emissary of the Pope and the house of Lorraine, and his proceedings were jealously watched by the ministers. Aubigny, however, continued to rise in favour with the king, who bestowed on him the earldom of Lennox; and, as his influence increased, that of Morton again began to decline. The distrust with which he was regarded was little diminished by his making a public profession of the Reformed religion in the beginning of the year 1580.

Acting chiefly by the advice of Lennox, and that of James Stewart, a younger son of Lord Ochiltree, the king broke off his intercourse with England, and entered into a correspondence with his mother. The Earl of Morton was encouraged by Elizabeth to rise against the government, but on this occasion his enemies were more prompt than himself. He was accused of participation in the murder of Darnley, and committed a prisoner to Dunbarton Castle. Elizabeth interceded in his favour, and, when she found that her remonstrances had no effect, endeavoured by means of Randolph, now employed in his former congenial occupation, to stir up a party of the nobles to make the king a prisoner. The plot was discovered; Randolph fled to England; and Morton was beheaded at Edinburgh, on the second of June, 1581. Lennox was soon afterwards created a duke, and the earldom of Arran, which the forfeiture of the Hamiltons had placed at the disposal of the crown, was bestowed on Stewart.[1]

The Duke of Lennox continued to be the most intimate friend and the chief adviser of his sovereign, but he was never able to allay the suspicions of the ministers. They endeavoured in every way to injure his character and diminish his power, and their efforts were eagerly seconded by the agents of Elizabeth. The imputations which were made against his personal conduct were evidently the result of party animosity, and may be entirely disregarded. The doubts which were entertained of the sincerity of his religious profession deserve more consideration. The most learned and temperate of our historians have generally entertained a favourable opinion of Lennox's honesty in this respect, but documents which have recently been discovered shew that the distrust of the Reformed was well founded. There can hardly now be a question that he acted from the beginning in concert with the princes of Lorraine; and it is certain that he was soon engaged in confidential communications with the envoys of Spain, and the Pope, for the purpose of delivering Mary from captivity, and re-establishing the Roman Catholic religion. He proposed to unite the two parties in Scotland, by associating the queen and her son in the government of the kingdom, and in this Lennox acted with the consent of James

[1] Tytler, vol. viii. p. 31-87.

and the co-operation of Arran: but there is no evidence that his designs in favour of the Roman Church were known to the king or the Protestant members of the council; he himself in a confidential letter to Mary implies the reverse. His Scottish associates in that more dangerous enterprise were the deprived bishops, and the missionaries who were now coming over in considerable numbers from the Continent.

As already mentioned, a short time before Lennox came over from France, the Roman communion was in a very depressed condition; but the revival of spiritual zeal and discipline, which had turned back the cause of the Reformation on the Continent, was now beginning to produce its effects in the Scottish kingdom. The most ardent and accomplished of those who had fled from the persecution of the Protestants had joined the regular orders, especially the institute of the Jesuits. Among the members of that body were Edmund Hay, who had formerly acted as a confidential agent at the court of Mary, Tyrie, the opponent of Knox, and James Gordon, brother of the Earl of Huntly. Most of the Scottish missionaries were Jesuits. They were ready to encounter any peril for the purpose of bringing back their country to the Roman Catholic Church, and they had already converted several of the Protestant teachers.

There can scarcely be a doubt that the attempt to bring about a counter-reformation in Scotland was mainly owing to the exertions and the influence of Lennox. In a sermon preached at Edinburgh, on the seventh of December, 1580, one of the Protestant ministers, Walter Balcanqual, pointed out the sudden change which had occurred. " Within these two years and less," he said, " our Papists stood in such awe of the laws of the realm, and discipline of the Church of God, that they durst not plainly profess their Papistry, but were constrained either to depart the realm, or subscribe to the religion; which sundry of them did hypocritically, and against their heart, and yet excuse their hypocrisy and dissimulation with this doctrine of the Papists, that it is lawful to a Catholic to deny his religion, being amongst heretics and Calvinists. But now, with the dolour of our hearts, we that fear God perceive that the Papists have cast off their wonted dissimulation and fear, and have taken such hardiness and boldness unto themselves, that not only were they bold in Paris, and other parts out of the country, plainly to preach Papistry, to impugn the truth of the Gospel, to quarrel and persecute their own countrymen for the same; but also, when they are come home here in Scotland, they dare not only profess their foresaid Papistry and impugn the truth, but likewise debate their quarrels upon the streets of Edinburgh, which for the religion they had begun in Paris. . . . Before this French court came to Scotland, there were either few or none that durst avow themselves for Papists, neither yet publicly in the country, neither in Reformed cities, neither in the king's palace. But since that time, not only begin the Papists within the realm to lift up their heads, but also our Scottish Papists that were out of the realm swarm home from all places like locusts; and have taken such hardihood unto them, that not only have they had access to the French court, but also in the king's palace, in the particular sessions of our kirks, and general assemblies thereof, durst plainly avow their Papistry, and impugn the truth, both against the laws of the realm and discipline of the Church, contrary to all practice that we have had before."[1]

In a general assembly held at Edinburgh on the twenty-fourth of April, 1578, at which Andrew Melville was chosen moderator, it was ordered that all bishops, and others bearing ecclesiastical functions, should be called by their own names, or simply brethren; and the chapters were prohibited from making further elections of bishops till the next assembly. At an assembly held at Stirling on the eleventh of June, this last regulation was made perpetual, and bishops already elected were required to make their submission.[2]

The assembly again met at Edinburgh on the twenty-fourth of October. The Bishop of Glasgow was called on to submit, and was accused of neglecting his duty in various points. He gave the following answer in writing:—" I understand the name, office, and modest reverence borne to a bishop, to be

[1] Calderwood, vol. iii. p. 773-775; vol. iv. p. 397-400. Spottiswood, vol. ii. p. 267. Mignet, vol ii. p 207-216, and appendix, p. 461-465. The evidence of the real character and objects of Lennox is to be found in the documents in the Spanish archives at Simancas, quoted by Mignet.

[2] Calderwood, vol. iii. pp. 398-405, 410-413. Book of the Universal Kirk, p. 172-181.

lawful and allowable by the Scriptures of God; and, being elected by the Church and king to be Bishop of Glasgow, I esteem my calling and office lawful. As touching the execution of the charge committed to me, I am content to endeavour, at my uttermost ability, to perform the same, and every point thereof, and to abide the honourable judgment of the Church from time to time of my offending, seeing the charge is weighty; and in laying anything to be laid to my charge, to be examined by the canon left by the Apostle to Timothy, First Epistle, chapter iii., seeing that place was appointed to me at my receiving, to understand therefrom the duties of a bishop. As towards my livings and rents, and other things granted by the prince to me and my antecessors for my serving of that charge, I reckon the same lawful. As to my duty to the supreme magistrate in assisting his grace in council or parliament, being craved thereto, I esteem I am bound to obey the same; and that it is no hurt, but a weal to the Church, that some of our number be at the making of good laws and ordinances. In doing whereof I protest, before God, I intend never to do any thing but that which I believe shall stand with the purity of the Scriptures, and a well reformed country; as also a good part of the livings which I possess hath been given for that cause." This answer was judged not to be satisfactory. The bishop afterwards submitted unconditionally to the assembly held at Edinburgh, on the seventh of July, 1579.

At the assembly of October, 1578, the bishops were specially called on to make their submission as to certain points, and farther to promise, "that, if the general assembly hereafter shall find farther corruption in the said estate than is hitherto expressed, they be content to be reformed by the said assembly, according to the word of God, when they shall be required thereto." The particular points mentioned were the following:—"That they be content to be pastors and ministers of one flock; that they usurp no criminal jurisdiction; that they vote not in parliament, in name of the Church, without advice from the assembly; that they take not up for maintenance of their ambition and riotousness the emoluments of the Church, which may sustain many pastors, the schools, and the poor, but be content with reasonable livings, according to their office; that they claim not to themselves the titles of lords temporal, neither usurp temporal jurisdiction, whereby they may be abstracted from their office; that they aspire not above the particular elderships, but be subject to the same; that they usurp not the power of presbyteries; that they take no farther bounds of visitation than the assembly committeth to them."[1]

It is manifest that the opponents of the titular Episcopacy, though determined to press their victory to the utmost, had not yet agreed, or were unwilling to let it be known, what actual measures were still to be adopted.

The assembly met at Dundee on the twelfth of July, 1580, and James Lawson was chosen moderator. At the fourth session of this assembly an act was passed, by which the Episcopacy then established in Scotland was formally condemned. It was to the following effect:—" Forasmuch as the office of a Bishop, as it is now used and commonly taken within this realm, hath no sure warrant, authority, or good ground out of the Book and Scriptures of God, but was brought in by the folly and corruption of men's invention to the great overthrow of the true Church of God, the whole assembly of the Church in one voice, after liberty given to all men to reason in the matter, none opposing themselves in defence of the said pretended office, findeth and declareth the same pretended office, used and termed as is above said, unlawful in itself, as having neither foundation, ground, nor warrant in the word of God; and ordaineth that all such persons as enjoy, or hereafter shall enjoy, the said office, be charged simpliciter to demit, quit, and leave off the same, as an office whereunto they are not called by God, and also to desist and cease from all preaching, ministration of the sacraments, or using any way the office of pastors, until they receive de novo admission from the general assembly of the Church, under the pain of excommunication to be used against them; wherein if they be found disobedient, or contravene this act in any point, the sentence of excommunication, after due admonition, to be executed against them."[2]

---

[1] Calderwood, vol. iii. pp. 426-433, 445. Book of the Universal Kirk, p. 181-185.
[2] Calderwood, vol. iii. p. 463-473. Book of the Universal Kirk, p. 193-201. Spottiswood, vol. ii. p. 272.

It is said that in January, 1581, certain papal dispensations were intercepted, by which the Roman Catholics in Scotland were allowed to subscribe or swear whatever should be required of them, provided they remained faithful to their religion, and ready to advance its interests. This circumstance, we are told by Spottiswood, gave occasion to what was called the King's Confession—a document prepared by Craig at the request of the king, and subscribed by James himself, and by the Duke of Lennox and others of his council and household; and which soon afterwards, by royal proclamation, was ordered to be signed by all the people. The following is the tenor of this document :—

"We, all and every one of us underwritten, protest that after long and due examination of our own consciences, in matters of true and false religion, we are now thoroughly resolved in the truth by the word and Spirit of God. And therefore we believe with our hearts, confess with our mouths, subscribe with our hands, and constantly affirm before God and the whole world, that this only is the true Christian faith and religion, pleasing to God and bringing salvation to man, which is now by the mercy of God revealed to the world by the preaching of the blessed Evangel, and is received, believed, and defended by many and sundry notable Churches and realms, but chiefly by the Church of Scotland, the king's majesty, and three estates of this realm, as God's eternal truth and only ground of our salvation ; as more particularly is expressed in the Confession of our Faith, stablished and publicly confirmed by sundry acts of parliament, and which now of a long time hath been openly professed by the king's majesty and whole body of his realm both in burgh and land. To the which Confession and form of religion we willingly agree in our consciences in all points, as unto God's undoubted truth and verity, grounded only upon his written word.

"And therefore we abhor and detest all contrary religion and doctrine, but chiefly all kind of Papistry in general and particular heads, even as they are now condemned and confuted by the word of God and Church of Scotland. But in special we detest and refuse the usurped authority of the Roman Antichrist upon the Scriptures of God, upon the Church, the civil magistrate, and consciences of men; all his tyrannous laws made upon indifferent things against our Christian liberty; his erroneous doctrine against the sufficiency of the written word, the perfection of the law, the offices of Christ, and his blessed Evangel; his corrupted doctrine concerning original sin, our natural inability, and rebellion to God's law, our justification by faith only, our imperfect sanctification and obedience to the law; the nature, number, and use of the holy sacraments; his five bastard sacraments, with all his rites, ceremonies, and false doctrine, added to the ministration of the true sacraments, without the word of God; his cruel judgment against infants departing without the sacrament; his absolute necessity of Baptism; his blasphemous opinion of Transubstantiation, or real presence of Christ's body in the elements, and receiving the same by the wicked for bodies of men; his dispensation with oaths, perjuries, and degrees of marriage forbidden in the word; his cruelty against the innocent divorced, his devilish mass, his blasphemous priesthood, his profane sacrifice for the sins of the dead and quick, his canonization of men, calling upon angels and saints departed, worshipping of imagery, relics, and crosses, dedicating of churches, altars, days, vows to creatures; his purgatory, prayers for the dead, praying or speaking in a strange language; his processions, and blasphemous litany, and multitude of advocates or mediators; his manifold orders; auricular confession; his desperate and uncertain repentance, his general and doubtful faith, his satisfaction of men for their sins; his justification by works, opus operatum, works of supererogation, merits, pardons, peregrinations, and stations; his holy water, baptizing of bells, conjuring of spirits, crossing, saining, anointing, conjuring, hallowing of God's good creatures, with the superstitious opinion joined therewith; his worldly monarchy and wicked hierarchy; his three solemn vows, with all his shavelings of sundry sorts; his erroneous and bloody decrees made at Trent, with all the subscribers and approvers of that cruel and bloody bond conjured against the Church of God: and, finally, we detest all his vain allegories, rites, signs, and traditions, brought into the Church without or against the word of God, and doctrine of this true reformed Church, to the which we join ourselves willingly in doctrine, faith, religion, discipline, and use of the holy sacraments, as lively members of the same, in Christ our Head: promising and swearing, by the great name of the Lord our God, that we shall continue in the obedience of the doctrine and discipline of this Church, and shall defend the same, according to our vocation and power, all the days of our lives, under the pains contained in the law, and danger both of body and soul in the day of God's fearful judgment.

"And seeing that many are stirred up by Satan and that Roman Antichrist to promise, swear, subscribe, and for a time use the holy sacraments in the Church deceitfully, against their own conscience, minding thereby, first, under the external cloak of religion, to corrupt and subvert secretly God's true religion within the Church, and afterward, when time may serve, to become open enemies and persecutors of the same, under vain hope of the Pope's dispensation, devised against the word of God, to his greater confusion, and their double condemnation in the day of the Lord Jesus; we, therefore, willing to take away all suspicion of hypocrisy, and of such double dealing with God and his Church, protest, and call the Searcher of all hearts to witness, that our minds and hearts do fully agree with this our confession, promise, oath, and subscription, so that we are not moved for any worldly respect, but are persuaded only in our consciences, through the knowledge and love of God's true religion, printed in our hearts by the Holy Spirit, as we shall answer to Him in the day when the secrets of all hearts shall be disclosed.

"And because we perceive that the greatness and stability of our religion and Church doth depend upon the safety and good behaviour of the king's majesty, as upon a comfortable instrument of God's mercy, granted to this country for the maintaining of his Church and ministration of justice among us, we protest and promise with our hearts, under the same oath, hand-writ, and pains, that we shall defend his person and authority with our goods, bodies, and lives, in the defence of Christ's Evangel, liberty of our country, ministration of justice, and punishment of iniquity, against all enemies within this realm or without, as we desire our God to be a strong and merciful defender to us in the day of our death, and coming of our Lord Jesus Christ; to whom, with the Father and the Holy Spirit, be all honour and glory eternally. Amen."[1]

James lived long enough to regret that he had been induced by the counsellors of his boyhood to encourage such violent and indiscriminate protests against the doctrines of Rome.

Soon after the promulgation of the King's Confession, a document appeared, bearing to proceed from the archbishops and bishops, chief heads of the ecclesiastical estate of Scotland, and having the signatures affixed of the Archbishops of St. Andrews and Glasgow, and the Bishop of Aberdeen. Grave and temperate in its language, and appealing to the Scripture for the proof of its statements, it contrasts favourably in various respects with the King's Confession, to which it was evidently meant to be an answer. But the shape in which it appeared was unjustifiable. Calderwood, to whom we are indebted for its preservation, says, that it was a forgery; and such undoubtedly it was, so far as it professed to come from the prelates whose names were attached to it. There can be little hesitation in agreeing with the opinion expressed in a document preserved by the same historian, that it was the production of some of those who acted in concert with the Duke of Lennox.[2]

The general assembly met at Glasgow on the twenty-fourth of April, and Robert Pont was chosen moderator. King James and his advisers, whatever their precise motives may have been, were anxious at this time to conciliate the ruling party in the Church. A royal letter was presented to the assembly, in which the sovereign expressed his desire to make better provision for the stipends of the ministers, and the exercise of ecclesiastical discipline, recommending for those purposes the erection of presbyteries throughout the kingdom. This proposal was gladly acceded to by the assembly, and presbyteries were ordered to be set up at Edinburgh, St. Andrews, Dundee, Perth, Stirling, Glasgow, Ayr, Irvine, Haddington, Dunbar, Chirnside, Linlithgow, and Dunfermline;

---

[1] Calderwood, vol iii. p. 501-505. Spottiswood, vol. ii. p. 268. M'Crie's Life of Melville, vol. i. pp. 262, 263. Dr. M'Crie styles this Confession the "National Covenant," a name which it does not appear to have received at the time when it was put forth, although the writers of the following century call it " the Covenant."

[2] Calderwood, vol. iii. p. 511-515; vol iv. p. 398.

and it was declared that these should serve as an example for others. This was the first establishment of presbyteries in Scotland, although the measure now agreed to had probably been contemplated for some time. The way to it had been prepared by an act of the assembly of October, 1576, by which the meetings of the exercise, which had ceased in most places, were restored and made obligatory, and by an answer of the assembly of July, 1579, to a proposal of the provincial assembly of Lothian for the erection of presbyteries, to the effect that the exercise might be held to be a presbytery.

The act against Episcopacy agreed to at Dundee was explained and ratified by the Glasgow assembly; the King's Confession was approved of; and the office of reader, which on a former occasion had been declared not to be an ordinary function in the Church, was now forbidden to be conferred on any one in time coming. Still more important than those measures was the act whereby the Book of Policy, which had been long in preparation, and which in its essential parts had already been approved of by various assemblies, now received a formal sanction. The state still refused to confirm it, but Melville's scheme for a reform in the ecclesiastical government, so carefully planned, and so laboriously and skilfully carried on, was thus brought to a successful termination in the highest court of the Church.

The Second Book of Discipline was divided into thirteen chapters.

The first chapter related to the Church and its policy in general, and to those points in which it differed from the civil policy. The Church of God, it was declared, is sometimes taken in a large sense for all who profess the Gospel of Christ, and so is a company and fellowship not only of the godly, but also of hypocrites professing outwardly a true religion. At other times it is taken for the godly and elect only, and sometimes for those who exercise spiritual authority in the congregation. In this last sense, the Church has a certain power granted by God, according to which it uses a proper jurisdiction and government for the comfort of the whole Church, and this power is to be put in execution by those to whom the spiritual government of the Church by lawful calling is committed. The policy of the Church, flowing from this power, is an order or form of spiritual government, exercised by the members appointed thereto by the word of God, and therefore is given immediately to the office-bearers, by whom it is exercised to the weal of the whole body. This power and policy ecclesiastical is different in its nature from the civil power, although they are both from God. For the power ecclesiastical flows immediately from God, and the Mediator, Jesus Christ, and is spiritual, not having a temporal head on earth, but only Christ, the sole spiritual King and Governor of his Church. Kings, princes, and magistrates, are properly called lords, but Christ alone is Lord and Master in the Church, and others who bear office therein ought only to be called ministers, disciples, and servants. As the ministers and others of the ecclesiastical state are subject to the civil magistrate, so ought the person of the civil magistrate to be subject to the Church spiritually, and in ecclesiastical government. The civil magistrate enforces obedience by the sword and other external means; the ministers by the spiritual sword and spiritual means. The magistrate ought neither to preach, minister the sacraments, nor execute the censures of the Church, nor yet prescribe any rule how it should be done; but should command the ministers to observe the rules enjoined in the Scriptures, and punish the transgressors by civil means. The ministers exercise not the civil jurisdiction, but teach the magistrate how it should be exercised according to the word.

The second chapter treated of the Policy of the Church and the persons or office-bearers to whom its administration was committed. As in the civil policy the whole commonwealth consists of those that are governors or magistrates, and those that are governed or subjects, so in the policy of the Church some are appointed to be rulers, and the rest to be ruled and obey. The policy of the Church consists of three things—doctrine, to which is annexed the administration of the sacraments; discipline; and distribution. And so there arises a threefold sort of office-bearers—ministers or preachers, elders or governors, and deacons or distributors; and all these may in a general sense be called ministers of the Church. In the times of the New Testament, our Lord used the ministry of the apostles, prophets, evangelists, pastors, and doctors, in the administration of the word; the eldership for good order and the exercise of discipline; and the deaconship to have the care of the ecclesiastical goods. The offices of apostle, evangelist, and prophet, are extraordinary, and now have ceased in the Church, except when God is pleased to stir some of them up extraordinarily. There are four ordinary functions—that of pastor, minister, or bishop; of doctor; of presbyter or elder; and of deacon. These offices are perpetual in the Church, and are necessary for the government of the same, and no others ought to be received in the true Church of God.

The third chapter explained how persons bearing ecclesiastical functions were admitted to their office. Vocation or calling is common to all who bear office in the Church, and without lawful calling no one is entitled to enter on any ecclesiastical function. There are two sorts of calling, extraordinary and immediate by God Himself, as in the case of the prophets and apostles, which has no place in Churches established and completely reformed; and ordinary, which, besides the calling of God and the testimony of a good conscience, has the lawful approbation and outward judgment of men, according to God's word, and order established in his Church. This ordinary calling has two parts, election and ordination. Election is the choosing of a fit person by the judgment of the eldership, and consent of the congregation to which the person chosen is to be appointed. No one ought to be intruded into any office contrary to the will of the congregation, or without the voice of the eldership. Ordination is the separation and sanctifying of the person appointed by God and his Church, after he is tried and found qualified. The ceremonies of ordination are fasting, earnest prayer, and imposition of hands of the eldership.

The fourth chapter related to the office-bearers in particular, and first to the Pastors or Ministers. Pastors or ministers are they who are appointed to particular congregations, which they rule by the word of God, and over which they watch. In respect of this they receive the names of pastors, episcopi or bishops, ministers, and presbyters or seniors. To the pastor appertains the preaching of the word of God, and the administration of the sacraments, both of which are appointed by God as means to teach us, the one by the ear, the other by the eye and the senses generally, that by both knowledge may be transferred to the mind. To the pastor also it appertains to pray for the flock committed to his charge, and to bless them in the name of the Lord; to watch over them; after lawful proceeding of the eldership to pronounce the sentence of binding and loosing on any one according to the power of the keys granted to the Church; and after like lawful proceeding to solemnize marriages.

The fifth chapter treated of Doctors and their office, and of the Schools. One of the two ordinary and perpetual functions that travail in the word is the office of the doctor, who also may be called prophet, bishop, elder, and catechizer. His office is to open up the mind of the Spirit of God in the Scriptures simply, without such applications as the minister uses, to the end that the faithful may be instructed, sound doctrine taught, and the purity of the Gospel preserved from corruption. Under this name and office is comprehended the order in schools, colleges, and universities. The doctor, being an elder, should assist the pastor in the government of the Church, and concur with the elders his brethren in all assemblies, but it pertains not to him to preach, minister the sacraments, and celebrate marriages, unless he also be orderly called thereto. The pastor, however, may teach in the schools, as the example of Polycarp and others testifies.

The sixth chapter treated of Elders and their office. The word elder in the Scriptures is sometimes the name of age, sometimes of office. When it is the name of an office, it is sometimes taken largely, and comprehends pastors and doctors, as well as those who are called seniors or elders. Here those are called elders whom the Apostle calls presidents or governors. The office is ordinary, perpetual, and always necessary in the Church. The eldership is a spiritual function like the ministry, and those once lawfully called to the office, and having the proper gifts for the same, may not leave it again. The number of elders in each congregation should be according to the number and necessity of the people. It is not necessary that all elders should be also teachers of the word, although they chiefly ought to be so, and so worthy of double honour. It pertains to them to watch over the flock, and to assist the pastor in the examination of those who come to the

Lord's Table, and in visiting the sick. Their principal office is to hold assemblies with the pastors and doctors, who are also of their number, for establishing of good order, and execution of discipline. To those assemblies all persons are subject that remain within their bounds.

The seventh chapter treated of the Elderships and Assemblies, and Discipline. Elderships and assemblies are commonly constituted of pastors, doctors, and those elders who labour not in the word and doctrine. Assemblies are of four sorts —of particular congregations, one or more; of a province; of a whole nation; or of all nations professing obedience to Christ. In all assemblies a moderator should be chosen by common consent, to keep order, and to see that ecclesiastical matters only are discussed. It is not intended that every particular congregation shall have its own particular eldership, but three or four may have an eldership common to all. This may be gathered from the practice of the primitive Church, where elders or colleges of seniors were constituted in cities and large places. This kind of assembly has the general care of ecclesiastical discipline, and to it belongs the duty of seeing that the ordinances of provincial, national, and general assemblies, are put in execution. It has the power of electing and deposing those who hold ecclesiastical charges within its bounds. Provincial assemblies are the lawful conventions of the pastors, doctors, and other elders of a province, gathered for the common affairs of the churches thereof. The national assembly is a lawful convention of the whole churches of a realm or nation. No persons may vote in this assembly except ecclesiastical persons, in such numbers as may be agreed on, though others may be present to propose, hear, and reason. The fourth sort of assembly is of all nations and estates of persons within the Church, representing the Universal Church of Christ, and may be called the general assembly or council of the whole Church of God. These assemblies were called together specially on the occasion of any great schism or controversy, and were convened by the order of godly emperors.

The eighth chapter treated of Deacons and their office. The word deacon is here taken for those to whom belong the collection and distribution of the alms of the faithful, and the ecclesiastical goods. It is an ordinary and perpetual function of the Church of Christ, and persons ought to be called and elected to it, as to other spiritual offices. They ought to make distribution according to the judgment of the elderships, of the which they themselves are not.

The ninth chapter treated of the Patrimony of the Church, and the distribution thereof. By the patrimony of the Church is meant whatever hath been or shall be granted by consent or universal custom to ecclesiastical uses, such as lands, buildings, the interest of money, and the like, given by kings or inferior persons, together with the continual oblations of the faithful; and also tithes, manses, glebes, and the like, which are possessed by universal usage. To take away any part of this patrimony by unlawful means, and convert it to particular or profane uses, is detestable sacrilege. In the apostolical Church, ecclesiastical goods were collected and distributed by the deacons; and the ancient canons also mention the four-fold distribution of this patrimony, one part to the pastor or bishop, another to the elders, deacons, and all the clergy, a third to the poor, the sick, and strangers, and the fourth to the upholding of the fabric of the church and other uses.

The tenth chapter related to the office of a Christian Magistrate in the Church. Though all members of the Church, according to their several vocations, are bound to advance the kingdom of Christ, Christian princes and other magistrates are chiefly called upon to do so. Thus it is the duty of a Christian magistrate to assist and defend the Church; to see that its ministers are properly sustained, and that it is not invaded by false teachers or hirelings; to maintain its discipline, and to punish civilly those who will not submit to ecclesiastical censure, without confounding the two jurisdictions; and to make laws and constitutions, agreeable to God's word, for the advancement of the Church, without usurping anything belonging to ecclesiastical offices, or any part of the power of the spiritual keys, which our Master gave to the apostles and their true successors. For although godly kings and princes, when the Church was corrupted, sometimes restored the true service of God, after the example of the godly kings of Judah, and divers emperors and kings under the Gospel, yet where the ministers are lawfully constituted, and discharge their duties faithfully, princes and magistrates ought to hear and obey their voice, and reverence the majesty of the Son of God, speaking by them.

The eleventh chapter referred to the abuses remaining in the Church, which it was desired should be reformed. As the godly magistrate should maintain the liberty which God has now granted to the preaching of His word, so he should take away what abuses still remain, among which may be reckoned the admission of men to Papistical titles and benefices which have no function in the Reformed Church, as those of abbots, commendators, priors, and the like; the offices of chapters and convents in abbey, cathedral, and other churches; deans, archdeacons, chanters, treasurers, chancellors, and others; the annexation of benefices; the possession of two thirds of the rents by persons coming in the place of the old beneficiaries; also the chapters of the new bishops, because true bishops should confine themselves to one particular flock, and should not usurp lordship over their brethren; the criminal jurisdiction of pastors, and sitting in council, or parliament, in the Church's name, without commission from the Church.

The twelfth chapter contained certain special heads of reformation which were craved. One or more pastors ought to be placed in every parish, and no pastor should be burdened with more flocks than one; doctors should be provided in universities, colleges, and other needful places; elderships and provincial assemblies should be properly constituted; general assemblies ought to be maintained in their true liberty, and all persons subjected to their judgment in ecclesiastical causes without appeal to any judge, civil or ecclesiastical; the liberty of election of persons holding ecclesiastical functions should be restored, so that none be intruded on any congregation, either by the prince or inferior persons, without lawful election, and the assent of the people, as the practice of the apostolical and primitive Church, and good order craves. And because this order cannot stand with patronages and presentations to benefices having cure of souls, as used in the Pope's Church, it ought to be considered by all, whether these should now have place in the light of the Reformation. The ecclesiastical goods ought to be distributed by the deacons, according to the four-fold division already mentioned.

The thirteenth chapter made some remarks on the utility which would flow from this reformation of all estates.[1]

The Second Book of Discipline differed from the First in several important details, and still more in the character which it was intended and fitted to impress on the polity of the Reformed Church. Matters of doctrine are only incidentally alluded to. While the sacraments are spoken of with less reverence than in the older book, a higher view is taken of ordination: imposition of hands, which had before been rejected as unnecessary, is now required to be used, and declared to be one of the appointed ceremonies for conferring the ministerial character. The most marked distinction, however, between the two books, is the change of opinion in regard to the authority of the civil power, and of the people, in matters ecclesiastical. Knox and his associates permitted, and even enjoined the sovereign to take a chief part in the counsels of the Church, though undoubtedly they were ready enough to resist when the royal authority was directed against themselves; and to the people they gave almost unlimited influence. According to their theory, the people were not only the source of all ecclesiastical power, but had also a chief part in its immediate exercise; and, in conformity with this, the office-bearers of the Church were subjected to the control of those whom nominally they ruled, the minister being periodically examined as to his life and the discharge of his duties by the kirk-session, and the superintendent by his provincial assembly. Knox's system was not expressly set aside by Melville, but the manifest purpose of the new discipline was to establish a hierarchy of ecclesiastical courts, resting on the will of the people as its foundation, but controlling that will in its actual exercise, and independent altogether of the civil magistrate. The right of patronage was taken from the crown and the nobility, and conferred on the eldership and the congregation, the consent of the latter being requisite to the appointment of a minister, but the former having the judicial power, both in election and deposition. It was also declared to be the duty of the magistrate to enforce the decisions of the

---

[1] Calderwood, vol. iii. p. 515-555. Book of the Universal Kirk, p. 206-220. James Melville's Diary, p. 86-116. Spottiswood, vol. ii. p. 233-256. Cook, vol. i. p. 283-288. M'Crie's Life of Melville, vol. i. p. 166-171.

ecclesiastical tribunals by civil penalties, but, in doing so, he was simply to execute the decrees of the spiritual estate. The discipline itself was held to be enjoined by the Scriptures, and to be in conformity with the example of the primitive Church; and its various offices were held to be of ordinary and perpetual authority in the Church, and therefore unalterable under any circumstances whatever. This was entirely opposed to the opinions held by the compilers of the First Book of Discipline, in common with most of the English and continental reformers.

It cannot, however, be said that the divine right of the Presbyterian system was even now distinctly set forth. A scriptural and apostolical sanction was claimed for the discipline, but the essential feature of Presbyterianism was still imperfectly developed. The Presbytery itself was not yet in actual existence, though its establishment in certain places had been agreed to; nor was such a body recognized, even in theory, as essential to the constitution of the Church. It formed no part of Knox's polity, where what was called the exercise bore less resemblance to the presbytery, than the superintendent did to the bishop; and in the new discipline there was but one sort of assembly subordinate to the provincial synod, and that assembly partook more of the nature of a kirk-session than of a presbytery, though it combined the functions of both. Melville and his friends had hitherto been unable to convert the exercise into the presbytery, and several drafts of the Second Book of Discipline had been approved of, before the presbytery or classical assembly was set up. Hence arose the incongruity of all notice of the presbytery being omitted in the very charter of the ecclesiastical polity of which that court was afterwards held to be the most essential part.

James Boyd, titular archbishop of Glasgow, died in the month of June, and was buried within the choir of his cathedral church, in the sepulchre of Archbishop Dunbar. Spottiswood describes him, and apparently with justice, as "a wise, learned, and religious prelate, and worthy to have lived in better times than he fell into." According to the same historian, during his last illness he professed his sorrow for having condemned episcopal government at the bidding of the assembly.[1]

[1] Spottiswood, vol. ii. p. 257.

The Duke of Lennox thought this to be a fitting opportunity for obtaining the revenues of the bishopric of Glasgow, by means of an arrangement with some minister, who would accept the see on condition of making over its emoluments, with the exception of a small pension, to himself. After offering the appointment to various persons who refused to enter into such a compact, he at last found a fit instrument for his purpose in Robert Montgomery, minister at Stirling, hitherto a vehement supporter of the anti-episcopal party, but who now consented to accept the bishopric on the duke's terms. This is the most open and flagrant instance that had yet occurred of those simoniacal compacts, which earned for the ecclesiastics concerned in them the opprobrious name, so well known in our history, of Tulchan bishops. That epithet has erroneously, or with an intentional disregard of facts, been connected by many writers with the titular episcopacy established at Leith. Had the system which was then agreed to been allowed to continue, it would have tended, as was the design of its authors, to check such improper appointments. Nominations of that kind had been made previous to the agreement at Leith, and they continued to take place after Melville had succeeded in overturning it. It is well known, however, that similar abuses have existed in different ages, and under all varieties of external circumstances, wherever the state has encouraged or permitted the making merchandize of ecclesiastical benefices.

The nomination to the see of Glasgow was intimated to the general assembly, which met at Edinburgh on the seventeenth of October. The members refused to sanction it, and ordered Montgomery to remain at his proper church of Stirling, without seeking any higher function, under the penalty of excommunication. At this assembly, certain brethren were appointed to labour diligently for the erection of presbyteries throughout the kingdom.[1]

---

[1] Calderwood, vol. iii. p. 281-284. Book of the Universal Kirk, p. 220-234. Spottiswood, vol. ii. p. 281-284. The meaning of the expression, "Tulchan bishops," may best be given in a passage from the report of the proceedings of the Edinburgh Assembly of 1639: "The moderator [David Dickson] craved liberty to expone what was meant by Tulchan bishops. It was a Scots word used in their common language. When a cow will not let down her milk, they stuff a calf's skin full of straw, and set it down before the cow,

The general assembly met in St. Mary's College, St. Andrews, on the twenty-fourth of April, 1582, and Andrew Melville, who, in December, 1580, had been appointed principal of that college, was chosen moderator. Montgomery made his submission, and agreed to give up all claim to the bishopric of Glasgow. Soon after this, however, he again endeavoured, with the assistance of the civil power, to retain possession of his see, and the sentence of excommunication was in consequence pronounced against him by the Presbytery of Edinburgh. An extraordinary meeting of the assembly was convened at Edinburgh, on the twenty-seventh of June, and Melville was continued as moderator. The post which he held in the assembly was no longer one of mere dignity. The ruling powers in Church and State were now openly opposed to each other. The dispute regarding the see of Glasgow still continued, and John Durie had been summoned before the council for language which he had used in a sermon preached during the month of May. He had denounced Montgomery as an apostate, asserted that Lennox wished to turn away the king from the true religion, and prayed, after his sermon, that God would either convert or confound thé duke. On account of this discourse, Durie was ordered to leave Edinburgh.

The opening of the assembly was ominous of what was to follow. Melville preached, and his words, as given by Calderwood, mark the spirit which now animated the ecclesiastical courts of Scotland :—" He inveighed against the bloody knife of absolute authority, whereby men intended to pull the crown off Christ's head, and to wring the sceptre out of his hand." Durie appeared before the assembly, and craved their advice how to act. Under the circumstances, it was not thought advisable that he should remain at Edinburgh in defiance of the royal authority, and he therefore left the city, after publicly protesting against the lawfulness of his expulsion. The assembly drew up a list of their grievances to be presented to the king, and appointed certain of their number to wait upon him for that purpose. These commis-

and that was called a Tulchan. So these bishops possessing the title and the benefice, without the office, they wist not what name to give them, and so they called them Tulchan bishops." (Peterkin's Records of the Kirk, p. 248.)

sioners went to Perth, where James then was, to present the document. When it was read, Arran exclaimed, "What! Who dare subscribe these treasonable articles?" Melville answered, "We dare and will subscribe them, and give our lives in the cause." Encouraged by his example, the other commissioners put their names to the paper. They were allowed to depart without molestation. In the meantime, however, Montgomery had been proclaimed Bishop of Glasgow at the cross of Edinburgh, and his excommunication declared null.[1]

Melville was never wanting in courage, but, when he defied Arran, he knew that he would be supported, if necessary, by a powerful party. The intrigues of Lennox had been discovered by Elizabeth, and her envoys encouraged the discontented nobles to prevent the execution of a design, as prejudicial to the influence of England, as it was to the independence of the Scottish barons, and the interests of the Reformed Church. The Earls of Mar and Gowrie, the Master of Glammis, and others, entered into a bond for the purpose of putting an end to the authority of Lennox. On the twenty-second of August, while the king was residing at Gowrie's castle of Ruthven, he was seized by the associated barons, and soon afterwards carried to Stirling Castle. The Earl of Arran was made prisoner while attempting to rescue his sovereign, and Gowrie and his friends, having assumed the direction of the government, sent a message to Lennox, in name of the captive king, ordering him to leave Scotland within fourteen days.[2]

[1] Calderwood, vol. iii. p. 598-631. Book of the Universal Kirk, p. 235-258. James Melville's Diary, p. 128-133. Spottiswood, vol. ii. p. 284-289. Tytler, vol. viii. pp. 382, 383.

[2] Calderwood, vol. iii. p. 637-647. Tytler, vol. viii. p. 104-115. Mignet, vol. ii. p. 220-223.

CHAPTER XLI.

FROM THE RAID OF RUTHVEN IN AUGUST, 1582, TO THE DEATH OF QUEEN MARY IN FEBRUARY, 1587.

Meetings of the General Assembly—Execution of the Earl of Gowrie—Robert Brown, the English sectary, in Scotland—Flight of Andrew Melville and other ministers—Archbishop Adamson's intercourse with the English bishops—His opposition to the Presbyterian discipline—Ecclesiastical Supremacy of the King ratified by Parliament—Royal declaration regarding the Supremacy—The Earl of Arran driven from power—Return of the ministers from exile—Archbishop Adamson excommunicated by the Synod of Fife—His appeal to the King and Parliament—Declaration by the General Assembly—Proceedings of the English Government against Queen Mary—Her trial and condemnation—Remonstrances of King James—Death of Mary.

THE Raid of Ruthven secured the complete ascendency of Melville and his party. The sentence against Durie was immediately recalled. He preached before the king at Stirling, on the second of September, and, on the fourth, he entered Edinburgh in triumph, a great crowd accompanying him from the Netherbow to St. Giles', singing the hundred and twenty-fourth Psalm. Before the end of the same month the decease took place of John Winram, who, as Sub-prior of St. Andrews, and as one of the Protestant superintendents, had taken an important part in so many ecclesiastical changes.[1]

The general assembly met at Edinburgh on the ninth of October. David Lindsay was chosen moderator, and two commissioners from the king were present. The members formally approved of what had been done by Gowrie and his associates; every minister was ordered to explain and recommend their proceedings in his own congregation; and all who opposed them by word or deed were declared liable to ecclesias-

[1] Calderwood, vol. iii. pp. 646, 647. Lee's Lectures on the History of the Church of Scotland, vol. i. p. 345.

tical censure. Injunctions were issued for the erection of presbyteries in the northern parts of the kingdom, and commission was given to certain specified presbyteries to call before them the Bishops of Murray, Aberdeen, Brechin, Dunkeld, St. Andrews, Dunblane, and the Isles, with instructions to accuse them of various offences, and after trial and conviction to take order with every one of them before the next assembly. Commission was also given to Melville and Smeaton to confer with the Bishop of Orkney, who had ceased altogether to exercise his office as a minister on the ground of sickness and infirmity.

The assembly again met on the twenty-fourth of April, 1583. Farther instructions were given about the bishops, as nothing definite had been done in the interval; and it was declared that baptism administered by lay persons, and such as had no ordinary function in the ministry, was no baptism, and that those so baptized should be baptized anew.[1]

The king was obliged to acquiesce for the most part in whatever was recommended by the Protestant nobles and their allies in the assembly of the Church, but he watched for an opportunity of freeing himself from the thraldom in which he was kept, and of recalling Lennox, towards whom he continued to cherish the most affectionate regard. His hopes in this last respect were frustrated by the death of that nobleman at Paris, in the month of May. Lennox, on his death-bed, recommended his children to the care of James, and requested that his heart should be embalmed and sent to the king. The duke had many amiable qualities. His devotion to the cause of Mary was chivalrous and sincere; and at the same time his loyalty and personal attachment to James are proved by his confidential letters, and the whole tenor of his actions, while engaged in his project of associating the queen and her son in the government of Scotland. But his pretended conversion to the Protestant religion cannot be too severely condemned.[2]

In the end of June, the king was successful in escaping

---

[1] Calderwood, vol. iii. pp. 675-689, 705-713. Book of the Universal Kirk, p. 259-277.

[2] Calderwood, vol. iii. pp. 714, 715. Tytler, vol. viii. pp. 386, 387. Mignet, vol. ii. pp. 464, 465.

from restraint. Arran was recalled to court, and a proclamation was issued, in which the Raid of Ruthven was declared to be treason. Before the end of the year, the Protestant lords made their submission, but in the spring of 1584 a new plot was devised by them and the agents of Elizabeth. Their plans, however, were discovered, and when their treasonable intentions had been openly manifested, the Earl of Gowrie was seized, and soon afterwards beheaded. The other conspirators were compelled to flee to England.[1]

The apprehensions of the ministers were now renewed, but it was not the interest of James to quarrel with so formidable a body. The only person who suffered at first in any way was Durie, who was ordered to retire beyond the Tay, and to fix his residence at Montrose.

In January, 1584, the English sectary, Robert Brown, came over from Flanders, and landed at Dundee. At St. Andrews he received from Melville a letter of commendation to Lawson, and went on to Edinburgh, where he remained for some time. It is probable that Melville, when he gave him the letter, knew little more of him than that he was at variance with the English bishops, and that he had been obliged to leave his own country on that account. He soon exhibited the true character of his opinions, by attacking the Scottish discipline, refusing to submit to the Edinburgh presbytery, and threatening to appeal from them to the civil magistrate.

In the beginning of February, Melville was summoned before the council, on account of a sermon which he had preached at St. Andrews, in June of the preceding year. He declined to answer, maintaining that whatever charge might be brought against a preacher for words spoken in his sermon, even although they should be alleged to be treasonable, he was entitled, in the first place, to be tried by the ecclesiastical court. He was in consequence ordered to enter himself to ward within the castle of Blackness, but, apprehensive that still more severe measures were intended, he fled to Berwick. After the execution of the Earl of Gowrie, several ministers followed Melville's example, and retired to England.

The general assembly met at St. Andrews on the twenty-fourth of April. The king called upon them to retract their

[1] Tytler, vol. viii. p. 149-173.

approbation of the Raid of Ruthven, but they waived considering the question on account of the small number of the members present.[1]

About this time, Archbishop Adamson returned from an embassy on which he had been sent to England. Calderwood mentions that he was well received by the English bishops, who were glad to see a brother of their order from Scotland, and accuses him of endeavouring to make the new discipline odious to Elizabeth and the Church of England, and to the Reformed communions on the Continent, by giving false representations of it. A person of Adamson's learning and accomplishments, holding the position he did, and professing ecclesiastical opinions similar to those maintained by most of the bishops, was sure of a welcome reception in England, where Whitgift had lately been raised to the see of Canterbury. He, no doubt, gave a sufficiently unfavourable account of the proceedings of Melville's party, and brought prominently forward those parts of the discipline which were most opposed to royal and episcopal authority. But the extracts from the writings which he circulated, as preserved by James Melville and Calderwood, clearly shew that there was no misrepresentation in the matter. It required nothing more than the enunciation of the principles of the new polity to make it offensive to the English queen and primate.

In opposition to the discipline, Adamson also put forth the following articles:—

"I. FOR THE PRINCE.

" 1. It is one of the greatest parts of the princely office to appoint a godly order to the Church, and to take heed that the same should be maintained and kept.

" 2. It proceedeth from the tyranny of the Pope to arrogate to the clergy the whole government of the Church, and to exclude therefrom Christian princes and godly magistrates, who should be nourishers of the Church, and keepers of both the Tables.

" 3. Princes in their own countries are chief heads under

[1] Calderwood, vol. iii. p. 764 ; vol. iv. pp. 1-14, 37, 38. Spottiswood, vol. ii. pp. 308, 309. M'Crie's Life of Melville, vol. i. p. 286-294.

Christ, as well in ecclesiastical polity as temporal, and their judgment in both is sovereign.

"4. If the rulers of the Church have done wrong, appellation is lawful to the princely power, by whose authority the same should be redressed.

"II. FOR THE MINISTRY.

"1. It is most necessary that a good order and form be prescribed in the Church, as well in the service of God, as in public doctrine, that all things may be done orderly, and no man transgress the limits and bounds appointed in the Scripture, under pretext of the liberty of the Spirit of God.

"2. The government of the Church does consist in the authority and power of the bishops, to whom are committed the dioceses and provinces in government.

"3. The office of bishop is of the apostolic institution, and most agreeable to the primitive purity of the Church of God.

"4. The ordination and ordinary judgment of pastors belongeth to the bishop, without whose authority whosoever does presume to the pastoral cure enters not at the door but over the wall.

"5. Doctors have no power to preach but by the appointment of bishops; neither have they any farther power in governing the Church.

"6. Seniors or elders of the laic sort are not agreeable with the Scriptures or ancient purity of the primitive Church.

"7. Presbyteries to be appointed of gentlemen, lords of the ground, and others associated with the ministers, do nothing else but induce a great confusion in the Church, and give occasion to continual sedition.

"8. The order of appointing moderators in presbyteries or assemblies, to be altered at their meeting, is neither canonical after the Scripture, nor agreeable to the order of the primitive Church, in the which it has been local in the bishop's seat, and not elective and variable as were the wardens of the friars.

"9. The synodal assembly should be moderated and governed by the bishop in every province and diocese; and by him should order be taken that the churches be well served.

"10. The general assembly of a realm has no power to

convene itself, but upon a great and weighty occasion, intimated to the Prince, and license granted thereto.

"11. There is no assembly that has power to establish laws and constitutions within the realm, but such as are allowed of the Prince and his estate.

"12. The resort of the prelates of the Church to the king's parliament and great council for the weighty affairs of the realm is most necessary; and that ministers shall presume to direct certain of their own number to the council and parliament, is an intolerable annoyance.

"13. Visitation is an office necessary in the Church, and proper to the function of a bishop, and such as are appointed by him for that effect.

"14. Benefices and patronages have been zealously and godly appointed by our antecessors, and Christian pastors may with a safe conscience enjoy the same; and the deacons to be appointed over the Church rents are a preposterous imitation of the primitive Church, without any kind of reason.

"15. The patrimony of the Church is that which by the laws and estates of countries belongs to the Church and entertainment thereof; and not that abundance wherewith the Roman Church did overflow."

These articles, we are told, were presented to the Archbishop of Canterbury and the Bishop of London, to the ministers of the French congregations at London, and to sundry other learned persons, as warranted by the Scriptures and primitive antiquity, with a request, in virtue of the commission which Adamson had from King James, that they would consider the same, and confirm them by their subscription and approval. The result of this application is not mentioned. Melville watched these proceedings, and apprized his friends in Scotland of what was going on to their prejudice. He afterwards wrote to the Churches of Geneva and Zurich, giving his own account of Scottish affairs, and denouncing the archbishop in language most offensive and unbecoming. The contrast is very great between the calm ecclesiastical propositions of Adamson, and the personal invective, and political discussions of Melville.[1]

---

[1] Calderwood, vol. iv. pp. 49-55, 157-167. James Melville's Diary, pp. 141, 148-164.

A parliament was held at Edinburgh on the nineteenth of May. In the roll of members present there appear the names of the Archbishop of St. Andrews, and the Bishops of Dunkeld, Aberdeen, Brechin, Orkney, Dunblane, Argyll, and the Isles. The róyal authority over all estates, spiritual as well as temporal, was confirmed; to decline the jurisdiction of the king and council was declared to be treason; all conventions, whether civil or ecclesiastical, held without the sovereign's license, were forbidden; and power was given to the Archbishop of St. Andrews, the bishops, and other commissioners, to take order in matters ecclesiastical within their dioceses, to visit the churches and ministers of the same, to reform the colleges, and to give collation of benefices. The excommunication pronounced against the Archbishop of Glasgow was declared to be irregular and invalid, and the bishops and commissioners to be appointed by the king for the deprivation of unworthy persons were ordered to investigate the charges brought against him. The general nature of these acts had previously become known, and David Lindsay was ready to protest against them; but he was seized, and imprisoned in Blackness Castle, on a charge of illegal correspondence with England. When they were proclaimed at the cross of Edinburgh, Pont and Balcanqual openly protested against their validity, in so far as they were prejudicial to the former liberties of the Church. Soon afterwards the latter of these two ministers, Lawson, James Melville, and others, fled to Berwick.[1]

In a parliament held at Edinburgh in the month of August, it was ordered, for the better observance of the statutes abovementioned, that all beneficed persons, ministers, readers, masters of colleges and schools, being required by their ordinary bishop or commissioner, should subscribe the following promise and obligation:—" We the beneficed men, ministers, readers, and masters of colleges and schools underwritten, testify and faithfully promise, by these our subscriptions, our humble and dutiful submission and fidelity to our sovereign lord the king's majesty, and to obey with all humility his highness' acts of his late parliament; and that according to the same we shall shew our obedience to our ordinary bishop or

---

[1] Acts of the Parliaments of Scotland, vol. iii. p. 290-312. Calderwood, vol. iv. p. 62-73. Tytler, vol. viii. p. 177-179.

commissioner, appointed or to be appointed by his majesty to have the exercise of the spiritual jurisdiction in our diocese;" and that under the pain of forfeiting their benefices.

In terms of this act, all the ministers between Stirling and Berwick were summoned to make their subscription at Edinburgh, on the sixteenth of November. A number of those who were called did not appear, and, according to Calderwood, of the others only eleven subscribed, with several readers who had formerly been priests. The stipends of those who refused were immediately withdrawn. Various ministers, however, were ready to subscribe, provided they were allowed to add to the formula, "according to the word of God;" and the king having expressed his willingness to accept of this qualification, Craig and others signed during the month of December.[1]

In the beginning of the year 1585, a very able paper, the composition of Archbishop Adamson, and containing a declaration of the king's intentions and meaning in regard to the late acts of parliament, was published by the royal command. It claimed for the sovereign the authority given in the Old and New Testament, and in the primitive Church, to godly kings and emperors, in virtue of which it was his duty to see that all estates discharged their several offices aright. It denounced the opinion that the king had no authority in matters ecclesiastical, as one of the chief errors of Rome, and accused Melville and his party of imitating the Pope in claiming exemption from all civil jurisdiction, and of creating a spiritual tyranny by means of the newly invented presbyteries. It defended the episcopal office now established, as a form of government continued in the Church from the Apostles' times by regular succession, and maintained in Scotland from the introduction of Christianity into the kingdom, until within a few years back when some curious and busy men laboured to introduce parity among the ministers. It was his majesty's intention that the bishops should hold their synodical assemblies twice every year, and that general assemblies should be allowed to meet, provided they were called with his knowledge and license, but he was determined not to permit the exercise

---

[1] Acts of the Parliaments of Scotland, vol. iii. p. 347. Calderwood, vol. iv. pp. 209-211, 246, 247.

of jurisdiction by presbyteries, consisting of a mixed body of ministers and laymen.

This paper was extensively circulated, and was reprinted in England, where it produced a great effect. Several answers to it were written by Melville and the members of his party. They maintained that the desire which the writer put forward of upholding good order in the realm was only an artifice for introducing a new popedom in the person of the king, who, being chief judge in all causes, might cast down religion at his pleasure; and that for this purpose the ecclesiastical jurisdiction given by God immediately to the Church was transferred to the bishops, who were the king's creatures.[1]

The answers to the king's declaration were skilfully written, but they were disfigured by the most unscrupulous personal charges, and by denunciations of divine vengeance against those whose measures they were intended to oppose. No adequate provocation to such language had been given by Adamson. "An ambitious man of a salt and fiery humour," is the severest expression which he uses of Melville; "a juggler, a Howliglass, a drunkard, a vile Epicurean," are but samples of the names which were applied to himself. There was much truth, however, in the accusations brought by each party against the principles maintained by the other. In what was now taking place, and in the proceedings for many years afterwards, the old contest between the Popes and the Emperors, with the faults on either side, seemed to be revived. The king, in virtue of his ecclesiastical supremacy, claimed a right to control the whole external system of the Church; the ministers denied that the sovereign had any ecclesiastical authority whatever, and, while refusing to sit in his civil courts, even at his own request, interfered in every political matter, on the pretence that spiritual interests were involved. The tendency of the one system was to make the Church wholly subservient to the State, and to allow it to act merely as the instrument of the temporal power; that of the other, to create within the kingdom an independent jurisdiction, checking the civil magistrate in the lawful use of his own authority, and exercising a domestic tyranny over every household. The contest at this time was farther aggravated

[1] Calderwood, vol. iv. p. 254-339.

by the circumstance that the king and his counsellors were endeavouring to free the royal authority from those limitations to which it had hitherto been subjected in Scotland, and that Melville and several of the leading ministers disliked the kingly office altogether, and were desirous of establishing a political system unknown to the ancient constitution of the realm, and opposed to the wishes of the great body of the people.

In the month of January, a commission was granted to various bishops, noblemen, and others, to call before them those ministers who had not yet submitted, and to require their subscription to the promise of obedience. The prelates named in the commission were the Archbishops of St. Andrews and Glasgow, and the Bishops of Argyll, the Isles, and Aberdeen; and these appear to have been the whole bishops at this time exercising ecclesiastical jurisdiction in the Reformed Church. The Bishop of Argyll was Neil Campbell, who had been appointed to that see about the year 1580, in room of James Hamilton. The commissioner for the diocese of Brechin was John Erskine of Dun, who thus shewed his steady adherence to the form of Episcopacy which had been established in a great measure by his exertions. He was accused, indeed, by the adherents of the banished ministers, of being particularly active in urging subscription. Thus matters went on during the greater part of the year 1585. Many of the ministers signed the obligation required of them; but in so doing a considerable number undoubtedly acted against their real belief.[1]

Another revolution was now approaching which was again to change the position of affairs in Scotland. The Master of Gray, a favourite of James yet more unscrupulous than Arran, and jealous of the superior influence of that nobleman, formed a plan for overturning the government, to which the English ambassador gave his strenuous support, and which was communicated to the banished nobles and ministers, and to Lord John and Lord Claud Hamilton. The Earls of Angus and Mar, the Master of Glammis, Lord John Hamilton, Melville, Balcanqual, and others, met at Berwick and arranged their proceedings.

[1] Calderwood, vol. iv. pp. 339-343, 351. Miscellany of the Wodrow Society, vol. i. pp. 432, 433.

The noblemen entered Scotland, where they were joined by the Earl of Bothwell, Lord Maxwell, and other barons; and James, unprepared to oppose them, and betrayed by the Master of Gray, was obliged to surrender at Stirling. Arran escaped with difficulty, and the associated lords assumed the chief direction of the government. This revolution took place in the beginning of November.[1]

These proceedings were fatal to the scheme which Arran had formed, and which, with the assistance of Archbishop Adamson, he had almost carried through, of assimilating the Scottish monarchy to that of England, and making the power of the crown supreme both in Church and State. There is no evidence that this design was connected with any plan for restoring the Roman Catholic religion. The reverse indeed is shewn by the whole course of Arran's policy, and by the character of the combination which overthrew his power. That combination was formed by a union of the exiled Protestant barons and ministers with the Hamiltons and other personal enemies of Arran, among whom were some of the leading Roman Catholic nobles, the Lord Claud Hamilton, the Lord Maxwell, and the Earl of Huntly.

The ministers expected that the change of government would immediately lead to a corresponding alteration in the condition of the Church. In this, however, they were disappointed. The nobles, having gained their own ends, had no wish to provoke the king further by an attack on Episcopacy, and the ministers who had signed the obligation defended the lawfulness of subscription, and even denounced the conduct of their brethren who had been in exile. The statutes were enforced both against the Roman Catholics, and the Protestants who denied the king's supremacy. The Lord Maxwell was warded in Edinburgh Castle for causing mass to be sung in the church of Lincluden, and James Gibson, minister at Pencaitland, was committed a prisoner to the same place for comparing the king to Jeroboam, and styling him a persecutor of the Church. All that the ministers could obtain was a declaration from the king explanatory of the acts of parliament complained of, and the restitution of their livings to those who had returned from England.[2]

[1] Tytler, vol. viii. p. 229-242.
[2] Calderwood, vol. iv. pp. 448-465, 484, 491.

In April, 1586, the provincial assembly of Fife met at St. Andrews, and Robert Wilkie, one of the professors of St. Leonard's College, was elected moderator. James Melville, as moderator of the last assembly, delivered a discourse, in which he animadverted severely on the conduct of Archbishop Adamson. Certain charges having also been brought against the archbishop, that prelate gave in answers, protesting at the same time both against the authority of the assembly, and the presence among its members of the Master of Lindsay and the two Melvilles, who were his personal enemies. His answers were not thought satisfactory, and a sentence of excommunication was pronounced against him. Some of the archbishop's retainers, on the other hand, excommunicated the two Melvilles and several of the brethren.

Adamson appealed to the king, the parliament, the privy council, and a lawful general assembly, and continued to preach notwithstanding the excommunication. In his appeal, he denied the authority of the convention at St. Andrews, because it was called without the sanction of the king or the bishop of the diocese; because a layman presided, and it was composed for the most part of barons, gentlemen, and masters of schools or colleges, who had no function in the ecclesiastical state; because even if composed of ministers, they were not lawful judges of their bishop, but he of them; because the sentence was pronounced irregularly and for insufficient reasons; and because it was doubtful whether synods could excommunicate, where the prince was a Christian.[1]

The general assembly, whose sittings were now resumed, met at Edinburgh on the tenth of May. The king attended in person at the election of a moderator, and gave his vote in favour of David Lindsay, who was accordingly chosen. When the proceedings at St. Andrews came before them, Adamson disclaimed seeking supremacy over the Church or its courts, promised to claim no more authority than was allowed by God's word, and to shew himself in all respects a moderate pastor, according to the definition of Paul, and offered to submit his life and doctrine to the judgment of the assembly. When this submission was made, the assembly,

[1] Calderwood, vol. iv. p. 494-547. James Melville's Diary, p. 245-247. Spottiswood, vol ii. p. 337-340.

out of respect to the king and to promote quietness in the Church, and without condemning what was done by the synod of Fife, declared that the excommunication should be accounted as not pronounced. Against this sentence a protest was entered by Melville and some of his supporters.

The members of assembly were divided in opinion, and were evidently desirous to avoid coming to a positive resolution on the one side or the other. Some time before, a conference had been held by the king's advisers and the ministers, at which an attempt was made to establish a sort of middle system between the Episcopacy recognized by law and the discipline sanctioned by the assembly; and, in conformity with this policy, Adamson had no doubt received the command of James to make the modified submission which led to the resolution agreed to by the majority of the ecclesiastical court. It was probably part of this compromise, that no opposition should now be made by the king to a decree of the assembly, by which the kingdom was formally divided into a specified number of provincial synods and presbyteries. It was also proposed to subject the bishops to the censure of these courts, but the king refused to agree to this, insisting that they should be tried only by the general assembly.[1]

The proceedings of this assembly were not satisfactory either to Melville or to his opponents, but the submission of Adamson, and the change of policy adopted by the court, were in their result fatal to the cause of titular Episcopacy.

During the latter part of the year 1586, the attention of the Scottish nation was directed to circumstances in the neighbouring kingdom in which they were deeply interested. Queen Mary had now been a prisoner for eighteen years, and every attempt to obtain her release had been unsuccessful. Depressed as she was by misfortune, worn out with infirmities and premature old age, she was still as much feared by Elizabeth, as when, in her youth, she was the sovereign of an independent kingdom, and the wife of one of the most powerful monarchs of Europe. The feelings of the English queen were shared by her Protestant subjects, who hated Mary for her religion, and as the cause of all the plots and conspiracies

[1] Calderwood, vol. iv. p. 547-583. Book of the Universal Kirk, p. 289-313. Spottiswood, vol. ii. p. 341-343. M'Crie's Life of Melville, vol. i. p. 351-360.

to which her imprisonment had given rise. They never seem to have thought that her detention was cruel and unjust, and that the wise course to prevent the evils they complained of would have been to restore her to freedom. The only remedies which occurred to them were increasing watchfulness and harsher captivity; and, when these were found to be ineffectual, her trial and execution were demanded by the popular voice. Although Elizabeth had connived at schemes for delivering Mary to certain death, she had hitherto refused to bring her to public trial in England, but, when Babington's conspiracy was discovered, she acquiesced in the course which was recommended by the majority of her council.

On the fifth of October a commission was issued for the trial of Mary as accessory to the plot against the Queen of England, and, nine days afterwards, the court met in the great hall of Fotheringay Castle. When the commission was read, Mary, addressing the court, said that she was a free princess, an anointed queen, subject to God only; and she therefore protested against the legality of the proceedings, and that under that protest her answers to the charges were to be given. She maintained her innocence, and argued against the sufficiency of the evidence which was brought against her. But conscious how little weight her assertions would have with her judges, she appealed to other motives. "Think," she said, "of the royal majesty which is wounded through me: think of the precedent you are creating. . . . I came into England, relying on the friendship and promises of the Queen of England. I came relying on that token which she sent me." Drawing a ring from her finger, she continued, "Trusting to this pledge of love and protection I came amongst you. You can tell me how it has been redeemed. . . . I desire that I may have another day of hearing. I claim the privilege of having an advocate to plead my cause; or, being a queen, that I may be believed on the word of a queen." Her entreaties and her pleas were disregarded. The court, after adjourning to Westminster, found her guilty of the crime of which she had been accused.

The intelligence of these proceedings excited a feeling of deep indignation among all in Scotland whose hearts were not hardened by fanaticism and political rancour. James had been separated from his mother in infancy, and been educated by those who had driven her from the throne, and who had used every endeavour to blacken her reputation. In such circumstances, it is rather matter of wonder that he had not lost altogether the feelings of a son, than that they were sometimes forgotten in his supposed duty or interest as a sovereign. So long as he thought his mother's life was not aimed at, he shewed little interest in her trial, but, when the true object of Elizabeth became apparent, his conduct was altered, and he remonstrated in the warmest manner against the threatened outrage. Unhappily for his good name, he still allowed himself to be influenced by the fear of losing the succession to the English crown, and sent, as one of his envoys to Elizabeth, the Master of Gray, who had already betrayed Mary, and whose true character he ought to have known. Full of anxiety, he also requested the ministers to pray for his mother. Many of them, especially those in Edinburgh, refused. In the king's own presence, and in the church of St. Giles, a minister, named Cowper, took possession of the pulpit to prevent the Archbishop of St. Andrews from officiating, and was hardly persuaded to come down.

After long hesitation, Elizabeth signed the warrant for the death of Mary. It was neither conscience nor pity that caused the delay, but dread of the consequences to herself; and she would have avoided a public execution, could she have persuaded Mary's keeper, Sir Amias Paulet, to assassinate her. A letter was written, at Elizabeth's request, urging him to shew his zeal for his sovereign by freeing her from her enemy; but Paulet, a stern Puritan, who believed that in putting Mary to death according to the forms of law he was doing a righteous act, at once refused to commit the base crime to which he was prompted.

On the seventh of February, 1587, the Earls of Kent and Shrewsbury repaired to Fotheringay, and intimated to Mary that she was to die on the morning of the following day. When the warrant for her execution was read to her, she made the sign of the cross, and exclaimed, "God be praised for the news you bring me. I could receive none better, for it announces to me the conclusion of my miseries, and the grace which God has granted me to die for the honour of his name, and of his Church, Catholic, Apostolic, and Roman. I did not expect such a happy end." She entreated to be allowed the assistance of her confessor, who had not been permitted to see her for some time. Her request was refused, and she declined to accept the services of the Dean of Peterborough, who had accompanied the earls.

She rose early next morning, and, entering her oratory, continued for some time in prayer before the altar. After taking a little food, she again proceeded with her devotions, till she was interrupted by a message that the lords were waiting for her. She was conducted to the great hall where the scaffold was erected, and, after urgent entreaty, some of her attendants were allowed to accompany her. While the Dean of Peterborough prayed in English, Mary, kneeling apart, repeated portions of the thirty-first, fifty-first, and ninety-first Psalms, in Latin, and afterwards continued her devotions in the English tongue. Then kissing the crucifix which she held in her hands, she said, " As thine arms, O my God, were spread out upon the cross, so receive me within the arms of thy mercy: extend thy pity, and forgive my sins!" The last words she was heard to utter as she knelt by the block were those of the thirty-first Psalm : " Into thy hands I commend my spirit, for Thou hast redeemed me O Lord, Thou God of Truth." [1]

[1] See Letters in Ellis, second series, vol. iii. p. 113-118, and in Robertson's appendix, vol. iii. p. 435-440 ; Tytler, vol. viii. p. 306-358 ; Mignet, vol. ii. p. 301-368 ; Jebb, De vita et rebus gestis Mariæ Scotorum Reginæ, vol. ii. p. 611-641. The account which Spottiswood gives (vol. ii. pp. 355, 356) of the general disobedience of the ministers to the injunctions of King James in regard to praying for his mother is perhaps exaggerated ; but the arguments and statements of Dr. Lee, (Lectures on the History of the Church of Scotland, vol. ii. p. 91-95) do not shew that it is substantially inaccurate. English writers, knowing how dangerous the life of Mary was to the civil and ecclesiastical constitution of their country, frequently attempt to defend or palliate her execution. With more truth, Mr. Keble (Preface to Hooker's Ecclesiastical Polity, p. lxiv.) says that " the chief hope of the Romanist party" was removed, "though at the cost of a great national crime."

CHAPTER XLII.

FROM THE DEATH OF QUEEN MARY IN FEBRUARY, 1587, TO THE ESTABLISHMENT OF PRESBYTERIANISM IN JUNE, 1592.

Indignation of the Scots on the death of Mary—The Spanish Armada—Insurrection of the Roman Catholic nobles—Marriage of King James with Anne of Denmark—Death of John Erskine of Dun—Letter from Elizabeth to James—General Assembly of August, 1590—Sermon of James Melville—Speech attributed to King James—Relations between the English and Scottish Churches—Rise of Puritanism—Bancroft's sermon at Paul's Cross—Irritation of the Scottish Presbyterians—Illness of Archbishop Adamson—His retractation—His death—General Assembly of May, 1592—Parliamentary ratification of the Presbyterian Church.

WHILE the bells were ringing in London for the death of Mary, Elizabeth pretended that the execution had taken place without her knowledge and against her wishes, and censured the ministers who had simply obeyed her orders. No one was deceived by these proceedings, but they afforded an excuse for continuing her previous intercourse with other kingdoms. Henry III. of France heard with anger of what had taken place in England, but was soon obliged to accept Elizabeth's apologies, in order to secure her assistance against the League and the princes of Lorraine. The English queen had a more difficult task to accomplish in appeasing the Scots. James was indignant; and all, except the more violent members of the Presbyterian party, were ready to support their sovereign in avenging what they thought an unpardonable insult to the Scottish nation. The Earl of Bothwell declared that the best mourning apparel on such an occasion was a coat of steel; and the border clans of the Scotts and Kers, without waiting for any formal declaration of war, ravaged the English marches. The trial and condemnation of the Master of Gray for various acts of treason, especially for his conduct during his late embassy to England, rendered the state of matters yet more threatening.

The position of Elizabeth, at this time, was very perilous. She had hoped to secure her throne by the death of her kinswoman, and that event had excited almost every nation in Europe against her. The King of Spain took advantage of this feeling to hasten the preparations which he had been making for the invasion of England, and, if James could be induced to open the Scottish ports to his fleet, and declare war against England, the expedition seemed assured of success. To this course the King of the Scots was urgently advised by a powerful party among his subjects. The Roman Catholics were now united, and were once more a formidable body. Their chief leaders were the Earls of Huntly, Errol, and Crawford, the Lord Maxwell, and Lord Claud Hamilton. Huntly, the grandson of the earl who fell at Corrichie, had subscribed the Protestant Confession, in order to avoid persecution, but now avowed his opinions, and promised to be stedfast to his faith. Errol and Crawford had lately been converted, the former by the Jesuit Edmund Hay, the latter by William Crichton, a priest of the same order. All these, as well as many who held Protestant opinions, were vehemently desirous of hostilities with England. The king was doubtful how to act, and, had he possessed greater resolution and higher principles than he did, his perplexity would not have been removed. He might have disregarded the risk of losing the succession to the English crown, but other considerations of the utmost importance were also to be kept in view. James had good reason to believe that the success of the Spanish invasion would be fatal alike to the Reformed Churches and the independence of the British kingdoms; and, when he finally yielded to the persuasions of Elizabeth, and resolved to assist her, he adopted the course which duty as well as interest pointed out.

It was fortunate for Britain that Huntly and his friends remained quiet till after the Armada was dispersed, but, in the spring of 1589, encouraged by promises of support from Spain, they broke out into open insurrection. The king exerted himself with unexpected vigour. Accompanied by the young Duke of Lennox, the chancellor Maitland, and others of his nobles, he advanced as far as Aberdeen. The northern lords, finding themselves unable to resist, were obliged to submit. Huntly and Crawford were committed to prison, and the same punishment was awarded to the Earl of Bothwell, who, though a Protestant, had joined in the rebellion.[1]

Soon after the restoration of tranquillity, James sent an embassy to request in marriage the princess Anne, daughter of Frederick II., King of Denmark. His suit was accepted. The princess sailed for Scotland, but was driven back by a hurricane, and James, impatient of the delay, embarked at Leith, and after a prosperous voyage arrived in Norway. On the twenty-fourth of November, 1589, the marriage was celebrated at Upslo, by David Lindsay, the royal chaplain. The king proceeded to Zealand, and remained there till the end of April, when he returned to Scotland. During his absence the kingdom had continued in a state of unusual tranquillity, under the administration of the nobles to whom he had entrusted the government. On Sunday the seventeenth of May, the queen was crowned in the abbey church of Holyrood. A dispute took place, similar to that which had occurred at the coronation of James himself. Several of the ministers objected to the unction as Judaical, Popish, and superstitious. The king insisted on its being used, and their scruples were at last overcome. The queen was anointed by Robert Bruce, one of the ministers of Edinburgh, and the crown was placed on her head either by the ministers, or by the Duke of Lennox and Lord Hamilton.[2]

John Erskine of Dun died on the twenty-second of March, 1590, having survived all his brethren who were appointed to the office of Superintendent on the establishment of the Reformed Church. This distinguished baron was one of the most estimable men of his time. Steadily attached to the Protestant opinions, and maintaining them consistently and courageously, he was always opposed to violent and extreme measures. The part which he took in connection with the agreement at Leith—a circumstance which many writers overlook or abstain from noticing—is sufficient to shew that the popular

[1] Tytler, vol. ix. p 1-27. Calderwood, vol. v. pp. 17, 25.
[2] Tytler, vol. ix. p. 27-34. Calderwood, vol. v. pp. 67, 72, 94-96. Spottiswood, vol. ii. p. 399-408.

opinion is mistaken which ascribes that arrangement solely to the covetousness of the regent and the nobility. When the nominal Episcopacy then established had been overthrown by Melville, and partially restored by King James and Archbishop Adamson, Erskine persevered in the same line of conduct, supporting the prelatical system, and enforcing obedience to it on the reluctant ministers of Angus and Mearns.

When, in 1571, the superintendent complained of certain bishops being intruded on the Church, it was not episcopal authority to which he objected, but the improper interference of the state in appointing bishops, and its sacrilegious invasion of ecclesiastical property. He held that the episcopal office was of divine institution, and to be conferred by the laying-on of hands of the pastors, but that individual bishops derived their powers from the Church, and were therefore responsible in the exercise of their function to the whole body of the faithful assembled in synod. He entertained a very high and reverential opinion of the authority of the Church and its ministers. This was an opinion which he did not acquire from the school of Knox, and which was distinctly promulgated by him before Melville's return to Scotland. Whence it was immediately derived cannot now be ascertained. If it were true, as is affirmed by Dr. M'Crie, that in his youth Erskine studied under Melancthon at Wittenberg, the origin of these opinions, and of his ecclesiastical principles generally, would admit of explanation. But the statement is erroneous; it was the superintendent's son, James Erskine, who was the scholar of Melancthon.[1]

---

[1] As to Erskine's ecclesiastical principles, see his letter to the regent Mar (Bannatyne, p. 279-288), and his "epistle written to a faithful brother," dated 13th December, 1571 (Miscellany of the Spalding Club, vol. iv. p. 92-101). The epistle is a very favourable specimen of the theological writings of the time. In regard to Dr. M'Crie's mistake above alluded to, compare Life of Melville, vol. i. pp. 10, 11, with James Melville's Diary, p. 14. The same writer (Life of Melville, vol. ii. pp. 21, 22) gives the 16th of October, 1592, as the date of Erskine's death, and states that Spottiswood is in error in fixing it on the 12th of March, 1592. Both are wrong, as appears from a contemporary obituary of the family of Dun (Miscellany of the Spalding Club, vol. iv. pp. lxxvii. lxxviii.), which is the authority for the date given in the text. The mistakes on the point are very excusable, being caused by confounding the superintendent with others of his family of the same Christian name. He attained a patriarchal age, and saw around him, grown up to manhood, a son named Robert, and a grandson and great-

Penry, the English Puritan, had taken refuge in Scotland, and the ministers there expressed their sympathy with his cause by praying for those who were persecuted in England. Some of them also seem to have made personal reflections on Queen Elizabeth, of the same character as those which they were in the way of using in regard to their own sovereign. Elizabeth was not disposed to tolerate such proceedings. On the sixth of July, 1590, she wrote a letter to James, in which, after referring to the good understanding existing between them, she said, " Lest fair semblances, that easily may beguile, do breed your ignorance of such persons as either pretend religion or dissemble devotion, let me warn you that there is risen, both in your realm and mine, a sect of perilous consequence, such as would have no kings, but a presbytery, and take our place, while they enjoy our privilege, with a shade of God's word, which none is judged to follow right, without by their censure they be so deemed. Yea, look we well unto them. When they have made in our people's hearts a doubt of our religion—and that we err if they say so— what perilous issue they may make I rather think than mind to write. Sapienti pauca. I pray you stop the mouths, or make shorter the tongues of such ministers as dare presume to make oraisons in their pulpits for the persecuted in England for the Gospel. Suppose you, my dear brother, that I can tolerate such scandals of my sincere government? No: I hope, however you be pleased to bear with their audacity towards yourself, yet you will not suffer a strange king receive that indignity at such caterpillars' hands, that instead of fruit I am afraid will stuff your realm with venom: of this I have particularized more to this bearer, together with other answers to his charge, beseeching you to hear them, and not to give more harbour to vagabond traitors and seditious inventors, but to return them to me, or banish them your

grandson, both named John, who all died within less than three years after himself; see Miscellany of the Spalding Club, vol. iv. pp. lxxvii. lxxviii., and two documents in the same volume, pp. 74, 75, 76, dated in the years 1586 and 1588, in the former of which "John Erskine of Dun, Superintendent of Angus and Mearns," alludes to his "oy, John Erskine of Logie," and in the latter of which " John Erskine, fiar of Dun, son and apparent heir to John Erskine of Logie," alludes to " John Erskine, elder, franktenementer of Dun," as his "grandsire," and to " Robert Erskine, fiar of Dun," as his " goodsire."

land." James willingly complied with the request of the English queen. The ministers were ordered to forbear praying for the Puritans, and Penry was commanded to leave Scotland.[1]

The struggle between the titular Episcopacy and Presbyterianism still continued, but the bishops, no longer supported by the court, were unable to check the measures of their opponents. In the general assembly which met at Edinburgh, on the twentieth of June, 1587, Melville was chosen moderator, and renewed instructions were given to proceed against the Archbishops of St. Andrews and Glasgow, and the Bishops of Aberdeen and Dunkeld. The Bishop of Dunkeld was Peter Rollock. He had succeeded, probably on the see becoming vacant by the death of Robert Crichton, the last canonical prelate, who had been restored to his temporalities during the administration of the Duke of Lennox. A question was also brought before this assembly in regard to the bishopric of Caithness. Robert, brother of Matthew Earl of Lennox, had held that see for many years. At the Reformation he conformed to the established religion, and in the year 1576 succeeded his nephew Charles as Earl of Lennox, a dignity which, at the king's request, he resigned in favour of Esmé Stewart, in exchange for the earldom of March. He died in 1586, and Robert Pont was presented by the king to the vacant see. Before accepting the appointment, he craved the judgment of the assembly, offering to act as minister of Dornoch, and to take the office of visitation only at the command of the Church.

The royal letter of nomination having been laid before the assembly, the following answer was transmitted to the king:—
"We have received your letter willing us to elect our brother, Mr. Robert Pont, to the bishopric of Caithness, vacant by the decease of umquhile Robert, Earl of March, your highness' uncle. We praise God that your majesty hath a good opinion and estimation of such a person as we judge the said Mr. Robert to be, whom we acknowledge indeed to be already a bishop according to the doctrine of St. Paul, and qualified to use the function of a pastor or minister at the church of

[1] Tytler, vol. ix. p. 46-48. Calendar of State Papers relating to Scotland, vol. ii. p. 579-581.

Dornoch, or any other church within your highness' realm, where he is lawfully called, and worthy to have a competent living appointed to him therefor, as also to use the office of a visitor or commissioner within the bounds or diocese of Caithness, if he be burdened therewith. But as to that corrupt estate or office of them who have been termed bishops heretofore, we find it not agreeable to the word of God, and it hath been condemned in divers others our assemblies: neither is the said Mr. Robert willing to accept the same in that manner: the which we thought good to signify unto your majesty, for answer of your highness' letter of nomination, and have ordained our brethren to be appointed commissioners to wait upon the next parliament to confer with your highness and council at more length, if need shall be, hereupon. Thus, after offering of our humble obedience, we earnestly wish the Spirit of the Lord to assist your highness in all good affairs."[1]

In the general assembly which met at Edinburgh on the fourth of August, 1590, it was agreed to discontinue the yearly election of commissioners for those districts in which presbyteries were properly constituted. The language used by James Melville, in a sermon preached at the commencement of this assembly, marks the complete victory which the new discipline had acquired. "Are we," said he, "the true Church? Are we the lawful ministry? Have we the authority and power of his sceptre? Have we that fire that devours the adversary, and that hammer that breaks the rocks? Yea, and have we not that sharp two-edged sword? Or is it sharp and drawn only against the poor and mean ones, and not potent in God for overthrowing of strongholds, for doing vengeance on whole nations, chastising of peoples, yea binding of kings in chains, and the most honourable

---

[1] Calderwood, vol. iv. pp. 398, 615-634. Book of the Universal Kirk, p. 314-322. Keith's Catalogue, pp. 215, 216. Acts of the Parliaments of Scotland, vol. iii. p. 373. The exact date of Bishop Crichton's decease is uncertain. He was alive, but very old, in 1585, and died probably before the 31st of July in that year, when Peter Rollock is styled bishop. In 1592, he is spoken of as "umquhile Robert, Bishop of Dunkeld." Compare the Acts of the Parliaments of Scotland, vol. iii. pp. 381, 625, and Calderwood, vol. iv. p. 338. The Christian name "Robert" given to the Bishop of Dunkeld in the third volume of the Acts, p. 423, is evidently a mistake for "Peter;" see p. 424 of the same volume.

princes in fetters of iron, to execute upon them the judgment written?"

It was at this assembly that the king is said to have concluded a speech, in which he professed his zeal for the welfare of the Church, by praising God "that he was born in such a time as the time of the light of the Gospel, to such a place as to be king in such a kirk, the sincerest kirk in the world. 'The Kirk of Geneva,' said he, ' keepeth Pasch and Yule: what have they for them? they have no institution. As for our neighbour kirk in England, it is an evil said mass in English, wanting nothing but the liftings. I charge you my good people, ministers, doctors, elders, nobles, gentlemen, and barons, to stand to your purity, and to exhort the people to do the same: and I, forsooth, so long as I possess my life and crown, shall maintain the same against all deadly.'"[1]

Neither the absurdity of this speech, nor its manifest insincerity, is a sufficient argument against its genuineness. It is very unlikely, however, that James would have affected sentiments which he did not feel, and proclaimed them in words which must have been offensive in England, while he was endeavouring, at Elizabeth's request, to repress the unbecoming language of the ministers. The earliest authority for his having thus spoken is Scot, who is copied, almost word for word, by Calderwood; and their statements are rendered suspicious by the silence, not of Spottiswood only, who would not have been unwilling to allow such a circumstance to be forgotten, but of James Melville, who would hardly have left the speech unrecorded. Melville's silence is the more marked from the circumstance that in his sermon he had referred to attempts on the part of the English bishops to bring about a conformity between the two realms, and to pervert the Scottish Kirk.

At the very time that the Presbyterian polity was acquiring a complete ascendency in Scotland, it came into direct and open collision with the Episcopacy of England. When the Confession of Faith received the sanction of parliament in 1560, most of the supporters of the Protestant opinions in the two British kingdoms looked on the communions to which

[1] Calderwood, vol. v. p. 100-111. Book of the Universal Kirk, p. 338-351. James Melville's Diary, p. 280-285. Scot's Apologetical Narration, p. 57. Spottiswood, vol. ii. pp. 409, 410.

they belonged as portions of the same Reformed Church, holding alike the great doctrines of the Gospel. So long as the superintendent system was maintained in Scotland, and the English bishoprics were chiefly filled by the exiles of Mary's reign, little occurred to disturb this harmonious feeling. Several of the English divines would even have preferred the northern establishment to their own. "The Scots," said Parkhurst, writing to Bullinger in August, 1560, "have made greater progress in true religion in a few months, than we have done in many years." Those who did not go so far still heartily rejoiced in the prosperity of the Scottish Reformation. Alluding to Scotland, in a letter to the same Swiss minister, dated in February, 1562, Bishop Jewel said, "Religion is most favourably received, firmly maintained, and daily making progress in that country."

By degrees, the different spirit which, though unknown to many of the chief actors, influenced the course of reformation in the two kingdoms, began to make itself felt. The rebellious tendencies of the Scottish system first excited suspicion among the more moderate of the English prelates. Parkhurst could describe the death of Riccio almost in the style of Knox himself, while Grindal, as became a Christian bishop, spoke of it as an atrocious act. When the vestment controversy began, the Scottish Protestants warmly sympathized with the clergy who scrupled to use the habits. But still there was no abatement in the general feeling of goodwill between the Reformed of the two countries. The fact that Knox sent his sons to England for their education, though it does not prove that he had any reverence for Episcopacy, shews that he had no serious objection to the system of the English Church as a whole.[1]

More serious differences, however, soon arose. When the English Puritans began to maintain the necessity of parity among the ministers of the Church, and to attack the Book of Common Prayer, the whole episcopal bench were seriously alarmed. When the supremacy of the sovereign in matters ecclesiastical was also denied, and when it was found that, on this point as well as on the others, the recusants in England were supported by the sympathy of a powerful party in the

[1] See Zurich Letters, vol. i. English Translation, pp, 91, 104, 166, 167, 170.

Scottish Church, the alienation between the two systems became apparent. It could not have been otherwise; for the changes in ecclesiastical polity, which Cartwright was attempting to introduce into England, were almost identical with those which Melville was successfully establishing in Scotland. There can be no doubt that the writings of Archbishop Adamson, and his personal intercourse with the English prelates, contributed to increase the jealousy with which the northern Presbyterians were now regarded. The ministers of Melville's party complained of the hospitable reception given to the archbishop as an injury to themselves; but, during their own banishment in England, their chief associates were the leaders of the Puritan faction, and when they recovered their ascendency at home, they shewed no wish to keep on good terms with the English Church. They openly proclaimed that the communion which they recognized in the southern kingdom was not the Church established by law, but the party which disregarded episcopal jurisdiction, and denounced the royal supremacy. The residence of Penry in Scotland has already been alluded to. Both he and Udall found refuge in that kingdom, though their connection with the Mar-prelate libels was notorious. The latter was treated with marked respect, sitting as an honoured spectator at the general assemblies, and preaching before the king in the church of St. Giles; and it was from Edinburgh that the former disseminated the writings for which he was afterwards executed.[1]

In 1589, an event had occurred which gave the controversy a new form. On the ninth of February, in that year, Dr. Bancroft preached his famous sermon at St. Paul's Cross, on the text, "Beloved, believe not every spirit, but try the spirits whether they are of God; because many false prophets are gone out into the world." In this discourse, he contrasted the excellence of the Book of Common Prayer with the absurdities and irreverence of extemporary worship; pointed out the essential distinction between bishops and presbyters; and maintained that the Puritan discipline was opposed to the Scriptures, and that it had never been heard of in the Church till the time of Calvin. The Scottish system and its founders

[1] Calderwood, vol. iv. p. 637; vol. v. p. 58. Collier's Ecclesiastical History, Lathbury's ed. vol. vii. p. 175-179.

were assailed. The opposition of Knox to the English Liturgy was censured, and an account was given of the manner in which the discipline had been established in the northern kingdom, chiefly on the authority of the royal declaration drawn up by Archbishop Adamson, and of a treatise written by Brown the Independent.

The opinions put forth in this sermon irritated the Presbyterians in both kingdoms, but in Scotland particularly the indignation which they excited was very great.. The Presbytery of Edinburgh, at a meeting held in April, appointed three of the brethren to draw up an answer to the discourse, and, in the month of December following, they agreed to direct a supplication to Queen Elizabeth, requesting her to "take order with Mr. Doctor Bancroft for that infamous sermon preached by him at Paul's Cross, traducing in it the whole discipline of the Church of Scotland." Two different supplications were prepared accordingly, but it would appear that neither of them was sent. They perhaps discovered how absurd it would be in those who refused to their own king the least authority in matters ecclesiastical, to call on a foreign sovereign to interfere with the clergy in the discharge of their religious functions. A formal answer to the sermon was written by a minister named John Davidson, and published at Edinburgh in 1590. Davidson denied the charges which Bancroft had brought against the loyalty of the Presbyterians, and blamed him in no measured language for relying on the declaration which the king had since disowned, and on the reports of such a person as Brown.[1]

Dr. Bancroft was no way intimidated by the clamour which his sermon excited. He afterwards put forth the same views in two other publications, "A Survey of the pretended Holy Discipline," and "Dangerous Positions and Proceedings, published and practised within this island of Britain, under pretence of Reformation, and for the Presbyterial Discipline." It was probably in order to obtain information regarding the subject of these works, that he caused certain inquiries to be made in Scotland. In February, 1590, an English stationer, of the name of Norton, then residing in Edinburgh, was ap-

[1] Miscellany of the Wodrow Society, vol. i. p. 469-520. Calderwood, vol. v. pp. 5, 6, 72-77.

prehended at the instance of Bruce and others of the ministers, on a charge of secret intelligence with Bancroft. He delivered up a paper containing several questions put by that divine in regard to Scottish ecclesiastical affairs. Among these inquiries were the following:—Why, notwithstanding the king's declaration, presbyteries had again been set up? What was the number of presbyteries, and of how many members they consisted? By whom children were baptized, and what was the form of public prayer on Sundays and week days? What kind of discipline was observed in their consistories? Whether dioceses were still kept up? What authority the king had in matters ecclesiastical? How the ministers were maintained and churches kept in repair? How ecclesiastical censures were respected, and what reformation of manners had proceeded therefrom, especially in prayer, fasting, obedience to superiors, humility, brotherly love, and patience? What had been done in regard to the Archbishop of St. Andrews, and whether Buchanan's treatise, "De jure regni apud Scotos," was approved of by the consistories?

These questions shew an honest and intelligent desire to ascertain the truth as to some points of great importance; and, had the ministers themselves furnished the desired information, instead of endeavouring to suppress all knowledge of their proceedings, they would have served their cause better, than by usurping the office of the civil magistrate.

In the beginning of the following year, a letter from Dr. Bancroft to Archbishop Adamson was intercepted, but the contents were not what was probably expected. Bancroft said that he had read the archbishop's works on the Apocalypse and on Job; advised him to bestow more honourable titles on Queen Elizabeth, and to praise the English Church above all others; and expressed his astonishment that he had not come to England, where he was expected, and where he would be well received by the Archbishop of Canterbury. The only account we have of these proceedings is the narrative of Calderwood.[1]

[1] Calderwood, vol. v. pp. 77-81, 118. Dr. M'Crie (Life of Melville, vol. i. p. 391) speaks of Bancroft's employing "an English bookseller at Edinburgh as a spy on the ministers," and transmitting to him "a string of officious queries respecting the conduct of the preachers, and the procedure of the church courts." The copy of the paper, as given by Calderwood, will certainly not bear out this interpretation.

Even if the Presbyterians had allowed the letter of Bancroft to reach its destination, it is not likely that Adamson could have availed himself of the generous offers of his English friends, as he was then oppressed with severe sickness. The king is said to have granted the revenues of the archbishopric to the Duke of Lennox, and had, at all events, with a forgetfulness of past services which deserves the severest condemnation, allowed Adamson to fall into a state of abject poverty. The unhappy prelate could ill bear the misery to which he was reduced, and which was aggravated by the liberal, or rather profuse disposition, which he had shewn during his prosperity. His bodily illness affected his mind, and, not knowing where to look for support, he applied for aid to Melville. We have no account of the circumstances of this application, except what is given by his enemies, but the main facts are sufficiently clear.

Adamson was visited by Melville, who gave him some relief, and, at his own urgent entreaty, he was afterwards loosed by the Presbytery of St Andrews from the sentence of excommunication which had been pronounced against him. At a meeting of the provincial assembly of Fife, held in April, certain articles were presented, written in the Latin language, in which the archbishop retracted his former opinions. These articles were not thought satisfactory, and a more clear and ample recantation in the vulgar tongue was demanded. To obtain this, Andrew Melville, Robert Wilkie, who had presided at the meeting of the presbytery which pronounced the excommunication, and Ferguson and Dalgleish, two ministers of the same party, were sent to the archbishop. They returned with the paper, signed by him, and attested by the persons who were present at his subscription. It set forth that, as he was unable from sickness to present himself before them, and because he wished to depart in the unity of the Christian faith, he therefore made his written confession. He declared that, since the time when it had pleased God to give him a knowledge of the truth, he had always held the true doctrine then taught in Scotland, in which he had walked uprightly till seduced by ambition, vain glory, and covetousness. He owned that he undertook the office of an archbishop, although it had been justly condemned, erroneously believing that the government of the Church was like to the kingdoms of the world; that he had laboured to subject churchmen to the king's ordinance in matters ecclesiastical; that he had believed and taught that presbyteries, the ordinance of Christ, were an invention of men; that he had written the declaration by order of the chancellor and secretary; that he had been the author of the statute by which the stipends of the ministers who refused subscription to the acts of parliament were taken away; that he had been more busy than became him with some bishops in England, while he was in that kingdom, and by his correspondence since; and that he had deceived the Church by confessions, subscriptions, and protestations.

An addition to the paper farther bore an answer to certain questions which seem to have been specially put to him, chiefly regarding the books which he had composed, and the opinions which they contained. He denied having any share in Sutcliffe's treatise against the form and order of presbyteries, and condemned the commentary which he himself had written on the First Epistle of St. Paul to Timothy, as containing divers offensive matters, and tending to allow the estate of bishops otherwise than God's word sanctioned it. In a second paper, dated the twelfth of May, he particularly retracted the declaration, admitting that it was false; confessing that he had wrongfully accused Melville as factious and seditious, and unadvisedly attributed to him a fiery and salt humour, and that he had condemned presbyteries, though their authority was recognized by the Gospel, and approved of bishops, whose office had no warrant in the Scriptures. He concluded with stating that, if he had omitted anything, it was not intentionally, but on account of weakness of memory, and his present sickness. The ministers seem to have been apprehensive that the reality of his confession would be called in question, for, in the month of June, they obtained from him a declaration of its genuineness, signed in the presence of several witnesses.[1]

Spottiswood asserts that Adamson complained of the wrong done to him in publishing his recantation. Whether this was the case or not, he never formally disavowed it, and there cannot be a doubt that the papers were signed by him. The

---

[1] Calderwood, vol v. p. 118-127. James Melville's Diary, p. 288-293. Row, p. 117-131. Spottiswood, vol. ii. p. 415.

whole proceeding is as little to the honour of the parties concerned, as were any of the forced retractations made at an earlier period by Protestants accused of heresy. The conduct of Melville, in particular, is very unbecoming. He urged his fallen enemy to a confession, the sincerity of which he must have doubted, and even allowed him to retract the supposed injurious expressions which he had used towards himself. There is in this an utter want of true magnanimity, and an evidence that he partook in one of Knox's worst faults—an extreme sensitiveness as to what was spoken of himself, although he habitually used the most reckless license of speech in regard to others.

The archbishop never recovered from his sickness. He died on the nineteenth of February, 1592. James Melville mentions that David Black, minister at St Andrews, visited him on his death-bed, but that he died as he had lived, " senseless of spiritual sanctification." The presence of Black could give little comfort. The dying prelate found better consolation in writing the Latin verses on his departing soul, which have so often been quoted.[1]

The memory of Archbishop Adamson has suffered from a cause which has been fatal to the character of many others in periods of controversy—the circumstance that his actions have come down to us chiefly in the writings of his opponents. His greatest fault was a want of firmness and sincerity in maintaining his ecclesiastical principles. The doctrine of Episcopacy, even in the imperfect form in which he believed it, should have been upheld with more consistency and courage. His moral character comes out unsullied by any one definite accusation, notwithstanding the ribald attacks to which he was subjected, so disgraceful to all who any way partook in them or encouraged them. His learning and literary accomplishments, his ability as a statesman, and his eloquence as a preacher, have seldom been disputed. His writings in opposition to Presbyterianism produced a great effect, and it is evident that his opponents dreaded their influence, although well aware of the advantage he gave by his

---

[1] Calderwood, vol. v. p. 147. James Melville's Diary, pp. 293, 294. Spottiswood, vol. ii. p. 415. Mackenzie's Lives, vol. iii. p. 376.

exaggerated opinion as to the ecclesiastical supremacy of the sovereign.¹

The general assembly, which met on the twenty-first of May, 1592, agreed to take steps for obtaining a repeal of the acts of parliament made against the discipline in the year 1584, and a ratification of the liberties of the Church. They had chosen a favourable time for the purpose. The country was distracted by the turbulent conduct of Francis, Earl of Bothwell, and the king had become unpopular in consequence of the suspicions entertained regarding the murder of the young Earl of Murray. James, anxious to secure the stability of his government, yielded to the advice of those counsellors who thought that this would best be effected by conceding some of the chief demands of the ministers.

The parliament assembled at Edinburgh in the beginning of June, and an act was passed by which the liberties, privileges, and immunities of the Church were ratified. General assemblies were allowed to meet once a-year, or oftener if there was occasion, the time and place of the next meeting to be fixed at each assembly by the king or his commissioner, and, failing their being present, by the members themselves. The provincial assemblies, presbyteries, and parochial sessions, were confirmed. It was farther declared that the second act of the parliament held at Edinburgh on the twenty-second day of May, 1584, should not derogate from the rights of the office-bearers of the Church concerning heads of religion, and matters of heresy, excommunication, collation, and deprivation of ministers. The twentieth act of the same parliament, granting commission to bishops and other judges in ecclesiastical causes, was expressly repealed, and presentations to benefices were ordered to be directed to the particular presbyteries, to whom full powers were given to grant collation, under the condition that they should be bound to receive and admit whatever qualified ministers were presented by his majesty, or other laic patrons.²

---

¹ A collection of the archbishop's works, with an account of his life written by his son-in-law, Thomas Wilson, was published at London, in 1619. Spottiswood mentions (vol. ii. p. 415) that " his prelections upon the Epistles to Timothy, which were most desired, falling into the hands of his adversaries, were suppressed."

² Acts of the Parliaments of Scotland, vol. iii. pp. 541, 542. Calderwood, vol. v. p. 156-166. James Melville's Diary, p. 294-298.

Such were the ample terms in which the privileges of the Church were ratified. In several important points, however, the triumph of Melville's party was incomplete. The Book of Discipline itself was not alluded to, and its provisions, as a whole, remained destitute of parliamentary sanction; the civil rights of the bishops and other prelates continued as before; and the law regarding the patronage of ecclesiastical benefices was expressly confirmed.

CHAPTER XLIII.

FROM THE ESTABLISHMENT OF PRESBYTERIANISM IN JUNE, 1592, TO THE ACCESSION OF KING JAMES TO THE CROWN OF ENGLAND IN MARCH, 1603.

Renewed insurrection of the Roman Catholic nobles—They are excommunicated by the Provincial Assembly of Fife—Suppression of the insurrection—Death of John Leslie, Bishop of Ross—Sermon of David Black—Tumult of the seventeenth of December at Edinburgh—Robert Bruce, minister at Edinburgh—Account of his conversion—Ecclesiastical convention at Perth—General Assembly at Dundee—Publication of the Basilicon Doron—General Assembly at Montrose—The Gowrie conspiracy—Vacant bishoprics filled up—Accession of James to the crown of England—Death of Archbishop Beaton.

THE connection between the ecclesiastical dignitaries in parliament and the actual office-bearers of the Church was now again as completely severed, as it was after the convention of 1560. The authority of the presbyteries, so long rejected by the king, was ratified as an essential part of the Church's system, but the prelates retained their civil rank and privileges. In the very parliament which established Presbyterianism, there appear as Lords of the Articles "pro clero" the Bishops of Orkney and Dunkeld, the Abbots of Culross, Lindores, Tungland, Kinloss, and Inchaffray, and the Prior of Blantyre; and subsequent parliaments were attended by various bishops, abbots, and priors, representing the spiritual estate, although the assembly of May, 1592, had declared that the prelates pretending to vote in name of the Church should not be allowed to do so in time coming. With the exception of some of the bishoprics, almost all the other higher dignities, and many of the inferior benefices, were enjoyed by persons who, without performing any spiritual function whatever, bore the old titles of abbots and priors, archdeacons, provosts, and parsons. This was the very state of matters which the agreement at Leith was intended to prevent.

The year 1593 beheld a renewal of the civil broils which had so often distracted Scotland. The great Roman Catholic lords, Huntly, Errol, and Angus, again broke out into rebellion, and were only suppressed by unusual exertions on the part of the king. James was urged by the ministers to subject all Roman Catholics, and especially the insurgent earls, to the penalties of treason, but he refused to adopt a measure so dangerous and so cruel. To have proscribed the whole adherents of the ancient religion would at this time have been a formidable attempt. Their leaders were persons of approved ability and resolution, and were encouraged by promises of support from Spain. In the northern provinces of the kingdom they had acquired the predominance, and it appears from a contemporary paper, of undoubted authority, that a third part of the whole Scottish nobility professed the Roman Catholic religion.[1]

The more zealous of the ministers were greatly dissatisfied with the king's moderation. At a meeting of the provincial assembly of Fife, held in the month of September, the members present claimed jurisdiction over the Roman Catholic leaders, because some of them had studied at the University of St. Andrews, and for other reasons, and solemnly excommunicated the Earls of Huntly, Angus, and Errol, the Lord Home, Sir Patrick Gordon of Auchindown, and Sir James Chisholm of Cromlix. The sentence so pronounced was ratified by the general assembly which met in the following year. Soon after this, Andrew Melville rebuked the king for speaking evil of his best friends, the regent Murray, Knox, and Buchanan; and requested that those who advised gentle measures towards Huntly and the Papists should be ordered to appear before the estates, offering to go to the gibbet if he did not convict them of treasonable and pernicious dealing against the Church and kingdom, provided they, if convicted, should be subjected to the same punishment. His nephew, James Melville, tells us, that on hearing this the king and his courtiers smiled, and said that the man was more zealous and choleric than wise.[2]

[1] Tytler, vol. ix. pp. 65-111, 376-382.
[2] Calderwood, vol. v. pp. 261-268, 288, 289, 309. James Melville's Diary, p. 313.

Adam Bothwell, Bishop of Orkney, died on the twenty-third of August, 1593.[1] On the twenty-sixth of September following, William Chisholm, Bishop of Dunblane, died at Rome. He had been appointed Bishop of Vaison by the Pope, but resigned his see, and joined the Carthusian order. After he became a monk, he was for some time in Scotland, aiding the adherents of the Roman Catholic religion with his counsels. When he resigned the bishopric of Vaison, his nephew, of the same name, was appointed his successor in that see. The latter prelate also took an active part in Scottish affairs, and the well-known letter addressed by Lord Balmerino to the Pope, in name of King James, contained a request that he should be made a cardinal. He died in the year 1629.[2]

On the nineteenth of February, 1594, Queen Anne gave birth to a son, who was baptized in the chapel-royal at Stirling, on the thirtieth of August, by the name of Frederick Henry. Notwithstanding the remonstrances of the Presbytery of Edinburgh, the baptism was celebrated by Cunningham, Bishop of Aberdeen.[3]

In the autumn of 1594, hostilities again commenced between the king and the Roman Catholic nobles. The Earl of Argyll marched northwards at the head of the royal army, but was defeated at Glenlivat by the troops of Huntly and Errol. When the king himself advanced as far as Aberdeen, the rebels offered no resistance, and Strathbogie, Slains, and other castles belonging to the insurgent chiefs, were levelled to the ground. In this expedition James was accompanied by the two Melvilles and others of the ministers. After a second vain attempt to rouse their followers, the northern earls lost heart, and prepared to leave the country. The Jesuit priest, James Gordon, Huntly's uncle, endeavoured to dissuade them. Mass was said, for the last time, within the cathedral of Elgin, and Gordon, ascending the pulpit, implored his kinsmen and

---

[1] Keith's Catalogue, p. 227. Note by Mr. Mark Napier, in Spottiswood's History, vol. ii. p. 79.

[2] Note by Bishop Russell, in Keith's Catalogue, p. 563. Calderwood, vol. iv. p. 663; vol. v. pp. 208, 209, 226, 740-744. Tytler, vol. ix. p. 350-353.

[3] Calderwood, vol. v. pp. 343, 346. Spottiswood, vol. ii. pp. 455, 456. Tytler, vol. ix. pp. 130, 140.

friends to risk all for the faith. His entreaties were vain. In March, 1595, the earls embarked for the Continent.[1]

On the thirty-first of May, 1596, John Leslie, Bishop of Ross, died at Brussels, in the sixty-ninth year of his age. This eminent prelate had long been absent from Scotland. He was one of the chief counsellors and defenders of Mary during her captivity, and was himself imprisoned, first in the Tower of London, and afterwards in milder confinement at Farnham Castle, under the custody of the Bishop of Winchester, on a charge of being implicated in Norfolk's conspiracy. While in prison, he wrote two devotional treatises for the use of his sovereign. Soon after his release he went to Rome, where his History of Scotland was published in 1578. He held for some time a commission as nuncio in Germany, and exerted himself in procuring the restoration of the old Scottish monasteries there, and securing them for his countrymen, in preference to the Irish who claimed them with more justice as the true representatives of the Celtic Scots. He afterwards resided in France, and was successively appointed vicar-general of the arch-diocese of Rouen, and Bishop of Coutances. Having taken part with the princes of Lorraine in the wars of the League, he was obliged to retire to the Low Countries, where he was treated with great honour by the command of King Philip, to whose protection he had been specially recommended by Mary immediately before her execution. Like other ecclesiastics of the day, Leslie appears more prominent as a statesman than as a bishop. But he deserves the highest praise, not only for his learning and ability, but for his zeal, piety, and worth, and for his uniform unswerving attachment to the religious and political principles which he maintained.[2]

James now directed his efforts with considerable success to the restoration of order and tranquillity in his kingdom. But whenever any of his measures were likely to soften the rigour of the laws against the Roman Catholics, or were even suspected of such a tendency, he was encountered by the violent opposition of the ministers. He was determined, however, to maintain his authority, and the old struggle for supremacy was

---

[1] Tytler, vol. ix. pp. 145-154, 165-167. James Melville's Diary, pp. 318, 319.
[2] Keith's Catalogue, p. 195-197. Spottiswood, vol. iii. pp. 55, 56. Irving's Scottish Writers, vol. i. p. 129-146.

renewed. In the month of October, 1596, David Black, minister at St. Andrews, preached a sermon in which he denounced Queen Elizabeth as an atheist, and the religion professed in her kingdom as an empty show; and asserted that all kings were the devil's children, that the lords of Session were miscreants and bribers, the nobility cormorants, and Anne of Denmark a woman, whom for fashion's sake they might pray for, but in whose time it was vain to expect any good. A complaint was made by the English ambassador on behalf of his mistress, and Black was summoned before the privy council. He declined to appear, claiming the right to be first judged in the ecclesiastical court. A committee of ministers, which now sat permanently in the metropolis, consisting of commissioners from various parts of the kingdom and certain members of the Presbytery of Edinburgh, approved of Black's proceedings, and ordered a copy of his declinature to be sent to every presbytery, with a request that the members would subscribe it. In consequence of this, a royal proclamation was set forth, declaring the sittings of the committee to be illegal, and ordering the commissioners to leave Edinburgh, and return to their own abodes. The commissioners, having met, agreed in thinking that " it was lawful to disobey any such unlawful charge, but, in respect of divers circumstances, it was not expedient to disobey for the present, namely because other good brethren might succeed to such as were discharged, and so the work go forward."

After some ineffectual attempts to bring about an accommodation, twenty-four burgesses of Edinburgh, distinguished for their zeal in the cause of the ministers, were also ordered to leave the capital. One of these went to Walter Balcanqual, who was then on his way to preach. In his sermon, Balcanqual attacked the measures of the court, and, when the discourse was finished, requested the noblemen, gentlemen, and others well affected to the cause, to assemble in the Little Kirk—as the chancel of St. Giles was then called—explaining that he had a warrant from his brethren to that effect. A large number of persons assembled accordingly, and Robert Bruce declared the great danger they were in from the Popish lords, who had been allowed to return home, and desired them, since they were met together, to hold up their hands and swear to defend the present state of religion against all opponents whatsoever. After this exhortation, two noblemen, two barons, two of the magistrates, and two ministers, were sent as a deputation to the king, who was then sitting in the Tolbooth, along with the lords of Session. James asked who they were that durst assemble against his proclamations. Lord Lindsay answered that they durst do more than that, and that they would not suffer religion to be overthrown. The king made no reply, but, as the people thronged in, commanded the doors to be shut. The deputies returned to their brethren in the church, where, in the meantime, one of the ministers had been reading the history of Haman and Mordecai, and similar passages from the Scriptures. It was now asked what course was to be taken. "There is no course," cried Lindsay, "but one; let us stay together that are here, and promise to take one part, and advertise our friends and the favourers of religion to come unto us; so it shall be either theirs or ours." The multitude now became furious. Some called to bring out Haman; others exclaimed, "The sword of the Lord and of Gideon." A person, who is alleged to have been an agent of a party of the courtiers that had all along inflamed the quarrel out of jealousy of the king's chief counsellors, cried out, "Armour, armour!" Part of the crowd went to the Tolbooth door, and demanded that the obnoxious counsellors should be delivered up, while the noblemen and barons appeared in arms outside the church. James sent some of those who were with him to remonstrate, and angry words passed between the Earl of Mar and Lord Lindsay, but it was agreed that another deputation should wait on the king, and request that he would rescind his late proceedings, and refuse any voice in ecclesiastical matters to certain counsellors whose religion was suspected. The king asked them to lay their wishes before a meeting of his council, and, tranquillity having now been restored by the assistance of the provost of the city, he went down to Holyrood.

These events took place in the forenoon of the seventeenth of December. In the afternoon, the noblemen, barons, and ministers, renewed their request, but James declined to receive it, and the next day departed for Linlithgow, after commanding a proclamation to be made, in which the ministers were denounced as the authors of the treasonable disturbance which had taken place, and the courts of law were ordered to remove from Edinburgh. The citizens were alarmed, but the ministers endeavoured to keep their supporters together, and for this purpose prepared a bond for their signature. A fast was also proclaimed, and sermons of preparation were enjoined to be made that afternoon. A minister, named John Welsh, preached in the church of St. Giles, and declared that the king had been possessed with a devil; that this one devil having been put out, seven worse spirits had entered in its place; and that his subjects might lawfully rise and take the sword out of his hand. This he confirmed by the example of a father, who, falling into a frenzy, may be seized by his children and servants, and bound hand and foot. "A most execrable doctrine," says Spottiswood, "and directly repugnant to Holy Scripture, which yet was taken by many of the hearers as a sound and free application." The preacher had married one of Knox's daughters, and the illustration he used was the same which that reformer had employed in defending his doctrine of resistance in his first interview with the king's mother. Those who had inherited the political principles of Knox at no time formed a majority of the ministers, but they were formidable by their zeal and union, and their unceasing efforts to make the person of the sovereign, and monarchy itself, hateful and contemptible to the people. It was only in times of great excitement that they came forward as a distinct party, but their continued existence requires to be kept in mind, in order to the due understanding of many important events in Scottish history.

On the day after the tumult, a letter, signed by Bruce, Balcanquhal, and two other ministers, was sent to Lord Hamilton, next heir to the crown after Prince Henry, in which they informed him that the godly barons and other gentlemen, who had undertaken the patronage of the Church's cause, lacked a chief nobleman to countenance them, and that his lordship was thought fittest for that honour. Hamilton, after some hesitation, carried the letter to the king. James heard of this proposal with deep indignation. He ordered the magistrates of Edinburgh to apprehend several of the ministers and their chief abettors; and Bruce and his friends, finding that they could expect no support from the burgesses, fled from the city. On the first of January, 1597, the king returned to Edinburgh, and was welcomed with professions of devoted loyalty.[1]

The tumult of the seventeenth of December has been excused as an accidental outburst of popular fury; but there were circumstances connected with it which plainly shewed a deliberate purpose of resistance to the royal authority. Its apologists have been able to speak of it as unimportant, only because it was an entire failure. Had the ministers, the citizens, and their supporters among the barons, been joined by the higher nobility, the insurrection in the capital might have ended in a revolution such as had occurred in the reign of Mary, or that which took place in the following century.

The suppression of the tumult enabled James to resume with better prospects of success his attempt to restore episcopal government in the Church; and the supporters of the Presbyterian discipline speak of the year 1596 as the time when it had attained its greatest purity and influence. " The Church of Scotland," says Calderwood, in commencing his narrative of the transactions of that year, " was now come to her perfection, and the greatest purity that she ever attained unto, both in doctrine and discipline, so that her beauty was admirable to foreign Churches. The assemblies of the saints were never so glorious nor profitable to every one of the true members thereof, as in the beginning of this year." The description is just, so far as it applies to the ascendency of the ecclesiastical opinions held by the historian, but, if it is understood to refer also to the religious and moral condition of the people, it can hardly be reconciled with what he relates a few pages farther on in the very words of the general assembly which met on the twenty-fourth of March, 1596. A more frightful state of corruption in a Christian nation has hardly ever been recorded, and, making every reasonable allowance for the exaggeration and mere words of form not unusual in such documents, the general faithfulness of the picture is attested by other writings of the time.[2]

One of the most suspicious circumstances connected with the

---

[1] Calderwood, vol. v. p. 447-536. Spottiswood, vol. iii. p. 10-37. Tytler, vol. ix. p. 204-225.

[2] Calderwood, vol. v. pp. 387, 388, 408-411.

events in the capital which have just been mentioned was the letter addressed by the ministers to Lord Hamilton. Bruce, instead of expressing regret for what he had done, wrote to Hamilton from the place of his concealment, upbraiding him for having laid his communication before the king, and assuring him that his sister's son, the Earl of Huntly, would not have done the like.[1] Next to Melville, Bruce was now the most distinguished among the Presbyterian leaders. He was descended from the ancient family of Bruce of Airth, and was born about the year 1559. He studied at St. Andrews, and afterwards at several of the continental universities, with the intention of adopting the profession of an advocate. On his return to Scotland, he practised for some time before the courts, but his mind gradually became averse to his occupation. It was his wish to study theology, and, having with considerable difficulty obtained permission from his parents, he went to St. Andrews, where he attended the lectures of the two Melvilles and other teachers.

The account which Bruce himself gives of his conversion deserves to be mentioned, as illustrating the state of religious feeling and opinion then prevalent among the Scottish Protestants. "As touching my vocation to the ministry," he says, "I was first called to my grace before I obeyed my calling to the ministry. He made me first a Christian before He made me a minister. I repugned long to my calling to the ministry; ten years at least I never leaped on horseback, nor lighted, but with a repugning and justly accusing conscience. At last it pleased God, in the fifteen hundred and eighty-first year of God, in the month of August, in the last night thereof, being in the place of Airth, lying in a chamber called the new loft chamber, in the very night while I lay, to smite me inwardly and judicially in my conscience, and to present all my sins before me in such sort, that He omitted not a circumstance, but made my conscience to see time, place, and persons, as vividly as the hour I did them. He made the devil accuse me so audibly, that I heard his voice as vividly as ever I heard any thing, not being sleeping but waking. So far as he spoke true, my conscience bare him record, and testified against me very clearly; but when he came

[1] Calderwood, vol. v. pp. 534, 535.

to be a false accuser, and laid things to my charge which I never had done, then my conscience failed him, and would not testify with him; but in those things which were true, my conscience condemned me, and the condemnator tormented me, and made me feel the wrath of God pressing me down as it were to the lower hell. Yea, I was so fearfully and extremely tormented, that I would have been content to have been cast into a cauldron of hot melted lead, to have had my soul relieved of that insupportable weight. Always so far as he spoke true, I confessed, restored God to his glory, and cried God's mercy for the merits of Christ; yea, I appealed ever to his mercy, purchased to me by the blood, death, and passion of Christ. This court of justice holden upon my soul, it turned of the bottomless mercy of God to a court of mercy to me; for that same night, ere ever the day dawned, or ever the sun rose, He restrained those furies and those outcries of my just accusing conscience, and enabled me to rise in the morning."

The zeal and acquirements of Bruce having become known, he was requested to accept the office of minister at Edinburgh, vacant by the death of James Lawson while in exile in England. He was at first unwilling to comply, and, when he did agree, it was by a temporary arrangement, and without being ordained as was required by the Book of Discipline. He preached for some time without administering the communion, and it is mentioned, on the authority of Livingstone, that it was only by an artifice of his brethren in the ministry that he was induced to dispense the sacrament. He was on one occasion purposely left alone in the middle of the communion, and, as no one else was present to officiate, he completed the celebration. Although he finally agreed to accept a sort of conditional ordination, he declined to do so for a number of years, alleging that he had the material part of it—the approval of all the ministers—and that he would not, by receiving it, alarm the people who had already partaken of the communion at his hands.

As one of the ministers of Edinburgh, Bruce took a leading part in all ecclesiastical proceedings. His advice and assistance were very useful to the noblemen whom James had intrusted with the government of the kingdom during his absence in Denmark, and for this he received the thanks of the king, and was selected to anoint Queen Anne at her coronation. When he was obliged to leave Edinburgh in December, 1596, he found refuge among those friendly to his cause in the north of England.[1]

King James ordered a meeting of the estates, and an ecclesiastical synod, to be held at Perth on the last day of February, 1597, in order to advise with them in regard to the jurisdiction and polity of the Church. That all persons might be the better prepared, he caused a number of questions to be previously circulated, embracing the chief points as to which he wished an answer. These questions were fifty-five in number. The most important of them were the following:— May not matters affecting the external government of the Church be disputed, salva fide et religione? Is it the king severally, or the pastors severally, or both conjunctly, who should establish the government of the Church, and what is the form of their conjunction in the making of laws? Is not the consent of the most part of the flock, and also of the patron, necessary in electing pastors? Is he a lawful pastor who wanteth imposition of hands? Is it lawful to pastors to express particular men's names in the pulpit, or to describe them so clearly that the people may understand who are meant, unless in the case of notorious declared vices, with private admonition preceding? Is it lawful to call the general assembly without the king's license, he being pius et Christianus magistratus? May any thing be enacted in the assembly to which the king does not consent? Is simple contumacy without probation of a crime, or is any crime without contumacy, a sufficient cause of excommunication? Is summary excommunication lawful in any case, without admonition and citation preceding? Have any others than the pastors of the Church a voice in excommunication? Is it lawful to excommunicate such Papists as never professed the Reformed religion? Has not a Christian king power to annul a notoriously unjust sentence of excommunication?

---

[1] Wodrow's Life of Bruce, prefixed to the Wodrow Society edition of his Sermons, p. 4-21. James Melville's Diary, pp. 147, 148, 254, 255. Calderwood, vol. iv. p. 634-638. See also Select Biographies, edited for the Wodrow Society, vol. i. pp. 305, 306.

When the pastors do not their duty, or when one jurisdiction usurps upon another, or when any other schism falleth out, should not a Christian king amend such disorders? Should any thing be treated in the ecclesiastical judgment prejudicial to the civil jurisdiction or private men's rights, and may not the civil magistrate lawfully stay all such proceedings?

It was evident from the nature of these questions that the king contemplated some change in the jurisdiction of the Church. The synods and presbyteries most zealously attached to the discipline were alarmed, and objections were made to the proposed ecclesiastical convention, because it was to be held at a different time and place from those which had been fixed at last general assembly. The provincial assembly of Fife ordered two members from every presbytery to meet at St. Andrews, on the twenty-first of February, to resolve on proper answers to the questions. They met accordingly, and, as Melville's adherents had the entire ascendency in this synod, the answers, which they agreed to, shew the opinions entertained by that party regarding the subjects under discussion. In every point of disputed jurisdiction between the Church and the State, their decision was in favour of the former.[1]

The brethren of the ministry met at Perth on the day appointed. From the commencement of the proceedings, the ministers of the northern districts shewed their jealousy of their southern brethren, especially of "the Popes of Edinburgh," who had hitherto taken a leading part in ecclesiastical affairs. The former, according to Calderwood, assembled in great numbers, having been well prepared beforehand for the part they were to take; and the same views were supported by the ministers of Angus. It is very likely that the royal influence had been freely used, but, independently of this, there were other causes sufficient to explain the differences in the assembly. The ministers in the diocese of Aberdeen were not averse to portions of the ancient system, and their inclinations in that direction were increased by the deference entertained by many of them to the house of Gordon. Those of Angus were no doubt favourably disposed towards Episco-

[1] Calderwood, vol. v. p. 577-596. James Melville's Diary, p. 390-403. Spottiswood, vol. iii. p. 40-45.

pacy, in consequence of their long connection with Erskine of Dun. In the absence of Andrew Melville, who was unable to attend the synod, his nephew, James, supplied his place as leader of the zealous Presbyterians. They endeavoured to prevent the adoption of any dangerous measures, by contending that the meeting was no proper assembly; but it was carried by the votes of eleven presbyteries to eight, that it should be recognized as an extraordinary general assembly of the Church. The king laid before them thirteen articles, most of which, after considerable discussion, were agreed to by a majority of the members. The principal of these were the following:—That ministers should not be allowed to meddle with matters of state in the pulpit; that they should not name or describe individual persons in their sermons, except in the case of notorious guilt, proved by a civil judgment or ecclesiastical excommunication; that no meetings of pastors should be held without the king's consent, except the ordinary sessions, presbyteries, and synods; that in all the chief towns the consent of the congregation and of the king should be requisite in the appointment of a minister; and that commission should be granted to seven or eight ministers to consider the remaining questions. On the other hand, the king, at the request of the assembly, agreed to allow Bruce and his friends to return, on their finding security to answer any charge which might be brought against them.[1]

In terms of special powers given to him at Perth, King James summoned an ordinary meeting of the general assembly at Dundee, on the tenth of May. Robert Rollock, Principal of the College of Edinburgh, who was highly esteemed by all on account of his learning and piety, was chosen moderator, and zealously supported the measures recommended by the king. At this assembly, the Earls of Huntly, Errol, and Angus, having professed their sorrow for former offences, and declared their adherence to the established religion, were absolved from the sentence of excommunication, notwithstanding the opposition of Melville's party. The assembly held at Perth was declared to be a lawful one; its proceedings were ratified; and it was provided that the king's assent should be

---

[1] Calderwood, vol. v. p. 606-622. Book of the Universal Kirk, p. 439-449. James Melville's Diary, p. 403-410. Spottiswood, vol. iii. p. 45-55.

required to every form of assembly, either general or special, permitted by the laws, and authorised by the word of God. The members agreed to various regulations connected with the rest of the king's questions. One of the most important of these was that all ministers should be ordained by imposition of hands. It was also agreed that commission should be given to a certain number of ministers to meet with the king, and consult as to matters ecclesiastical, at such time and place as his majesty might fix. This regulation was particularly offensive to Melville's party, who saw clearly to what it tended. While it prepared the way for Episcopacy, it took out of their hands the very instrument which they had themselves used with such success in governing the whole Church, by means of a permanent committee.[1]

At a parliament held in December, it was agreed, on the petition of the new commissioners of the Church, that any ministers provided by the king to the office of bishop or abbot, should have a vote in parliament as freely as any other prelates in times past, and that all bishopricks, vacant or to become vacant, should be bestowed only on ministers. At a meeting of the synod of Fife, both the Melvilles denounced this measure. David Ferguson compared it to the wooden horse by means of which Troy was taken; and John Davidson remarked, " Busk, busk, busk him as bonnily as you can, and bring him in as fairly as you will, we see him well enough, we see the horns of his mitre." In a general assembly held at Dundee in March, 1598, it was agreed that the ministers, as one of the three estates, ought to have a vote in parliament; but this was only carried by a small majority, the northern members, as before, strongly supporting the views of the king.[2]

In the following year an event occurred which shewed the feeling of dislike entertained by the zealous party towards the king, and the unscrupulous character of its leader. James had finished the composition of the Basilicon Doron, but, be-

---

[1] Calderwood, vol. v. p. 628-647. Book of the Universal Kirk, p. 450-463. Spottiswood, vol. iii. p. 58-60.

[2] Calderwood, vol. v. pp. 668-670, 680, 681, 695, 696. James Melville's Diary, pp. 436, 437. Spottiswood, vol. iii. p. 67-69. Acts of the Parliaments of Scotland, vol. iv. pp. 130, 131.

fore he had resolved on its publication, one of his attendants, whom he had employed to transcribe the work, shewed it to Melville, who caused several copies to be made and circulated among his friends. Certain passages were extracted and laid before the synod of Fife, as the work of an unknown author, in which the ecclesiastical authority of the king was maintained, parity declared to be the mother of confusion and inconsistent with monarchy, the restoration of Episcopacy advised as necessary for the welfare both of Church and State, and Puritans were denounced as pests in the commonwealth. The synod held these propositions to be seditious, wicked, and treasonable, and the king, much offended, endeavoured to discover by what means they had been laid before the meeting. The members disclaimed all knowledge of the matter—with what sincerity does not appear—but one of their number, named Dykes, by whom the articles had been presented, on being summoned before the council, failed to attend, and was proclaimed a rebel. The king himself, to prevent all farther rumours on the subject, published the book soon afterwards.[1]

At a general assembly summoned by royal proclamation to meet at Montrose, on the twenty-eighth of March, 1600, it was agreed, in regard to the ministers who were to have a vote in parliament, that each one of their number should be chosen by the king out of six to be named by the Church. Various restrictions were imposed upon them, among which were the following:—The persons selected were to receive their instructions from the assembly, and to give account to it of their proceedings; they were to have no more power in presbyteries, and provincial and general assemblies, and in the ecclesiastical government generally, than any other ministers; they were to attend to their own particular congregations, and, in the event of their being deposed by the ecclesiastical courts, were ipso facto to lose their vote in parliament, and their benefice; they were to be styled commissioners of the particular place to which they were appointed, and every year were to lay down their office at the meeting of the general assembly, and

---

[1] Spottiswood, vol, iii. pp. 80, 81. Calderwood, vol. v. pp. 744, 745. James Melville's Diary, p. 444-446.

to continue, or be removed, as the assembly, with the king's consent, should judge most expedient.

In connection with the restrictions thus imposed, Archbishop Spottiswood remarks, " It was neither the king's intention, nor the mind of the wiser sort, to have these cautions stand in force; . . . . . but, to have matters peaceably ended and the reformation of the policy made without any noise, the king gave way to these conceits, knowing that with time the utility of the government which he purposed to have established would appear, and trusting that they whom he should place in these rooms would, by their care for the Church, and their wise and good behaviour, purchase to themselves the authority which appertained." That such was the king's intention there can be no doubt, but the line of policy thus adopted for the re-establishment of Episcopacy was as blameable as that which Melville had used for its abolition.[1]

The month of August, in the last year of the sixteenth century, became memorable in Scottish history for the event known by the name of the Gowrie conspiracy. John, Earl of Gowrie, was a son of the earl who was beheaded in 1584, and grandson of Lord Ruthven, one of the chief actors in the murder of Riccio. In May, 1600, he returned to Scotland, after a residence abroad for several years, in the course of which he had made great proficiency in his studies, and distinguished himself by his ardour for the Protestant religion. During the previous year he had resided for three months at Geneva, in the house of Beza, and in passing through Paris was furnished by the English ambassador with letters of recommendation to Queen Elizabeth. He remained at her court for some time, and was admitted to frequent and confidential interviews with her. At this time the English and Scottish sovereigns viewed each other with feelings of mutual suspicion and dislike. There can be little doubt that the object of Gowrie's plot was to make the king a prisoner, and to administer the government in his name, with the assistance of Elizabeth and the violent Presbyterian party. The Edinburgh ministers shewed their sympathy with the earl by refusing to admit that there was a conspiracy at all, and even charging James with a plot

[1] Calderwood, vol. vi. p. 1-26. Book of the Universal Kirk, p. 477-490 Spottiswood, vol. iii. pp. 73-75, 82.

against the Ruthvens. The other preachers finally acknowledged their error, but Bruce persisted in maintaining that the king's narrative was untrue, and was banished from Scotland. Sometime afterwards, however, he was permitted by the king to return to his own country.[1]

Before the end of this year, several of the vacant bishopricks were filled up. The king had power by act of parliament to name bishops and other prelates, although the persons so appointed could not vote in behalf of the Church without its sanction. At the date of the rising of the Montrose assembly, the revenues of the archiepiscopal see of St. Andrews were in the possession of the Duke of Lennox, and those of Glasgow were divided between the duke and Archbishop Beaton. Lord Spynie had Murray; Orkney had been acquired by the Earl of Orkney; Dunkeld, Dunblane, and Brechin, were still held by the titular bishops, Rollock, Graham, and Campbell, though none of them at that time acted as ministers. David Cunningham was Bishop of Aberdeen, and Neil Campbell of Argyll. The dioceses of Galloway and the Isles were vacant, and their endowments had been entirely dilapidated. Ross and Caithness still retained a part of their revenues, and David Lindsay was now appointed to the former see, and George Gladstones, to the latter, both of these prelates, however, continuing to perform their ordinary duties as ministers at Leith and St. Andrews. On Bishop Cunningham's decease, Peter Blackburn, minister at Aberdeen, was appointed in his place, and he, along with Lindsay and Gladstones, received commission in the month of October to vote on behalf of the Church. They took their seats in the parliament which met in November, along with Alexander Douglas, who had then been named to the see of Murray.[2]

On the nineteenth of November, the queen gave birth, in the palace of Dunfermline, to a son, who was baptized on the thirtieth of December by the Bishop of Ross, and received the name of Charles.[3]

[1] Tytler, vol. ix. p. 271-321. Calderwood, vol. vi. pp. 56-59, 82-99. Spottiswood, vol. iii. p. 84-90.

[2] Calderwood, vol. vi. pp. 96, 99, 100. Spottiswood, vol. iii. p. 82. Preface to Original Letters of the reign of James the Sixth, p. xvii.

[3] Spottiswood, vol. iii. p. 91. Tytler, vol. ix. p. 327. Keith's Catalogue, p. 201.

Queen Elizabeth died on the twenty-fourth of March, 1603, and the King of the Scots was immediately acknowledged as her successor. On Sunday, the third of April, James attended divine service in the church of St. Giles, at Edinburgh. When the sermon was finished, he addressed the congregation in a homely and affectionate manner, bidding them think of him as a king going from one part of the isle to another, and expressing a wish that, as God had joined the right of both kingdoms in his person, so they might be "joined in wealth, in religion, in hearts and affections." Two days afterwards he began his journey southwards, and on the sixth of May entered London, amid the joyful acclamations of his English subjects.[1]

On the twenty-fourth of April, while the king was on his progress towards London, James Beaton, Archbishop of Glasgow, died at Paris, in the eighty-sixth year of his age; and thus, at the very time that the British kingdoms were united under one sovereign, the last member of the old Scottish hierarchy, the last of those bishops who had exercised canonical jurisdiction under the authority of the Roman see, was taken away. Beaton had remained abroad since the year 1560, but he had all along been the faithful servant of Mary and her son. In 1598, a special act of parliament had been passed in his favour, restoring and confirming his honours, dignities, and possessions, and dispensing with his acknowledgment of the established religion. Archbishop Beaton was a munificent benefactor of the Scottish College at Paris, and was reverenced as its second founder.[2]

[1] Tytler, vol. ix. p. 360-362. Calderwood, vol. vi. pp. 215, 216.
[2] Keith's Catalogue, pp. 259, 260. Acts of the Parliaments of Scotland, vol. iv. pp. 169, 170. Spottiswood, vol. iii. pp. 139, 140. Mackenzie's Lives, vol. iii. p. 466.

CHAPTER XLIV.

FROM THE ACCESSION OF KING JAMES TO THE CROWN OF ENGLAND IN MARCH, 1603, TO THE CONSECRATION OF THE THREE SCOTTISH BISHOPS IN OCTOBER, 1610.

Coronation of King James—Conference at Hampton Court—Convocation of 1604—John Spottiswood, Archbishop of Glasgow—General Assembly at Aberdeen—Imprisonment of John Forbes, and other Ministers—Treatise by James Melville—Trial of the Ministers—Parliament at Perth—Scottish Ministers summoned to London—Imprisonment of Andrew Melville—General Assemblies at Linlithgow—Court of High Commission erected—General Assembly at Glasgow—Episcopal Government restored—Consecration of the Scottish Bishops at London.

ON the twenty-fifth day of July, 1603, King James was enthroned on the royal chair at Westminster Abbey, and, with his queen, Anne of Denmark, was anointed and crowned by the Archbishop of Canterbury. James, thus acknowledged King of England in right of his great-grandmother Margaret Tudor, was also, through his descent from Malcolm Canmore and St Margaret, the representative both of the Saxon line, and of the royal Celtic race, which had received the blessing of St Columba. The sovereign of the two British kingdoms was desirous of effecting a still closer union between them. Had he been successful in this design, the union would probably have been carried through in a manner much more satisfactory than it afterwards was in the reign of Queen Anne; but the mutual jealousies of the English and Scots defeated his intentions.

Intimately connected with the proposed measure for a civil union was the assimilation of the ecclesiastical institutions of the two kingdoms, and the restoration of religious unity in both. The differences between the Reformed and the Roman Catholics seemed to be hardly capable of reconciliation, but there was some hope of agreement among the Protestants themselves. Towards such a result nothing seemed more important than the establishment of a common system of church government in England and Scotland. In this opinion the supporters of the hierarchy and of Puritanism were agreed, although each party wished to extend its own system over the whole island. James was not more anxious for the introduction of Episcopacy into Scotland, than the zealous Presbyterians of that country were for the overthrow of prelacy in England. Row expresses the feelings, not only of the Covenanters of his own day, but also of the Presbyterian party at the time of James's accession to the English crown, when he regrets that the king made no effort to establish the Scottish sessions, presbyteries, and assemblies in Southern Britain—a change, he says, "which all the well affected in England both looked and longed for," and towards which, " means were essayed, and the sincerest pastors and professors of the truth of God in both kingdoms, opposed to prelatical government, made all the help they could."[1]

The Presbyterians in Scotland must have been aware that their system would receive no support from the king, but the English Puritans expected that a sovereign, who came from a country in which Episcopacy was only recognized as a part of the civil constitution, would give his assistance to relieve them from subjection to the hierarchy, and their enforced obedience to the Book of Common Prayer. The result of the Hampton Court conference, held in January, 1604, shewed that James was resolved to maintain the Church of England as then established by law. The king expressed his ecclesiastical opinions at great length in a speech before the parliament, which met soon after the conference. He concluded by declaring his love of unity, and stating that, as his faith, founded on the Scriptures, was truly Catholic and Apostolic, so he should ever be ready to give all imaginable deference to antiquity in points of discipline and government, and thus hope, by the grace of God, always to preserve himself from heresy and schism.[2]

The convocation of the province of Canterbury met at the same time with the parliament, and Dr Bancroft, now Bishop of

---

[1] History of the Kirk of Scotland, pp. 220, 221.
[2] Collier, vol. vii. p. 273-318.

London, presided, in consequence of the death of Archbishop Whitgift. Among other canons agreed to by the synod, and ratified by the king, was one regarding the form of prayer to be used before sermons. Preachers were enjoined to move the people to join in prayer "for Christ's holy Catholic Church, that is, for the whole congregation of Christian people dispersed throughout the whole world, and especially for the Churches of England, Scotland, and Ireland," and for the king, "supreme governor in these his realms, and all other his dominions and countries, over all persons in all causes, as well ecclesiastical as temporal." Much needless controversy has taken place regarding the meaning of this canon, so far as applicable to the Church of Scotland. There can be no doubt that its framers meant to acknowledge the northern ecclesiastical establishment as a Christian Church; and such was the opinion held by Bancroft and most of the English prelates, although they believed the Scottish system to be defective in its ritual, in the ordination of its ministers, and in other points. With the exception of the Roman Catholics, it was the only Christian communion then existing in Scotland, and questions regarding any other state of matters than that actually before them could not have occurred to the convocation.

To the preference which James had always entertained for Episcopacy, as most suitable to a monarchical form of government in the state, was now added the belief that without it there was no regular and duly authorised polity in the Church. His accession to the crown of England enabled him to proceed with more confidence and vigour in the reform of the ecclesiastical system of his native kingdom. The distance to which he was removed was of itself conducive to success in this design. It saved him from the rude and violent attacks of the ministers, and it protected him also from what was one of his chief faults—an undignified familiarity with those among whom he had long resided, and a fondness for attempting to convince opponents by personal argument and persuasion.

The two points to which the attention of James was chiefly directed were the filling up of the vacant episcopal sees, and the regulation of the proceedings in the general assemblies. Soon after the death of Archbishop Beaton, he nominated John Spottiswood, minister at Calder, to the see of Glasgow. The letter of nomination, which is dated at Hampton Court, the twentieth day of July, 1603, mentions that the archbishoprick was vacant by the decease of "James Beaton, late lawful archbishop thereof;" and, in respect of the learning, loyalty, and good life of Spottiswood, appoints him to the benefice. The language used shews how completely the office was viewed as a civil dignity, to be bestowed indeed in time to come, as provided by the laws, on Protestant ministers only, but capable, in itself, of being held by a Roman Catholic prelate.[1]

John Spottiswood, thus named to the archiepiscopal see of Glasgow, soon became the king's chief ecclesiastical adviser, and the most vigorous supporter of his measures for the reestablishment of the hierarchy in Scotland. He was the son of John Spottiswood, Superintendent of Lothian, and was born in the year 1565. On his father's death he succeeded him as minister at Calder, and in 1601 was selected to act as chaplain to the Duke of Lennox, during his embassy to France. Calderwood asserts that he was at one time a zealous champion of Melville's party among the ministers, but on this point the statement of a violent personal enemy must be received with caution.[2]

Andrew Graham having resigned the see of Dunblane, George Graham, minister at Scone, was appointed to that bishoprick in 1604. Before the end of the same year, Bishop Gladstones was translated to the metropolitan see of St. Andrews, and, in his place, Alexander Forbes, minister at Fettercairn, was named Bishop of Caithness.[3]

A meeting of the general assembly had been appointed to take place at Aberdeen, on the last Tuesday of July, 1604,

---

[1] Spottiswood, vol. iii. p. 140. Preface to Original Letters of the reign of James the Sixth, pp. xxiii. xxiv.

[2] Bishop Russell's Life of Spottiswood, prefixed to his edition of the archbishop's History, pp. xxxii. xxxiii. Spottiswood, vol. iii. p. 100. Calderwood, vol. v. p. 560. Dr. M'Crie asserts (Life of Melville, vol. ii, p. 95) that, "according to the accounts of different writers," Spottiswood had shewn more than ordinary zeal for the party of the ministers ; but the only authorities which he quotes are Calderwood, and a dubious passage from the MS. Annals of Archibald Simson.

[3] Preface to Original Letters of the reign of James the Sixth, p. xxxvii. Calderwood, vol. vi. p. 272.

but it was adjourned by the king's command. On the day, however, which had been fixed, James Melville and two other ministers, commissioners from the Presbytery of St. Andrews, appeared within the church of St. Nicholas in Aberdeen, and solemnly protested that, as they were present and ready to attend to their duty, whatever loss the Church should sustain should not be attributed to them, or to the presbytery whose commission they bore.[1]

The assembly having been continued to the second day of July, 1605, but having again been forbidden to sit, a small number of the ministers met at Aberdeen on the day appointed, and, notwithstanding the absence of the moderator of last assembly, commenced proceedings by electing John Forbes, minister at Alford, to be moderator. Being ordered to depart by royal proclamation, they separated for the time, but agreed to assemble again at the same place on the last Tuesday of September ensuing. For this act of disobedience to the royal authority, Forbes, Welsh, and several other ministers, were committed prisoners to Blackness.[2]

These proceedings gave rise to an important ecclesiastical question—whether a general assembly could lawfully meet in opposition to the express injunction of the king. The imprisoned ministers asserted that they had not actually been forbidden to meet, but the real point at issue was apparent to every one. Under the title of "An Apology for the prisoners of the Lord Jesus, presently in the castle of Blackness," the whole question was discussed by James Melville; and the line of argument, by which he contended for the right to meet in general assembly without the royal authority, or even if necessary in opposition to it, deserves to be carefully considered. He maintained that the members of the late assembly were entitled to meet at Aberdeen, first, by the express warrant of the word of God; secondly, by the laws of their country; and, thirdly, by the constitution, practice, and discipline of the Reformed Church.

First, he says, our Lord, having received from the Father

---

[1] James Melville's Diary, p. 560-565. Calderwood, vol. vi. p. 264-268.

[2] Forbes's Records touching the estate of the Kirk, p. 386-407. James Melville's Diary, p. 570-575. Calderwood, vol. vi. p. 279-291. Spottiswood, vol. iii. p. 157-159.

all power in heaven and in earth, in like manner gave authority to the apostles to govern the Church, and promised to be with them to the end of the world. He breathed on them, saying, "Receive ye the Holy Ghost: whosesoever sins ye remit, they are remitted to them, and whosoever sins ye retain, they are retained." He conversed with them forty days after his Resurrection, instructing them in the matters pertaining to his kingdom, and on the day of Pentecost sent upon them the Holy Spirit, the Comforter. When He had founded the Church by the apostles, He gave it pastors, doctors, and elders, who also had the keys of the kingdom of heaven, and the power of binding and loosing; and all these ministers are bound to discharge their offices, not only as individuals, but conjunctly in their courts and synods, for the preservation of sound doctrine and discipline. And this power, so given, no mortal man, no king, prince, or magistrate, should any way impede. Therefore, the faithful men who assembled at Aberdeen had the power and warrant of Jesus Christ for so doing, and the attempt to hinder them was like that of the tyrant Licinius, who, in order to effect the overthrow of the Church, prevented the bishops from meeting in council.

Secondly, the freedom of the holy Church is expressly protected by various acts of parliament in the reigns of the first, second, third, fourth, and fifth James, and it was ever one of the special points of her freedom to meet in synod. And if this was granted to the Popish Church, much more should it be possessed by the true Church of Christ, as is shewn by the statutes made subsequently to the Reformation, especially by that golden act of the parliament held at Edinburgh, in the year 1592, by which general assemblies of the Church are ratified and approved, and it is declared lawful for them to meet every year at the least, or oftener if occasion requires. Therefore, had the brethren acted otherwise than they did, they would have betrayed the cause of Christ, and the liberties of the Church.

Thirdly, from the year 1560, when the Reformed religion was established, to the departure of the king from Scotland, it was the continual practice of the Church to meet in general assembly almost twice every year and sometimes thrice. And if it be said that it was wrong to contend with the king for a precise day, he having no intention to take away general assemblies, the answer is, there was great reason for so doing, unless another day had been appointed, because, failing that, the right to hold assemblies would be interrupted, and their possession broken by prescription. Therefore, the meeting in assembly is an essential part of the office of the ministry, which they have from no earthly king, but from Him who is King of kings and Lord of lords.[1]

The ministers in Blackness, having been summoned before the council to answer for the unlawful keeping of the assembly, gave in a declinature of its jurisdiction, on the ground that the approbation or the disallowance of a general assembly was a spiritual matter, to be judged of by the Church. For this they were indicted before the court of Justiciary, on a charge of treason. At the trial, they stated that they declined not to appear before his majesty and council in any case wherein their jurisdiction was lawful, neither did they decline his majesty as judge in matters ecclesiastical, provided he judged along with the general assembly, but it was never heard in any nation, Protestant or Papist, that the king and his council were judges in spiritual matters. The court having declared that a declinature, such as had been presented by the accused, was treasonable in point of law, the assize, by a majority, found them guilty; and they were remitted to prison till the king's pleasure should be known as to their punishment.[2]

The harsh and unjust sentence thus pronounced may be explained, but cannot be justified, by the conduct of the ministers, on former occasions, in declining the civil jurisdiction respecting matters plainly within its cognizance. The original offence —the holding of the assembly—might be imprudent or factious, but it could not be criminal, so long as the act of 1592 was unrepealed. The ministers did not probably expect that the meeting at Aberdeen would be attended with consequences so serious to themselves. There is no reason to doubt that they had received secret promises of support from some of the nobles, particularly from the chancellor, the Earl of Dunfermline,

---

[1] James Melville's Diary, p. 593-612. Calderwood, vol. vi. p. 297-322.

[2] Forbes's Records, p. 463-496. Calderwood, vol. vi. p. 342-391. Spottiswood, vol. iii. p. 161-163.

a Roman Catholic, and the possessor of extensive church lands, whom they promised not to call in question on account of his religion. Mutual recriminations afterwards passed between them and the earl, which caused the king to remark " that none of the two deserved credit, and that he saw the ministers would betray religion, rather than submit themselves to government, and that the chancellor would betray the king for the malice he carried to the bishops."[1]

A parliament was held at Perth in July, 1606, by the Earl of Montrose, as the king's commissioner. On this occasion, the bishops rode between the earls and the lords, clothed in silk and velvet. First came the two archbishops, and after them the Bishops of Dunkeld and Galloway, Ross and Dunblane, Murray and Caithness, Orkney and the Isles. Peter Blackburn, Bishop of Aberdeen, esteeming it unbecoming the simplicity of a minister to use such pomp, went on foot to the parliament house. The Bishops of Galloway, Orkney, and the Isles, had been appointed to their sees during the preceding year. The first of these prelates was Gavin Hamilton, minister at Bothwell; the second, James Law, minister at Kirkliston; and the third, Andrew Knox, minister at Paisley. At the parliament of Perth a statute was passed, abrogating the act of 1587, in so far as the estates of the bishops were thereby annexed to the crown, but confirming the grants which had been made of other prelacies and benefices.[2]

Soon after the dissolution of parliament, the king summoned to London the Archbishops of St. Andrews and Glasgow, the Bishops of Orkney and Galloway, and James Nicolson, minister at Meigle, on the one side, and Andrew and James Melville, and six ministers of their party, on the other side, in order to consult with them about the ecclesiastical affairs of Scotland. They waited on the king at Hampton Court, and various conferences took place. By the command of James, the Presbyterian ministers attended a course of sermons, preached by four English divines, on the rights of the episcopate, the supremacy of the crown, and the want of all authority in Scripture and antiquity for the office of lay-

[1] Spottiswood, vol. iii. pp. 157, 174, 175.

[2] Calderwood, vol. vi. pp. 493, 494. Preface to Original Letters of the reign of James the Sixth, pp. xxxix. xl. xlii. Acts of the Parliaments of Scotland, vol. iv. p. 281-284.

elders. The forced attendance of the Melvilles and their friends on such an occasion was an absurd and ill-advised measure. Spottiswood was aware of this, at least in after times. He says that the king took this course, "as conceiving that some of the ministers should be moved by force of reason to quit their opinions, and give place to the truth; but that seldom happeneth, especially where the mind is prepossessed with prejudice either against person or matter."

During the conferences, James asked the opinion of those present regarding the lawfulness of the Aberdeen assembly and other points. All the bishops condemned the assembly as turbulent, factious, and illegal. Melville and his friends declined to express a similar opinion, and craved that the questions might be put to them specifically and in writing, and that time should be allowed to answer them. This was agreed to, but, in the meantime, they were forbidden to return to Scotland without the royal license.

The ministers could not have given a direct and conscientious answer to the king's enquiries without compromising their own safety. It was otherwise, however, with the following questions put in private to two of their number by Bancroft, who had succeeded Whitgift in the see of Canterbury:—"Whether in any of the ancients the name of presbyter was found given to any that taught not the word, and ministered not the sacraments? Whether the name of Bishop in the ancients was found given to any one who had not superiority above the presbyters and the rest of the clergy? Whether ever among the ancients we read of a presbytery, or ecclesiastical senate, that had not in and above it a Bishop?" These questions the archbishop offered to give them in writing, but they declined to receive them, lest, says James Melville, they should be drawn into dispute. This can hardly be reconciled with what he immediately adds, that the archbishop "found these two brethren so hard of his learning, that he despaired to call for them again, or for any more of us."

Wearied with the delay, the ministers earnestly entreated permission to return home, or to be put to lawful trial for any crime which they had committed. They were all finally allowed to depart, except the two Melvilles. The younger of the kinsmen, though prohibited from returning to Scotland, was permitted to reside, first at Newcastle, and afterwards at Berwick, but his uncle suffered a more severe punishment. Andrew Melville having been summoned before the English privy council on account of his well-known verses on the altar in the chapel royal, his fierce ungovernable temper overpowered all sense of prudence and decency. He accused the Archbishop of Canterbury of encouraging Popery and superstition, of profaning the Sabbath, and of silencing faithful ministers. Seizing the sleeves of his rochet and shaking them, he told the primate that he esteemed him the capital enemy of all the Reformed Churches in Europe, and that he would oppose him and his proceedings to the last drop of his blood. He railed against Dr Barlow in similar terms, and only stopped when he was removed to another part of the room. The Lord Chancellor Egerton admonished Melville to join wisdom, gravity, modesty, and discretion to his learning and years. This rebuke would have been a sufficient punishment for Melville's verses and unbecoming language; but it did not satisfy the king, who caused him to be committed to custody with the Dean of St Paul's, and subsequently in the Tower.[1]

The whole proceedings of James in regard to these ministers gave reasonable ground for supposing that they had been summoned to England merely to prevent their resisting the ecclesiastical measures in progress in their own country. The detention of the others, and still more the imprisonment of Melville, was illegal and unjust. Their coming to England at the king's command should have protected them from all punishment for opinions expressed by them, or for mere ebullitions of temper.

James was equally severe in the sentences pronounced against the ministers in Scotland who had been tried for assisting at the Aberdeen assembly. Forbes, Welsh, and their four companions in Blackness, were condemned to perpetual banishment from the king's dominions, with the threat of capital punishment if they should presume to return without leave; and several of their supporters were ordered to be confined in various islands, or in remote parts of the kingdom.

---

[1] James Melville's Diary, pp. 644-683, 688-700, 705-711. Calderwood, vol. vi. pp. 477-480, 556-560, 567-583, 586-600. Spottiswood, vol. iii. pp. 176-183, 190. M'Crie's Life of Melville, vol. ii. pp. 221-247, 250, 260.

[2] Calderwood, vol. vi. pp. 590, 591. Spottiswood, vol. iii. pp. 181, 182.

The long promised general assembly was at last held at Linlithgow, on the tenth of December, 1606. The Earl of Dunbar was the royal commissioner; one hundred and thirty-six ministers, and thirty-three noblemen, barons, and others of the laity, were present; and James Nicolson was elected moderator. It was proposed, on the king's recommendation, that in every presbytery one of the members should be appointed to act as permanent moderator till the present dissensions should be at an end, the bishops to be moderators in the places of their residence; and that the bishops should be moderators in the diocesan synods. These proposals were agreed to, under certain conditions restricting the powers of moderators, and subjecting the moderators of presbyteries to the censure of the synods, and the moderators of synods to the censure of the general assembly.[1]

At a parliament held at Edinburgh, in August, 1607, a statute was passed, authorising the Archbishop of St Andrews to select the ministers of seven parishes within his diocese to act as the chapter of the archbishopric, in room of the Prior and canons, whose dignities were now secularised.[2]

In April, 1607, Alexander Campbell, who had so long held the titular office of Bishop of Brechin, resigned that dignity, and was immediately succeeded by Andrew Lamb, minister of the chapel royal. Peter Rollock, titular Bishop of Dunkeld, also resigned his see, and was succeeded by James Nicolson. The latter died in August, 1607, after holding the bishopric for a very short time, and, in December following, Alexander Lindsay, minister at St Madoes, was appointed in his room. In June, 1608, John Campbell succeeded his father Neil Campbell as Bishop of Argyll.[3]

On the twenty-sixth of July, 1608, another general assembly met at Linlithgow. The Earl of Dunbar was commissioner for the king, and the Bishop of Orkney, by a majority of votes, was elected moderator. At this assembly, the Marquis of Huntly was again excommunicated on account of his repeated relapses to Popery. The members were of opinion that

---

[1] Calderwood, vol. vi. p. 601-624. Book of the Universal Kirk, p. 567-574. Spottiswood, vol. iii. p. 183-189.

[2] Acts of the Parliaments of Scotland, vol iv. p. 372.

[3] Preface to Original Letters of the Reign of James the Sixth, pp. xxxvi. xxxviii. xxxix.

the increase of Roman errors was owing in part to the negligence of ministers in catechizing the young, and therefore ordered that all children of the age of six years should be carefully instructed in the Creed, the Lord's Prayer, and the Ten Commandments.[1]

At a parliament held in June, 1609, the consistorial jurisdiction was restored to the bishops, and an act was passed giving power to the king to regulate the habits to be worn by judges, magistrates, and churchmen. In virtue of the power so conferred, directions were soon afterwards issued that ministers should wear black gowns in the pulpit, and that bishops and doctors of divinity should wear black cassocks, with black gowns in the English form, and tippets.[2]

In February, 1610, a court of High Commission was erected by the king in each of the provinces of St. Andrews and Glasgow, the members of which, or any five of their number, the archbishop being always one, had power to call before them and try all scandalous offenders in life or religion, and to enforce their sentences by fine and imprisonment, and also by excommunication, to be pronounced by the minister of the parish where the criminal resided under pain of suspension and deprivation. The first person named in the Commission for the province of St Andrews was the archbishop, therein styled Primate and Metropolitan of the kingdom; and the Archbishop of Glasgow was the first person named in the Commission for that province. All the bishops were members in their respective provinces, and the other commissioners consisted of peers, barons, judges, and ministers.[3]

James Melville and Calderwood remark with justice on the arbitrary powers of these illegal courts, now first introduced into Scotland on the model of the similar institution in England, and on the anomaly that one archbishop, though himself, by the rules of the system then established, only a simple minister without spiritual authority over his brethren, could,

---

[1] Calderwood, vol. vi. p. 751-776. Book of the Universal Kirk, p. 575-587. Spottiswood, vol. iii. p. 193-195.

[2] Acts of the Parliaments of Scotland, vol. iv. pp. 430, 431, 435, 436. Calderwood, vol. vii. pp. 54, 55.

[3] James Melville's Diary, p. 786-792. Calderwood, vol. vii. p. 57-63. Original Letters of the Reign of James the Sixth, vol. i. pp. 242, 243.

along with four secular persons, suspend or deprive ministers. The erection of the court of High Commission was, indeed, a restoration of metropolitan jurisdiction, and a formal re-establishment of the old provinces and dioceses, by means of the royal prerogative. This and similar measures of the king could only be justified on the ground that the crown was the fountain of all ecclesiastical jurisdiction; and hence the opinion became common, both among the supporters and opponents of the hierarchy, that as episcopal authority had been conferred, so also it could be taken away by the civil power.

The Presbyterian form of church government was now in reality subverted, although the name and outward appearance remained. In a letter addressed to the Bishop of Orkney, Hume of Godscroft remarked, "If some shadow of old forms be yet left, as in the alteration of the Roman government when with Julius monarchy re-entered, though the people convened and had their form of comitia, though the senate was yet on foot, though consuls were chosen and had name and countenance, yet the force of authority and government, the liberty in choice of persons restrained from free choice to the recommendation of the emperor, and the truth of the old estate taken away, none denies but the government was altered from popular to monarchical. So, though presbyteries remain, though synods did, though general assemblies also, shadows and shows of our discipline, not the less that parity, freedom, and vicissitude taken away, or the force thereof broken and restrained, the essence and essential points thereof are also altered, or to be altered."[1]

It was obvious, however, to the bishops themselves, that the powers conferred upon them would be greatly strengthened by the sanction of the highest ecclesiastical authority recognized by the Scottish people, and it was probably at their suggestion that the king summoned a general assembly to meet at Glasgow, on the eighth of June, 1610. The influence of the crown was openly used in directing the choice of members, the king's desires in that respect being made known through the Archbishop of St. Andrews to the presbyteries. The Earl of Dunbar was again the royal commissioner, and various noblemen, barons, and commissioners of burghs,

[1] Calderwood, vol. vii. p. 68.

were present. The Archbishop of Glasgow preached at the opening of the assembly. He denounced the sin of sacrilege, blaming also the proceedings of lay patrons of benefices, and concluded by stating that religion ought not to be maintained after the manner in which it had been introduced into the kingdom. "It was brought in by confusion," he said, "it must be maintained by order; it was brought in against authority, it must be maintained by authority." In another discourse, the Bishop of Orkney undertook to prove the lawfulness of episcopal government. Without alluding to the jus divinum, he supported his argument by the three grounds of antiquity, universality, and perpetuity, appealing for his authorities to the continual practice of the Church, and the consent of the Fathers. In the afternoon, Dr. Hudson, an English divine who had accompanied the Earl of Dunbar, preached on the superiority of bishops over presbyters.

The Archbishop of Glasgow having been chosen moderator, after various discussions continued during three days, eleven articles were agreed to with little opposition from any of the members. By the first, it was acknowledged that the calling of general assemblies belonged to the king, and that all otherwise summoned, specially the conventicle at Aberdeen in 1605, were unlawful. By the second, it was agreed that synods should be held in every diocese twice in the year, in April and October, at which the bishop was to moderate. By the third, it was declared that no sentence of excommunication, or of absolution from excommunication, should be pronounced without the knowledge and approbation of the bishop of the diocese, and if he stayed the pronouncing of sentence, where the proceedings were just and regular, on his being convicted thereof in the general assembly, intimation was to be made to the king, that another might be appointed in his room. By the fourth, all presentations to benefices were to be directed to the bishop of the diocese; and by him, with the assistance of some of the ministers, the persons presented were, after due examination, to be ordained. By the fifth, in the suspension and deprivation of ministers, the bishop of the diocese was to associate with himself some of the ministers within the bounds where the delinquent served, and after just trial to pronounce sentence. By the sixth, every minister, at his ordination, was to swear obedience to the king and his ordinary, according to the form agreed upon in the year 1572. By the seventh, visitations of the diocese were to be made by the bishop himself, or, where the extent was too great, by one of the ministers acting under his commission. By the eighth, the bishop, or in his absence a minister to be named by him in diocesan synod, was to moderate at all meetings of the ministers for the exercise—the name of presbytery being purposely not used. By the ninth, it was declared that bishops should be subject in all matters regarding their life, conversation, office, and benefice, to the censure of the general assembly, and, if found culpable, should, with the king's advice and consent, be deprived. By the tenth, no bishop was to be elected till he was past the age of forty years at least, and till he had officiated as a minister for ten years. By the eleventh, it was ordered that no minister should speak in public against any of the foresaid articles, nor dispute the question of the equality or inequality of ministers.

When the proceedings were over, a sum of five thousand pounds Scots was distributed by the Earl of Dunbar among those ministers who had acted as moderators of presbyteries. The opponents of the synod asserted that the money was given to secure the votes of the members. There can be little doubt that its distribution was entrusted to the earl, for the purpose, at least, of rewarding the ministers who supported the measures recommended by the sovereign.[1]

Thus, after an interval of forty years, a polity similar to that which had been agreed to at Leith during the regency of Mar was again established. The chief features of that system were evidently copied by James, and express reference was made to one of them in the articles. A leading object with the king and his ecclesiastical advisers, as formerly with Erskine of Dun and the better part of the ministers, was the

[1] Calderwood, vol. vii. p. 91-103. Book of the Universal Kirk, p. 587-589. Spottiswood, vol. iii. p. 205-207. Cook, vol. ii. p. 227-237. Original Letters of the reign of James the Sixth, vol. i. p. 425. The articles, as given by Spottiswood, are not those agreed to by the assembly, but are substantially the same with the articles amended and ratified by the parliament of 1612. This can hardly have been unintentional on the part of the historian, and the suppression of those portions which limited the powers of the episcopate deserves the severe censure which Dr. Cook has bestowed upon it.

wish to rescue church property from lay spoliation, and to restore it to its proper use, and hence, at this time also, a powerful party among the nobility and barons were opposed to the re-establishment of Episcopacy, although they did not venture to make any open resistance.

At the Glasgow assembly, a petition was presented from the Marquis of Huntly, and the Earls of Angus and Errol, requesting to be freed from the excommunication which had been pronounced against them. These noblemen were in confinement, and liable to the severe civil penalties which followed the ecclesiastical sentence. The Marquis of Huntly, having subscribed the Confession of Faith, and professed his repentance, was absolved. The Earl of Angus, rather than conform, went beyond seas, and died in exile. The Earl of Errol was at first willing to submit, but, on the very night after he had offered to sign the Confession, he fell into such trouble of mind, that in despair he was about to kill himself. Early in the morning, on the Archbishop of Glasgow being sent for, he acknowledged his dissimulation with many tears, and beseeched those who were present to witness his remorse. This nobleman, says Spottiswood, who himself relates the circumstance in a manner honourable to his feelings, " was of a tender heart, and of all I have known the most conscientious in his profession; and thereupon to his dying was used by the Church with greater lenity than were others of that sect."[1]

The restoration of episcopal government and the civil rights of the bishops had now been accomplished. But there was yet wanting that without which, so far as the Church was concerned, all the rest was comparatively unimportant. The king was anxious that the bishops should receive a valid consecration, and the English prelates zealously assisted in carrying out his wishes. The Scottish prelates also, on their part, were desirous to receive consecration, although it is not easy to ascertain in what light they regarded the gift. The general feeling among them and those of the ministers who shared their sentiments was probably what Bishop Law had expressed at the late synod—that Episcopacy was both lawful and expedient, and most in accordance with the practice of the Apostles and the ancient Church, but

[1] Spottiswood, vol. iii. p. 208.

that it was not absolutely necessary as a form of ecclesiastical government, and that holy orders, and the grace of the Eucharist, might exist independently of episcopal ordination. Among the ministers, a large party looked on the proposed step as superstitious and antichristian, while others, though averse to it, were willing to submit. The great body of the people appear at this time to have been entirely indifferent, and ready to acquiesce in whatever measures of the kind the royal authority might prescribe.

Soon after the assembly, the Archbishop of Glasgow, and the Bishops of Brechin and Galloway, were summoned to court. They arrived in the middle of September, and, at their first audience, the king told them that he had now recovered the bishoprics out of the hands of those who possessed them, and bestowed them on such as he hoped would be worthy of their places; but, since he could not make them bishops, nor they assume that honour to themselves, and as no consecration could be obtained for them in Scotland, he had called them to England, that being consecrated themselves they might, on their return, give ordination to those at home, and so stop the mouths of the adversaries, who said that he took upon himself to create bishops, and bestow spiritual offices, which he could not presume to do, knowing that that authority belonged to Christ alone, and those on whom He had conferred the power. Spottiswood answered that they were willing to obey his majesty's desire, and only feared that the Church of Scotland might thereby be subjected to the Church of England, in consequence of similar usurpations of old. James assured them that he had guarded against that danger, by providing that neither of the English metropolitans should assist at the consecration.

Another question, however, was raised by Dr. Andrews, Bishop of Ely. He said that the Scottish prelates ought first to be ordained presbyters, as they had never received episcopal ordination. The English primate, Dr. Bancroft, answered that there was no necessity for this, because, where bishops were not to be had, ordination given by presbyters must be esteemed valid, otherwise it might be doubted whether there was any lawful vocation in most of the Reformed Churches. He farther mentioned that there was no necessity for the

Scottish prelates passing through the intermediate orders of priest and deacon, because the episcopal character could be given by one consecration, as was shewn by several examples in the ancient Church.

All difficulties being thus removed, the three prelates were consecrated, according to the form in the English ordinal, in the chapel of London House, on Sunday the twenty-first day of October, 1610, by the Bishops of London, Ely, Rochester, and Worcester.[1]

[1] Spottiswood, vol iii. pp. 208, 209. Wilkins's Concilia, vol. iv. p. 443. Collier, vol. vii. p. 363-365. Balfour's Historical Works, vol. ii. pp. 35, 36. Andrew Melville wrote some verses on the consecration, in his usual style. A scholar of far higher name, a personal friend of Melville, who was present on the occasion, was very differently affected. On the day of the consecration, Isaac Casaubon made the following entry in his diary: "This Lord's day, by God's blessing, was not ill spent. For I was invited to be present at the consecration of two bishops and an archbishop of Scotland. I witnessed that ceremony, and the imposition of hands, and the whole service. O God, how great was my delight. Do Thou O Lord Jesus preserve this Church, and give to our Puritans who ridicule such things a better mind." See Calderwood, vol. vii. p. 151, and Scottish Ecclesiastical Journal, vol. i. p. 9.

CHAPTER XLV.

FROM THE CONSECRATION OF THE THREE SCOTTISH BISHOPS IN OCTOBER, 1610, TO THE PERTH ASSEMBLY OF AUGUST, 1618.

Consecration of the other Bishops—Directions issued by the King—Acts of the Glasgow Assembly ratified by Parliament—William Cowper, Bishop of Galloway—Execution of John Ogilvie—Death of Archbishop Gladstones—John Spottiswood appointed Archbishop of St. Andrews—Absolution of the Marquis of Huntly—Creation of Doctors of Divinity—General Assembly at Aberdeen—New Confession of Faith—King James visits Scotland—Imprisonment of David Calderwood—New erection of Cathedral Chapters—General Assembly at St. Andrews—Patrick Forbes, Bishop of Aberdeen—His letter to Archbishop Spottiswood—General Assembly at Perth—Sermon of Archbishop Spottiswood—Five Articles agreed to by the Assembly.

SOON after the return of the three prelates to Scotland, the other bishops were consecrated. The first consecration was that of the Archbishop of St. Andrews, which took place at his own primatial city in the month of December, the consecrating prelates being the three newly ordained bishops. On the fifteenth of March, the Bishop of Murray was consecrated at Edinburgh by his metropolitan, the Archbishop of St. Andrews, assisted, there can be no doubt, by other bishops. The Bishops of Aberdeen and Caithness were consecrated in the cathedral church of Brechin by Archbishop Gladstones and the Bishops of Dunkeld and Brechin; and the primate, in a letter dated the third of May, 1611, mentions to the king that all the bishops of his province had then been consecrated.[1]

Certain directions were sent by the king to the clergy, and approved of at a meeting of the bishops and some of the lead-

[1] James Melville's Diary, p. 804. Original Letters of the reign of James the Sixth, vol. i. pp. 265, 270.

ing ministers held at Edinburgh in the month of February, 1611. Among the chief of these instructions were the following:—That every archbishop and bishop should reside at the cathedral church of his diocese, and endeavour, as far as he could, to repair the same; that bishops should make a visitation of their dioceses every three years, and archbishops of their provinces every seven years at least; that, inasmuch as lay elders were not sanctioned by the Scriptures or the primitive Church, but it was not the less necessary that fit persons should assist the minister in repairing the fabric of the church, providing the elements for the Holy Communion, collecting contributions for the poor, and such like services, the ministers should therefore make choice of wise and discreet persons within the parish, for the performance of those duties, and present their names to the ordinary for his approbation; that no minister should be admitted without trial and imposition of hands by the bishop and two or three ministers called in by him to assist, and that a form should be printed for that purpose and strictly adhered to; that the election of bishops should be made in the manner agreed to at the conference of 1572, and that the dean of the chapter should be vicar during a vacancy in the bishopric; that, when it was thought expedient to call a general assembly, a supplication should be made for his majesty's license to meet, and that the assembly should consist of bishops, deans, archdeacons, and of ministers to be elected by their brethren; that, to check the abuse of young men preaching before attaining years of discretion or receiving ordination, none should be permitted to preach except those who had received orders.[1]

At a parliament held at Edinburgh in October, 1612, the acts of the Glasgow assembly were ratified, with some important modifications. Nothing was said as to the new appointment in room of a bishop who impeded excommunication. The form of the oath of obedience to the ordinary was now prescribed. It was as follows:—"I A. B., now admitted to the church of C., promise and swear to E. F., Bishop of that diocese, obedience, and to his successors, in all lawful things. So help me God." The articles regarding the censure of bishops by the general assembly and their age before election

[1] Spottiswood, vol. iii. p. 210-212.

were omitted. The act of parliament of 1592, and all other statutes opposed to the articles so ratified, were repealed.[1]

Gavin Hamilton, Bishop of Galloway, died in July, 1612, and was succeeded by William Cowper, minister at Perth. Cowper was distinguished for his learning and piety, but he had at one time opposed the restoration of Episcopacy, and was now severely attacked by his former friends, particularly by Hume of Godscroft. He published two treatises in defence of his conduct, and in a letter addressed to Hume, marked by great candour and humility, and in which he thanked him for putting his name to what he had written, instead of assailing him anonymously like others, the bishop called God to witness the sincerity of the change in his opinions. He was consecrated in the cathedral church of Glasgow, on the fourth of October, 1612.[2]

John Campbell, Bishop of Argyll, died in January, 1613, and was succeeded by Andrew Boyd, parson of Eaglesham, a natural son of the Lord Boyd.[3]

On the fourteenth of August, 1613, David Lindsay, Bishop of Ross, died at Leith, where he had officiated as minister since the year 1560. He was the last survivor of the original Reformed ministers. His successor in the see of Ross was Patrick Lindsay, minister at St. Vigeans, who was consecrated at Leith on the first of December.[4]

On the fourth of March, 1614, a royal proclamation was made at the cross of Edinburgh, enjoining all ministers to celebrate the Communion on Easter-day following, and the people to communicate at that time in their own parish churches. This was justly supposed to be a preparation for other measures which were soon to follow.[5]

Towards the end of the same year, a Jesuit priest, named

---

[1] Acts of the Parliaments of Scotland, vol. iv. pp. 469, 470. Calderwood, vol. vii. p. 165-173.

[2] Original Letters of the reign of James the Sixth, vol. i. pp. 346, 347, and preface, p. xxxix. Calderwood, vol. vii. pp. 179, 180. Note by Mr. David Laing, in Row's History, p. 259.

[3] Preface to Original Letters of the reign of James the Sixth, p. xxxvi. Calderwood, vol. vii. p. 176.

[4] Preface to Original Letters of the reign of James the Sixth, p. xli. Spottiswood, vol. iii. p. 220. Calderwood, vol. vii. p. 178.

[5] Calderwood, vol. vii. p. 191.

John Ogilvie, who had lately come over from Gratz, was apprehended at Glasgow. He was examined before Archbishop Spottiswood and others, and, on his declining to mention with whom he had resided since his arrival in Scotland, was ordered to be kept from sleep for several nights. The sufferings which he thus underwent made him discover various circumstances; but, as soon as he was allowed to take any rest, he denied the whole. By the king's express desire, certain questions were put to him, through the archbishop, concerning the power of the Pope to excommunicate and depose princes, and to loose their subjects from their oaths of allegiance; particularly, whether he had such power in the case of the King of Great Britain, and whether it was murder to slay his majesty, if so excommunicated and deposed. Ogilvie said that he thought the Pope had power to excommunicate the king, but declined to give his opinion as to the other questions, unless to the Pope, as judge of controversies in religion.

In consequence of this declinature, on the twenty-eighth of February, 1615, Ogilvie was tried at Glasgow for high treason, under the acts establishing the king's supremacy. On being warned of the danger to which he exposed himself, he answered, "I am a subject as free as the king is a king; I came by commandment of my superior into this kingdom, and, if I were even now forth of it, I would return; neither do I repent any thing, but that I have not been so busy as I should in that which you call perverting of subjects. I am accused for declining the king's authority, and will do it still in matters of religion, for with such matters he hath nothing to do; and this which I say the best of your ministers do maintain, and, if they be wise, will continue of the same mind. Some questions were moved to me which I refused to answer, because the proposers were not judges in controversies of religion, and therefore I trust you cannot infer anything against me." "But I hope," said the archbishop, "you will not make this a controversy of religion, whether the king, being deposed by the Pope, may be lawfully killed." Ogilvie answered, "It is a question among the doctors of the Church: many hold the affirmative not improbably; but as that point is not yet determined, so, if it shall be concluded,

I will give my life in defence of it; and to call it unlawful I will not, though I should save my life by saying it."

Ogilvie was found guilty by the jury, and condemned to be hanged and quartered. When sentence was pronounced, he asked if he might speak to the people. The archbishop answered that he might, if he would acknowledge the justice of his condemnation, and request the king's pardon for his treasonable speeches, but that otherwise he could not be allowed. "Then," said the priest, "God have mercy upon me;" and added, with a loud voice, "If there be here any hidden Catholics, let them pray for me; but the prayers of heretics I will not have."

He was allowed a few hours to prepare for death, and was then led to the scaffold. Two ministers, who were in attendance, exhorted him to disburden his conscience, if anything troubled him, and to seek mercy of God through Jesus Christ, but did not enter on disputed points of religion. He answered that he was prepared and resolved. After ascending the scaffold, he said in a low voice, so that there was some difficulty in hearing him, "Maria, mater gratiæ, ora pro me; omnes angeli, orate pro me; omnes sancti sanctæque, orate pro me." He then commended his soul to God, and suffered death in terms of his sentence. The quartering of his body was dispensed with.

In the account of the execution published by the government, it was correctly stated that Ogilvie died for maintaining an erroneous and dangerous opinion regarding the authority of the Pope, not for saying mass, or for any direct point of religion. But to punish capitally a mere expression of opinion, given in answer to questions put by his judges, was a cruel and wicked act; and the whole proceedings connected with the trial were disgraceful to all concerned, especially to Archbishop Spottiswood, who took so active a part in them. Another Jesuit, named Moffat, who had been apprehended at St. Andrews about the same time, is said to have disclaimed the temporal authority of the Pope, and was allowed to depart from the kingdom.[1]

---

[1] Spottiswood, vol. iii. p. 222-227. Pitcairn's Criminal Trials, vol. iii. p. 330-354. Calderwood, vol. vii. pp. 193, 196. Original Letters of the reign of James the Sixth, vol. ii. pp. 385-391, 399-401, 424, 446-448, 795-797. I have

On the second of May, 1615, Archbishop Gladstones died at St. Andrews. He was a prelate of a good life and benevolent disposition, but not distinguished in any particular way for learning or ability. To guard against the calumnies which the Puritans systematically spread abroad regarding the deathbed of their opponents, he left in writing a declaration of his opinions respecting ecclesiastical government, and a statement that his conscience had never accused him for what he had done. Archbishop Spottiswood was appointed his successor in the primacy, and was inaugurated at St. Andrews, on Sunday the sixth of August, in presence of most of the suffragan bishops. The Bishop of Orkney was translated to Glasgow, and the Bishop of Dunblane to Orkney; and Adam Bellenden, parson of Falkirk, was elected and consecrated Bishop of Dunblane.[1]

Peter Blackburn, Bishop of Aberdeen, died on the fourteenth of June, 1616, and was succeeded by Bishop Alexander Forbes, who was translated from Caithness. John Abernethy, minister at Jedburgh, was appointed to the see of Caithness.[2]

In December, 1615, the two courts of High Commission were united, five members, including one of the archbishops, continuing to be a quorum.[3]

The Marquis of Huntly, having again relapsed to Popery, and having again been excommunicated, was committed to ward by the court of High Commission, but after a short imprisonment was released in virtue of a warrant from the Chancellor. The prelates remonstrated against this proceeding, and sent Bishop Forbes of Caithness to explain their views to the king. The marquis also went to London, and professed

not seen the Roman Catholic account of Ogilvie's trial and execution, published at Douay before the end of 1615. It has been conjectured that the narrative published at Edinburgh in the same year, and reprinted by Mr. Pitcairn, was the composition of Archbishop Spottiswood; see Original Letters, vol. ii. p. 424. Calderwood, who condemns so severely and so justly the imprisonment and banishment of the Presbyterian ministers, speaks with scornful indifference of the death of the Jesuit.

[1] Original Letters of the reign of James the Sixth, vol. ii. p. 437, and preface p. xxxvii. Spottiswood, vol. iii. p. 227. Calderwood, vol. vii. pp. 197, 201, 203.
[2] Preface to Original Letters of the Reign of James the Sixth, pp. xxxvi. xxxvii. Calderwood, vol. vii. pp. 216, 217. Selections from the Ecclesiastical Records of Aberdeen, p. 84.
[3] Calderwood, vol. vii. p. 204-210.

his readiness to communicate with the Church of England. James wished to avoid extreme measures against so powerful a nobleman, to whom personally he was much attached, but was also anxious not to encroach on the rights of the Scottish Church, by allowing the English bishops to absolve a person who lay under a sentence of excommunication in Scotland. The Bishop of Caithness, however, having expressed his assent on the part of the Scottish prelates, although he had no authority to do so, in July, 1616, the marquis was absolved in the chapel of Lambeth palace by Dr Abbot, Archbishop of Canterbury. The form used on that occasion was the following:— "Whereas the purpose and intendment of the whole Church of Christ is to win men unto God, and frame their souls for heaven, and that there is such an agreement and correspondency betwixt the Churches of Scotland and England, that what the bishops and pastors in the one, without any earthly or worldly respect, shall accomplish to satisfy the Christian and charitable end and desire of the other, cannot be distasteful to either; I, therefore, finding your earnest entreaty to be loosed from the bond of excommunication, wherewith you stand bound in the Church of Scotland, and well considering the reason and cause of that censure, and also considering your desire on this present day to communicate here with us, for the better effecting of this work of participation of the holy sacrament of Christ our Saviour his blessed Body and Blood, do absolve you from the said excommunication, in the Name of the Father, and of the Son, and of the Holy Ghost; and beseech Almighty God, that you may be so directed by the Holy Spirit, that you may continue in the truths of his Gospel unto your life's end, and then be made partaker of his everlasting kingdom."

The king and the Archbishop of Canterbury wrote to Archbishop Spottiswood, explaining the reason for this proceeding, and mentioning their anxious wish to avoid doing anything which might interfere with the just rights of the Scottish Church.[1]

On the twenty-ninth of July, the principals of the three colleges at St Andrews, and some other ministers, were inaugurated as doctors of divinity in that university, Dr Young, Dean of Winchester, assisting on the occasion. Degrees in

[1] Spottiswood, vol. iii. p. 230-235. Calderwood, vol. vii. pp. 212, 218, 219.

theology had been given up by the Scottish reformers as tending to Popery and superstition, and this was the first time they were again used.[1]

The king and his advisers had for some years contemplated the restoration of certain important points of primitive order and ritual, and, in 1612, a draft of a new Confession of Faith had been submitted to the two archbishops. The following articles, apparently drawn up by Spottiswood while absent in England in the year 1615, shew what were then considered to be the chief defects of the Scottish Church:—

" There is lacking in our Church a form of Divine Service; and while every minister is left to the framing of public prayer by himself, both the people are neglected, and their prayers prove often impertinent.

" A public Confession of Faith must be formed, agreeing as near as can be with the Confession of the English Church.

" An order for election of Archbishops and Bishops in time hereafter must be established by law; and, in the meanwhile, if his majesty propose the translation of any by occasion of this vacancy of St Andrews, the form used in the translating of Bishops here in England should be kept.

" A uniform order for electing of ministers and their receiving.

" The forms of Marriage, Baptism, and Administration of the Holy Supper, must be in some points amended.

" Confirmation is wanting in our Church, whereof the use for children is most profitable.

" Canons and Constitutions must be concluded and set forth, for keeping both the clergy and churches in order.

" These things must be advised and agreed upon in a general assembly of the clergy, which must be drawn to the form of the convocation house here in England."

At the request of the bishops, a general assembly was summoned to meet at Aberdeen on the thirteenth of August, 1616. The Archbishop of St Andrews presided, in virtue of his metropolitan authority, and the Earl of Montrose was the royal commissioner. Among the recommendations submitted to the assembly, and agreed to by them, were the following:—That a true and simple Confession of Faith should be prepared, to

[1] Calderwood, vol. vii. p. 222.

which all should swear before being admitted to any office in the Church or commonwealth; that a short Catechism should be compiled for the instruction of children previous to Communion; that a Liturgy and form of Divine Service should be made, to be said by the Reader before the Sermon every Sabbath, or, where there was no Reader, by the Minister before conceiving his own prayer, that the common people might learn it and by custom serve God rightly; that the Communion should be celebrated four times in the year in towns, and twice in country parishes, one of these times to be at Easter; that, to promote uniformity of discipline, the canons of former councils and assemblies should be collected, and their deficiencies supplied; that all ministers, under the pain of deposition, should administer the sacrament of Baptism whenever required so to do, the godfather promising to instruct the infant in the faith.

The new Confession of Faith was presented to the assembly and approved of, after being revised by a committee of the members. This Confession was subscribed by the Marquis of Huntly, who was thereupon formally loosed from his excommunication. Calderwood states that he subscribed it without reading it over, on being assured that it was all one with the old Confession. If such was the case, the assertion was substantially correct. The new Confession agrees with the old one in all important points; the chief difference being in its more marked enunciation of the doctrine of Calvin in regard to election and predestination. It is not easy to see what was the precise object in bringing it forward. The old Confession was not abrogated, but it was perhaps intended that both that formulary, and the Negative Confession of Craig, should gradually be set aside.[1]

The king soon afterwards expressed his desire that five articles should be received by the Church, by which kneeling at the reception of the Communion, private Communion to the sick, private Baptism in cases of necessity, the Commemoration of the Birth, Passion, Resurrection, and Ascension of our Lord, and of the Descent of the Holy Ghost, and the

---

[1] Original Letters of the reign of James the Sixth, vol. i. p. 293; vol. ii. pp. 445, 446, 481-488. Calderwood, vol. vii. p. 220-242. Book of the Universal Kirk, p. 589-599. Spottiswood, vol. iii. pp. 235, 236.

Confirmation of children, were to be restored. The Archbishop of St. Andrews remonstrated against this, pointing out that these articles had never been sanctioned by the clergy; and the king agreed to withdraw them in the meantime.[1]

James had long intended to visit his native kingdom, and in the year 1617 he was enabled to do so. Great preparations were made for his reception, and, by his own express command, directions were given to fit up the chapel royal at Holyrood for the celebration of divine service in the English form. Organs were sent for that purpose; and sculptured figures of the twelve Apostles and four Evangelists were prepared, in order to be placed as ornaments in the stalls, but, at the request of the Bishop of Galloway, who in virtue of the ancient privilege of his see was now dean of the chapel, the king reluctantly consented to forbear setting them up. He was accompanied in his journey by several English prelates and divines, among others, by Bishop Andrews, and by Dr. Laud, then Dean of Gloucester. He entered Edinburgh on the sixteenth of May, and, on Saturday the seventeenth, the service of the Church, according to the English rite, was celebrated in the chapel royal. On the eighth of June, being the feast of Whitsunday, Bishop Andrews preached, and the Holy Communion was celebrated in the English form, the Archbishops of St. Andrews and Glasgow and several of the bishops being present.[2]

The parliament met at Edinburgh on the seventeenth of June. The Lords of the Articles having agreed to an act, by which whatever the king, with the advice of the archbishops, bishops, and a competent number of the ministers, should determine regarding the external government of the Church was to have the force of law, if not repugnant to the word of God, a protestation was drawn up and presented in name of several of the ministers who had assembled for the purpose. Three of those who took a leading part in this matter were summoned before the court of High Commission.

---

[1] Spottiswood, vol. iii. p. 236-238.
[2] Original Letters of the reign of James the Sixth, vol. ii. p. 496-500. Calderwood, vol. vii. p. 242-247. Spottiswood, vol. iii. pp. 238, 239. Lawson's History of the Episcopal Church of Scotland from the Reformation to the Revolution, p. 365-368.

Two of them were deprived; the third, David Calderwood, minister at Crailing, who on former occasions had distinguished himself by his opposition to the bishops, was treated with more severity. The king himself was present at his examination, and asked what moved him to protest. He answered that it was the article conferring the new powers on the king. "What fault was there in that?" asked James. "It cutteth off our general assemblies," was the answer. "Hear me, Mr. Calderwood," continued James, "I have been an older keeper of general assemblies than you. A general assembly serves to preserve doctrine in purity from error and heresy, the Church from schism, to make confessions of faith, to put up petitions to the king and parliament. But as for matters of order, rites, and things indifferent in church policy, they may be concluded by the king, with advice of the bishops, and a chosen number of ministers. Next, what is a general assembly but a competent number of ministers?" Calderwood answered, "As to the first point, Sir, a general assembly should serve, and our general assemblies have served, these fifty-six years, not only for preserving doctrine from error and heresy, the Church from schism, to make confessions of faith, and to put up petitions to the king or parliament, but also to make canons and constitutions of all rites and orders belonging to church policy. As for the second point—as by a competent number of ministers may be meant a general assembly, so also may be meant a fewer number of ministers convened than may make up a general assembly. It was ordained in a general assembly, with your majesty's own consent, your majesty being present, that there should be commissioners chosen out of every presbytery, not exceeding the number of three, to be sent to a general assembly, and so the competent number of ministers is already defined." "What needed farther," said the king, "but to have protested for a declarator what was meant by a competent number?" Calderwood answered, "In pleading for the liberty of the general assembly, we did that in effect." He was deprived, and ordered to be confined in the tolbooth of St. Andrews, till he should find caution to leave the kingdom.[1]

When the other acts were submitted to the estates for their

[1] Calderwood, vol. vii. p. 249-282. Spottiswood, vol. iii. p. 240-247.

ratification, the king, afraid of farther opposition, withdrew the obnoxious article. Several of the statutes agreed to at this parliament were of importance in connection with ecclesiastical matters. One of them regulated the mode of election of archbishops and bishops. It was declared that, when any see became vacant, the king should grant license to the dean and chapter to proceed to the election of a bishop, and that they should be bound to choose the person nominated by the king, such person being always an actual minister of the Church. On the election being assented to by his majesty, a mandate was to be issued to a competent number of the bishops of the province to proceed with the consecration of the bishop-elect.

This act, which gave the absolute right of nomination to the king, took away the ecclesiastical control over the appointment of bishops which had been secured by the agreement at Leith.

By another act, the deans and members of cathedral chapters were restored to their ancient manses, glebes, and possessions, which were for that purpose given up, so far as they remained with the crown. The same statute provided that the chapter of St. Andrews should consist of the Prior of Portmoak, who was also Principal of St. Leonard's College, as dean, the archdeacon, and the ministers of twenty-two parishes of the diocese therein specified, who were to discharge the functions of the former Prior and canons, except in regard to the election of an archbishop, which privilege was conferred on the eight bishops of the province, the Dean and Archdeacon of St. Andrews, and three other members of the chapter, the Bishop of Dunkeld being vicar-general for convening the electors. It was also declared that the Archbishop of Glasgow should be elected by the three bishops of his province—viz., the Bishops of Galloway, Argyll, and the Isles, and by the ordinary chapter of the metropolitan see, the Bishop of Galloway being convener of the electors, and the ancient and ordinary chapter of Glasgow retaining all its former rights and privileges, except that of election.

By another statute, a new chapter was established for the see of the Isles. The preamble bore that the ancient writs of the bishopric had been lost, so that it was not known how many dignitaries there were, or who were the members of the chapter, whereby a new foundation was rendered necessary. It was therefore enacted that the parson of Sorbie in Tyree, who was also vicar of Iona, should be dean, the parson of Rothsay, sub-dean, and that they, along with the parsons of four other churches in the diocese, should be the members of the convent and chapter.

Another act of the same parliament declared that the Principal of King's College, Aberdeen, should be dean, and the Sub-principal sub-chanter of the cathedral church of Aberdeen.[1]

After arranging that a general assembly should be called for the purpose of giving its sanction to the five articles which he had formerly agreed to withdraw, James returned to England in the beginning of August. The assembly met at St. Andrews on the twenty-fifth of November, and Lord Binning and others acted as royal commissioners in place of the Earl of Montrose, who excused himself on the ground of sickness. More opposition was made than the king and the bishops expected. The majority of the members resolved to delay coming to a final determination till another assembly, but they agreed to allow private Communion in cases of urgent necessity, and it was ordered that, in the administration of that sacrament, the ministers should give the bread and wine out of their own hands directly to the people.

When these proceedings were reported to the king, he was much displeased, and wrote angry letters to the two archbishops, commanding them to preach on Christmas-day, and enjoin the bishops also to do so, and forbidding any stipend to be paid to those ministers who had opposed the articles. This prohibition, however, was suspended at the request of the bishops, who promised to use every exertion at their diocesan synods to prevail on the ministers to comply with the king's wishes.[2]

The observance of the five holy-days having been enjoined by royal proclamation, on Easter-day, 1618, several of the bishops administered the Holy Communion in their cathedral churches, the people kneeling to receive the sacrament; and

---

[1] Acts of the Parliaments of Scotland, vol. iv. pp. 529, 530, 554, 555, 577.

[2] Original Letters of the reign of James the Sixth, vol. ii. p. 520-526. Calderwood, vol. vii. p. 284-286. Spottiswood, vol. iii. p. 248-252.

on Whitsunday some members of the privy council communicated at the chapel royal of Holyrood.[1]

Alexander Forbes, Bishop of Aberdeen, died on the fourteenth of December, 1617, and the king intimated his intention of appointing Patrick Forbes, minister at Keith, to the vacant see. The person thus selected was one of the most distinguished of the Scottish clergy. He was the eldest son of William Forbes, laird of Corse in Aberdeenshire, and was born at the castle of Corse on the twenty-fourth of August, 1564. He was educated at the grammar school of Stirling under Thomas Buchanan, a nephew of the celebrated poet, and afterwards at the University of Glasgow under Andrew Melville, who was his relative. When Melville removed to St Andrews, Forbes accompanied him, and, in common with most of the young students, zealously adopted the opinions of his master. He was with him during his banishment to England in 1584, and returned with him to Scotland in the following year. In 1589, he was married to Lucretia Spense, a daughter of the laird of Wormiston, and resided for some time in the neighbourhood of Montrose. On his father's death in 1598, he removed to the castle of Corse, where he continued to abide, pursuing his theological and literary studies, and discharging at the same time his duties as a Scottish baron.

During the course of years, the opinions of Forbes regarding ecclesiastical government were greatly modified. Retaining his strong attachment to the Protestant doctrines, he was disposed, like many other good men of that time, to acquiesce in the sovereign's claim to regulate the external polity of the Church, differing in this from his brother John, who was minister at Alford, and was banished for the part which he took in the Aberdeen assembly of 1605. In the beginning of the seventeenth century many parishes in the diocese of Aberdeen were destitute of ministers, and the barbarism of the people increased from the want of religious instruction. At the request of Bishop Blackburn and others, the laird of Corse preached for some time in the parish church near his own residence, to the great edification of the people, but declined to accept the office of pastor. On this being reported to Arch-

[1] Original Letters of the reign of James the Sixth, vol. ii. p. 562. Calderwood, vol. vii. pp. 297, 298.

bishop Gladstones, he ordered Forbes to abstain from preaching until he should be regularly admitted as a minister; and the primate's injunction was immediately obeyed. In February, 1610, Forbes wrote to King James, explaining the motives of his conduct; and the prudence and moderation with which he expressed himself laid the foundation of the favourable opinion which the king ever afterwards entertained of him.

In the following year, Forbes was induced to accept ordination, and to undertake the office of a parish minister by a circumstance which he viewed as a providential call. The minister at Keith, in the diocese of Murray, attempted to kill himself, and a wound which he inflicted proved mortal; but he survived for some time, and expressed deep penitence for his crime. Having been visited by the laird of Corse, the dying minister, who received much comfort from his exhortations, entreated him to become his successor in the parish, and so prevent, as far as possible, the evil consequences of the act which he himself had committed. The people and the neighbouring ministers earnestly joined in this request, and Forbes, yielding to their entreaties, was ordained, and became minister at Keith, being then in the forty-seventh year of his age.

On the death of Bishop Blackburn, the clergy and people of the diocese of Aberdeen were anxious to have Forbes for their bishop. They were disappointed at the time, but, at the next vacancy, he was judged by all the fittest person to succeed. On the twenty-seventh of January, 1618, the king intimated his choice to the Scottish bishops, by whom the intelligence was joyfully communicated to Forbes. He was as reluctant to accept the episcopal office as he had formerly been to become a parochial minister, and, in a letter addressed to Archbishop Spottiswood, mentioned his scruples and unwillingness. The letter is evidently the sincere expression of his feelings and convictions. It contains a reference to the opinions which he held respecting the episcopate, and the position of ecclesiastical affairs in Scotland at that time. "I am so far," he says, "from disallowing the office and degree of a bishop (as hereupon men might apprehend), that they being rightly elected, and defined with such moderation of place and power as may put restraint to excessive usurpation, and practising accordingly, I think it not only a tolerable, but even a

laudable and expedient policy in the Church, and very well consisting with God's written word, the only rule whereto all the affairs of his house should be levelled." He then explained the cause of his refusal: "This is that, my good lord, which maketh all my scruple, the present condition and course of things (and we cannot tell how far a further novation in our Church is intended) so peremptorily and impetuously urged on the one part, and so hardly received on the other, as betwixt these extremities and the undertaking of a bishopric, I see no option left to me but either to incur his majesty's displeasure, which is the rock under Christ I am loathest to strike on, or then to drive both myself and my ministry in such common distaste as I see not how henceforth it can be any more fruitful. I dispute not here of the points themselves; but I am persuaded, if so wise, so learned, and so religious a king, as God hath blessed us with, were fully and freely informed, or did thoroughly conceive the sad sequel of enforcing our Church, that neither in the points already proposed, nor in any which we fear yet to ensue for this intended conformity, would his majesty esteem any of such fruit or effect as therefore the state of a quiet Church should be marred, the minds of brethren, who for any bygone distraction were beginning again to warm in mutual love, should be of new again and almost desperately distracted, the hearts of many good Christians discouraged, the resolution of many weak ones shaken, matter of insulting ministered to Romanists, and to profane epicureans of a disdainful deriding of our whole profession.
. . . . . . If wherein our Church seemeth defective his majesty would so far pity our weakness, and tender our peace, as to enforce nothing but what first in a free and national council were determined, wherein his highness would neither make any man afraid with terror, nor pervert the judgment of any with hope of favour, then men may adventure to do service. But if things be so violently carried as no end may appear of bitter contention, neither any place left to men in office, but instead of procuring peace and reuniting the hearts of the brethren, to stir the coals of detestable debate; for me, I have no courage to be a partner in that work. I wish my heart's blood might extinguish the ungracious rising flame in our Church. But if I can do nothing for the quenching of

it, then I would be heartily sorry to add fuel thereto. And this it is, my very good lord, which only terrifieth me from undertaking that which otherwise, for the zeal of God's house, with all hazard and with all my heart I would embrace."

The Archbishop of St. Andrews entreated Forbes to accept the bishopric; and, his election having taken place, the dean and chapter, and the commissioners of presbyteries within the diocese, added their solicitations that he would obey the call which they had unanimously given. He finally yielded to their wishes, and, on the seventeenth of May, was consecrated at St. Andrews by the primate and the Bishops of Dunkeld and Brechin.[1]

The bishops, having found the clergy more conformable to their wishes at their several diocesan synods than when last convened in one body, obtained the king's license to summon another general assembly. It met at Perth, on the twenty-fifth of August, 1618. The Lord Binning, secretary of state, Lord Scone, and Lord Carnegie, were the royal commissioners, assisted by four assessors. The bishops, the ministers who were commissioners for presbyteries, a minister representing the University of St. Andrews, and several noblemen, barons, and commissioners of burghs, were present. The Bishop of Aberdeen preached on the morning of the first day of the assembly, and the Archbishop of St. Andrews on the forenoon. The sermon of the latter has been preserved. The text was from the sixteenth verse of the eleventh chapter of the First Epistle of St. Paul to the Corinthians, " But if any man seem to be contentious, we have no such custom, neither the Churches of God." Its subject was the consideration of the five articles for the establishment of which the assembly had been convened. In the very beginning of his discourse the primate admitted that the introduction of those changes was ordered by royal authority, that they were in themselves

[1] See Mr. C. Farquhar Shand's Biographical Memoir of Bishop Forbes, prefixed to the Spottiswood Society edition of his Funerals, p. xxv.-lxv., and the authorities there cited. See also the Funerals, p. 193-216, where the various documents connected with the election and consecration of Bishop Forbes shew how the recent statute regarding episcopal elections was carried out in practice. It appears from one of these records that a shadow of the ancient form of enthroning was kept up, but the only ceremony used was the delivery of a Bible by the archdeacon to the bishop.

indifferent, and that many persons, not without cause, were doubtful as to their expediency at that time. He added that himself and the other bishops would, if in their power, have avoided proposing such alterations, but that the choice now lay between the evil of introducing new rites and ceremonies, and the far greater evil of disobeying lawful authority; and what the Apostle says of contention he would say of disobedience—" We have no such custom, neither the Churches of God." Men ought to contend for the faith, and that earnestly, but to contend for matters of ceremony, as for some main point of religion, is to injure the truth of God.

After defining the nature of ecclesiastical ceremonies generally, and enforcing the duty of conformity to them when once established by authority, he entered upon an explanation and defence of the five articles. He observed that, as it was the duty of ministers to visit the sick and comfort them in other respects, there could be no reason why the Holy Communion, which is the seal of God's promises and a special means of binding up our communion with Christ, should be denied to them. It was now proposed that it should be given, not to all the sick, but to those only whose recovery was desperate, and as a comfort to the dying, not superstitiously as a viaticum. Baptism was to be administered in private in certain cases, not from an opinion of the absolute necessity of that sacrament, but because to withhold it was to bring Christ's ordinance into contempt. Confirmation was one of the most ancient customs of the Church, and had continued from the days of the Apostles. It was evident from all antiquity that the power of confirming had always belonged to the Bishop, although it did not follow from this that Confirmation was a greater sacrament than Baptism. In regard to the holy days which were to be enjoined, they were originally observed by all the Reformed Churches, and still were observed by most of them. Many objections had been made to the article which required kneeling as the most reverent gesture at receiving the Communion, but without any good cause. It was not meant by this to agree with the Papists; but some of those who opposed it seemed to differ little from the Arians. As Christians, they had learned to honour the Son as they honoured the Father, and he that honoured not the Son in every place, especially in the participation of the Holy Supper, should be to them as a Jew or a Pagan. "It is an excellent passage, that of St. Augustine upon the ninety-eighth Psalm, ' Nemo carnem illam manducat, nisi prius adoraverit': that is, no man can eat that flesh, unless first he have adored. For myself, I think sitting in the beginning was not evilly instituted, and since by our Church continued, for we may adore while we are sitting as well as kneeling; yet the gesture which becometh adoration best is that of bowing of the knee, and the irreligion of these times craves that we should put men more unto it than we do."

On the commencement of the proceedings, the primate assumed the moderator's chair, and, when one of the ministers requested that a free election to that office should take place, he answered that the synod was convened within his province, wherein he trusted, so long as he served, no man should take his place. It was asked whether all noblemen, barons, and ministers, who were present, had a right to vote. The archbishop answered that no minister could vote without a commission, but that a voice could not be denied to noblemen and barons who had come in obedience to his majesty's missives. The king's letter to the assembly was then read by Dr. Young, Dean of Winchester. It blamed the ministers severely for their proceedings at St. Andrews, declared that the king by his own authority alone had a right to enjoin the observance of the articles, and stated that he would be content with nothing save a direct simple acceptance of them. Much discussion took place which was continued during three days, partly in presence of the whole assembly, partly at a conference of particular members appointed to consider the articles. When the vote was taken, the question was put whether the assembly would receive or refuse the articles, and a proposal of one of the members that they should be voted for separately was rejected. The royal commissioners and their assessors, the bishops, the noblemen except one, the barons and commissioners of burghs, and a considerable number of ministers, agreed to the articles, the whole number of those so agreeing being eighty-six; one nobleman and forty-one ministers, or, according to another account, forty-five, voted against the articles; and four declined to express an opinion.

The five articles were the following:—

"1. Seeing we are commanded by God Himself, that, when we come to worship Him, we fall down and kneel before the Lord our Maker, and considering withal that there is no part of divine worship more heavenly and spiritual than is the holy receiving of the blessed Body and Blood of our Lord and Saviour, Jesus Christ, like as the most humble and reverent gesture of our body in our meditation and the lifting up of our hearts best becometh so divine and sacred an action; therefore, notwithstanding that our Church hath used since the Reformation of religion to celebrate the Holy Communion to the people sitting, by reason of the great abuse of kneeling used in the idolatrous worship of the sacrament by the Papists, yet seeing all memory of by-past superstitions is past, in reverence of God, and in due regard of so divine a mystery, and in remembrance of so mystical an union as we are made partakers of, the assembly thinketh good that the blessed sacrament be celebrated hereafter meekly and reverently upon their knees.

"2. If any good Christian visited with long sickness, and known to the pastor by reason of his present infirmity to be unable to resort to the church for receiving the Holy Communion, or, being sick, shall declare to his pastor upon his conscience that he thinks his sickness to be deadly, and shall earnestly desire to receive the same in his house, the minister shall not deny him so great a comfort, lawful warning being given to him the night before, and that there be three or four of good religion and conversation, free of all lawful impediments, present with the sick person to communicate with him, who must also provide a convenient place in his house, and all things necessary for the reverent administration thereof, according to the order prescribed in the Church.

"3. The minister shall often admonish the people that they defer not the baptizing of infants any longer than the next Lord's day after the child be born, unless, upon a great and reasonable cause declared to the minister and by him approved, the same be continued. As also they shall warn them that, without great cause, they procure not their children to be baptized at home in their houses; but where great need shall compel them to baptize in private houses, (in which case the minister shall not refuse to do it upon the knowledge of the great need, and being timely required thereto,) then baptism shall be administered after the same form as it should have been in the congregation: and the minister shall, the next Lord's-day after any such private baptism, declare in the church that the infant was so baptized, and therefore ought to be received as one of the true flock of Christ's fold.

" 4. Forasmuch as one of the special means for staying the increase of Popery and settling of true religion in the hearts of people is, that a special care be taken of young children, their education, and how they are catechized, which in time of the primitive Church most carefully was attended, as being most profitable to cause young children in their tender years drink in the knowledge of God and his religion, but is now altogether neglected in respect of the great abuse and errors which crept into the Popish Church by making thereof a sacrament of Confirmation; therefore, that all superstition built thereupon may be rescinded, and that the matter itself, being most necessary for the education of youth, may be reduced to the primitive integrity, it is thought good that the minister in every parish shall catechize all young children of eight years of age, and see that they have the knowledge, and be able to make the rehearsal of the Lord's Prayer, Belief, and Ten Commandments, with answers to the questions in the small Catechism used in our Church, and that every bishop, in his visitation, shall censure the minister who shall be found remiss therein; and the said bishops shall cause the said children to be presented before them, and bless them with prayer for the increase of their knowledge, and the continuance of God's heavenly graces with every one of them.

" 5. As we abhor the superstitious observation of festival days by the Papists, and detest all licentious and profane abuses thereof by the common sort of professors, so we think that the inestimable benefits received from God, by our Lord Jesus Christ, his Birth, Passion, Resurrection, Ascension, and sending down of the Holy Ghost, were commendably and godly remembered at certain particular days and times by the whole Church of the world, and may also be now; therefore, the assembly ordaineth that every minister should upon these days have the commemoration of the foresaid inestimable benefits, and make choice of several and pertinent texts of Scripture, and frame their doctrine and exhortations thereto; and rebuke all superstitious observation and licentious profanation thereof."

On the twenty-first of October, the acts of the Perth assembly were ratified by the privy council.[1]

[1] Lindsay's True Narrative of the Proceedings in the Perth Assembly, p. 19-72. Spottiswood, vol. iii. p. 252-257. Calderwood, vol. vii. p. 303-339. Original Letters of the reign of James the Sixth, vol. ii. p. 567-583. The primate's sermon is reprinted from Dr. Lindsay's work in the Spottiswood Miscellany, vol. i. p. 65-87.

CHAPTER XLVI.

FROM THE PERTH ASSEMBLY OF AUGUST, 1618, TO THE DEATH OF KING JAMES VI. IN MARCH, 1625.

Synod of Dort—Death of Bishop Cowper—Scottish Ordinal of 1620—The Perth Articles ratified in Parliament—Dissatisfaction in consequence of the Perth Articles—Popular feeling at Edinburgh—John Cameron, Principal of the College of Glasgow—Death of Andrew Melville—His character—Death of John Welsh—English Service introduced at St. Andrews—Dr. William Forbes—His teaching at Aberdeen—His removal to Edinburgh—His dispute with the Puritans there—His return to Aberdeen—Death of King James—His character and ecclesiastical policy.

THE Synod of Dort, which had been called together to settle the controversies between the Calvinists and Arminians, met in November, 1618, and continued its sittings till April in the following year. It was attended by deputies from all the Churches of the Reformed, strictly so called, except those of France. King James sent thither four English divines, and Walter Balcanquhal, son of the minister of Edinburgh of the same name, as representatives of the British Churches, but these envoys had no commission of any kind beyond the sovereign's appointment.[1]

William Cowper, Bishop of Galloway, died on the fifteenth of February, 1619. He was an eloquent preacher, and, in the opinion of Dr. M'Crie, his discourses are probably superior to any sermons of that age. He never recovered the popularity which he enjoyed before he accepted the bishopric; and this circumstance, and the libels with which the Puritans unceasingly attacked him, weighed too much on his mind. Spottiswood, while recording his ability and his goodness, condemns his anxiety for popular applause. He left an account of his own life, in which he mentions his deliberate

[1] Collier, vol. vii. p. 408-416.

opinion regarding the episcopal office, and speaks of his trials in the discharge of it. "I esteem it," he said, "a lawful, ancient, and necessary government. I see not, nor have I read of any Church which wanted it before our time; only the abuses of it by pride, tyranny, and idleness, have brought it into misliking. From those evils I pray the Lord preserve his servants that now are, or hereafter shall be called to these places. But there is no reason why a thing good in itself should be condemned or rejected for the evil of abuse, for no good thing at all would be retained in the Church; and in this calling, how I have walked, and what my care was to advance the Gospel, I trust I shall not nor do want witnesses. In this estate I now live, my soul alway in my hand, ready to be offered to my God. Where or what kind of death God hath prepared for me I know not, but sure I am there can be no evil death to him that liveth in Christ, nor sudden death to a Christian pilgrim, who, as Job says, 'every day waits for his change.' Yea many a day have I sought it with tears, not out of impatience, distrust, or perturbation, but being weary of sin, and fearful to fall into it. Concerning those who have been my enemies without cause, and charged me with many wrongful imputations from which my conscience clears me, excusing me of these things, love of gain and glory, and such like, whereof they accused me, the Lord lay it not to their charge. I go to my Father, and seek his blessing to them, to rectify their judgments, and moderate their affections, with true piety from faith and love."

On Bishop Cowper's death, the Bishop of Brechin was translated to Galloway, and Dr. David Lindsay, minister at Dundee, was nominated to the see of Brechin, and consecrated at St. Andrews, on the twenty-third of November.[1]

During the vacancy of the bishopric of Galloway, the deanery of the chapel royal was transferred from that see to Dunblane. This alteration was ratified by parliament in 1621. The emoluments of the dean and prebendaries were

[1] See Spottiswood, vol. iii. p. 258; Calderwood, vol. vii. pp. 349-351, 396; Preface to Original Letters of the reign of James the Sixth, pp. xxxvii. xxxix.; Keith's Catalogue, pp. 167, 280; M'Crie's Life of Melville, vol. ii. p. 316. See also Lawson's History, p. 324-334, where an account is given of Bishop Cowper, derived from his own memoir and the writings of Mr. Scott of Perth,

derived from the remains of the magnificent foundation of King James IV. The chapel itself, however, was no longer at Stirling, but within the palace of Holyrood—in the same place, probably, which had been used as a private chapel from the time of Queen Mary's return to Scotland.[1]

In 1610, Andrew Knox, Bishop of the Isles, had been translated to the see of Raphoe, in the province of Armagh, but it is supposed that he continued to retain both bishoprics for some years. His son, Thomas Knox, was appointed to the see of the Isles in February, 1619.[2]

Among the directions issued by the king, and approved of by the bishops and others of the clergy in 1611, one was, that an uniform order should be observed in the admission of ministers, and that a form thereof should be printed and followed by every bishop. It was probably in consequence of this resolution that an Ordinal was printed by authority in 1620, entitled, "The form and manner of ordaining Ministers, and consecrating Archbishops, and Bishops, used in the Church of Scotland." As the order of Deacon had not yet been restored in Scotland, those known by that name being mere laymen, provision was only made for the ordination of the two highest degrees of the clergy.

The form for the ordination of ministers was similar to the English office for the ordering of priests, and was evidently framed on its model. After sufficient trial of the qualifications of the person to be admitted, on the day appointed for the ordination a sermon was to be preached declaring the duties and office of ministers, their necessity in the Church, and how the people ought to esteem them and their vocation. After the sermon, the Archdeacon, or his deputy, was to present the person to be admitted to the Bishop, who was then directed to enquire into his qualifications, and to address the people in words almost the same as those of the English ordinal. The oath of the king's supremacy having been administered, questions were put to the person to be ordained,—and answers were required, also similar to the English form. In giving

---

[1] Original Letters of the reign of James the Sixth, vol. ii. p. 721, note. Acts of the Parliaments of Scotland, vol. iv. p. 649.

[2] Original Letters of the reign of James the Sixth, vol. i. pp. 427, 428, and preface, p. xlii. Book of the Thanes of Cawdor, p. 246.

ordination, the Bishop and the ministers present were to lay their hands on the head of the person to be admitted, kneeling before them, and the Bishop was then to say, "In the Name of God, and by the authority committed unto us by the Lord Jesus Christ, we give unto thee power and authority to preach the word of God, to minister his holy sacraments, and exercise discipline in such sort as is committed unto ministers by the order of our Church; and God, the Father of our Lord Jesus Christ, who has called thee to the office of a watchman over his people, multiply his graces with thee, illuminate thee with his Holy Spirit, comfort and strengthen thee in all virtue, govern and guide thy ministry, to the praise of his holy name, to the propagation of Christ's kingdom, to the comfort of his Church, and to the discharge of thy own conscience in the day of the Lord Jesus; to whom, with the Father and the Holy Ghost, be all honour, praise, and glory, now and ever, Amen." The Bishop was next to deliver the Bible into the hands of the person admitted, saying, "This is the Book of Scripture, which thou must study continually, and make the ground and rule of thy doctrine and living."

The office was concluded with an exhortation by the Bishop, the singing of the twenty-third Psalm, and a prayer of thanksgiving. Before the ordination, an oath of canonical obedience to the ordinary, an oath against simony, an oath of residence, and an oath against granting leases of the benefice, were to be administered. Neither the hymn Veni Creator Spiritus, nor the Litany was used, and there was no celebration of the Holy Communion.

At the consecration of a Bishop, three bishops at least were to be present, and four at the consecration of an Archbishop. After public prayers, and a sermon on the office and duty of a Bishop, and a call to those to come forward who had any objections to the life or doctrine of the prelate to be ordained, the bishop elect was to be presented to the Archbishop, or to another bishop acting by his commission. The king's mandate for the consecration was then read, and the oath of the king's supremacy, and, in the case of a bishop, the oath of obedience to the Metropolitan, were administered. The Archbishop, sitting in his chair, was then to put questions to the bishop-elect, and to require answers, similar to those in the English ordinal. The Archbishop was next to say a prayer, the same as in that formulary, and the Veni Creator Spiritus was to be sung. An address by the Archbishop to the congregation followed, after which the Archbishop and bishops present were to lay their hands on the head of the elected bishop, the Archbishop saying, " We, by the authority given us of God, and of his Son, the Lord Jesus Christ, give unto thee the power of ordination, imposition of hands, and correction of manners, within the dioceses whereunto thou art or hereafter shalt be called. And God Almighty be with thee in all thy ways, increase his grace unto thee, and guide thy ministry to the praise of his holy name, and the comfort of his Church, Amen." After this, the Archbishop was to deliver the Bible to the bishop-elect, using words almost the same as those in the English office. The Archbishop and bishops, the newly consecrated bishop, and others present, were then to receive the Holy Communion.

There was appended to the form an advertisement regarding the translation of bishops, setting forth that in such a case no new consecration was to be made, but the bishop or archbishop elect was to be confirmed, and an order given to the archdeacon of the diocese for his induction.[1]

A considerable number of the ministers refused to obey the Perth articles, and several of those who were most active in resisting were suspended or deprived by the court of High Commission. The dispute was carried on in a series of controversial works, the chief writer on one side being Calderwood, on the other, the Bishop of Brechin. The king, finding that every effort was made by the opponents of the articles to stir up the nation against them, resolved to have their authority confirmed by parliament. The estates of the kingdom met at Edinburgh, in July, 1621. The Marquis of Hamilton was the royal commissioner, and succeeded, with some difficulty, in obtaining the desired ratification, seventy-eight voting for it, and fifty-one against it. In the minority were a considerable number of the lesser barons and the burgesses; all the bishops and most of the peers were in the majority. But though the articles were

[1] See the Ordinal, as reprinted in the Miscellany of the Wodrow Society, vol. i. p. 597-615.

now sanctioned by the highest civil as well as ecclesiastical authority, the opposition still continued, and the bishops were obliged in many cases to connive at their partial observance, or their entire disuse. The recusant ministers shewed themselves prepared to undergo any suffering in defence of their principles. Their conduct would call forth more sympathy, if it had not frequently been marked by the want of Christian charity, and even of the ordinary courtesies of society.[1]

The measures of King James had all along been opposed by the party of which Melville was formerly the leader, but, for many years, the nation generally acquiesced in them without shewing much feeling on the one side or the other. This admits of an easy explanation. There was no attempt to interfere either with doctrine or worship; and in regard to church government the people were indifferent, sometimes even shewing a preference for the supremacy of the sovereign to that of the ecclesiastical courts. A great change, however, had begun with the enactment of the Perth articles. There was now for the first time an alteration in the forms of worship to which the people had become accustomed. Three of the articles gave little offence. Private Baptism and Private Communion were simply privileges to those who were willing to avail themselves of them, and Confirmation seems never to have been insisted on. But the observance of the five holy-days was enjoined by the privy council, and caused much discontent. Still more offensive was the article which required kneeling at the Communion. The posture thus commanded was new to all, and, in the opinion of many who did not belong to the extreme Presbyterian party, it was supposed to be connected with the Roman doctrine of Transubstantiation. Religious persons were offended during the most sacred part of Christian worship, and those who were anxious to find an opportunity of assailing royal and episcopal authority were now able to identify themselves with

---

[1] Spottiswood, vol. iii. p. 261-263. Calderwood, vol. vii. p. 488-504. Original Letters of the reign of James the Sixth, vol. ii. p. 656-662. Acts of the Parliaments of Scotland, vol. iv. pp. 596, 597. Most of the works written in connection with the Perth articles are mentioned in a list appended to Dr. Irving's Life of Calderwood—Lives of Scottish Writers, vol. i. p. 318-322.

some of the most devout and conscientious of their countrymen.

Edinburgh continued to be the head-quarters of Presbyterianism, although the ministers were now obedient to the sovereign; and there the changes excited much dissatisfaction. At Easter, 1619, many persons deserted the churches in the town, and resorted to those in the neighbourhood. Calderwood asserts that the ministers had promised to allow the people to sit, stand, or kneel, at the Communion, as they might think best, but that at the celebration they used all means in their power to make them kneel. "Some," he says, "kneeled, but with shedding of tears for grief. Cold and graceless were the Communions, and few were the communicants." "In some churches," he adds, "the people went out, and left the minister alone; in some, when the minister would have them to kneel, the ignorant and simple sort cried out, 'The danger, if any be, light upon your own soul, and not upon ours.' Some, when they could not get the sacrament sitting, departed, and besought God to be judge between them and the minister."

The discontented party at Edinburgh, not satisfied with deserting the churches during the celebration of the Communion, or with refusing to kneel when present, began to hold private meetings at other times, at which the deprived and suspended ministers officiated. These meetings were denounced by the clergy as conventicles, and their supporters as Brownists and Anabaptists; and the frequenting of them was forbidden by royal proclamation.

The feeling so prevalent in the capital was shared by many in the south-western counties and in Fife. In the other principal towns, and in the central and northern provinces generally, there was little resistance to the articles. The citizens of Perth and Dundee appear to have made no complaints; those of St Andrews were gradually becoming attached to the hierarchy, the restoration of which added to their importance; and at Aberdeen the influence of the bishop and the university, aided by old prepossessions, caused the changes not only to be submitted to but to be welcomed. Even in the West the prevalence of extreme Presbyterian opinions was not universal. At Glasgow, except in the university, there was no marked opposition; while Paisley, at this time, is described as "a nest of Papists."[1]

King James took a great interest in the universities, and endeavoured to prevail on men of ability to fill the highest offices in them. He had another motive for this in addition to his love of learning; he was thereby enabled to select those who were most disposed to aid in carrying out his ecclesiastical reforms. St. Andrews was safely left to the superintendence of the primate, and Aberdeen to that of Bishop Forbes. At the time of the Perth assembly, Robert Boyd, son of James Boyd, titular Archbishop of Glasgow, was Principal of the College of Glasgow. He was a learned and good man, but he had not inherited his father's love for Episcopacy. He was compelled to resign his office in 1622, and John Cameron was appointed in his place. The new principal was a native of Glasgow, and was educated in that city, but had long resided in France. His knowledge was very great, especially in the Greek and Latin languages, and none of the many Scotsmen in the continental universities possessed a higher character as a scholar and a theologian. He was a zealous advocate of the royal prerogative, was favourably disposed to Episcopacy and the Perth articles, and had even begun to question the authority of Calvin on grace and free-will. It was unfortunate for the objects which James had so much at heart, that Cameron, who appears to have been of a restless disposition, resigned his office within a twelvemonth, and returned to France, where he died in 1625. He had the gift of attracting the warmest devotion of his pupils, and, brief as his sojourn

---

[1] See Calderwood, vol. vii. pp. 359, 360, 4444-47, 449, 611-614; Original Letters of the reign of James the Sixth, vol. ii. pp. 626, 627; Row, p. 438. The Autobiography of Robert Blair throws considerable light on the state of Scotland in the latter years of the reign of James. Referring to the period after the Glasgow assembly of 1610, the writer says (Life of Robert Blair, Wodrow Society ed. p. 12), "At this time I observed little controversy in religion in the Kirk of Scotland; for though there were bishops, yet they took little upon them, and so were very little opposed until Perth assembly." It was not uncommon for persons to receive the Communion at an early age. Blair was a communicant in his twelfth year, and Livingstone communicated for the first time when at school, between his tenth and fourteenth year; see Life of Robert Blair, pp. 6, 7, and Select Biographies, edited for the Wodrow Society, vol. i. p. 132. In connection with the same circumstance, Blair mentions that "it was then a generally received opinion that the sacrament behoved to be received fasting."

was at the Scottish university, it appears to have left a permanent impression on many. It was from him that Baillie derived those opinions in regard to royal and episcopal authority, which made him shrink for a considerable time from fully adopting the principles of the Covenanters.[1]

In the year 1622, when the cause of Presbyterianism seemed most hopeless, Andrew Melville died in exile. He had been released from the Tower in 1611, through the intercession of the Duke of Bouillon, but not being allowed to return to Scotland, he accepted the office of professor of divinity in the University of Sedan. At that place he spent the rest of his life. The exact date of his decease, and the particular events of his later years, have not been accurately ascertained. His nephew James had died at Berwick, in 1614.[2]

The political and ecclesiastical character of Andrew Melville can best be judged from the part he took in the transactions of the time. He was more fitted to be the head of a college than the chief of a great party. The influence which he had acquired by his zeal and ability was frequently lost by his arrogance and want of temper. In prosperity he shewed little moderation, but in adversity he was patient, constant, and courageous. His private life was upright and irreproachable, and, in his intercourse with his nephew and the familiar friends who shared his opinions, he shewed a tenderness of feeling, and a hearty, cheerful sympathy, contrasting strongly with his austere bearing towards others.

[1] See Irving's Lives of Scottish Writers, vol. i. p. 333-340; Original Letters of the reign of James the Sixth, vol. ii. p. 692; Life of Robert Blair, p. 37-46; Baillie's Letters, Laing's ed. vol. i. pp. 53, 189.

[2] M'Crie's Life of Melville, vol. ii. pp. 411-421, 440, 458. Archbishop Spottiswood, after mentioning the death of Melville (History, vol. iii. p. 183), adds, "Whilst I am writing this, there cometh to my mind the hard and uncharitable dealing that he and his faction used towards Patrick, sometime Archbishop of St. Andrews, who not content to have persecuted that worthy man in his life, made him, a long time after his death, the subject of their sermons; interpreting the miseries whereunto he was brought to be the judgment of God inflicted upon him for withstanding their courses of discipline. If now one should take the like liberty, and say, that God, to whom the bishop at his dying did commend his cause, had taken revenge of him who was the chief instrument of his trouble, it might be as probably spoken, and with some more likelihood, than that which they blasted forth against the dead bishop. But away with such rash and bold conceits; the love of God either to causes or persons is not to be measured by the external and outward accidents."

The Presbyterian party seemed now to be left without a leader. Their chief men had been removed by death, imprisonment, or banishment. Walter Balcanqual died in 1616. The decease of John Welsh, who had come over from the Continent, took place at London, in the same year with that of Melville. A story, first published by Dr. M'Crie, containing a minute account of an interview between King James and Welsh's wife, a daughter of John Knox, at which she is said to have petitioned the king to permit her husband's return to Scotland, rests on very doubtful authority. John Forbes was still in exile. Calderwood, on being released from confinement, lurked for some years in Scotland, and afterwards retired to Holland, where he wrote his largest controversial treatise, the "Altare Damascenum." Bruce was allowed to remain in Scotland sometimes at his own house, at other times in a mitigated form of banishment at Inverness.[1]

In January, 1623, in terms of an order sent by the king, the regular use of the Morning and Evening Service of the

[1] See Calderwood, vol. vii. pp. 219, 511, 583; M'Crie's Life of Knox, p. 372; Life of John Forbes, prefixed to his Records touching the estate of the Kirk, p. xlix.— lii.; Wodrow's Life of Bruce, p. 124-133. The earliest, and what really seems to be the only authority, for the alleged conversation between King James and the wife of Welsh, is a manuscript "account of several passages in the lives of some eminent men in the nation, not recorded in any history," written by a minister, named Robert Trail, and "inserted in the heart of a common-place book, containing notes of sermons, &c., written by him when a student of divinity at St. Andrews between 1659 and 1663." "He received the account from aged persons, and says that the conference between King James and Mrs. Welsh 'is current to this day in the mouths of many.'" Dr. M'Crie adds, that he had seen the same story in Wodrow's MS. Collections. Calderwood, who was careful in collecting every story to the discredit of King James, says nothing on this subject; and Kirkton, who wrote a Life of Welsh, and was himself connected with Knox's family, is also silent. Compare M'Crie's Life of Knox, p. 372; Calderwood, vol. vii. p. 511; and Select Biographies, edited for the Wodrow Society, vol. i. pp. 41, 42. There is an evident mis-statement in the narrative. Knox is there said to have left only three children, all daughters. It is well known that he left also two sons, but, if that circumstance had been mentioned, a chief point of the story would have been lost. Legends of this description are very common in the ecclesiastical history of the sixteenth and seventeenth centuries. Dr. M'Crie, who has given currency to a considerable number of them, is almost always careful to mention the sources of his information; but those who copy from him generally convert a tradition of more or less probability into a well ascertained and undoubted fact, and suppress the references which would enable their readers to judge for themselves.

Church of England began in the chapel of St. Mary's College, St. Andrews, where the students of the university attended.[1]

Alexander Douglas, Bishop of Murray, died in May, 1623, and was succeeded by John Guthrie, one of the ministers of Edinburgh, who was consecrated during the following autumn.[2]

A short time before Easter, 1624, a commotion arose at Edinburgh, originating in the Perth articles, but mixed up with the dissatisfaction excited among the Puritans of that city by the doctrines of one of their ministers, Dr. William Forbes. It could hardly have failed that the teaching of this eminent theologian should have displeased the inhabitants of the capital, to whose opinions he was in every respect so much opposed. This will best be explained by a brief account of his previous life. His father was Thomas Forbes, a burgess of Aberdeen, descended from the family of Corsindae; his mother was sister to Dr. James Cargill, an eminent physician in the same city. He was born at Aberdeen in the year 1585, and educated at the grammar school, and afterwards at the college there, recently founded by George, Earl Marischal. In his twenty-first year he went abroad in order to complete his education, and, after residing for some time in Poland, studied in several of the universities of Germany and Holland, where he acquired the friendship of Scaliger, Grotius, and other distinguished scholars. Leaving the Continent, he paid a visit to Oxford, and then returned at the end of five years to his native city. Having been ordained, probably by Bishop Blackburn, he became minister, first at Alford and afterwards at Monymusk, and in November, 1616, was appointed one of the ministers of St. Nicholas' church, in the burgh of Aberdeen. In the following year he was created doctor of divinity, and in 1618 was present at the Perth assembly, where he was selected to defend the lawfulness of kneeling at the Communion against the objections of its opponents.

The opinions of Dr. Forbes went far beyond those maintained by most of the bishops. He was favourable to the

[1] Calderwood, vol. vii. p. 569.
[2] Keith's Catalogue, p. 152. Original Letters of the reign of James the Sixth, vol. ii. p. 714. Calderwood, vol. vii. p. 580.

restoration of various primitive doctrines and practices which hitherto had found few supporters in Scotland. He even believed that the differences between the Church of Rome and the Protestants, in some important points, were more nominal than real, and capable of being reconciled without much difficulty. During the year 1618, a formal dispute took place at Aberdeen between him and Andrew Aidie, Principal of Marischal College, regarding the lawfulness of prayers for the dead; and it shews how far the ancient doctrines had already been received in the theological schools of Aberdeen, that Aidie was looked upon with suspicion for maintaining the negative opinion in the controversy. In connection with this discussion, the Bishop of Aberdeen wrote to the king, that his majesty had not " a more learned, sound, sanctified, and diligent divine " in his kingdom than Dr. Forbes. Aidie, being in various respects not well qualified for the office which he held, was induced to resign, and Forbes was appointed his successor as principal of the college.

In the end of the year 1621, Dr. Forbes was chosen one of the ministers of Edinburgh. He was reluctant to leave Aberdeen, and his fellow-citizens were as unwilling to lose their pastor; but it was thought expedient for the good of the Church that divines of approved ecclesiastical principles should be placed in the congregations of the capital, which had so long furnished leaders to the Presbyterian party. He therefore submitted, and was duly instituted to his new office. His doctrines, which were received with favour or without opposition at Aberdeen, excited the strongest dislike among many of the citizens of Edinburgh, and he became involved in frequent controversies with the disaffected, which finally excited general attention on the occasion which has been referred to.[1]

Dr. Forbes had strenuously enforced the duty of submission to the Perth articles, not only as enjoined by authority, but as sanctioned by the practice of the universal Church. He

[1] See Life of Bishop William Forbes, prefixed to his Considerationes Modestæ et Pacificæ, ed. 1658; Garden's Life of Dr. John Forbes, in the Amsterdam edition of that author's works, p. 19; Original Letters of the reign of James the Sixth, vol. ii. pp. 589, 590, 634; Selections from the Ecclesiastical Records of Aberdeen, p. 85; Lindsay's Perth Assembly, p. 62; and Calderwood, vol. vii. pp. 516, 542, 543, 571, 572.

had taught that Episcopacy was not an institution of human appointment, but a divine ordinance, founded on the word of God, the practice of the Apostles, and the authority of the primitive Church. These doctrines must have been very displeasing to many of his hearers, but, when he also maintained that several of the points in dispute with the Roman Catholics, especially those regarding Justification, were capable of being reconciled with the doctrines of the Reformed Church, the popular feeling became excited. The usage of making periodical inquisition into the character and teaching of the ministers was still kept up at Edinburgh. The town council, the kirk session, and the citizens, assembled for that purpose in March, 1624, and two burgesses, a butcher and a merchant, objected to the teaching of Dr. Forbes. He peremptorily refused to submit to the judgment of his own flock; and the other ministers, encouraged probably by his example, denied that the people had any right to examine into their doctrine, although they had hitherto, for form's sake, allowed the old custom to continue. The citizens, on the other hand, maintained that, as God's people, they had a right to try the doctrine of their pastors, even as the inhabitants of Berea had tried the teaching of St. Paul and compared it with the Scriptures. They farther proceeded to demand that the Communion should be administered in the manner used before the Perth assembly.

The Communion was to be celebrated on Easter-day, the twenty-eighth of March; and, on the previous Thursday, Dr. Forbes censured some of the elders and deacons who had intimated their intention not to be present. The conversation which took place between them is mentioned by Calderwood, but the accuracy of his report cannot be relied on. It is very probable, however, that Forbes rebuked his parishioners with considerable severity. The chief person among them was William Rigg, one of the magistrates of the town, to whom Forbes said that he had need to be catechized himself in place of admonishing his teacher.

The ministers having complained of the disorderly proceedings of the people, Rigg and five other burgesses were summoned before a committee of the privy council, consisting of the Chancellor, the Archbishop of St. Andrews, and others specially named by the king to inquire into the matter. Rigg was ordered to be warded in Blackness, and various punishments were inflicted on his associates.

It was the wish of Forbes to convince opponents by gentler methods than those which were used to vindicate his authority. His learning and eloquence proved insufficient for the purpose, and, finding also that his health was suffering, he resigned his charge, and returned to Aberdeen, where he resumed his former pastoral office, to the great joy of the clergy and people.[1]

On the twenty-seventh of March, 1625, King James died at Theobald's. The unfavourable points of this sovereign's character are very obvious, and have been dwelt upon by most historians. His good qualities have also been admitted both by the writers of his own day and by those of succeeding times. But the great improvement which his government effected in the condition of Scotland has seldom been sufficiently acknowledged. When he grew up to manhood, he found his kingdom torn by civil dissensions, his people discontented and miserable, and the authority of the law utterly set at nought. At his death he left his subjects quiet and prosperous, and the country accustomed to the steady administration of justice. The wild borderers had become an obedient and orderly peasantry; the inhabitants of the Highlands and the remotest Isles had begun to learn that there was a power above their chiefs by which they could be protected or punished; the clergy no longer claimed exemption from obedience to the laws by which their fellow subjects were governed; and the proudest nobles had been taught by severe examples that rank was not an immunity for crime. On the other hand, much evil had been done for which the king himself was chiefly responsible. Having been successful in repressing aristocratical tyranny, he had exceeded his lawful prerogatives, and assumed to himself and his council an authority which he had no right to exercise without the consent of parliament. So also in the government of the Church, in room of the ecclesiastical democracy of the ministers, he had claimed for the crown a sort of metropolitan au-

[1] Calderwood, vol. vii. p. 596-620. Spottiswood, vol. iii. pp. 268, 269. Original Letters of the reign of James the Sixth, pp. 740-745, 748-756. Life of Bishop William Forbes, prefixed to the Considerationes Modestæ et Pacificæ.

thority, by virtue of which all matters of external order, the regulation of rites and ceremonies, and the appointment of offices for divine worship, were subjected to the control of the sovereign. It was through this usurped power that some of the most important of the ecclesiastical changes were effected; and so it came about that the very restorations, which in themselves were good and praiseworthy, became inseparably connected, in the minds of the Scottish people, with the unconstitutional means by which they were introduced.

CHAPTER XLVII.

FROM THE DEATH OF KING JAMES VI. IN MARCH, 1625, TO THE RATIFICATION OF THE BOOK OF CANONS IN MAY, 1635.

Accession of Charles I.—Ecclesiastical instructions issued by the King—Arrangement in regard to Tithes—David Dickson—Religious movement in the West of Scotland—Robert Blair—John Livingstone—Voyage of Blair and Livingstone—The King's journey to Scotland—His Coronation—Meeting of Parliament—Service at the Chapel Royal—Foundation of the see of Edinburgh—Dr. William Forbes, Bishop of Edinburgh—His sermon before the King—His death—His character and opinions—His writings—Archbishop Spottiswood appointed Chancellor of Scotland—Patrick Forbes, Bishop of Aberdeen—His diocesan administration—His restoration of the University of Aberdeen—His illness and death—His character—Ratification of the Book of Canons.

CHARLES, the only surviving son of James VI., was proclaimed King of Scotland at the cross of Edinburgh, on the thirty-first of March.

Before the late king's decease, arrangements had been made for dividing the town of Edinburgh into four parishes, each to be provided with two ministers; and these were carried through and received the royal sanction soon after the accession of Charles. The ministers were to be chosen, not by the people, but by the magistrates and town council; and they were to be presented to the Archbishop of St. Andrews, the ordinary of the diocese, for collation. The king having required that the usage of the people to try and censure their ministers should be given up, the magistrates and town council expressed their willingness to obey, but remarked that the practice had been introduced at the Reformation, and enjoined by the superintendents. The written note made on this by the king might have been sufficient to dispel the hopes which the Presbyterians entertained of a change of ecclesiastical policy in the new reign. It was in these words:—" The conclusion of this answer satisfies the article, but the narrative, if it be true, sheweth what a Reformation that was, and how evil advised; yet we believe not that either superintendent or minister would ever subject their doctrine to the trial of the popular voice: this is an Anabaptistical frenzy."[1]

In July, 1626, the king sent to the archbishops and bishops certain instructions regarding ecclesiastical affairs, chiefly in reference to the Perth articles. By these, permission was to be given to such ministers as had scruples about the articles, and had been admitted before the Perth assembly, to forbear observing them, provided they did not openly speak against them, or dissuade others from their observance, or refuse the Communion to any who wished to partake of it kneeling, or receive any from other congregations without testimonials from their pastors. The banished, imprisoned, and suspended ministers were to be restored on similar conditions, but all who had been admitted subsequently to the synod were to be obliged to observe the articles. The bishops were enjoined to plant schools in every parish, and to cause the ministers catechize the people weekly.[2]

King Charles continued in other respects to pursue his father's ecclesiastical policy; nor did he neglect to attend carefully to Scottish affairs, even during the distraction caused in the early years of his reign by his disputes with the English House of Commons. James had greatly improved the temporal condition of the clergy, and had secured moderate endowments for several of the bishops by purchasing portions of the alienated church lands with his own money. Charles restored to the two metropolitan sees a farther share of their old endowments, by acquiring the abbacy of Arbroath from the Marquis of Hamilton, and the lordship of Glasgow from the Duke of Lennox. Various estates were bought in the same way and given to others of the bishoprics; and it is said that, encouraged by these voluntary surrenders, he contemplated a formal revocation of all the grants of church lands made during his father's minority. Burnet states that, in the third year of the king's reign, the Earl of Nithsdale was

[1] Original Letters of the reign of James the Sixth, vol. ii. p. 780-791.
[2] Balfour, vol. ii. p. 142-145.

sent down to Scotland, with a commission to obtain gratuitous surrenders, but that he was intimidated by the threatened opposition of the chief impropriators, and returned to court without executing his instructions. The historian adds that, if Nithsdale had persevered, it was the intention of the nobles opposed to him to massacre him and his friends. This last statement, however, would require better evidence, than he gives, to support it.[1]

The king was more successful in accomplishing his design of procuring a better maintenance for the clergy and relieving the smaller landholders of the kingdom from the exactions of the impropriators. The tithes at this time were more rigidly exacted by their lay-owners, than ever they had been during the most corrupt times of the hierarchy; yet these persons grudged the small portion which the law compelled them to bestow on the clergy. This grievance gave rise to many complaints, and the king obliged the impropriators, as well as the other parties concerned, to enter into an arbitration, by which they agreed to abide by the judgment to be pronounced by himself in the matter. After long and deliberate consideration, he gave forth his sentence in a series of decrees, which still continue to regulate the right to tithes, and the payment of the stipends to the ministers of the established Church in Scotland. By these judgments, relief was given to the persons aggrieved, and the clergy were provided with a regular permanent endowment, derived from the fund set apart for their maintenance in former days; but many of the nobility were indignant at being deprived of a portion of their sacrilegious gains, and thenceforth watched for an opportunity of requiting the fancied injury on their sovereign. The arrangement as to the tithes was ratified by parliament in 1630; and its justice and benevolence are now acknowledged by all parties.[2]

Thomas Knox, Bishop of the Isles, died in 1628, and was succeeded by Dr John Leslie, a descendant of the house of Balquhain in Aberdeenshire, and at that time rector of St Faith's, London. In 1633, Dr. Leslie was translated to the

[1] Burnet's History of his Own Time, Routh's ed. vol. i. pp. 34, 35.
[2] Acts of the Parliaments of Scotland, vol. v. pp. 189-207, 218, 219. Cook, vol. ii. p. 330-332. Napier's Montrose and the Covenanters, vol. i. p. 78-91.

see of Raphoe, vacant by the decease of Andrew Knox, formerly Bishop of the Isles; and, on the seventeenth of October in that year, the usual royal license to elect was issued to the chapter of the Isles, accompanied by a recommendation of Neil Campbell, minister at Kilmichael, in the deanery of Glassery, and son of Neil Campbell, sometime Bishop of Argyll, who was accordingly chosen. During the episcopate of Bishop Campbell, King Charles gave directions for restoring the cathedral of Iona, but the execution of this pious design was prevented by the breaking out of the rebellion.[1]

James Law, Archbishop of Glasgow, died in the beginning of November, 1632, and was succeeded by Patrick Lindsay, Bishop of Ross. Dr. John Maxwell, one of the ministers of Edinburgh, was nominated to the see of Ross.[2]

During the earlier years of the reign of Charles, the practical toleration in regard to the Perth articles, which prevailed in most of the dioceses, was producing a good effect. Kneeling at the Communion became more common, and the holy-days were better observed; and, if the people had not been alarmed by the dread of farther innovations, the articles might gradually have been established. But they had good reason to believe that a wish was still entertained by the king and his advisers of bringing the Scottish Church to an entire conformity with that of England; and a numerous and increasing political party, which was dissatisfied with the government, eagerly strove to inflame the ecclesiastical controversies. There seemed, however, but little prospect of successful opposition to royal and episcopal authority.

The decease of Bruce took place in August, 1631; and John Forbes, formerly minister at Alford, died in Holland, about the year 1634.[3] The most learned men in the Church were

[1] Original Letters of the reign of James the Sixth, preface, p. xlii. Keith's Catalogue, p. 308-310. Calendar of State Papers, Domestic Series, of the reign of Charles the First, 1628-29, p. 211. Collectanea de rebus Albanicis, pp. 184, 188. In one of the documents printed in the Collectanea, the king orders Sir Lachlan Maclean of Duart to restore to the see of the Isles the island of Iona, which his family had unjustly seized. In another he enjoins the Bishop of Raphoe to deliver to Bishop Campbell two bells which Bishop Andrew Knox had carried with him from Iona to Ireland.

[2] Keith's Catalogue, pp. 202, 264, 265. Balfour, vol. ii. p. 192.

[3] Wodrow's Life of Bruce, p. 140. M'Crie's Life of Melville, vol. ii. p. 448.

now arrayed among the defenders of Episcopacy and the Perth articles, and very few of those who opposed them had much reputation for ability. One name, however, was now attracting attention. David Dickson, the son of a merchant in Glasgow, after teaching for some years in the university of that city, had been appointed minister at Irvine in 1618. His resistance to the ceremonies, as the Perth articles were called, brought him under the notice of his diocesan, the Archbishop of Glasgow. In the year 1622, he was summoned before the court of High Commission, deprived of his benefice, and ordered to reside at Turriff in Aberdeenshire. This sentence was remitted, within little more than a year, at the intercession of his congregation at Irvine and of the Earl of Eglinton, and he was allowed to return to his former ministry.

The account which Wodrow gives of the effects of Dickson's teaching was written nearly a century afterwards, and is marked by the phraseology of the school to which its author belonged, but there is no reason to question its substantial accuracy. "At Irvine," he says, "Mr. Dickson's ministry was singularly countenanced of God. Multitudes were convinced and converted; and few that lived in his day were more honoured to be instruments of conversion than he. People, under exercise and soul concern, came from every place about Irvine, and attended upon his sermons; and the most eminent and serious Christians, from all corners of the Church, came and joined with him at his communions, which were indeed times of refreshing from the presence of the Lord of these amiable institutions; yea, not a few came from distant places and settled in Irvine, that they might be under the drop of his ministry. Yet he himself used to observe, that the vintage of Irvine was not equal to the gleanings, and not once to be compared to the harvest at Ayr, in John Welsh's time, when indeed the Gospel had wonderful success, in conviction, conversion, and confirmation."[1]

The people of the south-western counties which formed of old a portion of the British kingdom of Cumbria were now developing that peculiar ecclesiastical character by which they were long distinguished. They were ardently attached to the

[1] Wodrow's Life of Dickson—Select Biographies, edited for the Wodrow Society, vol. ii. p. 5-8. Calderwood, vol. vii. pp. 530-542, 567, 568.

Presbyterian discipline and worship, and their devotional feelings were easily excited to fanaticism. Dickson preached on Mondays as well as on Sundays, and many persons came to hear him, not only from the town of Irvine, but from the neighbouring country. The inhabitants of Stewarton, a parish near Irvine, were particularly affected by his sermons and those of other ministers who sympathized with him; and hence the state of mind and feeling, which was thus produced, received the name of the Stewarton sickness, and those who shared in it were called by their opponents the mad people of Stewarton. The excitement appears to have reached a height in June, 1630, at a great gathering on the occasion of a communion in the parish of Shotts, in Clydesdale, which was attended by Bruce and others. The communions were the chief seasons of preaching among the Presbyterians, and they were used as opportunities for collecting together the adherents of the party, not only ministers, but professors also, as the lay people were styled. Archbishop Law did what he could to discourage these proceedings in his diocese, which were dangerous in a political, as well as in an ecclesiastical point of view, but it does not appear that he attempted actually to prohibit them. The preachers were supported, not only by the popular feeling, but by the encouragement of several men of high rank, and still more by that of the female members of various noble families.[1]

Among those present at the communion at Shotts were two ministers, Robert Blair and John Livingstone. The former, the son of a gentleman of good family residing at Irvine, was born in 1593. He was educated at the University of Glasgow, and was afterwards one of the regents in the college there. He was a diligent student; and a careful examination of the controversies of the day confirmed the Presbyterian opinions in which he had been brought up. His zeal was increased by a journey which he made to the North in order to confer with Bruce and Dickson, then in their temporary exile at Inverness and Turriff. He was intimate with Robert Boyd, the principal of his college; but on Cameron being ap-

[1] Wodrow's Life of Dickson—Select Biographies, edited for the Wodrow Society, vol. ii. p. 8. Life of John Livingstone, ibid. vol. i. pp. 138, 145. Wodrow's Life of Bruce, p. 140. Life of Robert Blair, p. 19.

pointed in room of Boyd, a dispute arose between them, and Blair resigned his office.

A Scottish gentleman of the name of Hamilton had, through the favour of King James, acquired large possessions in Ireland, and had been ennobled in that country by the title of Viscount Claneboy. By him Blair was invited to come over to Ulster, and to take an appointment as minister at Bangor. After hesitating for some time, he accepted the invitation. The sea-coast of Ulster was at that time filled with Scottish colonists, most of them adventurers of broken fortune and dissolute character, and whose religion, so far as they had any, was the Presbyterianism of their own country. Blair was willing to labour among them, but he informed his patron that he could not submit to episcopal government, or use any part of the English Liturgy. According to his own account, he was equally plain with Bishop Echlin of Down, in whose diocese his new residence was. That prelate, who was a Scotsman by birth, made no objection. "I hear good of you," he said, " and will impose no conditions upon you ; I am old, and can teach you ceremonies, and you can teach me substance. Only I must ordain you, else neither I nor you can answer the law, or enjoy the land." Blair answered that that was contrary to his principles, to which the bishop replied, "Whatever you account of Episcopacy, yet I know you account a presbyter to have divine warrant ; will you not receive ordination from Mr. Cunningham and the adjacent brethren, and let me come in amongst them in no other relation than a presbyter ?" " This," Blair says, " I could not refuse, and so the matter was performed."

Blair appears to have seen nothing wrong in obtaining admission to a cure in the Irish Church in this manner; but he went still farther, and endeavoured to impose his own Presbyterian usages on others. He mentions that, at his first celebration of the Lord's Supper at Bangor, the noble lord his patron, and his lady, wished to communicate kneeling; that he endeavoured, in vain, to dissuade them ; and that he finally arranged the matter by a sort of compromise.

In 1630, Blair made a visit to Scotland, and assisted at the communion at Shotts. His presence there having become known, Bishop Echlin suspended him from his office on that account, or for some other irregularity. The suspension, he says, was taken off at the request of Archbishop Usher; but he was soon afterwards cited before his diocesan and deposed. He attempted to obtain a reversal of the sentence by a personal application to the king. He succeeded in procuring a temporary relaxation, but was finally deposed a second time in 1634. On this occasion, he says, " I cited the bishop to appear before the tribunal of Jesus Christ, to answer for that wicked deed. To which he replied, ' I appeal from justice to mercy.' ' But,' said I, ' your appellation is like to be rejected, seeing you act against the light of your conscience.' " The bishop died in the following year, and was succeeded by Henry Leslie, Dean of Down, also a Scotsman by birth, but whose ecclesiastical principles were very different from those of his predecessor.[1]

John Livingstone, like Blair, wrote an account of his own life. He was the son of William Livingstone, minister at Kilsyth, who could trace his descent from the chief branch of the family whose name he bore. Livingstone was born in 1603, and was educated at the grammar school of Stirling and the University of Glasgow. He was brought up in strong aversion to Episcopacy and the ceremonies, and, when a student at Glasgow, refused to kneel at the communion, though enjoined to do so by Archbishop Law. He began to preach in 1625, and, having been prevented by the bishops from obtaining a parochial charge, officiated for some time at the house of Cumbernauld, under the protection of the Earl and Countess of Wigton. Soon after the communion at Shotts, he was invited by Lord Claneboy to accept a call to the parish of Killinshie, in the diocese of Down. As Bishop Echlin required that he should be ordained, and was now more strict than he was some years before, Livingstone applied to Andrew Knox, Bishop of Raphoe, formerly Bishop of the Isles. He states that he brought letters to the bishop from Lord Claneboy, the Earl of Wigton, and others; and that he was ordained in the same irregular fashion as Blair, Knox saying that he thought his old age was prolonged

[1] Life of Robert Blair, pp. 7, 16, 39-46, 51, 54, 58-60, 90,91, 101, 102, 112. See also M'Crie's Life of Melville, vol. ii. p. 293, and Mant's History of the Church of Ireland, vol. i. p. 514.

for little other purpose than to do such offices, and desiring him to draw a line through any passage in the Ordinal which he objected to.

At Killinshie Livingstone conducted everything in the Presbyterian manner, even appointing elders and deacons, and going to Antrim once a month to attend a sort of presbytery which met there, consisting of ministers who held similar opinions. He was suspended at the same time with Blair; and he confirms the statement of the latter that the suspension was taken off by means of Archbishop Usher, whom he calls " not only a learned but a godly man, though a bishop." When Blair was deposed for the first time, the same sentence was pronounced against Livingstone. He says that they were accused both of non-conformity, and of stirring up the people to " extasies and enthusianisms." He denies the latter charge, stating that he and his friends did not encourage such practices, because they suspected that they did not proceed from the Spirit of God; adding that few of those so affected made any solid increase in religion, but continued ignorant and profane. While application was made to the king for a reversal of the sentence, Livingstone went to Scotland and preached in various places, sometimes in the parish churches, at other times at the private meetings of the Presbyterians in Edinburgh, being supported by pecuniary assistance which he received from the Countesses of Wigton and Eglinton, and two other ladies. In November, 1635, he was finally deposed by Bishop Henry Leslie.[1]

Blair and Livingstone, having been deprived of their benefices in Ireland, and seeing no prospect of a change of ecclesiastical policy in Scotland, agreed, along with several of

[1] Life of John Livingstone—Select Biographies, edited for the Wodrow Society, vol. i. pp. 129, 130, 133, 134, 136-138, 141-143, 145-148, 152. Bishop Mant says (History of the Church of Ireland, vol. i. p. 453), "Among the records of the Sovereign's Court of Prerogative in Dublin, is deposited a regal Visitation Book of the diocese of Down and Connor in the year 1633. From this it appears that amongst several other clergymen, ordained by Robert Echlin, the bishop of the diocese at that period, Robert Blair had been admitted by him in 1623 to the holy orders of deacon and of priest, and John Livingstone had been admitted in 1630 to the same orders, by Andrew, Bishop of Raphoe. This authentic document takes no notice of any deviation from the regular form of ordination prescribed by law." He expresses a doubt, in consequence, how far the narratives of Blair and Livingstone are to be trusted on this point.

their friends, to emigrate to New England, whither they were invited by letters from the governor and council. They built a ship near Belfast, to which they gave the name of the Eagle Wing, and sailed in September, 1636, accompanied by their wives and families. After being detained for some time, they had a favourable gale which carried them so far across the Atlantic that they were nearer Newfoundland than any part of Europe; but they were then driven back by a hurricane, and obliged to return to Ireland. "We could not imagine," says Livingstone, "what to make of such a dispensation, yet we were confident that the Lord would let us see something that would abundantly satisfy us." [1]

The king, who had proposed to visit Scotland in the beginning of his reign, but had been prevented by various causes from doing so, was able to carry out his intention in the summer of 1633. He was accompanied by Dr. Laud, Bishop of London, Dr. White, Bishop of Ely, and a numerous retinue of English and Scottish nobles and gentlemen, and arrived at Edinburgh on Saturday the fifteenth of June. On the following day he attended divine service at the chapel royal, when the Bishop of Dunblane officiated. On Tuesday the eighteenth, his coronation took place in the abbey church of Holyrood. It was celebrated with the greatest solemnity and magnificence. The king was received at the western door of the church by the Archbishop of St. Andrews and other prelates, and the choristers of the chapel royal, and was conducted into the nave by the dean of the chapel. The sermon was preached by the Bishop of Brechin, and the coronation oath was administered by the archbishop, after which the hymn Veni Creator Spiritus was sung. The Litany having been said by the Bishops of Murray and Ross, the king was anointed by the archbishop, and invested with the royal robes, and girt with the sword. The archbishop then placed the crown on the king's head, and the sceptre in his hand, and blessed and enthronized him, while the peers and bishops did homage, and the people promised obedience. The ceremony was concluded with the celebration of the Eucharist, the king receiving the Communion with great reverence. The whole ritual resembled that used in

[1] Life of Robert Blair, p 104-108. Life of John Livingstone—Select Biographies, edited for the Wodrow Society, vol. i. p. 153-156.

England, from which it was no doubt taken; but it is probable that in this office, as in others, the ancient Scottish use differed little from the English form, and that the coronation of King Charles was in its chief circumstances similar to the ceremonial used in crowning his royal predecessors from the time of David II.[1]

The parliament met immediately after the coronation, and various acts were passed, among others, a statute ratifying the powers formerly conferred on the sovereign to regulate the apparel of churchmen. This provision was opposed by a considerable number of the members. Burnet asserts that a majority actually voted against it, and that the king, though aware of this, forbade the contrary declaration of the Clerk Register to be questioned, unless those who did so would undertake to prove that the record was falsified—an averment which, if proved, inferred a capital offence in the official accused, and, if not proved, a like crime in the person accusing him. Row mentions that the negative votes were thought by some to equal the affirmative, and, without questioning the king's sincerity, adds a statement about his forbidding all inquiry. A rumour to a similar effect was circu-

[1] Balfour, vol. ii. p. 193-198. See also Balfour, vol. iv. p. 383-403, where a minute and most interesting account is given of the coronation of King Charles—the only occasion on which a Scottish sovereign was crowned by a primate of the Reformed Church. Balfour was present at the solemnity as Lord Lion, King-at-Arms. Compare the English offices of Coronation in the third volume of Mr. Maskell's Monumenta Ritualia. Rushworth mentions (Historical Collections, vol. ii. p. 182) that at the coronation Laud was "high in his carriage, taking upon him the order and management of the ceremonies;" and, in particular, that the Archbishop of St. Andrews being placed at the king's right hand, and the Archbishop of Glasgow at his left, he thrust the latter away, saying, "Are you a churchman, and want the coat of your order?" and put the Bishop of Ross in his place. There can be no doubt that the Bishop of London had been consulted in regard to the whole arrangements; and the special circumstance mentioned is not improbable in itself. Laud's hasty temper and his love of ceremonial are sufficient to explain it. But it does not appear what authority Rushworth had for his statement, and it may only have been one of those untrue or exaggerated stories so frequently circulated at the time. In Sir James Balfour's minute narrative of the coronation it does not appear that any special place was assigned to Archbishop Lindsay; and Spalding (Memorials of the Troubles, Spalding Club ed. vol. i. pp. 36, 37), after referring to those bishops who took part in the ceremony, adds that "the Archbishop of Glasgow and remanent of the bishops there present, who were not in service, changed not their habit, but wore their black gowns without rochets or white sleeves."

lated after the king's return to England by the party in opposition to the court, and the accusation called forth an indignant denial from Charles. Even had he been capable of doing such a thing, it is improbable that the attempt would have been made in the face of a hostile majority to whom the fact must have been known. Under the powers conferred by the statute, the king, in the month of October following, sent an order to Scotland, by which the archbishops and bishops were enjoined to wear in church a rochet and lawn-sleeves, as they had done at the coronation, and the inferior clergy to preach in their black gowns, but to wear the surplice when reading divine service, christening, burying, or celebrating the Communion. So far as the inferior clergy were concerned, there is no appearance of any attempt having been made to enforce this order.[1]

On Sunday, the twenty-third of June, when the king attended the church of St. Giles, two of his English chaplains read the service in the Book of Common Prayer, and the Bishop of Murray preached in his episcopal habit. On the following day, being the feast of St. John the Baptist, he went in state to the chapel royal, and, after making his offering, touched more than a hundred persons for the king's evil. On Sunday, the thirtieth of June, Dr. Laud, Bishop of London, preached in the chapel royal. His discourse, Clarendon says, was chiefly "upon the benefit of conformity, and the reverend ceremonies of the Church, and was received with all the marks of approbation and applause imaginable." On the first of July, Charles left Edinburgh, and made a progress as far as Perth. While he was on this journey, the Bishop of London visited St. Andrews and Dunblane. The king returned to England about the middle of July, and soon afterwards, on the death of Archbishop Abbot, Laud was translated to the see of Canterbury.[2]

---

[1] Acts of the Parliaments of Scotland, vol. v. pp. 20, 21. Burnet, vol. i. pp. 36, 37. Row, p. 367. King Charles's Large Declaration, p. 12. The charge against the king is examined by Mr. Napier (Montrose and the Covenanters, vol. i. p. 521-526), who shews that Burnet's version of the story, which has so often been repeated, has no authority whatever.

[2] Balfour, vol. ii. p. 201-204. Laud's Works, Anglo-Catholic Library, vol. iii. p. 218. Clarendon, ed. 1826, vol. i. p. 147. Row, pp. 363, 369. Row mentions that Laud was made a burgess of Perth, but that he refused to take the usual

On the eighth of October, certain articles were issued by the king regarding the mode of celebrating divine service in the chapel royal. This was done, according to Rushworth, at the request of the newly appointed Archbishop of Canterbury. The articles ordered that the dean of the chapel should always assist the Archbishop of St. Andrews at the coronation of the kings of Scotland, and that the form recently used should be carefully preserved by him. Choral service was to be said twice a day according to the English Liturgy, until a Scottish office should be prepared. The Communion was to be celebrated the first Sunday of every month; communicants were to receive the sacrament kneeling; and copes were to be used at the celebration.[1]

One important ecclesiastical occurrence is connected with the visit of King Charles to Scotland. More than four hundred years had elapsed since a bishopric had been founded in the northern kingdom. That portion of the diocese of St. Andrews, which was formerly the archdeaconry of Lothian, was now erected by the king into a separate diocese, having for its cathedral the collegiate church of St. Giles in Edinburgh. By the charter of erection and endowment, which is dated the twenty-ninth day of September, 1633, he declared that, at the request of the Archbishop of St. Andrews, he had established the new diocese for the glory of God, and the good of the Church, in his ancient and native kingdom of Scotland.

burgher oath "to defend the true Protestant Reformed religion," saying that it was his part rather to exact of them an oath for religion. The historian adds that, when the archbishop visited the cathedral of Dunblane, he said it was a goodly church; and, on a bystander adding, "Yes, my lord, this was a brave church before the Reformation," Laud exclaimed, "What, fellow! Deformation, not Reformation."

[1] Rushworth, vol. ii. p. 205. In regard to the arrangements of the choir of the chapel royal, the following information is given in a document presented to the king, dated, Whitehall, 24th January, 1632, and printed from the original in the Register House:—"In time of service within the chapel, the organist and all the singing men are in black gowns, the boys are in sad coloured coats, and the usher, and sexton, and vestry keeper, are in brown gowns. The singing men do sit in seats, lately made, before the noblemen, and the boys before them, with their books laid as in your majesty's chapel here. One of the great Bibles is placed in the middle of the chapel for the reader, the other before the dean. There is sung before sermon a full anthem, and after sermon an anthem alone in versus with the organ." See Dauney's Ancient Scottish Melodies, p. 365-367.

Its bishop was to be styled Bishop of Edinburgh, and to be one of the suffragans of the primatial see. He was to give special assistance in matters ecclesiastical to his metropolitan, and to discharge in some measure the office of Chancellor to him, and on that account was to have precedence among the prelates, immediately after the two archbishops. In the same way the Bishop of Galloway was to assist the Metropolitan of Glasgow, and to take precedence next to the Bishop of Edinburgh. The principal minister of the church of St. Giles as dean, and twelve other ministers of the diocese as prebendaries, were to form the chapter of the bishopric.[1]

In order that the church of St. Giles might be better fitted to be the cathedral of the new see, the magistrates of Edinburgh received special injunctions from the king to cast down the partition wall between the chancel and the nave, by means of which, according to the common Presbyterian fashion, it had been divided into two portions, called the Great and the Little Kirk. The prescribed restoration took place accordingly.[2]

Soon after the erection, Charles intimated the choice which he had made in the nomination of a bishop. Dr. William Forbes had preached before him at Edinburgh. An abstract of the sermon has been preserved, and it is important, not only on account of the solemnity of the occasion, but also as marking the character which Scottish theology was now beginning to assume. The text was from the twenty-seventh verse of the fourteenth chapter of St. John's Gospel, "Peace I leave with you; my peace I give unto you: not as the world giveth give I unto you. Let not your heart be troubled, neither let it be afraid." The preacher described the nature of that peace which our Lord left to his Church, and then alluded to the grievous change which had come over Christendom in his own day—to the disputes among princes, the tyranny of the Bishop of Rome, and the quarrels of the Reformed with each other. Referring to particular matters of controversy, he condemned the eagerness with which positive opinions were laid down regarding Predestination, and Divine Grace, and the manner in which the Body of Christ was present in the Eucharist. He pointed

---

[1] See charter of erection in Keith's Catalogue, p. 44-60.
[2] Row, pp. 369, 370.

out the folly of resisting the voice of the universal Church, and the decrees of lawful authority, in respect of rites and ceremonies, and the absurdity of opposing a uniform Liturgy, and prescribed form of administering the sacraments, especially where the offices thus set at nought were derived from the ancient Liturgies of the Christian Church. He denounced the prevalence of sacrilege, and the covetousness of those who, professing to abhor idolatry, robbed the Church and the poor of their property; declaring that such conduct was like the persecution of Julian, which was worse than that of Diocletian, inasmuch as the one destroyed priests, while the other overthrew the priesthood.[1]

The king was much pleased with this sermon, and, as the high attainments and eminent virtues of the preacher were well known to his ecclesiastical advisers, Dr. Forbes was nominated to the see of Edinburgh. His appointment took place in January, 1634; and, once more leaving Aberdeen, he repaired to his cathedral city, and, in the beginning of February, was consecrated in the chapel royal at Holyrood.

The first bishop of Edinburgh had hardly an opportunity of shewing how far he possessed the qualities necessary for the episcopate at that trying period. In the beginning of March he sent a mandate to his clergy to celebrate the Communion on the Easter day following, enjoining them to take it themselves on their knees and so give a good example to the people, and to minister the elements out of their own hands to every one of the communicants. He was soon afterwards seized with a severe illness, for which the skill of his physicians could find no remedy. He prepared himself for his departure by confession of his sins with priestly absolution, and by the reception of the Eucharist, and expired on the twelfth of April, being the Saturday after Easter. He was buried within the cathedral church of St. Giles, near the place where the

[1] See the abstract of the sermon, printed by Dr. Garden as an appendix to his Life of Dr. John Forbes, p. 290-294. It was preached in the chapel royal, on the twenty-fifth of June: and Spalding mentions (Memorials of the Troubles, vol. i. pp. 39, 40) that he preached in his black gown; that the English service was said before and after the sermon; that the chaplains and novices wore their surplices; that the Bishop of Dunblane, as dean of the chapel, had his rochet and lawn sleeves; and that the other Scottish bishops wore their black gowns.

altar formerly stood, and his funeral sermon was preached by his friend Thomas Sydserf, then Dean of Edinburgh.[1]

Few, except the Puritans of his own day, have spoken of this prelate otherwise than in terms of the highest commendation. Often as his character by Bishop Burnet has been quoted, no notice of his life can be complete without it. "William Forbes," he states, "was promoted by the late king, while he was in Scotland in the year 1633, to the bishopric of Edinburgh, that was then founded by him, so that that glorious king said on good ground, that he had found out a bishop that deserved that a see should be made for him. He was a grave and eminent divine; my father that knew him long, and being of counsel for him in his law matters had occasion to know him well, has often told me that he never saw him but he thought his heart was in heaven, and he was never alone with him, but he felt within himself a commentary on these words of the Apostle, 'Did not our hearts burn within us while He yet talked with us, and opened to us the Scriptures?' He preached with a zeal and vehemence that made him often forget all the measures of time; two or three hours was no extraordinary thing for him; those sermons wasted his strength so fast, and his ascetical course of life was such, that he supplied it so scantily that he died within a year after his promotion; so he only appeared there long enough to be known, but not long enough to do what might have been otherwise expected from so great a prelate. That little remnant of his that is in print shews how learned he was. I do not deny but his earnest desire of a general peace and union among all Christians has made him too favourable to many of the corruptions in the Church of Rome; but, though a charity that is not well balanced may carry one to very indiscreet things, yet the principle from whence they flowed in him was so truly good, that the errors to which it carried him ought to be either excused, or at least to be very gently censured."[2]

---

[1] Life of Bishop William Forbes, prefixed to the Considerationes Modestæ et Pacificæ. Garden's Life of Dr. John Forbes, p. 19. Spalding, vol. i. p. 45. Row, p. 370-373. According to the writers of the Lives, Bishop Forbes died on the first of April; but the twelfth of April is the true date, as is evident from Row and Spalding.

[2] Preface to the Life of Bishop Bedell. The opinions of various writers regarding Bishop Forbes are collected by Mr. Joseph Robertson and myself, in a

Allusion is made in this passage to a work written by Bishop Forbes. Its full title is "Considerationes Modestæ et Pacificæ Controversiarum de Justificatione, Purgatorio, Invocatione Sanctorum et Christo Mediatore, Eucharistia." It formed a part of his divinity lectures at Marischal College, and was first published at London in 1658, with a Life of the author, by Sydserf, Bishop of Galloway. The opinions maintained in this work were in several respects peculiar to the writer, and not shared by the rest of the Aberdeen divines. There is no reason whatever to suppose that he thought of joining the Church of Rome, and the charge is denied in the strongest manner by his biographer; but it is probable that he allowed himself in some points to extenuate the errors of that communion, and to speak of a reconciliation with it in terms much more hopeful than the circumstances warranted. We know that he disapproved altogether of the manner in which the Reformation had been carried on. He often said that if there had been more like Cassander and Wicelius, there would have been no need for Luther and Calvin.

Bishop Forbes's treatise was the first Scottish theological work in which the writings of the Anglican divines were constantly appealed to as authorities. Among those repeatedly quoted are Andrews, Field, Jackson, White, and Montague. The opinions of Forbes himself, on some important points, may be understood from the high terms in which he speaks of the first Prayer Book of King Edward VI., and the regret

note to Gordon's History of Scots Affairs, vol. iii. p. 241-243. The account Bishop Forbes, given by Burnet in the History of his Own Time, is one of the many instances of the different spirit evinced by that writer in his earlier and later works. It is as follows :—" While the king was in Scotland, he erected a new bishopric at Edinburgh, and made one Forbes bishop, who was a very learned and pious man ; he had a strange faculty of preaching five or six hours at a time ; his way of life and devotion was thought monastic, and his learning lay in antiquity; he studied to be a reconciler between the Papists and Protestants, leaning rather to the first, as appears by his Considerationes Modestæ; he was a very simple man and knew little of the world: so he fell into several errors in conduct, but died soon after, suspected of Popery, which suspicion was increased by his son's turning Papist." (History, vol. i. p. 38.) What the errors of conduct were into which Bishop Forbes fell, Burnet leaves his readers to conjecture. Even in matters of small importance the difference between the Preface to Bedell's Life and the History is apparent. The two or three hours' sermons of the former become five or six in the latter.

which he expresses that the English bishops had yielded to the suggestions of Bucer in the adoption of a less primitive Liturgy.[1]

Bishop Forbes's biographer and Dr. Garden mention that, besides the Considerationes, he wrote Animadversions on the works of Bellarmine. These Animadversions, written on the margins of a copy of the cardinal's works, were, after the author's death, in possession of Dr. Baron, who thought them superior to any other answers to the great Roman doctor, and intended to prepare them for the press, but was prevented by the troubles which ensued. Garden adds that it was not known what had become of them. It is probable that they were carried off by the Covenanters when they took possession of Dr. Baron's papers.[2]

---

[1] The orthodoxy and impartiality of Bishop Forbes's work are defended in the preface to it, written by Bishop Sydserf, and in the Life of the author, which probably was also the composition of the same prelate; and by Dr. Garden in his Life of Dr. John Forbes. The following is the judgment of a vehement adversary regarding the opinions maintained by Dr. Forbes :—"If this man had left in legacy a confession of his faith, ye would have seen a strange miscellany, farrago, and hotch-potch of Popery, Arminianism, Lutheranism, and what not. Maxwell, Sydserf, and Mitchell, were never heard to utter any unsound heterodox doctrine, except in relation to prelacy and the ceremonies, till Forbes came to Edinburgh. But then it was taught—the Pope is not Antichrist—a Papist living and dying such may be saved—Christ descended locally to hell—Christ died for all, intentionally to redeem all—there is universal grace—the saints may fall from grace finally and totally—Christ is really present in the Sacrament; verbum audimus, motum sentimus, modum nescimus ; so they would neither as yet speak out Consubstantiation or Transubstantiation—in honorem sacerdotii, why not a minister meddle with secular affairs, be on parliament, court, council, session, exchequer, commission, &c. ?—ministers' doctrine should not be examined by the people, but seeing they watch for their souls, as they that must give account, the people should believe what they preach to them. All these doctrines and many more, we heard with our ears uttered in that most eminent watch-tower of this kirk." (Row, pp. 371, 372.) A writer, well qualified to appreciate both the strength and the weakness of Bishop Forbes's arguments, expresses the following opinion :—" William Forbes wrote his Dissertations, and Herbert Thorndike his Weights and Measures, with the prospect of effecting such a measure [reunion with the Roman Catholic Church] on terms not wholly inconsistent with their Church-of-England feelings. This, however, was visionary ; it was, in truth, the fruit of despair, and, perhaps, cherished by insidious assurances from Roman Catholic emissaries." (Remains of Alexander Knox, second ed. vol. i. p. 62.)

[2] Life of Bishop William Forbes, prefixed to the Considerationes Modestæ et Pacificæ. Garden's Life of Dr. John Forbes, p. 20. Gordon's Scots Affairs, vol. iii. p. 235-237.

The successor of Bishop Forbes in the diocese of Edinburgh was Dr. Lindsay, Bishop of Brechin; and Thomas Sydserf, Dean of Edinburgh, was appointed to the see of Brechin. The installation of Bishop Lindsay, and the consecration of Bishop Sydserf, took place at Edinburgh on the same day—the twenty-ninth of July.[1]

On the decease of the Earl of Kinnoul, Chancellor of Scotland, the Archbishop of St. Andrews was named Chancellor, in January, 1635. No churchman had held that dignity since the Reformation; and the promotion of Spottiswood excited great murmurs, not only among the Presbyterians, who professed to condemn the union of ecclesiastical and secular functions in the same person, but also among the nobles, who had become accustomed to regard the high offices of state as exclusively their own. The chancellors had frequently thwarted the ecclesiastical policy of the sovereign, and hindered the execution of measures which were thought conducive to the good of the Church. The new appointment was probably made to obviate such evils, but the dissatisfaction which it caused was much more than sufficient to counterbalance any good that could have resulted in this respect. No one knew the prevalent feeling of the country better than the primate himself. On a former occasion he had expressed his reluctance to accept the office, and in consenting to take it at a more advanced age, and in a more perilous time, he either allowed his usual prudence to be overmastered by his ambition, or yielded to what the command of his sovereign left him no means of avoiding.[2]

Andrew Lamb, Bishop of Galloway, died in the beginning of the year 1635. In the month of June, Bishop Sydserf was translated to Galloway, and Dr. Walter Whitford, Sub-dean of Glasgow, was appointed Bishop of Brechin.[3]

Patrick Forbes, Bishop of Aberdeen, died in the same year. From the time of his appointment, this eminent prelate devoted his whole attention to the government of his diocese. He exerted himself to obtain fit persons for the vacant bene-

---

[1] Row, p. 375.

[2] Balfour, vol. ii. p. 222. Row, p. 385. See also Original Letters of the reign of James the Sixth, vol. ii. p. 690.

[3] Row, p. 388.

fices, and to disjoin the parishes which had been united to gratify the avarice of the gentry. In order to ascertain how his clergy discharged their duties, it was his practice to visit the various cures without previous notice, the first intimation being generally his appearance in church on the Sunday. He held his diocesan synods twice in the year; and on these occasions, before any other business was taken up, he requested his clergy, if they knew anything wrong in his conduct, to use all freedom with him, to warn him in private of secret errors, and, if they were public, to mention them openly. He devoted particular attention to the restoration of the University of Aberdeen, and of Bishop Elphinstone's foundation of King's College. The ancient usages of the university had been abolished by the reformers, and it had become a mere school for the teaching of languages and philosophy. The bishop, in virtue of his office of chancellor of the university, re-established its former constitution, so far as compatible with the change of religion, and used his influence to procure the most eminent scholars and divines to fill the various offices both in the university and in the churches of his cathedral city.

The personal conduct of Bishop Forbes was in all respects a model to the clergy and people of his diocese. He was particularly careful to preach every Sunday, knowing how important that duty was, and how much harm was done by the remissness of those prelates who neglected it. His original opinions in matters of doctrine remained for the most part unchanged. He was averse to any alterations in ritual, but, when they had once been established by authority, he strenuously enforced submission to them throughout his diocese, and supported their observance by his influence in the Church.

The approach of old age did not abate the vigorous exertions of Bishop Forbes. Even after being struck with paralysis, which disabled him entirely on one side, and made it necessary for him to be carried from place to place in a chair, he continued to preach, and to preside at the meetings of his diocesan synod. He was afterwards entirely confined to bed, but retained the power of speech and the full use of his mental faculties to the last. Although suffering great pain, he allowed no impatient word to escape his lips, but conversed cheerfully with all who came to him, exhorting them, as their father and pastor, to do their duty. In March, 1635, when he saw that his last hour was approaching, he expressed his desire that the "health-giving viaticum of the Holy Eucharist" should be ministered to him. His son, Dr. John Forbes, who received the Communion with him, asked whether he fully tasted the life-giving sweetness of the bread of life. He answered, that he could say with Simeon, "Lord now lettest Thou thy servant depart in peace, according to thy word, for mine eyes have seen thy salvation." When the clergy and his family and domestics who were present implored his blessing, he laid the hand which he could still use on the head of each of them, and, as they knelt, blessed them, and commended them to God, in brief and fervent prayer. When he was told of the general supplications that were made for his restoration to health, he answered in the words of St. Ambrose, "I have not so long lived among you, that I am ashamed to live, nor do I fear to die, since we have a just God."

On Good Friday, while they were engaged in meditating on the Passion, his son reminded him of the prayer of our Lord, "Father, into thy hands I commend my spirit," and remarked that Christ not only commended to the Father his own spirit, hypostatically united to his Godhead, but also the soul of every faithful dying Christian. The bishop lifted up his eyes, and said, "Without doubt, this is the true interpretation, and the very sense of the Lord's words, who prays for us, and is always heard by the Father."

These circumstances are related by Dr. John Forbes; and what follows may best be told in his very words—"The evening before his death I said to him, 'Father, your soul now hears these most grateful words of our Saviour, Well done, thou good and faithful servant, enter thou into the joy of thy Lord. He will now give you the rest of the blessed, and will put upon your head the unfading garland of glory.' He answered in a very few words, for he had not strength to speak much, 'May God grant this.' I then reminded him of the words of Scripture, 'Rise up my love, my fair one, and come away.' I said, with this dearest call, and most gracious invitation, his Saviour now called him, that he might hasten from this world of sin and sorrow to heaven, the abode of the happiness and glory of God, that this night he would be with Christ in Paradise. I earnestly besought him to rest and rely upon this so consolatory and precious invitation now, as he had often done before, when the journey to his house, to the Lord Jesus, through the valley of death, was drawing to a close. He answered, 'Best of journeys, the blessedness of which so far beyond comparison transcends that of all others.'

"Subsequently, when the use of speech failed him, as long as he was able to follow our words, while we spake of the mercy of God, of the blessed death of those who die in the Lord, of the heavenly mansions prepared for him by Christ, in which he would soon be, and join the company of angels and patriarchs, and apostles and martyrs, and of the other blessed saints, and of the plenitude of joy which is there in the presence of God, and of the eternal pleasure at his right hand —as long, I say, as he was able to perceive our voices, he shewed how much he was gratified by our meditations on such heavenly subjects, whither his mind and all his wishes were then tending, and how constantly he trusted in God, by frequently lifting up the hand which was free from paralysis, and raising his eyes to heaven. When I asked him, if we who were present might kneel down, and together pour out our souls before our heavenly Father, that He, of his boundless grace and unchangeable love of his servants in Christ, would render his departure, which we all now saw was near, a happy one, he raised himself as well as he was able, and lifting his hand and his quivering eyes to heaven, he shewed us by the most anxious and evident signs how agreeable and acceptable this was to him, how deeply grateful our prayers on his behalf were to him. We could clearly perceive by the motion of his hand and eyes, and by the whole expression of his countenance, that he joined in our prayers. After prayer was ended, when we spoke close to his ear, he raised his hand and eyes a little, but soon his sense of hearing, and all power of motion left him. We stood around, looking on in tears, and pouring out our whole souls to God, in prayer to God, having the consoling assurance, from what we had seen and heard, of the certain happiness of his change. He most placidly, as if in sleep, breathed out his blessed spirit, already ripe for heaven, into the hands of his heavenly Father. I myself, as if I had looked on the dying patriarch Jacob of old, kissed his soulless body, and moistening it with my tears closed his eyes. There only remained for me the care of his funeral obsequies."

Bishop Forbes died on the morning of Easter Eve, the twenty-eighth day of March, 1635, being then in the seventy-first year of his age. According to the usage of Aberdeen at that time, his body was removed from the episcopal palace to St. Ninian's chapel on the Castle-hill, where it lay in state for some days. It was then carried back to Old Aberdeen, and interred within the south transept of the cathedral, close by the grave of Bishop Dunbar.[1]

It is almost needless to add anything regarding the character of Bishop Forbes. His good deeds and his holy life have been an abiding memorial. A volume was published at Aberdeen soon after his decease, containing funeral sermons and other tributes of regard and affection in Latin and English, in prose and verse, by the most distinguished Scottish divines and scholars of the time. Among these, no one spoke with more sincerity than the primate, who knew that in the Bishop of Aberdeen he had lost a counsellor and a friend, who shared his opinions, and was ever ready to afford his sympathy and support. On the second of April, he thus wrote to Dr. John Forbes—" In so necessary a time, to be bereaved of such counsel and comfort as God had furnished him with—I mean your worthy father — for the directing of some and the strengthening of others, I know not what it portendeth to our Church. When Bishop Elphinstone, the founder of your college, was laid in his grave, the tradition is, that a voice was heard cry, 'Tecum, Gulielme, mitra sepelienda,' and that the pastoral staff brake in pieces. He was certainly an excellent man, and I may truly say, since him, unto your father, there arose not the like in that church. What, say I, in that church? Every man can speak of that he hath known and seen; and for myself I speak truth—so wise, judicious, so

[1] Garden's Life of Dr. John Forbes, p. 3-6. Burnet's Preface to the Life of Bishop Bedell. Funerals of Bishop Patrick Forbes, Spottiswood Society ed. p. 297-302, and Biographical Memoir by Mr. C. Farquhar Shand, p. lxxv.-xciv. Mr. Shand s translation of the Latin sermon by Dr. John Forbes, containing the account of the bishop's death, has been used in the text.

grave and graceful a pastor, I have not known in all my time, in any church."[1]

Bishop Forbes wrote several works on theological subjects, and chiefly in connection with the Roman controversy, but his merits as an author are of little account in comparison with his high reputation as a prelate.[2] He was succeeded in the see of Aberdeen by Adam Bellenden, Bishop of Dunblane. Dr. James Wedderburn was appointed to the bishopric of Dunblane, and was consecrated in the beginning of the year 1636. He was a native of Dundee, but was educated in England. He resided for a long time with Isaac Casaubon, afterwards taught divinity in St. Mary's College, St. Andrews, and was made a prebendary of Ely by Bishop Andrews.[3]

On the twenty-third day of May, 1635, the king granted his royal warrant, authorizing and enjoining a new Book of Canons for the government of the Church of Scotland. These canons were not published till the following year, but their ratification was the first step in the series of ecclesiastical measures which have become so memorable in the history of our country.

---

[1] Funerals of Bishop Patrick Forbes, pp. 217, 218.

[2] See an account of these works in Mr. Shand's Biographical Memoir, p. xcviii.-cxvi.

[3] Keith's Catalogue, p. 133. Heylin's Life of Archbishop Laud, ed. 1719, part ii. p. 49. Laud's Works, vol. iii. p. 374; vol. vi. p. 455. Baillie's Canterburian's Self-Conviction, ed. 1641, p. 11.

CHAPTER XLVIII.

FROM THE RATIFICATION OF THE BOOK OF CANONS IN MAY, 1635, TO THE ACT OF THE PRIVY COUNCIL REGARDING THE BOOK OF COMMON PRAYER IN DECEMBER, 1636.

State of the Scottish Church—Its Government, Ritual, and Doctrines — The cathedral and parish churches — The Book of Canons—Objections to the Canons—The Ordinal of 1636—New warrant for the Court of High Commission — Alleged diocesan Commission Courts — Samuel Rutherford—Andrew Boyd, Bishop of Argyll— John Durie's attempt to unite the Lutheran and the Reformed—Judgment of the Theological Faculty of Aberdeen on this subject—The divines of Aberdeen—Dr. Alexander Scroggie—Dr. William Leslie—Dr. James Sibbald—Dr. Alexander Ross—Dr. Robert Baron—Dr. John Forbes—Education of Dr. John Forbes—His ordination—His theological teaching—Publication of his Irenicum—Act of the Privy Council regarding the Book of Common Prayer.

A VALID episcopate had now been established in Scotland for twenty-five years, and various portions of the English ritual had been introduced, but the ecclesiastical system still retained many traces of the institutions of Knox and Melville. The government of the Church was a mixture of Episcopacy and Presbyterianism. In outward appearance the hierarchy was again what it had been of old. The two archbishops presided in their provinces over the same suffragan sees, and the chapters discharged their former functions in the election of bishops and the administration of the temporalities of the cathedrals. But it was rather as the chief ecclesiastical ministers under the king, than in virtue of their metropolitan authority, that the archbishops claimed any peculiar rights; the clergy did not meet in provincial council; and the privilege of the chapters in the election of bishops was merely a matter of form, the nomination belonging to the crown. The titles of Dean and Archdeacon, and of the other capitular dignitaries, had been restored, but the persons who held these offices appeared in the ecclesiastical courts as mere parish ministers: the bishops were the only prelates in the Reformed communion.

Along with the archbishops and bishops, the deans and chapters of the ancient Church, the new hierarchy of ecclesiastical synods, established by Melville, continued to exist. The lowest of these was the Parochial Consistory or Kirk Session, composed of the minister and his lay elders and deacons. Above them was the Presbytery or Exercise, which was justly regarded as the distinguishing feature of this system. It had been proposed to take away the powers, and even to suppress the name of the presbyteries, but these courts remained as before, except that the bishop had the right of appointing the moderator who presided at their meetings, and that their members were the ministers of the parishes which formed the presbytery, without lay elders. The court immediately above the presbytery was that which was formerly called the Provincial Assembly, but which was now known as the Diocesan Synod. It was composed of all the parochial ministers within the diocese, and the bishop presided, either in person, or through a moderator specially appointed by him. It was chiefly by means of this court that the episcopal authority was maintained among the clergy and laity. Highest of all was the General Assembly, which could only meet when summoned by the king. The supporters of Episcopacy held that the Primate was entitled to act as moderator of the assembly, and that the bishops were not subject to its jurisdiction. They were also desirous to restrict its members to ecclesiastics, but, except in so far as lay elders from the presbyteries were concerned, this could hardly be reconciled with the constitution of the last assembly at Perth, at which noblemen, barons, and the representatives of burghs, had voted. Their opponents, on the other hand, maintained that the members of the assembly were entitled to choose their own moderator; that its authority over the bishops was expressly reserved, even by the acts of the Glasgow synod of 1610; and that lay elders from the presbyteries had as much a right to vote as ministers.

The ritual of the Reformed Church partook still less of the

ancient forms. The only proper liturgical office which had been introduced was the Ordinal, and, as its use was a matter entirely within the power of the bishops, it was no doubt strictly enforced. The daily offices, and the order for the ministration of the Holy Communion, in the Book of Common Prayer, were regularly observed in the chapel royal at Holyrood, and the former at least in St. Mary's College, St. Andrews. The English Liturgy had also been used for some time by Bishop Maxwell at Fortrose, and probably by some others of the bishops in their cathedrals, but it does not appear that it had been introduced into any of the parish churches. The Book of Common Order, or what was called Knox's Liturgy, was still in general use, though now in less esteem, from the knowledge of its manifold deficiences on the one side, and the increasing aversion to forms of prayer on the other. The ancient ecclesiastical music was unknown, except in the chapel royal, and the Psalter was only used in the shape of a metrical translation.

The five articles of Perth had been established both by the ecclesiastical and the secular authority, but they were still far from being universally adopted. In certain cases the non-observance of the two articles regarding holy-days and kneeling at the Communion was expressly permitted; in many more it was connived at by the bishops. It does not distinctly appear how far the other articles were in use. Private Baptism was probably not uncommon; but Confirmation was entirely neglected by the bishops themselves,[1] and private Communion seems to have been sought only in those cases where it was recommended by individual clergymen, as it is known to have been by Dr William Forbes, and the other divines of Aberdeen.

A change of opinion, in a direction opposed to the Calvinistic views, had already begun regarding various matters of doctrine, but the general belief both of the clergy and the people was still in conformity with the Confession of Faith agreed to at the beginning of the Reformation. That formulary continued to be the established rule of faith, the Confes-

---

[1] This is expressly asserted by the Covenanting ministers in their Answer to the Replies of the Doctors of Aberdeen, and its correctness is admitted by the Doctors in their Duply.

sion approved by the assembly at Aberdeen having apparently never superseded it. The new opinions were condemned by the Puritans under the name of Arminianism. They were known to be favoured by the English primate, and, in Scotland, those who carried on an intimate correspondence with him now openly avowed their dislike to the prevailing Calvinism.

The cathedral and monastic churches still remained in the state of desolation to which the excesses of Knox and his followers had reduced them, and those which were capable of being used were fitted up in the Presbyterian fashion. The parish churches had been miserably neglected. The lay beneficiaries paid no attention to the obligations incumbent upon them as coming in place of the old parsons, and time had done its work as effectually as violence. An attempt had been made by Archbishop Spottiswood to begin the work of restoration by rebuilding the church of Dairsie, which was situated on his own estates in Fifeshire. Its division into nave and chancel, and its internal decorations, approached as nearly as circumstances would allow to the ancient rule.

Such was the state of matters which Charles and Laud beheld when they visited Scotland, and, however much they may have been prepared for it by their former knowledge and experience, it excited a deep feeling of disappointment. There can be no doubt that, after their return, the king and the primate devoted themselves, with the ardent zeal which marked their character, to the task of completing the restoration of the Scottish Church. The bishops were exhorted to encourage orthodox principles, and to uphold conformity; Puritanical practices, such as fasting on the Sunday, were forbidden; the liturgical worship in the chapel royal was carefully maintained; and the king's intention was announced of rebuilding the once venerated cathedrals of Iona and St. Andrews. Above all, the preparations were urged on for completing a Book of Canons and a Liturgy.

The Book of Canons, which had been ratified by the king in May, 1635, was printed at Aberdeen, and published in the beginning of the year 1636. It bore the following title:—
" Canons and Constitutions Ecclesiastical, gathered and put in form for the government of the Church of Scotland, ratified

and approved by his majesty's royal warrant, and ordained to be observed by the clergy, and all others whom they concern."[1]

The book was divided into nineteen chapters. The first chapter, under the title "Of the Church of Scotland," related chiefly to the king's supremacy, and contained the following declarations :—" Whosoever shall hereafter affirm that the king's majesty hath not the same authority in causes ecclesiastical that the godly kings had amongst the Jews, and Christian emperors in the primitive Church, or impeach in any part his royal supremacy in causes ecclesiastical, let him be excommunicated, and not restored but only by the archbishop of the province, after his repentance, and public revocation of these his wicked errors." "Whosoever shall hereafter affirm that the doctrine of the Church of Scotland, the form of worship contained in the Book of Common Prayer and Administration of the Sacraments, the rites and ceremonies of the Church, the government of the Church under his majesty by archbishops, bishops, and others which bear office in the same, the form of making and consecrating archbishops, bishops, presbyters, and deacons, as they are now established under his majesty's authority, do contain in them any thing repugnant to the Scriptures, or are corrupt, superstitious, or unlawful, in the service and worship of God, let him be excommunicated, and not restored but by the bishop of the place, or archbishop of the province, after his repentance, and public revocation of such his wicked errors."

The second chapter was entitled, "Of Presbyters and Deacons, their nomination, ordination, function, and charge." It enjoined that no person should be ordained without having been educated in some university or college, and taken a degree there, and without examination by the bishop of the diocese or his chaplains. No one was to be ordained deacon till he was twenty-one years of age, or presbyter till he was twenty-five. Bishops were forbidden to ordain any out of their own diocese, except on letters dimissory, and a certificate of honest conversation ; and the persons ordained were in all cases to have a particular place or charge, where they

[1] The Scottish canons are reprinted in the fifth volume of Archbishop Laud's Works.

were to exercise their functions. Orders were to be conferred according to the form in the Book of Ordination, at four seasons in the year, the first weeks of March, June, September, and December.

The third chapter was, " Of residence and preaching." Divine service was to be celebrated according to the Book of Common Prayer in all cases before sermons. No person of the laity, whatever might be his gifts of learning, knowledge, or holiness, was to exercise any of the functions of Presbyters or Deacons without previous ordination, and the licence of the ordinary. Preachers were not to impugn the doctrine of neighbouring preachers, unless with permission of the bishop; they were not to speak against his majesty or his laws, or allude reproachfully to any one by name, except in the case of notorious offenders. All presbyters, as their text should give occasion, were to urge on their hearers the necessity of good works. They were to visit the sick according to the form in the Book of Common Prayer; and, when any person was passing out of this life, a bell was to be tolled, that the people might pray for him as a fellow-member of Christ's body, and the presbyter was not then to neglect to do his last duty. Every presbyter was to be careful to provide himself with good books, especially the Holy Scriptures and the writings of the ancient Fathers and Doctors of the Church. All presbyters and preachers were to move the people to join with them in prayer, using few and convenient words, and were always to conclude with the Lord's Prayer.

The fourth chapter, " Of the conversation of Presbyters," contained various rules similar to those in the canons of other Christian Churches.

The fifth chapter, " Of Translation," forbade translation to another benefice, except with consent of the ordinary.

The sixth chapter, " Of the Sacraments," forbade all lay persons to minister the sacraments under the pain of excommunication, and enjoined presbyters to give private Baptism in cases of necessity. The sacrament of the Lord's Supper was to be celebrated four times every year, the feast of Easter being always one, and every person was to communicate with his own presbyter once in the year at least. In the ministration of that sacrament, what was reserved of the elements was to be distributed to the poorer persons among the communicants, to be consumed by them before leaving the church. The sacrament was to be received with bowing of the knee, to testify the devotion and thankfulness of the receivers for that most excellent gift.

The seventh chapter, "Of Marriage," laid down rules regarding marriage and divorce.

The eighth chapter, "Of Synods," ordered diocesan synods of the clergy to be held twice a year; forbade all conventicles and secret meetings of churchmen; and declared that national synods, called by the king's authority, should bind all persons, whether absent or present, to obedience to their decrees in matters ecclesiastical.

The ninth chapter, "Of meetings to Divine Service," enjoined reverence in time of divine service. All persons were to kneel when the confession and other prayers were read, and to stand up at the saying of the Creed. No presbyter or reader was to conceive prayers extempore, or to use any other form in the public Liturgy than that which was prescribed, under the pain of deprivation.

The tenth, eleventh, and twelfth chapters, contained brief rules regarding Schoolmasters, Curates and Readers, and Printers. The last of these forbade any thing to be printed till allowed by visitors appointed for the purpose.

The thirteenth chapter ordered that all Christenings, Weddings, and Burials, should be registered.

The fourteenth chapter, "Of Public Fasts," forbade any solemn fasts to be kept by clergymen, except with consent of their ordinary, and declared it unlawful to keep fasts on Sundays.

The fifteenth chapter enjoined the clergy and members of the universities to use apparel beseeming their degrees.

The sixteenth chapter, "Of things pertaining to the Church," ordered that every church should be provided at the expense of the parish with a Bible and a Book of Common Prayer, and with a Font, to be placed near the door, and a cloth of fine linen for Baptism; with a comely and decent Table for the Holy Communion, to be placed at the upper end of the church or chancel, and to be covered during divine service with a carpet of decent stuff, and during ministration with a white linen cloth; with basins, cups or chalices of some pure metal to be set on the Table, and reserved to that use only, and with a pulpit and an alms chest. All these were to be carefully preserved by the ministers and church wardens. The church and churchyard were to be kept in careful repair. Visitations were to be held by the archdeacon once every year, and by the bishop once every three years; the archbishop was to be entitled to visit his province metropolitically, but only once during his life, and that at such times as the ordinaries might think best for the good of the Church.

The seventeenth chapter laid down regulations regarding tithes, and lands dedicated to churches.

The eighteenth chapter was entitled, " Of Censures Ecclesiastical." It forbade ecclesiastical judicatories to meddle with anything beyond their jurisdiction. It declared that excommunication was only to be pronounced after lawful citation and due admonition preceding, and with the knowledge and consent of the ordinary. If any person wished to unburden his conscience by confession to a bishop or presbyter, he was to receive all spiritual consolations, and absolution after the manner prescribed in the Visitation of the Sick, if truly penitent and desirous to be absolved. Any person injured by his metropolitan was entitled to appeal to delegates, or immediately to the king.

The nineteenth chapter was entitled, " Of Commissaries and their Courts ;" and the book concluded with a declaration that " wheresoever there is no penalty expressly set down, it is to be understood that (so the crime or offence be proved) the punishment shall be arbitrary, as the ordinary shall think fittest."

Such were the Scottish canons of 1636. It had been proposed on several occasions, and especially at the Aberdeen assembly of 1616, to compile a body of canons from the acts of the general assembly, and from other sources; but the new constitutions bore little resemblance to any Scottish ecclesiastical enactments subsequent to the Reformation. They are said to have been drawn up by the Bishops of Galloway, Aberdeen, Ross, and Dunblane. Nothing certain, however, is known as to this. They were revised by Archbishop Laud, and by Dr. Juxon, Bishop of London, and were evidently framed on the model of the English canons of 1604. They were not, so far as appears, discussed at any synod, nor were they promulgated with any sanction whatever except that of the king. Their whole authority, therefore, depended on the royal supremacy, and on such right as the bishops might have to enjoin their observance in their own dioceses.

The canons made express reference to the Book of Common Prayer, and the Book of Ordination, neither of which was yet published. Attention was called at the time to the singular circumstance, that obedience was required to a Liturgy which was still in the course of preparation. This has never been satisfactorily explained. It was quite reasonable in itself that a Code of Canons should be issued before a Service Book, but it was a proceeding equally absurd and tyrannical to denounce the penalty of excommunication against the infringers of a book, the contents of which were not yet known. Had the Scottish Church been reformed on the same principle as that of England, there would have been little to object to in the canons themselves, but, as it was, they established a system, both of ecclesiastical government and of ritual, very different from that which was then in existence and recognized by law. The change in the former respect is thus stated by a contemporary Presbyterian writer, in language which, no doubt, faithfully represents the prevalent feeling of his party:—" In all the canons, not one mention of a ruling elder, an office which bishops detest, because they love to see profanity grow, increase, abound, that theirs may be the less taken notice of; no word of a session or congregational consistory; no word of a presbytery, or classical judicatory; yea now also the brethren of the exercise are buried in deep oblivion; instead of a provincial free synod, ye have twice a year a bishop's court, where he not only usurped moderation, but also a negative voice, and many times would command the whole to write what he pleased though the voices had carried otherwise, yea often would not refer the matter to voicing; and, lastly, the general assembly, the great bulwark under God of this kirk, from which only ecclesiastical canons can by the law of this land flow, and not from some particular persons, is in effect abolished."[1]

Some of the persons concerned in framing the canons appear to have expected opposition when their contents became known. Considerable alarm was certainly excited, but no public demonstration of any kind took place.[2] Those who afterwards took a leading part against the king and the prelates were not prepared for resistance, and the canons themselves did not afford a sufficient ground for an appeal to popular feeling. They were as yet mere written rules, not practically enforced in any way; and, on more than one occasion in late years, royal injunctions issued in matters ecclesiastical had been quietly recalled, or allowed to become an empty form.

Before the end of the year 1636, a Book of Ordination was printed. It appears to have differed from the book of 1620 in containing a form for the ordering of Deacons.[3]

In October, 1634, a new warrant had been granted for establishing the High Commission, in virtue of which any seven of the members, an archbishop or bishop being one, were empowered to exercise the jurisdiction conferred upon the court.[4]

It is asserted by Burnet that the bishops, not satisfied with the general High Commission court, procured warrants from

[1] Row, pp. 394, 395. Strange accounts of the canons have been given by some historians. Their ignorance of ecclesiastical language may have led to misapprehensions, but various statements have been made, which can only be explained by supposing that the authors never read the book which they were condemning; see, for instance, the remarks of Mr. Brodie in his History of the British Empire from the Accession of Charles I. to the Restoration, vol. ii. p. 439. Dr. Cook, while censuring the canons themselves, gives a very fair account of their contents; see his History of the Church of Scotland, vol. ii. p. 358-364.

[2] Compare Baillie's Letters, vol, i. p. 4, and appendix, pp. 438, 439.

[3] Row, p. 391. Gordon's Scots Affairs, vol. ii. pp. 92, 93. The king's instructions, quoted by Heylin (Life of Archbishop Laud, ed. 1719, part ii. p. 50), shew that the Ordinal was not published till after the middle of October. I have not been able to discover the existence of any copy of this Book of Ordination. Heylin mentions (Life of Archbishop Laud, ibid.) that Bishop Wedderburn had brought under the notice of the English primate certain defects in the Ordinal of 1620, viz. "That the order of Deacons was made but a lay office at the best, as by that book might be understood, and that at the admission to the priesthood the very essential words of conferring orders were left out."

[4] Baillie, vol. i. appendix, p. 424-428.

the king for setting up commissions in their several dioceses, in which, with ministers and gentlemen of their own nomination as assessors, they might punish offenders; and he adds that the Bishop of Galloway was the only prelate who availed himself of the powers thereby conferred. This statement has frequently been repeated; but I am not aware of any record which supports it, and it seems to be a mistake arising from the circumstance that any bishop, with six other members, was entitled to exercise the powers of the High Commission.[1]

In July, 1636, Samuel Rutherford, minister of Anwoth, was summoned before the High Commission at Edinburgh, at the instance of his ordinary, the Bishop of Galloway. The bishop had in vain previously endeavoured at various private conferences to prevail upon him to submit to the ecclesiastical laws. He was ordered by the court to leave his parish, and take up his residence at Aberdeen. Rutherford, one of the most learned of the Puritan ministers, had for some time been a regent in the College of Edinburgh, and was afterwards appointed minister of Anwoth, at least as early as the year 1624. In that remote parish, and in the immediate neighbourhood, he was as popular as Dickson was at Irvine. He was an especial favourite with the female sex, his chief patroness in the first years of his ministry being the Viscountess of Kenmure, a daughter of the Earl of Argyll.

---

[1] See Memoirs of the Dukes of Hamilton, ed. 1677, pp. 30, 31. Burnet makes the same assertion in the History of his Own Time, and mentions, in connection with the diocesan court set up by Sydserf in Galloway, that the Earl of Argyll having complained in council of his proceedings, the bishop gave him the lie. According to Baillie, however, it was a court of High Commission which Bishop Sydserf held on this occasion for punishing the laird of Earlston and other Nonconformists; and that writer gives it as his own opinion that Argyll, or, as he more correctly designates him, the Lord Lorn, exaggerated for his own purposes a hasty expression of Sydserf. In regard to its being a court of High Commission, we have the authority of Earlston and Argyll themselves. Compare Burnet's History, vol. i. p. 44; Baillie, vol. i. p. 16; and Peterkin's Records of the Kirk, p. 150. The only contemporary authority of any kind which I have found, in the least degree resembling the statement of Burnet, is a notice in the Life of Robert Blair (p. 107), made in connection with the proceedings of Sydserf, that "now every bishop, having got up a High Commission, with a small quorum of their own creatures, could, in one harvest (for no one was excepted), fine and confine at their pleasure (no limits being set to them), in an arbitrary way, the lieges throughout the whole kingdom."

While at Anwoth, Rutherford wrote and published a Latin work on divine grace, in opposition to the Arminian opinions; and that publication was asserted by his friends to be the true cause of Sydserf's enmity. At Aberdeen, he had several discussions with the divines of that city regarding the disputed points of belief, but he found much more congenial occupation in writing a portion of that extraordinary series of letters, chiefly addressed to his female disciples in the South, which excited great attention at the time, and in connection with which his name is now chiefly remembered. There is no reasonable ground to question the sincerity of the excited feelings described in these compositions, but there is as little doubt as to the presumptuous fanaticism which dictated them, and the gross impropriety of the language in which they are written.[1]

Andrew Boyd, Bishop of Argyll, died on the twenty-second of December, 1636. Burnet gives the following character of this prelate:—"He found his diocese overrun with ignorance and barbarity, so that in many places the name of Christ was not known; but he went about that apostolical work of planting the Gospel, with a particular industry, and almost with equal success. He got churches and schools to be raised and endowed everywhere, and lived to see a great blessing on his endeavours; so that he is not so much as named in that country to this day but with a particular veneration, even by those who are otherwise no way equitable to that order. The only answer that our angry people in Scotland used to make, when they were pressed with such instances, was, that there were too few of them; but some of the severest of them have owned to me, that if there were many such bishops they would all be Episcopal."[2]

Boyd's successor in the see of Argyll was James Fairley, one of the ministers of Edinburgh, who was consecrated in the chapel royal at Holyrood, on the eighth day of August 1637.[3] No other bishop was consecrated in Scotland till after the Restoration.

In a letter from Rutherford to a friend in Ireland, written from his place of banishment at Aberdeen in the beginning of

---

[1] Row, pp. 396, 397. Select Biographies, edited for the Wodrow Society, vol. i. pp. 320, 321.

[2] Preface to the Life of Bedell. Keith's Catalogue, p. 291.

[3] Row, p. 410.

the year 1637, and containing reference to a proclamation regarding the Liturgy, which will afterwards be mentioned, the following information is given: " Our Service Book is ordained, by open proclamation and sound of trumpet, to be read in all the kirks of this kingdom. Our prelates are to meet this month for it and our canons, and for a reconciliation betwixt us and the Lutherans. The professors of Aberdeen University are charged to draw up the articles of an uniform confession, but reconciliation with Popery is intended."[1] Rutherford here alludes to the attempt which was going on at this time to bring about a reconciliation between the Lutherans and the Reformed. The person who chiefly endeavoured to effect this object was John Durie, son of Robert Durie one of the ministers who had been banished by King James on account of the Aberdeen assembly of 1605. Durie devoted his life to the task. He came over to England soon after Laud was appointed to the primacy, and was favourably received by the archbishop and other English prelates. He applied also to the Scottish bishops, and, by the advice of Archbishop Spottiswood, wrote to the divines of Aberdeen, requesting their opinion as to the points in dispute. On the twentieth of February, 1637, the members of the theological faculty in the University of Aberdeen sent a paper to the Scottish primate, containing their formal judgment. Drawing a distinction between absolute consent in every thing, and agreement in essential points, they declared that both the Lutherans and the Reformed, rightly understood, agreed in those matters of faith as to which the ancient Church had been of one opinion.[2]

This judgment was subscribed by six doctors, John Forbes, Robert Baron, Alexander Scroggie, William Leslie, James Sibbald, and Alexander Ross. The names of all these

---

[1] Rutherford's Letters, Aberdeen ed. p. 362.

[2] See Garden's Life of Dr. John Forbes, pp. 28, 29, and the Instructiones Historico-Theologicæ, p. 673-682. Baillie entertained a very different opinion of these proceedings from that which was expressed by Rutherford. He approved of the charitable attempt, and commended the prudence of Archbishop Spottiswood in keeping the matter quiet in Scotland, where it would be misinterpreted as a proposal to yield, first to the Lutherans, and after that to the Papists—the very charge made by the minister of Anwoth. (Baillie, vol i. pp. 9, 10.)

divines were already well-known in Scotland, and the reputation of two of them had extended to other Churches. Dr. Scroggie was minister of the cathedral church of St. Machar, to which he had been translated from the cure of Drumoak, in the same diocese, by Bishop Patrick Forbes. Dr. Leslie, who is said to have been brother of John Leslie, formerly Bishop of the Isles, and at this time Bishop of Raphoe, was successively one of the regents, sub-principal, and principal of King's College. Dr. Sibbald, a descendant of the ancient family of that name in the Mearns, was for some time a regent at Marischal College, and afterwards one of the ministers of the church of St. Nicholas in Aberdeen. Dr. Ross was first minister at Insch, in the diocese of Aberdeen, afterwards at St. Clement's chapel in the burgh of Aberdeen, and finally colleague to Dr. Sibbald in the church of St. Nicholas. He has sometimes been confounded with another Scottish divine of the same name, who wrote the View of all Religions and many other works. Dr. Baron was still more widely distinguished. He was of the house of Kinnaird in Fife, and was educated at St. Andrews. After having taught for some time in that university, he succeeded Bishop Patrick Forbes as minister at Keith, and afterwards became one of the ministers of the church of St. Nicholas, and professor of divinity in the Marischal College, Aberdeen.[1]

But of all the northern divines, Dr. John Forbes was the one who was best known in his own day, and whose name has still the highest reputation. He was the second son of Bishop Patrick Forbes, and was born on the second of May, 1593. His boyhood was passed under the care of his father, and in 1607 he was sent to the University of Aberdeen. He afterwards went abroad, and studied at Heidelberg, Sedan, and other Protestant universities, devoting his particular attention to theology. His opinions were at first those of the schools which he frequented, and, though they underwent a gradual change as his studies in the writings of the Fathers drew him more towards the model of the ancient Church, he never ceased to identify himself in all essential points with the continental Protestants. His views regarding Epis-

[1] See notices of these divines by the editors of Gordon's Scots Affairs, vol. iii. pp. 209, 227, 230, 231, 232, 235, 236.

copacy and Holy Orders were no doubt affected by the circumstance, that he himself had received only Presbyterian ordination. He was called to the ministry at Middleburg, on the fourth of April, 1619, and, among those who subscribed the certificate of his call, was his uncle, John Forbes, the deprived minister of Alford, at that time preacher to the English factory at Middleburg. He returned soon afterwards to his own country, and in the following year was appointed professor of divinity in King's College, Aberdeen.

In the discharge of his important duties as a teacher in the university, Dr. Forbes laboured to bring up those entrusted to his care in a strict religious life as well as in the knowledge of theology. The Bishop and clergy of Aberdeen made it their particular request that he would carefully instruct his scholars in ecclesiastical history. They were especially induced to do so, from observing that the adherents of the Roman see made many converts by claiming for their doctrine the support of the Fathers, and that others disregarded altogether the voice of Christian antiquity as contrary to the Scriptures. Forbes diligently attended to this request, and the learned works which he left behind him shew how well qualified he was for the required course of instruction.

In the year 1629, he published at Aberdeen his Irenicum, a treatise addressed to all lovers of truth and peace in the Scottish Church. It was dedicated to his father, and contained a defence of the lawfulness of the Perth articles, of Episcopacy, and of prescribed forms of prayer. In a letter written to the author in December, 1632, Archbishop Usher spoke of this treatise in the highest terms, esteeming his country happy that in him it had produced a second Irenæus, whose task it was, like that of the ancient Bishop of Lyons, to appease the strife which had arisen in the Church. The eldest son of Bishop Forbes having died before his father, Dr. Forbes, on the decease of the latter, became laird of Corse, and from that time was frequently referred to under his baronial title.[1]

The assistance which the doctors of Aberdeen gave to the attempt to restore concord in the Protestant communions of

---

[1] Garden's Life of Dr John Forbes, p. 6-16. Gordon's Scots Affairs, vol. iii, p. 234, note.

the Continent was their last peaceful labour. The conflict was now approaching which was to end in the overthrow of the ecclesiastical system they had endeavoured with such zeal to build up in their own land. On the eighteenth of October, 1636, the king had signed a warrant to the Scottish privy council, containing his instructions regarding the Liturgy. In terms thereof, on the twentieth of December, the council made an act ordering his majesty's subjects to conform themselves to the new Service Book, and enjoining all archbishops, bishops, presbyters, and other churchmen to take care that it should be observed, and especially that every parish should provide two copies before the following Easter.[1]

[1] Baillie, vol. i. appendix, pp. 440, 441.

CHAPTER XLIX.

FROM THE ACT OF THE PRIVY COUNCIL REGARDING THE BOOK OF COMMON PRAYER IN DECEMBER, 1636, TO THE THREE PROCLAMATIONS OF 17TH OCTOBER, 1637.

Difficulties in the introduction of a Liturgy—Alleged abandonment of such a design by King James—Proposal to introduce the English Liturgy—Resolution to prepare a Liturgy for Scotland—Delays in its publication—Supposed differences of opinion among the Bishops—The Scottish Service Book—The Communion Office—The reading of the Service Book—The tumult at Edinburgh—The authors of the tumult—Proceedings of the Privy Council—Diocesan Synod of Glasgow—Petitions against the Service Book—Conversation between the Primate and the Earl of Rothes—Increased agitation—Proclamations of the seventeenth of October.

AT the Aberdeen assembly of 1616, it had been agreed that a uniform order of Liturgy or Divine Service should be prepared for the use of the Scottish Church, and certain ministers were appointed to revise the Book of Common Order for that purpose. This resolution was agreed to at the king's express recommendation. There can be no doubt that James intended to introduce the English Liturgy, or a form as near to it as possible; but it is equally evident that many of the members of the assembly merely contemplated a book on the model of that which had been used since the Reformation. We hear of no steps taken by the ministers as a body; but the bishops and others in the king's confidence prepared a Book of Common Prayer, which was submitted to James by Archbishop Spottiswood, and afterwards returned to the primate with several alterations and additions. Nothing farther was done during the reign of James. It is probable that he saw the great difficulties which had to be overcome before his object could be carried out, and that he hesitated again to disturb the prejudices of his Scottish subjects; but there is no good reason to believe that he ever wholly abandoned a design which he had so much at heart.[1]

A story, indeed, is told, which, if true, would shew that James had relinquished all intention of introducing a Liturgy into Scotland. Bishop Hacket, in his Life of Archbishop Williams, relates a conversation between King James and Williams, in which the former excused himself from promoting Laud to the see of St. David's, on account of the restless spirit of that divine, and his love to bring things to an ideal pitch of reformation; giving as an example that he had himself been urged by Laud to assimilate the Liturgy and canons of the Scottish Church to those of England, although he had promised after the Perth assembly to force no more changes upon the Scots. It is certain, however, that James made no promise at the Perth assembly. Such a promise was undoubtedly made by the Marquis of Hamilton, the royal commissioner, at the parliament of 1621, when the Perth articles were ratified; and to the latter circumstance accordingly Bishop Hacket makes express reference in proof of the statement given in his book. But it could not have been to Hamilton's promise that James alluded, for Laud was presented to the see of St. David's on the twenty-ninth of June, 1621, while the Scottish parliament did not meet till the end of July. The only authority for the statement was evidently Williams's own report. The hostility of that prelate to Laud, and his well-known practice of attributing words to others which they never used, joined to the improbability of the narrative itself, render the authenticity of the conversation as reported extremely suspicious. It has often been quoted as a proof of James's sagacity: it appears rather to be an illustration of the unscrupulous ingenuity of Williams.[2]

King Charles, after his accession, resumed his father's design, examined the book which had been prepared, and

---

[1] Large Declaration by King Charles the First, pp. 16, 17. Baillie, vol. i. appendix, pp. 443, 444.

[2] See Hacket's Life of Archbishop Williams, part i. pp. 63, 64; Calderwood, vol. vii. pp. 488, 489; Spottiswood, vol. iii. p. 263. Compare what Clarendon says of Williams (History, vol. ii. p. 105): "He had a faculty of making relation of things done in his own presence, or discoveries made to himself or in his own hearing, with all the circumstances of answers and replies, and upon arguments of great moment, all which upon examination were still found to have nothing in them that was real, but to be the pure effect of his own invention."

gave instructions regarding it to the Archbishop of St. Andrews, and through him to others of the clergy. In the year 1629, Dr. Maxwell, then one of the ministers of Edinburgh, waited by the king's command on Bishop Laud, and explained to him what was proposed in regard to the Liturgy. On that occasion, Laud expressed his opinion that the English Book of Common Prayer should be adopted without any variation, that so the same Service Book might be used in all his majesty's dominions. Maxwell answered that the Scottish bishops thought differently; that they believed their countrymen would be better satisfied with a Liturgy framed by their own clergy; but that they had no objection that it should be drawn up on the English model. The king was of the same opinion as Laud, and for a considerable time entertained the design of introducing the English Liturgy. Afterwards, however, on the urgent remonstrances of the Scottish prelates, this plan was given up, and it was agreed that a Liturgy should be prepared in Scotland, similar, on the whole, to that used in England, but differing in some particular points. Laud received the king's command to give his assistance in framing the book on this principle.

It is probable that the new Liturgy was drawn up chiefly by Dr. Maxwell and Dr. Wedderburn, Bishops of Ross and Dunblane. The latter prelate appears to have been mainly instrumental in obtaining the restoration, in the order for the ministration of the Holy Communion, of portions of the office which had been lost in the Church of England since the first Liturgy of King Edward VI. The whole was entrusted for revisal to Archbishop Laud, Dr. Juxon, Bishop of London, and Dr. Wren, Bishop of Norwich. There can be no doubt that the English primate was one of the chief promoters of the book. He himself tells us that, after it had been finally agreed to give up the literal adoption of the English Liturgy, he gave the matter the best help he could.

On the eighteenth of October, 1636—the same day on which warrant was given to the privy council for enjoining the use of the Service Book—the king sent certain special instructions regarding it to the archbishops and bishops in Scotland. One of these was, that in the Calendar they should retain such Catholic saints as were in the English

Calendar, adding the Scottish saints, especially those of the royal blood, and some of the most holy bishops, and in no case omitting St. George and St. Patrick.[1]

It is probable that, at the date of the proclamation following the act of the privy council in December enjoining the use of the Liturgy, the printing of the book was completed; but various circumstances occurred, which did not allow of its distribution so early as was intended. In order to prepare the way for its reception, the king had enjoined the archbishops and bishops to cause the English Book of Common Prayer to be read in their cathedrals, and to be said daily in their own houses, and in the colleges, according to the practice in the chapel royal; but, on their requesting that everything should remain as before till their own book was published, the order was withdrawn. When proclamation was made at the market crosses of the various burghs in terms of the act of council, considerable alarm was caused. As copies of the Liturgy were not yet given out, strange rumours were circulated regarding its contents; and the national and religious feelings of the people were excited also by assertions that it differed in no respect from the English book, except in the addition of other Popish rites. Persons of more moderate views were startled by its promulgation without any synodical authority. Robert Baillie, then minister at Kilwinning, and as yet favourably disposed to Episcopacy though averse to ritual changes, in a letter written at the time, speaks of this as contrary to the English rule, by which the convocation was always consulted, and quotes the opinion of Bishop Andrews, "the semigod of the new faction," that all church laws and canons ecclesiastical should always be made in church assemblies and not elsewhere.

Before Easter, copies of the book were ready for distribution. A letter, addressed about this time by the Scottish primate to the Bishop of Norwich, indicates the opinion of Spottiswood regarding the Liturgy. "I was desired," he says, " to present your lordship with one of the copies of our Scottish Liturgy, which is formed so nigh to the English as we could, that it might be known how we are nothing different

---

[1] Laud's Works, vol. iii. pp. 356-359, 427-429; vol. vi. p. 456-459. Heylin's Life of Laud, part ii. pp. 49, 50. Large Declaration, p. 17-19. Baillie, vol. i. appendix, pp. 443, 444.

in substance from that Church. And God I beseech to keep us one, and free us from those that crave divisions. Your lordship will be pleased to accept this little present as a testimony of our Church's love, and sent by him who truly loveth your lordship." Certain circumstances, which are not explained, prevented the Bishop of Edinburgh from beginning the use of the Liturgy at the time appointed, and it also appeared that a number of the ministers had not provided copies for the parish churches, as ordered by the proclamation. Easter accordingly passed over without the Liturgy being used. In the end of April, the Bishop of Edinburgh wrote to the ministers of his diocese, warning them to attend his diocesan synod on the last Wednesday of May, and informing them that he was then to make a communication regarding the Service Book, which, in the meantime, he enjoined them to purchase. Several of the other bishops, about the same time, laid the book before their synods, and finally, on the thirteenth of June, the privy council ordered letters to be issued, charging all presbyters and ministers to provide themselves with copies of the Service Book for the use of their parishes within fifteen days, under the pain of rebellion. At a meeting of the bishops, it was agreed that the public reading of the Liturgy should begin at Edinburgh, on Sunday, the twenty-third of July, and intimation to that effect was accordingly made on the previous Sunday in all the churches of the capital. The prelates were empowered, however, in virtue of instructions from the king, to dispense with the practice of some portions of the book in those cases where they found the ministers doubtful as to using it, and willing to be better informed regarding it.[1]

Such were the circumstances connected with the introduction of the Liturgy, as derived from the official records and other contemporary authorities. Several points are obscure and, in particular, the reasons for the delay which occurred are not very clearly stated. But an account has been given by Bishop Guthrie in his Memoirs, which, if correct, would explain these difficulties. According to that writer, the

[1] Baillie, vol. i. pp. 1, 2, 4, 16, 17, and appendix, p. 441-447. Large Declaration, p. 21. Gordon's Scots Affairs, vol. i. p. 3-6. The Bishop of Norwich, to whom Archbishop Spottiswood's letter was written, was not Bishop Hall, as mentioned in the appendix to Baillie, but Bishop Wren.

bishops were misled and betrayed by several of the lay counsellors, and the prelates themselves were divided in opinion, a considerable number of them being wholly averse to introducing the Liturgy at this time. It is sufficiently evident that most of the noblemen in the privy council disliked the bishops, and bore no good-will to the proposed ecclesiastical changes, and it is also certain that among the bishops there were some differences of opinion; but there appears to be much exaggeration in Guthrie's narrative. He tells us that it was the practice of king James, when a bishopric fell void, to order the Archbishop of St. Andrews to convoke the prelates, and name to him three or four persons whom they thought qualified for the vacant dignity, out of whom his majesty chose one, whereby the Church was always supplied with able bishops: but that this was altered in the reign of Charles who, without consulting the bishops, preferred those clergymen to the vacant sees who were recommended by some powerful courtier or statesman; and of those so appointed, that none were esteemed fit for the office, except Bishop Maxwell, whose great parts were rendered useless by as great ambition. The statement regarding King James's mode of selecting bishops is not borne out by the original ecclesiastical documents which have been preserved; and the prelates appointed in his time were certainly not superior either in learning or ability to those promoted in the reign of Charles. A similar inaccuracy prevails in the statement respecting the alienation between the elder and the younger bishops, and the marked dependence of the latter on the Archbishop of Canterbury. It is very probable that some of the bishops were opposed to a Liturgy altogether, and that others may have wished for a different method of introducing it; but there is no sufficient ground for believing that there were two parties, one composed of the elder bishops, averse to the changes, the other of the younger bishops, desirous to hurry on these changes, and relying on the support of Laud. There were political divisions among the prelates, as among the lay counsellors, immediately before the introduction of the Liturgy, but in these we find Maxwell and Sydserf, the two most strongly opposed to the Puritans, taking opposite sides.

Guthrie also asserts that, when the Liturgy was completed,

an entirely different line of proceeding was recommended by the two parties; that Spottiswood and the elder bishops, alarmed by the symptoms of popular hostility, wrote to the Archbishop of Canterbury, requesting that the book should be kept back till the nation was better prepared to receive it; while the younger bishops, encouraged by the treasurer, the Earl of Traquair, insisted that there was no danger, and that the work should go on. He adds that the latter furnished Traquair with letters to the English primate, and that that nobleman, whose real object was to ruin the prelates, hastened to court, and, on his representations, Laud obtained for himself a warrant from the king, commanding the bishops to go on at all hazards, and threatening, if they delayed longer, to turn them out of their places, and appoint resolute persons who would not fear to do their duty. When this order was brought to Scotland, the elder bishops, we are told, seeing that no other course was left to them, now threw all moderation aside, and acted as recklessly and imprudently as the others.

How far Traquair deserved the great trust reposed in him by the king and the Archbishop of Canterbury has frequently been questioned, and, perhaps, cannot now be ascertained. Laud himself afterwards suspected him: Clarendon believed in his constant loyalty. But however this may have been, the narrative of Guthrie is improbable in itself, and unsupported by evidence. Had such a warrant as he speaks of been obtained by Laud, it could hardly have escaped the notice of those who subsequently preferred the charges against him. In estimating the value of Guthrie's testimony, it should be kept in mind that, though favourable to Episcopacy, and a member of the court of High Commissson, and himself a bishop after the Restoration, he subscribed the Covenant, and for a number of years acted with the prevailing party. And in weighing the whole circumstances connected with the introduction of the Liturgy, caution must be used in giving belief to accusations of treachery or incapacity regarding particular proceedings, which were perhaps well considered at the time, and only condemned when they were found to be unsuccessful.[1]

The Scottish Service Book of 1637 was framed on the model of the English Book of Common Prayer, from which it

[1] See Guthrie's Memoirs, p. 13-18.

did not differ in any material respect, except in the office for the Holy Communion. Prefixed to it was the royal proclamation enjoining its use, as ordered in council on the twentieth of December, 1636. A preface followed, which made reference to the constant use of some prescribed order of prayer in the Church; to the desirableness of uniformity; and to the propriety of adhering to the English form, even as to some festivals and rites which were not yet received in Scotland. Next came, in terms for the most part similar to those used in the present English Prayer Book, remarks on Ceremonies—why some should be abolished and some retained; the order how the Psalter was appointed to be read; the order how the rest of Holy Scripture was appointed to be read; a Table of proper Psalms and Lessons for Sundays and other Holy-days; a Table for the order of the Psalms at Daily Prayer; an Almanac for thirty-four years, commencing with 1637; a Table and Calendar for the daily Psalms and Lessons; and a list of Holy-days which were to be observed. In the Calendar, the king's instructions had been attended to regarding the insertion of the principal Scottish saints. Among these were St. David, St. Kentigern, St. Colman, St. Patrick, St. Gilbert, St. Columba, St. Palladius, St. Ninian, St. Adamnan, and St. Margaret. In the Table of daily Lessons the Apocryphal books were omitted, and the place which they occupy in the English Table was supplied by additional Lessons from the Pentateuch, the Prophets, and the Books of Chronicles, the Lessons from Isaiah being read in the order of the Books in the Old Testament, and not during Advent. Prefixed to the Daily Service was a rubric that Morning and Evening Prayer should be used in the accustomed place of the church, chapel, or chancel, except it should be otherwise determined by the Ordinary; that the chancels should remain as in times past; and that presbyters or ministers, at the time of the Communion and at other times in their ministrations, should use such ornaments in the church as were or should be prescribed by his majesty and his successors, according to the act of parliament in that behalf.

After these came the Order for Morning and Evening Prayer daily throughout the year. The Daily Services hardly differed in anything from those in the English Book of Common Prayer, except in the substitution of "Presbyter" for "Priest" in the rubrics, and of the Psalm Dominus regit me for the Benedicite. The Creed of St. Athanasius and the Litany followed, and after these the Collects, Epistles, and Gospels to be used throughout the year.

The Order of the administration of the Holy Communion differed in several important respects from the present English office, and still more from the office as it stood in the Book of Common Prayer before the Restoration. By the rubric, it was enjoined that "the Holy Table, having at the Communion time a carpet and a fair white linen cloth upon it, with other decent furniture meet for the high mysteries there to be celebrated," should stand at the uppermost part of the chancel or church. The Presbyter, standing at the north side or end of the Table, was to say the Lord's Prayer and the collect of preparation; and afterwards, turning to the people, was to rehearse the Ten Commandments, the people kneeling, and asking God's mercy for the transgression of every duty therein, either according to the letter, or the mystical import of the commandment. After the Nicene Creed, if there was no sermon, there was to follow one of the Homilies afterwards to be set forth by authority. In the offertory sentences, there were none from the Apocryphal books. A commemoration of the faithful departed was inserted at the end of the prayer for the Church militant. In the prayer of Consecration there was an express Invocation of the Holy Spirit. The Memorial or prayer of Oblation followed, after which came the Lord's Prayer, and the collect of humble access. In the benedictions to be said at delivering the Bread and the Cup, the latter part of the English form was omitted.

After the Order for the Communion, came the Form of ministration of Public Baptism. The first prayer contained the following words:—"Sanctify this fountain of Baptism, Thou which art the Sanctifier of all things:" and a rubric ordered the water in the font to be changed twice in the month at least; and the words above mentioned were to be said before any child was baptized in the water so changed.

The Order for Private Baptism followed; then the Office for Confirmation and the Catechism; and the Form of Solemnization of Matrimony. By a rubric at the end of the Marriage

Service, the newly married persons were enjoined to receive the Holy Communion on the day of the marriage. Next after these came the Order for the Visitation and Communion of the Sick, and for the Burial of the Dead. In the Burial Office, the Psalms were omitted, and the Lesson was to be read beside the grave. The Office for the Churching of Women followed, the Psalms appointed for it being the hundred and twenty-first, and the twenty-seventh. The book concluded with the Commination. The edition of the Psalter to be used along with the Prayer Book had been printed in 1636, and in it, as well as throughout the book itself, the Psalms and Hymns were according to the translation of the Bible made in the reign of King James.[1]

As already mentioned, it was finally agreed that the Service Book should be read in the various churches at Edinburgh on Sunday the twenty-third of July. When intimation was made on the previous Sunday, there was no appearance of any opposition. On the day appointed, being the seventh Sunday after Trinity, in order that the service should be celebrated with the utmost solemnity, the Archbishop of St. Andrews, chancellor of the kingdom, the Archbishop of Glasgow, the Bishop of Edinburgh, with several other bishops, lords of the privy council, and judges of the supreme court, and the magistrates of the city, attended at ten in the forenoon,

---

[1] The rumours spread abroad at the time regarding the contents of the Liturgy were not more absurd than some accounts of it which have been given since. Mr. Brodie's remarks upon it (History, vol. ii. p. 445-449), are as extraordinary as his observations on the Canons. He adds, in reference to the meeting of the privy council on the twentieth of December when the Liturgy was enjoined— "The council, though a lay meeting, was in reality composed of the bishops. Eleven members constituted a quorum, and that number was expressly selected for the occasion. Nine of them were ecclesiastics, and the other two were unprepared to vote, as they had not even seen the book which the meeting authorized and enforced." Those present were indeed eleven in number, but they were all laymen except the chancellor and the Archbishop of Glasgow ; see the names given in the appendix to Baillie, vol. i. p. 440. A contemporary Covenanting pamphlet, entitled, "A short relation of the State of the Kirk of Scotland," which was chiefly intended for circulation in England, contains a similar assertion, though not in such specific terms, that approbation was given to the Book of Common Prayer, "when few but bishops were present at Council." Many statements, made at the time in this way by unscrupulous partizans, have since been repeated, as if they possessed all the weight due to impartial authority.

at the cathedral church of St. Giles. The old service had already been used at an earlier hour. As soon as Dr. Hanna, Dean of Edinburgh, began the new service in the reading desk, a tumult arose among the meaner sort of the congregation, especially the women; and, when the dean continued to read, the noise and confusion increased, so that the prayers could not be heard. The Bishop of Edinburgh, who was to preach on the occasion, ascended the pulpit, and endeavoured to appease the uproar, putting the people in mind of the place where they were, and of the solemn duty for which they had come together. His address only caused further hootings and confusion, in the course of which a stool was thrown at him, which might have inflicted serious injury if the blow had not been diverted by one of the by-standers. The primate and others of the council then interposed, but to no purpose, till the magistrates descended from the gallery set apart for them, and with considerable difficulty thrust out the rioters. The dean then proceeded with the service, and the bishop preached, although the noise still continued outside. When the congregation were dismissed, Bishop Lindsay, on his way home, was surrounded by the rabble, and was only rescued by the intervention of the Earl of Wemyss.

Similar disturbances took place in the other churches of the city, especially in the Greyfriars' Church, where Bishop Fairley, elect of Argyll, was obliged to give up reading the service after finishing the absolution. Between the hours of service, the privy counsellors assembled in the chancellor's lodging, and, sending for the magistrates, took such precautions that the Evening Service was said at St. Giles, and some of the other churches, without interruption. The Bishop of Edinburgh, however, was again attacked while returning from church in the Earl of Roxburgh's coach, and his life would have been in danger had he not been protected by the armed servants of that nobleman.[1]

[1] Large Declaration, p. 23-25. Row, pp. 408,409. Baillie, vol. i. p. 18. Gordon's Scots Affairs, vol. i. p. 7-12. Appendix to Rothes's Relation, p. 198-200. Brodie, vol. ii. p. 452-456. The "Brief and true relation of the Broil which fell out on the Lord's day, the 23d of July, 1637, through the occasion of a black, Popish, and superstitious Service Book, which was then illegally introduced and impudently vented within the churches of Edinburgh," printed in the appendix to the Earl of Rothes's Relation of Proceedings concerning the

It was suspected at the time, and it has frequently been maintained since, that the riot of the twenty-third of July was no accidental explosion of popular feeling, but the result of a deliberate plan, contrived by the leaders of the Presbyterian party. Nothing certain can be known as to this, for the privy council and the magistrates of Edinburgh never made any proper attempt to discover who were the real authors of the tumult. But the conjecture is probable in itself, and affords the best explanation of the events which took place. There would be no room for doubt if the accounts given by Spalding and Guthrie could be relied on. The former writer mentions that the whole was arranged by the Lords Lindsay, Loudon, Balmerino, Cupar, and other noblemen, including the Marquis of Hamilton, and "a menzie of miscontented Puritans," of whom Henderson, Dickson, and Cant, were the ring-leaders. Guthrie tells us that a consultation was held at Edinburgh, in the month of April, at which Henderson attended on behalf of his brethren in Fife, and Dickson for those in the West; that they communicated with Sir Thomas Hope, and Lord Balmerino, and, having obtained their approbation, afterwards met in the house of Nicholas Balfour in the Cowgate, with several matrons whose names are given, one of them being Elspet Craig, the mother of Johnstone of Warriston. All this may be correct, except in regard to the participation of the Marquis of Hamilton, but there is little to support it beyond the assertions of the writers themselves. Spalding may always be trusted in his narrative of what took place in the neighbourhood of Aberdeen, but his information regarding events at a distance is frequently inaccu-

affairs of the Kirk of Scotland, from August, 1637, to July, 1638, is the narrative which Mr. Brodie quotes under the name of "Stopic-field-day," and which he erroneously ascribes to Sir James Balfour; see appendix to Rothes, p. 201. It bears to be dated "From Stonefield, at the sign of the Flaming Fire which might have burned up the Bishop of Argyll's house the day of his solemn festival consecration, being the eighth of August, 1637." It is a scurrilous and indecent account of what is alleged to have taken place, written by some Puritan at the time, and its accuracy has been too much relied upon. Bad as the tumult was, the details of this narrative are evidently exaggerated. It is composed in the very spirit of Knox's account of the murder of Cardinal Beaton, and, if Sir James Balfour had really been the author, it would form a strange contrast to his recital of the gorgeous ceremonial of the Coronation of King Charles.

rate; while Guthrie's statements, on this as on some other points, must be received with caution.[1]

The privy council met on the twenty-fourth of July, and issued a proclamation denouncing the rioters. The magistrates of Edinburgh made a submissive apology for what had occurred, apprehended some persons suspected to be implicated, and professed their readiness to do everything in their power to promote the quiet establishment of the Service Book. At a meeting on the twenty-ninth of July, the chancellor, in his own name and that of the other bishops, reported that, on account of the late tumults and for other reasons, it was thought good to forbear reading the Service Book till his majesty's pleasure should be known, and that, in the meantime, orders had been given that sermons should be preached in all the churches of the city at the accustomed hours, with a prayer before and after, but without either the old or the new service. This report was approved of by the council.

Baillie, evidently referring to this proceeding, mentions that Edinburgh was put under an episcopal interdict, that there was no preaching or prayers on the week days, and no reading or prayers on Sunday; and Spalding asserts that after the tumult all the church doors were locked, and no more preaching heard, and that the zealous Puritans flocked every Sunday for their devotions to Fife. The latter statement is exaggerated. What the bishops suspended was the use both of the old Book of Common Order and of the new Liturgy, but not the accustomed preaching.[2]

On the fourth of August, a letter from the king, dated the thirtieth of July, was laid before the council. The letter exhorted them to search for and punish the authors of the late tumult, and to support the clergy in establishing the Service Book. The council again met on the following day, and agreed that the use of the Liturgy should be resumed on Sunday, the thirteenth of August, and that, in the meantime, the ministers should preach on the ordinary days without service. Notwithstanding this resolution, the Liturgy was

[1] See Spalding, vol. i. pp. 78, 79, and Guthrie, pp. 20, 21.
[2] Large Declaration, p. 26. Baillie, vol. i. p. 18, aud appendix, p. 448. Spalding, vol. i. p. 80.

not used on the day named, the difficulty in finding readers to officiate, and other reasons, being alleged in excuse.

On the nineteenth of August, the magistrates of Edinburgh wrote to Archbishop Laud, expressing their regret on account of the tumult, mentioning their readiness to concur with their ordinary and ministers for settling the Service Book, appealing for their justification to the Lord Treasurer, and the Bishops of Galloway and Dunblane, and soliciting the archbishop's good offices with the king.[1]

Differences, in the meantime, had arisen between the bishops and the lay members of the privy council. Instead of using their united endeavours to restore tranquillity, they wrote separately to the king, each blaming the other for what had occurred—the prelates complaining of the want of hearty support from the noblemen, and referring to the absence of the treasurer from Edinburgh on the twenty-third of July, with no better pretext than the marriage of a kinsman; while Traquair and the others accused the bishops of precipitation, and of not giving due notice of their intentions to the lay lords. On the seventh of August, Archbishop Laud wrote to Traquair, blaming both the nobles and the bishops for their conduct, and especially censuring the latter for having put an interdict on divine service. The Earl of Traquair was the person on whom Laud placed his chief reliance, and this letter contains an exposition of the principles on which the archbishop professed to act in the affairs of the Scottish Church. "I think you know," he says, "my opinion how I would have church business carried, were I as great a master of men as, I thank God, I am of things. It is true the Church, as well there as elsewhere, hath been overborne by violence both in matters of maintenance and jurisdiction. But if the Church will recover in either of these, she and her governors must proceed not as she was proceeded against, but by a constant temper she must make the world see she had the wrong, but offer none. And since law hath followed in that kingdom, perhaps to make good that which was ill done; yet, since a law it is, such a reformation or restitution would be sought for, as might stand with the law, and some expedient be found out how

[1] Peterkin's Records of the Kirk of Scotland, pp. 52, 53. Large Declaration, pp. 28, 29.

the law may be by some just exposition helped, till the state shall see cause to abolish it."[1]

The bishops now proceeded to enjoin the use of the Liturgy in other dioceses, and for that purpose to order copies to be purchased by the ministers. Little is known of what took place in the North. Some ministers in the diocese of St. Andrews disregarded the injunction, and in consequence were charged to obey under the pain of rebellion. One of these was Alexander Henderson, whose proceedings in consequence of the charge will immediately be adverted to. The correspondence of Baillie supplies full details of what took place at Glasgow. The diocesan synod had been appointed by Archbishop Lindsay to be held on the last Wednesday of August, and Baillie himself was requested to preach on the occasion, and to urge on his hearers the duty of conforming to the canons and the Service Book. Baillie, in answer, thanked the archbishop for the honour proposed to be conferred upon him; and for his many past favours, but asked to be excused from the duty imposed, in respect of his not being at all satisfied with the new formularies, so far as he had yet been able to examine them. The archbishop, in reply, commanded him on his canonical obedience to preach, but left the subject of the sermon to his own discretion. He prepared to submit, but was relieved from the disagreeable task by the archbishop altering his arrangements, and requesting William Annand, minister at Ayr, to preach at the opening of the synod. Annand, a learned and orthodox divine, defended the Liturgy in his sermon, as well, according to Baillie's own testimony, as any man in Britain could have done under the circumstances. The discourse excited the wrath of the female Puritans of Glasgow, and on the following evening Annand was attacked by a large number of them, and hardly escaped with his life. Next day, to prevent a threatened renewal of the outrage, the magistrates and some of his friends conducted him out of the city. " This tumult," says Baillie, " was so great, that it was not thought meet to search either in plotters

---

[1] Baillie, vol. i. pp. 18, 19. Rushworth, vol. ii. pp. 389, 390. See also the letter of 27th August, from the Earl of Traquair to the Marquis of Hamilton, in Burnet's Memoirs of the Dukes of Hamilton, pp. 31, 32.

or actors of it, for numbers of the best quality would have been found guilty."[1]

On the twenty-third of August, a petition from Henderson and two other ministers in Fife, and several petitions from the West, were presented to the council. The supplication of Henderson and his associates set forth, that they had been required by the moderator of their presbytery to accept two copies of the Book of Common Prayer; that they had declared their willingness to receive one copy in order that they might know its contents before promising to use it; that this proposal had not been agreed to; and that, in consequence, they had been charged to provide themselves with two copies. They therefore prayed the lords of council to suspend the charge against them for the following reasons:—first, because the book was warranted neither by the general assembly nor by act of parliament; secondly, because the liberties of the true Church, and the form of worship and religion received at the Reformation, and universally practised since, were warranted by various acts of assembly and acts of parliament; thirdly, because the Church of Scotland was a free and independent Church, and its pastors were best able to provide what was for the good of the people; fourthly, because it was well known what disputes there had been respecting a few of the many ceremonies contained in that book, which, when examined, would be found to depart from the established form of worship, and to draw near to the antichristian Church of Rome; fifthly, because the people had been always taught a different doctrine since the Reformation, and would not agree to such changes, even if their pastors were willing to submit.

These petitions were supported by the written and personal solicitations of many noblemen and gentlemen. On the twenty-fifth of August, the council declared that their intention regarding the former acts had been mistaken, and that they had only meant that ministers should buy copies of the Liturgy. This interpretation could not be reconciled with the plain meaning of the act of the twentieth of December, and the proclamation prefixed to the Service Book. In a letter written to the king the same day, the council represented the discontent which prevailed even among those formerly obedient

[1] Baillie, vol. i. p. 19-21.

to the civil and ecclesiastical authority, and the clamours and fears of all parts of the kingdom; and stated that they had therefore agreed to let the matter rest till they had his majesty's instructions, after he should have summoned to his presence some of their own number, both clergy and laity, or otherwise, as to his majesty might seem proper, and that they had also agreed to meet again on the twentieth of September. The letter, which was signed not only by Traquair and other lay counsellors, but also by the Archbishop of St Andrews and several of the prelates, said nothing of the interpretation put on the former acts.

The king answered this letter on the tenth of September. He declined to call up any of the council to London, and expressed his dissatisfaction with the delay in causing the Service Book to be read, and the remissness in discovering and punishing those who had been accessory to the tumult in July. He farther intimated his pleasure that every bishop should cause the Liturgy to be read in his own diocese, as had already been done by the Bishops of Ross and Dunblane.

Meanwhile the popular agitation continued to increase. Petitions against the Liturgy had been circulated through the kingdom, and, on the twentieth of September, were presented to the council. A general supplication to the same effect was given in by the Earl of Sutherland, in name of the nobility, barons, ministers, and burgesses, who had assembled in great numbers at Edinburgh. The council were much perplexed how to act. They finally agreed to decline answering the supplications till they heard from the king. This resolution they communicated to the Earls of Sutherland and Wemyss on behalf of the petitioners. They farther appointed a committee of their own number to attend to what was necessary to be done during the vacation of the courts, and requested the Duke of Lennox, who had come down to Scotland to attend his mother's funeral, to represent to his majesty the actual state of matters, and the great difficulties which had arisen. In a letter to the king, they mentioned that more than sixty-eight petitions had been presented against the Service Book.[1]

---

[1] Baillie, vol. i. pp. 21, 22, and appendix, p. 449-454. Balfour, vol. ii. p. 233-235.

The Earl of Rothes, one of the leading persons among the petitioners, in his narrative of these proceedings, gives an account of a conversation which he had with the Archbishop of St. Andrews on the twentieth of September. On his mentioning that the Liturgy was irregularly brought in, and that it was unsound, the archbishop asked what evidence he had of the latter charge. Rothes referred to the Communion Office, and also to the Office for Baptism, in which it was asserted that all baptized infants were regenerated. Spottiswood maintained that the book was not fairly interpreted, and stated that the Bishop of Derry had approved of it, declaring that Scotland had therein the advantage of England; and that it was commended also by the prince's tutor, both he and the bishop saying that there had been no such Liturgy since the first six hundred years after Christ. Rothes answered that the Bishop of Derry was reputed to be the most unsound man in Ireland, and that he and the prince's tutor were known Arminians. In conclusion, Spottiswood asked, with a smile, "What needed this resistance? If the king would turn Papist we behoved to obey. Who could resist princes? When King Edward was a Protestant and made a reformation, Queen Mary changed it, and Queen Elizabeth altered it again. And so there was no resisting of princes, and there was no Church without troubles." Rothes replied, "They got it soon changed in England; the two professions were nearly equally divided; but there were few here to concur in such a change, all being reformed, and would never yield. The reformation of England was not so complete as that of Scotland, and had not so much law for it; it was but half reformed."[1]

On the twenty-sixth of September, the magistrates of Edinburgh again wrote to Archbishop Laud, mentioning the great

---

[1] Rothes's Relation, p. 10. The Bishop of Derry was Dr. Bramhall; the tutor of the Prince of Wales was Dr. Duppa. Spottiswood had sent a copy of the Book of Common Prayer to Bramhall; and it is probable that besides that prelate and Wren, other bishops in England and Ireland had also received copies. Bramhall, writing to Spottiswood on the 13th of August, says, "I humbly thank your grace for your high favour, the Book of Common Prayer; glad I was to see it, and more glad to see it such as it is; to be envied in some things perhaps if one owned." (Bramhall's Works, Anglo-Catholic Library, vol. i. p. lxxxvi.)

change for the worse which had taken place since the date of their former letter; the confluence of large numbers both of clergy and laity to the capital; and the necessity they had finally been under of petitioning the council not to urge the Service Book upon them, farther than upon the rest of the kingdom. The state of matters had now indeed become alarming. The whole of the south of Scotland was roused to a degree of excitement which had not been known since the early days of the Reformation. The persons whose task it had been to stir up the passions of the people were completely successful. The exhortations of the nobles, the sermons of the preachers, the deputations sent through the country, the tracts which were busily circulated, had done their work, and made a great part of the nation indifferent to all the horrors of rebellion and civil war. The Canons and Liturgy had been introduced without legal authority; and now authority of every kind was to be set at defiance in resisting them. Baillie, who had himself taken an active part in the agitation and cannot be supposed to exaggerate the evil, tells his correspondent in Holland what was going on, in language which marks his foreboding consciousness of the issue towards which he and others were allowing themselves to be hurried: " What shall be the event," he says, " God knows. There was never in our land such an appearance of a stir: the whole people think Popery at the doors; the scandalous pamphlets which come daily new from England, add oil to this flame; no man may speak anything in public for the king's part, except he would have himself marked for a sacrifice to be killed one day. I think our people possessed with a bloody devil, far above any thing that ever I could have imagined, though the Mass in Latin had been presented. The ministers who have the command of their mind do disavow their unchristian humour, but are noways so zealous against the devil of their fury, as they are against the seducing spirit of the bishops. For myself, I think, God, to revenge the crying sins of all estates and professions, which no example of our neighbours' calamities would move us to repent, is going to execute his long denounced threatenings, and to give us over unto madness, that we may every one shoot our swords in our neighbours' hearts. Our dregs are like to be more bitter than was the brim of God's cup either to the French or to the Dutch; ye and all your neighbours had much need to pray for us, as we have oft done for you, in your dangers. The barricades of Paris, the Catholic League of France is much before my eyes, but I hope the devil shall never find a Duke of Guise to lead the bands." [1]

On the ninth of October, the king wrote to the council, postponing an answer to their petitions; and, the lords having met on the seventeenth of that month, three proclamations were issued. By the first of these, it was declared that nothing would be done that day regarding church matters; and the petitioners, who had assembled in great numbers in expectation of an answer, were ordered to leave Edinburgh within twenty-four hours, unless they could show just cause, in connection with their private affairs, for remaining. By the second, the courts of justice were ordered to be removed first to Linlithgow, and afterwards to Dundee. By the third, all copies of a book entitled "A Dispute against the English Popish Ceremonies obtruded upon the Church of Scotland," were ordered to be brought to the council, and publicly burned. [2]

[1] Large Declaration, pp. 29, 30. Baillie, vol. i. p. 23.
[2] Balfour, vol. ii. p. 236. Large Declaration, p. 32-34.

CHAPTER L.

FROM THE THREE PROCLAMATIONS OF 17TH OCTOBER, 1637, TO THE PROCLAMATION OF 19TH FEBRUARY, 1638.

Gillespie's Book against the English Ceremonies—Objections to the Liturgy—Unreasonable expectations of the King—Causes of the opposition to the Liturgy—Opinions of the Clergy—Conduct and Character of the Bishops—The Nobility—Riot at Edinburgh—Complaint against the Bishops—Proceedings of the Privy Council—The King's determination to adhere to the Service Book—Proclamation of the nineteenth of February.

THE book against the English ceremonies, which was prohibited by the third of the proclamations of the seventeenth of October, was published without the author's name, and is supposed to have been printed in Holland. It was afterwards known to be the composition of George Gillespie, a young man then living in the family of the Earl of Cassillis, and subsequently one of the ministers of Edinburgh. Its object was to prove that the Perth articles and certain other ceremonies were neither necessary, expedient, nor lawful. It is a dull, tedious work, but, though sufficiently severe in its language, is not composed in the offensive tone which distinguishes some of the books written by the English Puritans, at this time, against the government and ritual of the Church. Except that it was the latest work on the subject, there appears to have been no sufficient reason why it should have been singled out in the proclamation. As it was, the prohibition caused it to be more eagerly read, and gave it an importance much beyond its real merits.

The objections which now began to be circulated against the Liturgy were more calculated to produce an injurious effect on the popular mind. They generally assumed the form of two assertions—first, that the Service Book was mainly taken from the English Book of Common Prayer, which was itself in various respects erroneous and superstitious; secondly, that in the points wherein it differed from the English form, the differences were such as to bring it nearer to the offices of the Church of Rome, or, as the common expression was, to the Mass.

In so far as the objections applied both to the English and Scottish books, they were of that kind which had all along been maintained by the Puritans of both kingdoms; and, if even the arguments of Hooker had failed to convince his countrymen, it was still less probable that any attempt to persuade the Presbyterians of Scotland would be successful. The accusation that the changes introduced into the Scottish Service Book brought it nearer to the Roman forms and doctrines was unjust; and, so far as the daily offices were concerned, its injustice must have been obvious even to the objectors themselves. The changes were manifestly in the opposite direction, and were intended to conciliate the popular feeling. Such was the substitution of "Presbyter" for "Priest" in the rubrics, and the omission of the Benedicite, and of the Apocryphal Lessons except on a few holy-days. There was, however, one important difference between the two books, in which it need excite no surprise that the Puritans of the seventeenth century could only see an approach to the teaching of Rome. The Scottish office for the ministration of the Holy Communion varied considerably, both in words and arrangement, from the English Liturgy, and the change undoubtedly indicated an opinion regarding the Eucharist, different from that which had generally prevailed in England. Laud and the Scottish bishops, who introduced the alteration, must have foreseen that the charge of departing from the established doctrine would be brought against them, but they were content to encounter the danger, for the sake of accomplishing a practical restoration of the belief once held by the universal Church on a subject of so much importance.

King Charles was not prepared for the determined opposition which the Liturgy encountered. In the Large Declaration he mentions the reasons which he had for believing that his injunctions would be obeyed, and that the Book of Common Prayer would be received. These were that the nobility and gentry, and his Scottish subjects generally, who resorted to England, attended the churches in that country without ever objecting to the Liturgy as unlawful and antichristian; that the English Service had been regularly celebrated in the chapel royal at Holyrood since the year 1617, and had been attended by all classes without dislike; that it had been used by the bishops while conferring orders, and for several years back had been also read in some cathedral churches, and in the New College at St Andrews; that many families had used it in private; and that, during his visit to Scotland, it had been publicly read in all churches where he was present, and many of the people had then resorted to it. He also states that, inasmuch as the Scottish Service Book was in substance the same with that of England, he never expected a charge of Popery or superstition would be brought against a Liturgy, which had been compiled by the bishops and other divines who in Queen Mary's reign had preferred banishment and death to submission to Rome, and which had since been cherished by the English clergy who had done so much to oppose Popery.[1]

Expectations founded on such reasons ought not to have deceived Charles and his counsellors. They should have been aware that a powerful, unscrupulous party would raise the cry of Popery against any ecclesiastical measure supported by the court; and, knowing how difficult it was to maintain the Book of Common Prayer in England, they should have been prepared for much more formidable obstacles to the introduction of a new Liturgy in Scotland. But, independently of mere political adversaries, resistance of another kind might have been anticipated, from the manner in which the Liturgy was introduced, and from the character of the book itself. Not only the Presbyterians who refused to acknowledge any ecclesiastical supremacy in the sovereign, but all who held that the crown was not entitled to exercise its prerogative without the concurrence of the Church, would naturally be averse to so important an alteration introduced by the authority of the king. If the very words in which the clergy were to minister the sacraments and offer the daily prayers of the Church were to be dictated by the crown, it was not easy to see why the temporal authority might not also proceed to define articles of faith.

Farther, the new Liturgy itself contained doctrines very

[1] Large Declaration, p. 19-21.

different from those which hitherto had been generally received in Scotland. The king and his advisers believed in the truth of these doctrines; but the majority of the Scottish people were of a different opinion, and it was very unlikely that they would be willing to abandon their convictions at the bidding of an authority which they did not recognise. The king thought that, because the Scots in England frequented the churches there, and because in Scotland the English Service had been used in a few particular places, and on some solemn occasions, without objection, the Liturgy would therefore be willingly received as the only authorized form of public worship in the kingdom. The expectation was an unreasonable one. Although individual Scotsmen had made no objection to a foreign ritual which they were at liberty to attend or not as they pleased, it did not follow that the nation would submit to the same ritual when made obligatory on all. The change sought to be introduced was very great. It was not, indeed, as has frequently been supposed, an alteration from a form of worship wholly extemporaneous; but it was the substitution of a Liturgy with its rubrics, and calendar, and services, adapted to the course of the Christian year, its offices in which priests and people took part, and from which they were not allowed to deviate, for a meagre form, in which the prayers and confession were said by the minister alone, and might be varied by him at his own discretion, and the people took no part except in the singing of some metrical psalms. Those who like Charles and Laud loved the Church's ritual, and to whom it was a never-failing well-spring of the deepest and most fervent devotion, could hardly understand how any reasonable persons to whose knowledge it was brought could fail to appreciate so excellent a gift. They did not make allowance for the effects of the peculiar religious system which had grown up in Scotland in the course of eighty years, and which had now alienated the national mind from what had been the common heritage of Christendom for fifteen centuries. They utterly disregarded the lesson which they might have learned from the establishment of the Perth articles. If it was hardly possible to reconcile the people to a few ceremonies only occasionally used, what was to be expected from an absolute subversion of their whole system of worship?

The introduction of the English Liturgy in Scotland must, under any circumstances, have been a work of difficulty, but it was perilous to an extreme degree at the time chosen by King Charles. During the latter years of his father's reign, a zealous and powerful party had opposed the measures of the sovereign; and the influence and numbers of that party were now greatly increased. It was composed of those who from whatever motive were hostile to the royal supremacy, and to the restoration of Episcopacy. A considerable proportion of the gentry and burgesses had always belonged to that party, although the authority of the king had repeatedly protected them from the tyranny of the nobles. The ministers had formerly been its chief supporters, and among them some of its most zealous champions were still to be found, but a great change had taken place in that respect. The strenuous exertions made by the sovereign to recover the alienated possessions of the Church, and the influence acquired by the bishops since the restoration of episcopal government, had won over many of the ministers who would otherwise have opposed their measures. Had the clergy been left to themselves, the majority of them, though opposed to ritual innovations, and submitting to Episcopacy rather than heartily embracing it, would not have taken active steps against the king and their ecclesiastical superiors. The discontented minority, however, were prepared to encounter all dangers in order to overthrow a ceremonial and government which they detested. They were encouraged by the sympathy of those of their countrymen who now formed a powerful colony in Ireland, and they were in frequent communication with the English Puritans. Their authority was great among the lower classes of the people in the southern districts of the kingdom, and they had been particularly successful in acquiring an influence over the women of all ranks.

While most of the clergy were either faint defenders or vehement adversaries of the established system, there was, however, an increasing, though still comparatively small party, who loved Episcopacy and liturgical forms, and who appealed to the practice and authority of the ancient Church in support of their views. Such were the doctors of Aberdeen, and many of the clergy of that diocese; and such generally were the members of the theological faculties in the other universities, and some of the ministers in almost every diocese of the kingdom.

There is some difficulty in arriving at a true estimate of the conduct and character of the Scottish bishops themselves at this time. Many writers, even among those attached to the cause of royalty and Episcopacy, relying on the authority of Guthrie and Burnet, have spoken in very unfavourable terms of the prelates. If what is mentioned by the former of these historians be correct, the blame should chiefly be bestowed on the younger bishops, who are said to have owned a dependence on Laud. The doubtful character of Guthrie's assertions has already been referred to; and there seems to be no reason, so far as the canons and Liturgy are concerned, for excusing one portion of the hierarchy at the expense of another. Burnet's remarks are still more severe. He speaks of the prelates in the time of King James in the following language :—" The bishops themselves did their part very ill. They generally grew haughty : they neglected their functions, and were often at court, and lost all esteem with the people. Some few that were stricter and more learned did lean so grossly to Popery that the heat and violence of the Reformation became the main subject of their sermons and discourses." He describes them in the reign of Charles as lenient to the errors of Rome; as generally favourable to Arminianism ; as neglecting the due observance of the Lord's day, not careful to prevent simony, proud, ambitious, and overbearing; and he farther speaks of them, immediately before the commencement of the civil war, as so lifted up with the king's zeal, and encouraged by Archbishop Laud, that they lost all temper, as was acknowledged, he says, by Sydserf himself in his old age.[1]

There is some truth in these remarks, but the statement as a whole is greatly exaggerated. The charge of a gross leaning to Popery is a manifest calumny. Not one of the Scottish bishops joined the Church of Rome; and, unless William Forbes and Sydserf be exceptions, not one of them expressed himself favourably towards the Roman doctrines. There is reason to believe that some of them lost temper in their discussions with the nobility; but, in their intercourse

[1] Burnet's History of his Own Time, vol. i. pp. 17, 18, 44, and Memoirs of the Dukes of Hamilton, pp. 29, 30.

with the clergy, they were generally mild and conciliatory, and, unless when the law was openly and systematically defied, were far from severe in enforcing the penalties on non-conformity. Had they been as tyrannical as they are frequently represented, some of the most distinguished Puritans would not have been allowed to retain the parochial cures of which we find them in possession at the commencement of the revolution. In the discharge of their religious duties, the bishops appear for the most part to have been careful and attentive; some of them, as has been seen, were models of humility and devotion.

The charge of ambition is the one most commonly brought against the episcopal order. In evidence of its truth, reference is generally made to the appointment of Archbishop Spottiswood as Chancellor on the death of the Earl of Kinnoul, and to the proposal to confer the office of Treasurer on Bishop Maxwell on the resignation of the Earl of Morton; to the large number of prelates who held seats in the privy council; to their controversies with the nobility for power and precedence; to their attempts to recover the lands belonging to their sees; and to the plan for re-establishing the ancient abbacies and priories in the persons of ecclesiastics, and restoring the original constitution of the College of Justice, under which half of the judges were churchmen. How far some of these specific accusations are correct it is not easy to ascertain. Most of them rest on mere conjecture, and on the reports of adversaries, rendered more or less probable by the circumstances of the time. Thus the intention of naming Maxwell to be Treasurer is mentioned by Baillie, Burnet, and Guthrie; yet there does not seem to be sufficient authority for it, although the report was readily believed by those who saw Juxon holding the same office in England, and Spottiswood a yet higher one in Scotland. The only secular offices of any importance held by the bishops, in addition to the chancellorship, were the seats in the privy council; and these conferred more dignity than power. But such appointments were unfortunate and impolitic. It was not that the bishops were unfit for those duties, or inferior in ability and experience to their lay rivals; but offices of that description were now rightly held, as a general rule, to be inconsistent with spiritual functions, and the giving them to the clergy was sure to provoke the jealousy and opposition of the nobles.

That the bishops wished to recover the lands which had belonged to their predecessors, and the other ecclesiastical property which had been alienated at the Reformation, is certain; but they only proposed doing so by lawful purchase or voluntary resignation, and even to this extent the attempt appears to have been abandoned when it was discovered to be very unpopular. The proposal to restore the other ecclesiastical prelacies and to nominate churchmen to fill them is mentioned by Row; and also by Baillie and Burnet in connection with the presentation of a person named Learmonth to the abbacy of Lindores. There is no certainty, however, that such a plan was really contemplated. Learmonth was not appointed to the abbacy; and it is evident that Laud, the supposed prime mover of all these schemes, was entirely ignorant of this great contrivance, and only sought to procure the restoration of some particular abbey lands for specific ecclesiastical purposes. It is possible that the nobles may have believed in the existence of such a design; it is more probable that they spread the report in order to increase popular feeling against the bishops.[1]

The nobles, during the reign of Charles, were the chief opponents of the king and the Church. Had they supported the measures of the sovereign, as they did for a considerable time after the accession of James to the English crown, the Puritanical party among the ministers and people could not have attempted open resistance with any prospect of success. But various circumstances had contributed to make the nobility the most discontented portion of the king's subjects; and they were now ready, as at the era of the Reformation, to make common cause with those who were hostile to the established Church. Their power was not so great as it had been during the minority of James, but it was still very for-

---

[1] See Row, pp. 389, 395; Baillie, vol. i. pp. 6, 7; Burnet's Memoirs of the Dukes of Hamilton, p. 30, and History, vol. i. p. 34; Guthrie, p. 14; and Laud's Works, vol. iii. p. 312-314. King James had allowed his right to nominate ministers to abbacies and priories to fall into disuse. The last person who held such an office seems to have been Peter Hewat, Abbot of Crossraguel, one of the two ministers who were deprived for their concurrence in the protestation to parliament in 1617. See Acts of the Parliaments of Scotland, vol. iv. pp. 523, 524, and Spottiswood, vol. iii. p. 244.

midable, and sufficient to check the designs of a sovereign, who, within Scotland, had nothing to rely on for the support of his authority except the reverence which the royal name could command.

The party among the nobility opposed to the court had acquired greater strength in consequence of the proceedings regarding the tithes, and the apprehended revocation of church lands. The former of these measures, however beneficial to others, was disadvantageous to the nobles, and, if the latter had been carried out, many of them would have lost the best part of their property. They looked on the ecclesiastics as rivals who were seeking both to deprive them of their possessions, and to share with them those political offices and emoluments which for many years they had regarded as exclusively their own. They dreaded also the influence of the bishops in parliament. The race of lay commendators was extinct, their abbacies and priories having been converted into temporal baronies; and the bishops, who now formed the whole estate of the clergy, were able, while acting in a body, to be the real electors of the Lords of the Articles. All these circumstances drew the discontented nobles into a close alliance with the Puritans, and at least from the time of the king's visit the two parties had been acting in concert. Their common object was the ruin of the bishops, and the overthrow of the existing ecclesiastical establishment.

The dislike to the bishops, and to everything which tended to increase the authority of the Church, was not confined to the nobles who appeared in opposition to the measures of the court. It was shared by many of those who made zealous professions of loyalty, and even by the majority of the members of the privy council. Although the charge of actual treachery should be disregarded, there can be no doubt that this hostile feeling prevented the adoption of the proceedings best calculated to restore confidence and tranquillity after the tumults about the Liturgy. Had the council been really anxious to obey the king's injunctions, month after month would not have been wasted in inaction, while their opponents were openly preparing for the conflict. Many of the nobles did not see, till it was too late, that the struggle was for something more than church lands and ecclesiastical ceremonies.

The narrative of events may now be resumed. The first of the three proclamations of the seventeenth of October had commanded all strangers to leave Edinburgh. On the morning of the eighteenth, the Bishop of Galloway, while on his way to the council-house to discharge some judicial duties, was surrounded by the rabble, who followed him to the door, and who would have torn him to pieces had he not been defended by Francis Stewart, son of the Earl of Bothwell. A report had been spread abroad that the bishop wore a crucifix beneath his vest, and this added to the fury of the people. After he had found refuge within the council-house, Traquair and other lords of the council sent to the magistrates of Edinburgh, requiring them to disperse the rioters. These officials answered that they were beset by the multitude within their own place of meeting, and that they had been obliged for their safety to sign a paper against the Service Book. The treasurer, upon this, repaired to the magistrates, but, on his return, was attacked by the rabble, and thrown down on the street, and his white staff was pulled from him. With great difficulty he reached the council-house, and it was only by the assistance of some lords of the popular party that he and the Bishop of Galloway were enabled to return to their lodgings. The council met at Holyrood in the afternoon, and issued another proclamation against unlawful meetings, which was as little regarded as the former.[1]

In the meantime, a considerable number of the nobility, gentry, and ministers opposed to the Service Book, had assembled to deliberate regarding the terms of a complaint against the bishops, which was to be presented to the council. Baillie's narrative supplies an interesting detail of the proceedings. He had been requested to come to Edinburgh at this time by his patron, Lord Montgomery, eldest son of the Earl of Eglinton. The resolution to prepare the complaint was taken after the three proclamations were issued on the seventeenth. The nobles, and a few of the ministers in whom they confided, were the devisers of this step, the rest of the ministers and the gentry being kept in ignorance of the purport of the paper till it was ready. Two forms were prepared, one by Henderson and Lord Balmerino, the other by Dickson and

[1] Large Declaration, p. 34-39. Baillie, vol. i. pp. 37, 38.

Lord Loudon. The latter was preferred, and, without farther deliberation, was immediately signed by about twenty-four earls and lords, and by more than a hundred gentlemen. Some of the ministers were in the act of subscribing when Baillie entered the room. He asked what they had signed, but they could give him no answer. "It seems," he says, "too many went in fide implicita." He requested that it should be read over, and he finally brought himself to subscribe it, because he agreed in its general import though not in all the particulars. He admits, however, that there was also another reason—that, had he refused his signature, he would have been as infamous that day by marring a good cause through his example, as he had been famous the day before, by furthering it by his discourse. He adds that he had not repented of his subscription, and that after much study he thought he could defend every word of the paper. Baillie belonged to that numerous class among the clergy who disliked the canons and the Service Book, without any wish to alter the established government in Church or State, but who, once induced to join with the violent faction, continued in a downward course, till they had taken part in deeds which at first they would have shrunk from with abhorrence.

The supplication, thus drawn up, set forth in name of the noblemen, barons, ministers, burgesses, and commons, who signed it, that they were constrained by the tenor of the late proclamation to remonstrate against the archbishops and bishops of the realm, who, being entrusted by his majesty with the government of the Church, had drawn up and enjoined two books; in one of which—the Book of Common Prayer—not only were sown the seeds of divers superstitions, idolatry, and false doctrine, but also the English Service Book was abused, especially in the Communion, in a manner quite contrary to the intentions of the blessed reformers of religion in England; while in the other—the Book of Canons—the Liturgy was enforced under the pain of excommunication, and many regulations were enacted tending to foster superstition and error; that they were satisfied these proceedings were contrary to the pious intentions of their gracious sovereign, who had been much wronged by the prelates: therefore, out of their bounden duty to God, their king and their country, they craved that the matter should be put to trial, and those parties taken order with according to the laws of the realm, and that they should not in the meantime be suffered to sit as judges.

At the same time, another petition was presented to the chancellor, in name of the men, women, children, and servants in Edinburgh, stating that, being urged with the Service Book, and having considered the same, they had found many things therein different from the form of public worship professed within the kingdom, and craving that his lordship would find some way of delivering them from this and similar innovations.

In answer to the first of these supplications, the council intimated that they would communicate it to the king, and report his answer. In the Large Declaration, the insincere expressions used regarding the English Liturgy in the former paper, and the circumstance that in the latter even the children are stated to have considered the Service Book, are pointed out. These things are sufficiently obvious, but the language of the appeals was really addressed to the people themselves, rather than to the sovereign or his counsellors.[1]

Before parting, the petitioners agreed to meet again on the fifteenth of November. On the fourteenth of that month, the privy council having assembled at Linlithgow, some of their number had a conference with the leading persons among the petitioners. Complaints were made by the counsellors regarding the multitudes congregated at Edinburgh, which threatened the peace of the kingdom; and the petitioners suggested that, to obviate this inconvenience, certain commissioners of their number, as representing the whole body, should receive any communication from the council, and report the result to their constituents. This proposal was most imprudently agreed to, and the consent thus given eventually led to the appointment of the committee, which became known by the name of the Tables. In all these matters, Baillie tells us, the ministers, generally, were not consulted. The persons who managed every thing were three or four noblemen, along with Henderson and Dickson, whom he styles the " two archbishops."[2]

[1] Baillie, vol. i. p. 34-38. Large Declaration, p. 41-44.
[2] Baillie, vol. i. p. 38-42.

On the seventh of December, the council issued a proclamation at Linlithgow, which announced that the king had delayed giving an answer to the petitioners, and set forth his majesty's abhorrence of Popery, and his determination to allow nothing which was opposed to the true religion then professed in his ancient kingdom of Scotland. About the same time the Earl of Roxburgh, Lord Privy Seal, returned from England with instructions from the king, in consequence of which the courts of justice were ordered to be removed from Linlithgow to Stirling on the first of February, and the council, till then, to sit at Dalkeith.

In the meantime, the petitioners continued to pursue their measures with increased boldness. They resolved to admonish the universities to beware of the Service Book, and not to suffer any corrupt doctrine to be taught, lest parents should be forced to remove their children. They had recourse also to an old device of their party—the appointing of a day of fasting. They did not, however, yet venture to usurp the supreme authority by ordering an universal public fast, but agreed that each minister, with consent of his session, should fix a day in his own parish. On the twenty-first of December, the petitioners were admitted to the presence of the council, and Lord Loudon, in a formal speech, recapitulated their grievances in connection with the Books of Canons, Ordination, and Common Prayer, and the court of High Commission, and again requested that order should be taken with the prelates, the authors of all these innovations; mentioning that they did not crave the bishops' blood, nor revenge on their persons, but only that the wrongs done by them should be remedied. None of the bishops were present on this occasion, and, by permitting such language to be used without censure, the lay lords of the council shewed plainly enough that they sympathized to a considerable extent with the petitioners.[1]

The king, more and more perplexed, ordered Traquair to come up to court. Anxious consultations took place regarding what was next to be done, and it was finally resolved to adhere to the Service Book. It is very doubtful whether any concession would now have restored tranquillity to Scotland,

[1] Large Declaration, p. 45-47. Baillie, vol. i. pp. 25-27, 42-46, and appendix, p. 454-458.

and prevented the meditated attack on the Perth articles and Episcopacy, but the king's determination was certainly an unfortunate one. Had he declared his willingness not to urge the Liturgy and canons, till duly sanctioned by law, and announced his resolution to maintain firmly the ecclesiastical government and the ceremonies then established, although he would neither have conciliated the Puritans, nor have won back the disaffected nobility, he would have obtained the sympathy of the greater number of the clergy, and secured the support of all whose opposition to the obnoxious measures was not a mere cloak for other designs.

The treasurer returned to Scotland, and a proclamation in accordance with the royal opinion was signed at Stirling on the nineteenth of February, 1638. This proclamation declared that the Liturgy had been compiled with the full and deliberate sanction of the king; censured severely the conduct of the petitioners, both in respect of the matter of their complaints, and the manner in which they had been brought forward; but promised to excuse the same in all who should now conduct themselves as faithful subjects, and forbade unlawful convocations of the people under the pain of treason, specially commanding all strangers to leave Stirling.

The petitioners, having contrived to learn both the import of the proclamation and the day on which it was to be made, immediately prepared a protestation against it. This document bore to be in name of the noblemen, barons, ministers, and burgesses appointed to attend his majesty's answer to their humble petitions, and to bring forward new grievances, and to do whatever else might lawfully conduce to their humble desires. It referred to their former supplications and complaints, and to their declinature of the bishops as their judges till the matters objected against them should be tried: and it contained a protest that, as these requests had been rejected, they should have immediate recourse to their sovereign, to present and prosecute their grievances in a legal way; that the bishops should not be esteemed their lawful judges, till they should purge themselves judicially of the crimes laid to their charge; that no act or proclamation made in presence of the bishops should be prejudicial to the petitioners; and that neither they, nor any others whom the Lord should move to join with them, should incur any penalty or danger for not observing the unlawful acts, books, or proclamations, and that any evil consequences which might follow should not be attributed to them.

When the proclamation was made at Stirling, and afterwards at Linlithgow, this protestation was publicly taken against it; and at Edinburgh, when the royal heralds and pursuivants attended in their coats of arms at the market-cross, to announce the king's resolution by sound of trumpet and with all the formalities observed on such occasions, the proclamation was received with jeering and laughter, and the officers were compelled to remain till the protestation was read in presence of a large number of noblemen, barons, ministers, and others.[1]

This open defiance of the royal authority, and the other measures which the petitioners immediately adopted, shewed that they were now determined to persist in their course at all hazards.

[1] Large Declaration, p. 47-52.

www.ingramcontent.com/pod-product-compliance
Lightning Source LLC
Chambersburg PA
CBHW030547300426
44111CB00009B/883